W9-BMZ-334

Microsoft® Windows®
Communication Foundation
Step by Step

John Sharp

content●master

PUBLISHED BY
Microsoft Press
A Division of Microsoft Corporation
One Microsoft Way
Redmond, Washington 98052-6399

Library of Congress Control Number: 2006939802

Printed and bound in the United States of America.

2 3 4 5 6 7 8 9   QWE   2 1 0 9 8 7

Distributed in Canada by H.B. Fenn and Company Ltd.

A CIP catalogue record for this book is available from the British Library.

Microsoft Press books are available through booksellers and distributors worldwide. For further information about international editions, contact your local Microsoft Corporation office or contact Microsoft Press International directly at fax (425) 936-7329. Visit our Web site at www.microsoft.com/mspress. Send comments to mspinput@microsoft.com.

Acquisitions Editor: Ben Ryan
Project Editor: Valerie Woolley
Editorial and Production: Custom Editorial Productions, Inc.
Technical Reviewer: Jon Flanders; Technical review services provided by Content Master, a member of CM Group, Ltd.

Body Part No. X13-24119

Contents at a Glance

Table of Contents

What do you think of this book? We want to hear from you!

Microsoft is interested in hearing your feedback so we can continually improve our books and learning
resources for you. To participate in a brief online survey, please visit:

www.microsoft.com/learning/booksurvey/

What do you think of this book? We want to hear from you!

Microsoft is interested in hearing your feedback so we can continually improve our books and learning resources for you. To participate in a brief online survey, please visit:

www.microsoft.com/learning/booksurvey/

Acknowledgments

Before I started work on this book, my wife used to *think* I was slightly mad. After my usual bout of late nights, gallons of hot sweet tea, and the occasional burst of interesting vocabulary (I had to initially explain that the term "WCF" is not an expletive, no matter how loudly I shout it), she has now reformed her opinion of me and *knows* I am quite insane. That said, I wouldn't swap the experience of writing books for anything in my professional life—there are much harder ways to earn a living, and I thank all at Content Master for allowing me to spend a significant amount of my time doing it.

Writing a book is a team effort. However, although you don't actually meet many people face to face, you work closely with so many people electronically that you feel they are old friends. Certainly the team of professionals I have had the pleasure of working with at Microsoft Press has been superb and I would like to thank them all, especially editor Valerie Woolley, who has guided me through the authoring process and put up with me making change after change to the titles of chapters, and Julie Hotchkiss, who worked patiently behind the scenes liasing with the editing staff and the technical reviewers. I must also make special mention of Jon Flanders, who has done sterling work reviewing each chapter, setting me straight when I did not make sense or when I was just plain wrong!

As ever, I must acknowledge the support given to me by my family: to Diana, who supplied the gallons of tea and now understands what WCF is even if she didn't want to know before; to James, who suddenly grew taller than me while I was writing Chapter 4; and to Francesca, who thinks I am an unfashionably dressed, sad geek.

And finally, "Up the Gills!" (If they don't get promoted soon I shall have to switch my allegiance to Forest Green Rovers.)

John Sharp

Introduction

Microsoft Windows Communication Foundation (WCF), alongside Windows Workflow Foundation (WF) and Windows Presentation Foundation (WPF), is intended to become the primary framework for building the next wave of business applications for the Microsoft Windows operating system. WCF enables you to build powerful service-oriented systems, based on connected services and applications. You can use WCF to create new services, as well as augment and interoperate with the functionality available through many existing services created by using other technologies. When designing distributed applications in the past, you frequently had to choose a specific technology, such as Web services, COM+, Microsoft Message Queue, or .NET Framework Remoting. This choice often had a fundamental impact on the architecture of your solutions. WCF provides a consistent model for using a variety of technologies, enabling you to design and architect your solutions without being restricted by a specific connectivity mechanism.

Who This Book Is For

This book will show you how to build connected applications and services by using WCF. If you are involved in designing, building, or deploying applications for the Microsoft Windows operating system, then sooner or later you are going to have to become familiar with WCF. This book will give you the initial boost you need to quickly learn many of the techniques required to create systems based on WCF. Its approach is pragmatic, covering the concepts and details necessary to enable you to build connected solutions.

To get the most from this book, you should meet the following profile:

- You should be an architect, designer, or developer who will be creating solutions for the Microsoft Windows family of operating systems.

- You should have experience developing applications by using Visual Studio 2005 and C#.

- You should have a basic understanding of concepts such as transactions, Web services, and message queuing.

Finding Your Best Starting Point in This Book

This book is designed to help you build skills in a number of essential areas. It assumes that you are new to WCF and takes you step by step through the fundamental concepts of WCF feature by feature. It is recommended that you follow the chapters in sequence and perform each of the exercises, as the techniques and ideas that you see in one chapter are extended by those in subsequent chapters. However, if you have specific requirements or are only interested in certain aspects of WCF, you can use the table below to find your best route through this book.

If you are	Follow these steps
New to Web services and distributed applications and need to gain a basic understanding of WCF.	1. Install the code samples as described in the "Code Samples" section of this Introduction. 2. Work through Chapters 1 to 5 sequentially and perform the exercises. 3. Complete Chapters 6 to 16 as your level of experience and interest dictates.
New to Web services and distributed applications and need to learn how to use WCF to implement solutions using common Web services features such as sessions, transactions, and reliable messaging.	1. Install the code samples as described in the "Code Samples" section of this Introduction. 2. Work through Chapters 1 to 9 sequentially and perform the exercises. 3. Complete Chapters 10 to 16 as your level of experience and interest dictates.
Familiar with Web services and distributed applications, and need to learn about WCF quickly, including its advanced features.	1. Install the code samples as described in the "Code Samples" section of this Introduction. 2. Skim the first chapter to get an overview of WCF, but perform the exercises. 3. Read Chapter 2 and perform the exercises. 4. Skim Chapter 3. 5. Read Chapters 4 and 5 and complete the exercises. 6. Skim Chapters 6 to 9, performing the exercises that interest you. 7. Complete the remaining chapters and exercises.
Familiar with security concepts but need to understand how to use the security features that WCF provides.	1. Install the code samples as described in the "Code Samples" section of this Introduction. 2. Skim the first three chapters. 3. Read Chapters 4 and 5 and perform the exercises. 4. Skim Chapters 6 to 14. 5. Read Chapter 15 and complete the exercises. 6. Skim Chapter 16.
Referencing the book after working through the exercises.	1. Use the index or the Table of Contents to find information about particular subjects. 2. Read the Summary sections at the end of each chapter to find a brief review of the concepts and techniques presented in the chapter.

Conventions and Features in This Book

This book presents information using conventions designed to make the information readable and easy to follow. Before you start, read the following list, which explains conventions you'll see throughout the book and points out helpful features that you might want to use.

Conventions

- Each exercise is a series of tasks. Each task is presented as a series of numbered steps (1, 2, and so on). A bullet (■) indicates an exercise that has only one step.

- Notes labeled "tip" provide additional information or alternative methods for completing a step successfully.

- Notes labeled "important" alert you to information you need to check before continuing.

- Text that you type appears in bold.

- A plus sign (+) between two key names means that you must press those keys at the same time. For example, "Press Alt+Tab" means that you hold down the Alt key while you press the Tab key.

System Requirements

You'll need the following hardware and software to complete the practice exercises in this book:

- Microsoft Windows XP with Service Pack 2, Microsoft Windows Server 2003 with Service Pack 1, or Microsoft Windows Vista.

- Microsoft Visual Studio 2005 Standard Edition or Microsoft Visual Studio 2005 Professional Edition, including SQL Server 2005 Express.

> **Note** You can perform all the exercises in this book using Visual Studio 2005 Standard Edition, *except* for the final set of exercises in Chapter 2, which creates a Windows Service and requires Visual Studio 2005 Professional Edition. However, this project is not required in any subsequent chapters, so you can omit this exercise if you have only Visual Studio 2005 Standard Edition.

- 600-MHz Pentium or compatible processor (1-GHz Pentium recommended).

- 192 MB RAM (256 MB or more recommended).

- Video (800 × 600 or higher resolution) monitor with at least 256 colors (1024 × 768 High Color 16-bit recommended).

- CD-ROM or DVD-ROM drive.
- Microsoft mouse or compatible pointing device.

Some of the exercises require that you have installed Internet Information Services (IIS) and Message Queuing (MSMQ).

You will also need to have the following additional software installed on your computer. This software is available on the companion CD supplied with this book. Installation and configuration instructions are provided later in the Introduction:

- Microsoft .NET Framework 3.0.

> **Note**   If you are using Windows Vista, the .NET Framework 3.0 is automatically installed as part of the operating system. You do not need to install it again.

- Visual Studio 2005 Extensions for .NET Framework 3.0.
- Microsoft SQL Server AdventureWorks database.
- Microsoft Enterprise Library (January 2006 version recommended).
- Microsoft Windows XP Service Pack 2 Support Tools (only required if you are using Microsoft Windows XP).

You will additionally require the Microsoft Windows Software Development Kit for Windows Vista and .NET Framework 3.0 Runtime Components. You can download this software from the Microsoft Download Center site at *http://www.microsoft.com/downloads/details.aspx?FamilyId=C2B1E300-F358-4523-B479-F53D234CDCCF&displaylang=en.*

> **Important**   The exercises in Chapter 5 use a tool called FindPrivateKey.exe. Not all releases of the Microsoft Windows Software Development Kit include this tool. A copy of it is provided on the companion CD.

Code Samples

The companion CD inside this book contains the code samples that you'll use as you perform the exercises. By using the code samples, you won't waste time creating files that aren't relevant to the exercise. The files and the step-by-step instructions in the lessons also let you learn by doing, which is an easy and effective way to acquire and remember new skills.

Installing the Code Samples

Follow these steps to install the code samples and required software on your computer so that you can use them with the exercises:

1. Remove the companion CD from the package inside this book and insert it into your CD-ROM drive.

 Note An end user license agreement should open automatically. If this agreement does not appear, open My Computer on the desktop or Start menu, double-click the icon for your CD-ROM drive, and then double-click StartCD.exe.

2. Review the end user license agreement. If you accept the terms, select the accept option, and then click Next.

   A menu will appear with options related to the book.

3. Click Install Code Samples.

4. Follow the instructions that appear.

   The code samples are installed to the following location on your computer if you are using Windows XP:

   My Documents\Microsoft Press\WCF Step By Step

   The code samples are installed to the following location on your computer if you are using Windows Vista:

   Documents\Microsoft Press\WCF Step By Step

Installing and Configuring the Microsoft .NET Framework 3.0 (Windows XP only)

The exercises and samples in this book have been tested against the RTM version of the .NET Framework 3.0. If you have previously installed an earlier version of the .NET Framework 3.0, you must uninstall it and use the software provided on the companion CD. Follow these instructions to install the Microsoft .NET Framework 3.0:

1. Using Windows Explorer, move to the \Software folder on the companion CD.

2. Double-click the file dotnetfx3.exe. If the Open File – Security Warning dialog appears, click Run.

> **Note**   A 64-bit version of the .NET Framework 3.0 is available in the file dotnextfx3_x64.exe.

3. In the Welcome to Setup page, read the license agreement. If you agree with the license terms, click I have read and ACCEPT the terms of the License Agreement, and then click Install.

   Installation continues in the background.

4. When the Setup Complete page appears, click Exit.

> **Important**   You should download and install the Microsoft Windows SDK before installing the Visual Studio 2005 Extensions for .NET Framework 3.0.

> **Important**   If your copy of the Windows SDK does not include the FindPrivateKey utility, copy the file FindPrivateKeye.exe from the \Software\FindPrivateKey folder on the companion CD to the bin folder under the Microsoft Windows SDK installation folder (C:\Program Files\Microsoft SDKs\Windows\v6.0\Bin).

Installing the Visual Studio 2005 Extensions for .NET Framework 3.0

The exercises and samples in this book have been tested against the November 2006 Customer Technical Preview version of the Visual Studio 2005 Extensions for .NET Framework 3.0. Follow these instructions to install this software:

1. Using Windows Explorer, move to the \Software folder on the companion CD.

2. Double-click the file vsextwfx.exe. If the Open File – Security Warning dialog appears, click Run.

3. In the Welcome to the Visual Studio 2005 extensions for .NET Framework 3.0 (WCF WPF) November 2006 CTP Setup Wizard page, click Next.

4. In the License Agreement page, read the license agreement. If you agree with the license terms, click I Accept, and then click Next.

5. In the Confirm Installation page, click Next.

6. When the Installation Complete page appears, click Close.

7. Close the Internet Explorer window displaying the release notes.

Installing and Configuring the Microsoft Enterprise Library

The exercises and samples in this book have been developed and tested using the January 2006 release of the Microsoft Enterprise Library. Follow these steps to install the Enterprise Library:

1. Using Windows Explorer, move to the \Software folder on the companion CD.

2. Double-click the file Enterprise Library January 2006.exe. If the Open File – Security Warning dialog appears, click Run.

3. In the Welcome to the Enterprise Library for .NET Framework 2.0 – January 2006 Installation Wizard page, click Next.

4. In the License Agreement page, read the license agreement. If you agree with the license terms, click I accept the license agreement, and then click Next.

5. In the User Information page, enter your full name and organization, and then click Next.

6. In the Destination Folder page, click Browse, change the Destination Folder to C:\Program Files\Microsoft Enterprise Library\, and then click OK. Select the Compile Enterprise Library check box, and then click Next.

> **Note**   The exercise instructions throughout this book assume you have installed the Enterprise Library in the C:\Program Files\Microsoft Enterprise Library\ folder.

7. In the Installation Configuration page, accept the default values, and then click Next.

8. In the Ready to Install the Application page, click Next.

    While the Enterprise Library installs, you will see a console window appear as the installation program compiles and builds the library.

9. When the Enterprise Library for .NET Framework 2.0 – January 2006 has been successfully installed page appears, click Finish.

Installing and Configuring the *AdventureWorks* Database

The exercises and examples in this book make use of the *AdventureWorks* sample database. If you don't already have this database installed on your computer, a copy of the database installation program is supplied on the companion CD. Follow these steps to install and configure the database:

1. Using Windows Explorer, move to the \Software folder on the companion CD.

2. Double-click the file AdventureWorksDB.msi. If the Open File – Security Warning dialog appears, click Run.

3. In the Welcome to the InstallShield Wizard for AdventureWorksDB page, click Next.

4. In the License Agreement page, read the license agreement. If you agree with the license terms, click I accept the terms in the license agreement, and then click Next.

5. In the Destination Folder page, accept the default location, and then click Next.

6. In the Ready to Install the Program page, click Install.

7. When the InstallShield Wizard Completed page appears, click Finish.

    The InstallShield Wizard only copies the database files on to your computer. You must attach the database files to SQL Server to make the database available, as described in the following steps.

8. On the Windows Start menu, point to All Programs, point to Accessories, and then click Command Prompt.

9. In the Command Prompt window, move to the \Setup folder on the companion CD, and then type the following command:

    ```
    osql -E -S .\SQLEXPRESS -i attach.sql
    ```

    This command should complete without any errors (it will display a series of prompts, "1> 2> 1> 2> 3> 4> 5> 1>").

> **Note**   The script attach.sql contains a CREATE DATABASE statement that assumes that you have installed the *AdventureWorks* database in the default location on the C: drive (C:\Program Files\Microsoft SQL Server\MSSQL.1\MSSQL\Data). If you have installed it elsewhere, you will need to create a copy of this file, update the paths it contains, and run this updated script instead. For example, if you are using the 64-bit version of Windows Vista, the database will be installed in the C:\Program Files (x86)\Microsoft SQL Server\MSSQL.1\MSSQL\Data folder by default.

By default, IIS uses the ASP.NET account when executing Web services. Follow these steps to grant the ASP.NET account access to the *AdventureWorks* database.

10. Copy the file aspnet.sql in the \Setup folder on the companion CD to your My Documents folder if you are using Windows XP, or to your Documents folder if you are using Windows Vista.

11. Using Notepad, edit the file aspnet.sql in your My Documents (or Documents) folder.

    If you are using Windows XP, replace the four occurrences of the text YOUR_COMPUTER with the name of your computer.

    If you are using Windows Vista, replace the four occurrences of the text [YOUR_COMPUTER\ASPNET] with the text [NT AUTHORITY\NETWORK SERVICE] (including the square brackets and spaces).

    Save the file and close Notepad when you have finished.

12. In the Command Prompt window, move to your My Documents (or Documents) folder and type the following command:

    ```
    osql –E –S .\SQLEXPRESS –i aspnet.sql
    ```

    This command should complete without any errors (it will display a series of prompts, "1> 2> 1> 2> 1> 2> 1> 2> 1> 2> 1>").

13. Close the Command Prompt window.

Installing the Microsoft Windows XP Service Pack 2 Support Tools (Windows XP only)

Some exercises make use of the httpcfg utility. If you are using Windows XP, you need to install the Support Tools. If you are using Windows Vista this is not necessary, as Vista provides its own utility called netsh. Follow these steps to install the Microsoft Windows XP Service Pack 2 Support Tools:

1. Using Windows Explorer, move to the \Software folder on the companion CD.

2. Double-click the file WindowsXP-KB838079-SupportTools-ENU.exe. If the Open File – Security Warning dialog appears, click Run.

3. In the Welcome to the Windows Support Tools Setup Wizard page, click Next.

4. In the End User License Agreement page, read the license agreement. If you agree with the license terms, click I Agree, and then click Next.

5. In the User Information page, enter your name and organization, and then click Next.

6. On the Select An Installation Type page, select Complete, and then click Next.

7. On the Destination Directory page, accept the default folder, and then click Install Now.

8. When the Completing the Windows Support Tools Setup Wizard page appears, click Finish.

Granting Access to Your Documents Folder

The practice files and exercises are installed under your My Documents (or Documents) folder. Some of the exercises require IIS to be able to run services installed with the practice files. IIS executes Web services using the ASPNET account under Windows XP, or the NETWORK SERVICE account under Windows Vista. This account must be able to read the contents of the folder holding the files for the service, as well as the parent folder hierarchy. Follow these steps to grant the ASPNET or NETWORK SERVICE account access to your My Documents folder.

If you are using Windows XP, perform the following steps:

1. Using Windows Explorer, move to the Documents and Settings folder, and then move to your folder. Right-click your My Documents folder, and then click Sharing and Security.

2. In the My Documents Properties window, click the Security tab.

> **Tip**   If the Security tab is not present, close the My Documents Properties window. In the Tools menu of Windows Explorer, click Folder Options. In the Folder Options dialog box, click the View tab. Scroll to the bottom of the tree-view in the Advanced Settings list, uncheck Use simple file sharing, and then click OK. Right-click your My Documents folder, and then click Sharing and Security. The Security tab should now appear.

3. Click Add.

4. In the Select Users or Groups dialog box, type **ASPNET,** and then click OK.

5. In My Documents Properties window, accept the default permissions, and then click OK.

If you are using Windows Vista, perform the following steps:

1. Using Windows Explorer, move to the Documents and Settings folder, and then move to your folder. Right-click your Documents folder, and then click Share.

2. In the "Choose people on your network to share with" window, type **NETWORK SERVICE** in the text box, and then click Add.

3. Click Share.

4. In the "Your folder is shared" window, click Done.

Using the Code Samples

Each chapter in this book explains when and how to use any code samples for that chapter. When it's time to use a code sample, the book will list the instructions for how to open the files. The chapters are built around scenarios that simulate real programming projects, so you can easily apply the skills you learn to your own work.

For those of you who like to know all the details, following is a list of the code sample Visual Studio projects and solutions, grouped by the folders where you can find them.

> **Important**   Many of the exercises require administrative access to your computer. Make sure you perform the exercises using an account that has this level of access.

Solution Folder	Description
Chapter 1	
ProductsService	This solution gets you started. Creating the ProductsService project leads you through the process of building a simple WCF service hosted by IIS. The service enables you to query and update product information in the *AdventureWorks* database.
	The ProductsClient project is a console-based WCF client application that connects to the ProductsService service. You use this project for testing the WCF service.
Chapter 2	
ProductsServiceHost	This solution contains Windows Presentation Foundation application that provides a host environment for the ProductsService service. You use this application to manually start and stop the service.
	You configure the ProductsClient application to connect to the service hosted by this application by using a TCP endpoint.
WindowsProductService	This solution contains a Windows Service that hosts the ProductsService service. You can start and stop the service from the Services applet in the Windows Control Panel.
	You reconfigure the ProductsClient application to connect to this service by using an endpoint based on the Named Pipe transport.
	This exercise requires Visual Studio 2005 Professional Edition.
Chapter 3	
ProductsServiceFault	The ProductsService service in this solution traps exceptions and reports them back to the client application as Simple Object Access Protocol (SOAP) faults. It defines fault contracts and specifies faults that each operation can throw.
	You modify the ProductsClient application to catch the SOAP faults thrown by the service.
Chapter 4	
ProductsService	When building this solution, you see how to configure security for the ProductsService service and the ProductsClient application. The techniques you use are appropriate for WCF client applications and services running inside the same organization over a corporate intranet. You learn how to:
	■ Apply message level security over a TCP binding.
	■ Implement transport level security over an HTTP binding.
	■ Implement message level security over an HTTP binding.
	■ Implement user authentication by using Windows credentials.
	■ Implement user authorization by using declarative and imperative .NET Framework security.

Solution Folder	Description
Chapter 5	
ProductsService	When creating this solution, you see how to configure security for the ProductsService service and the ProductsClient application using techniques that are appropriate to the Internet. You learn how to:
	■ Implement authentication and authorization by using the SQL Server Role Provider.
	■ Authenticate and authorize users by using certificates rather than usernames and passwords.
	■ Reconfigure the service to authenticate itself to the client application by using a certificate.
Chapter 6	
ProductsService	In this solution, you modify the service contract in the ProductsService and run the ProductsClient application to understand which modifications constitute breaking changes and which don't.
ProductsServiceV2	When creating this solution, you update the ProductsService service and modify the data contract defining the data structures one of its operations returns. You also use the solution to examine how to implement data contract compatibility with client applications that use an older version of the data contract.
Chapter 7	
ShoppingCartService	This solution contains a new service that implements shopping cart functionality and a client application that exercises this functionality. You use this solution to understand how to implement services based on sessions and how to maintain state information between operation calls.
Chapter 8	
ShoppingCartService	This solution contains a version of the ShoppingCartService service that uses transactions to maintain database integrity.
	You modify the client application to initiate a transaction and control the outcome of the transaction.
Chapter 9	
ShoppingCartService	You configure the ShoppingCartService service and client application in this solution to implement reliable messaging. You run the client application and use the WCF Service Trace Viewer utility to examine the messages passing between the client application and service.
	You then add a custom binding to the ShoppingCartService service that enables you to configure replay detection and test it by using the client application.

Solution Folder	Description
Chapter 10	
ShoppingCartService	This solution contains an implementation of the ShoppingCart-Service service that programmatically creates a custom binding rather than using one of the WCF predefined bindings. When building this solution, you also create a custom service behavior that enables you to inspect request messages sent to the service and response messages that it sends back to client applications.
ProductsServiceV2	This solution contains a copy of the ProductsService service from Chapter 6. The client application connects to the service by creating a binding and a channel programmatically rather than using a generated proxy class.
SimpleProductsService	This solution contains a stripped down version of the Prod-uctsService service. The client application connects to the service by creating a binding and a channel and then manually creates and sends a SOAP message to the service. It receives the response also as a SOAP message.
Chapter 11	
OneWay	This solution contains a new service called AdventureWorksAd-min. The AdventureWorksAdmin service exposes an operation that can take significant time to run, and you see how to implement this operation as a OneWay operation.
	You also use this solution to understand the circumstances under which a OneWay operation call can block a client application and how to resolve this blocking.
Async	This solution contains a version of the AdventureWorksAdmin service that implements an operation that can execute asynchronously.
	You also modify the client application in this solution to invoke the operation asynchronously.
MSMQ	This version of the solution contains an implementation of the AdventureWorksAdmin service that uses a message queue to receive messages from client applications. You run the client application and service at different times and verify that messages sent by the client application are queued and received when the service runs.
Chapter 12	
Throttling	This solution contains the ShoppingCartService service and a multi-threaded client application that establishes a number of concurrent sessions with the service. You use this service and client application to test the way in which you can configure WCF to conserve resources during periods of heavy load.

Solution Folder	Description
MTOM	This solution contains the ShoppingCartPhotoService that retrieves images of products from the *AdventureWorks* database. The client application displays these images in a WPF form. The service encodes the binary data constituting the image by using the Message Transmission Optimization Mechanism (MTOM).
Streaming	This solution contains a version of the ShoppingCartPhotoService that uses streaming to send the image data to the client application rather than MTOM.
Chapter 13	
Load-Balancing Router	This solution contains a WCF service that acts as a load-balancing router for two instances of the ShoppingCartService service. The client application connects to the router, which transparently redirects requests to one instance or the other of the ShoppingCartService service.
Chapter 14	
ProductsServiceV3	This solution contains a version of the ProductsService service that implements a callback contract. The service uses this callback contract to enable a client application to register an interest in an event and provide a reference to a method that the service can invoke when that event occurs.
Chapter 15	
ShoppingCartService	The ShoppingCartService service in this solution implements claims-based security. The client application uses Windows CardSpace to manage user credentials and send claims information to the service. The service uses verified claims to authorize access to users.
Chapter 16	
ASPNETService	This solution contains an ASP.NET Web service and client application. You examine the Web Services Description Language (WSDL) description of ASP.NET Web service to implement a WCF Web service that can support the ASP.NET client application.
WCFService	This is a WCF Web service that implements the same WSDL interface as the ASP.NET Web service. You reconfigure the ASP.NET client application to connect to this service, but you do not modify any code in the client application.
ProductsServiceHost	This is the host application for the WCFService. You use this application to start and stop the service.
Products	This solution contains a COM+ application that you configure to appear to client applications as a WCF service.
ProductsClient	This solution contains a test client application that connects to the Products COM+ application by using WCF.

In addition to these projects, all of the projects have solutions available for the practice exercises. The solutions for each project are included in the folder for each chapter and are labeled Solution.

Uninstalling the Code Samples

Follow these steps to remove the code samples from your computer.

1. In Control Panel, open Add Or Remove Programs.
2. From the list of Currently Installed Programs, select WCF Step By Step.
3. Click Remove.
4. Follow the instructions that appear to remove the code samples.

Support for This Book

Every effort has been made to ensure the accuracy of this book and the contents of the companion CD. As corrections or changes are collected, they will be added to a Microsoft Knowledge Base article.

Microsoft Press provides support for books and companion CDs at the following Web site:

http://www.microsoft.com/learning/support/books/.

Questions and Comments

If you have comments, questions, or ideas regarding the book or the companion CD, or questions that are not answered by visiting the sites above, please send them to Microsoft Press via e-mail to:

mspinput@microsoft.com.

Or via postal mail to:

Microsoft Press
Attn: Microsoft Windows Communication Foundation Step by Step Editor
One Microsoft Way
Redmond, WA
98052-6399.

Please note that Microsoft software product support is not offered through the above addresses.

Chapter 1
Introducing Windows Communication Foundation

After completing this chapter, you will be able to:

- Explain the purpose of Windows Communication Foundation (WCF).

- Use the .NET Framework 3.0 and Visual Studio 2005 to build a WCF service.

- Deploy a WCF service to Microsoft Internet Information Services (IIS).

- Build a client console application to test the WCF service.

- Describe the principles underpinning a Service-Oriented Architecture (SOA) and how WCF facilitates building applications and services for an SOA.

This chapter provides you with an introduction to WCF and shows you how to create, deploy, and access a simple WCF service. This is very much a "scene-setting" chapter. During its course, you will meet many of the features of WCF. In subsequent chapters, you will expand your knowledge of the various topics presented here.

What Is Windows Communication Foundation?

I assume that you are reading this book because you want to know how to build distributed applications by using WCF. But what actually is WCF, and why should you use it anyway? To answer these questions, it is helpful to take a few steps back into the past.

The Early Days of Personal Computer Applications

In the early days of the personal computer, most business solutions comprised integrated suites of applications, typically consisting of word processing software, a spreadsheet program, and a database package (much like Microsoft Office does these days). A skilled user could store business data in the database, analyze this data using the spreadsheet program, and maybe create reports and other documents integrating the data and the analyses by using the word processor. More often than not, these applications would all be located on the same computer, and the data and file formats they used would be proprietary to the application suite. This was the classic desktop business platform; it was single-user, usually with very limited scope for multi-tasking.

As personal computers became cheaper and more widely adopted as business tools, the next challenge was to enable multiple users to share the business data stored on them. This was not actually a new challenge, as multi-user databases had been available for some time, but they ran predominantly on mainframe computers rather than PCs. However, networking solutions and network operating systems (NOS) soon started to appear for the PC platform, enabling departments in an organization to connect their PCs together and share resources. Database management system vendors produced versions of their software for the networked PC environment, adapted from the mainframe environment, enabling networked PC solutions to share their business data more easily.

Inter-Process Communications Technologies

A networked platform is actually only part of the story. Although networking solutions enabled PCs to be able to communicate with each other and share resources such as printers and disks, applications needed to be able to send and receive data and coordinate their actions with other applications running at the same time on other computers. Many common inter-process communications mechanisms were available, such as named pipes and sockets. These mechanisms were very low-level and using them required a good understanding of how networks work. The same is true today. For example, building applications that use sockets to send and receive data can be a challenging occupation; ostensibly the process is quite simple, but factors such as coordinating access (you don't want two applications to both try and read from the same socket at the same time) can complicate matters. As computers and networks evolved, so did the variety and capabilities of the inter-process communications mechanisms. For example, Microsoft developed the Component Object Model, or COM, as the mechanism for communicating between applications and components running on the Windows platform. Developers can use COM to create reusable software components, link components together to build applications, and take advantage of Windows services. Microsoft itself uses COM to make elements of its own applications available as services for integration into custom solutions.

Microsoft originally designed COM to enable communications between components and applications running on the same computer. COM was followed by DCOM (distributed COM), enabling applications to access components running on other computers over a network. DCOM was itself followed by COM+. COM+ incorporated features such as integration with Microsoft Transaction Server, enabling applications to group operations on components together into transactions so that the results of these operations could either be made permanent (committed) if they were all successful, or automatically undone (rolled back) if some sort of error occurred. COM+ provided additional capabilities, such as automatic resource management (for example, if a component connects to a database, you can ensure that the connection is closed when the application finishes using the component), and asynchronous operations (useful if an application makes a request to a component that can take a long time to fulfill; the application can continue processing, and the component can alert the application by sending it a message when the operation has completed). COM+ was followed in turn by the .NET Framework, which further extended the features available and renamed the technology as Enterprise Services. The .NET Framework also provided several new technologies for building networked components. One example was Remoting, which enabled a client application to access a remote object hosted by a remote server application as though it was running locally, inside the client application.

The Web and Web Services

Technologies such as COM, DCOM, COM+, Enterprise Services, and .NET Framework Remoting all work well when applications and components are running within the same local area network inside an organization. They are also specific to the Microsoft Windows family of operating systems.

While Microsoft was developing COM and DCOM, the World Wide Web appeared. The World Wide Web is based on the Internet, which has been around for several decades. The World Wide Web provides an infrastructure that enables developers to build applications that can combine components and other elements located almost anywhere in the world, running on computers of varying architectures, and executing using a bewildering array of operating systems (not just Windows). The first generation of "Web applications" was quite simple, consisting of static Web pages that users could download and view using a Web browser application running on their local computer. The second generation provided elements of programmability, initially through the use of components, or applets, that could be downloaded from Web sites and executed locally in the users' Web browser. These have been followed by the third generation—Web services. A Web service is an application or component that executes on the computer hosting the Web site rather than the user's computer. A Web service can receive requests from applications running on the user's computer, perform operations on the computer hosting the Web service, and send a response back to the application running on the user's computer. A Web service can also invoke operations in other Web services, hosted elsewhere on the Internet. These are global, distributed applications.

You can build Web services that execute on Windows by using Visual Studio 2005 and the .NET Framework. You can create Web services for other platforms by using other technologies, such as Java and the Java Web Services Developers Pack. However, Web services are not specific to any particular language or operating system. To establish Web services as a global mechanism for building distributed applications, developers had to agree on several points, including a common format for data, a protocol for sending and receiving requests, and handling security. All of these features had to be independent of the platform being used to create and host Web services.

Using XML as a Common Data Format

Different types of computers can store the same values by using different internal representations—computers based on a "big-endian" 32-bit processor use a different format for numeric data than a computer based on a "small-endian" 32-bit processor for example. So, to share data successfully between applications running on different computers, developers had to agree on a common format for that data that was independent of the architecture of the computer they were using. To cut a long story short, the currently accepted universal data format is eXtensible Markup Language, or XML. XML is text-based and human-readable (just), and lets you define a grammar for describing just about any type of data that you need to handle. In case you have not seen XML data before, here is an example:

```
<Person>
  <Forename>John</Forename>
  <Surname>Sharp</Surname>
  <Age>42</Age>
</Person>
```

> **More Info**   For detailed information about XML and how you can use it, visit the XML.org Web site at *http://www.xml.org*.

Without trying too hard, you can probably guess what this data actually means. An application that needs to send information about a person to another application could format the data in this way, and the receiving application should be able to parse the data and make sense of it. However, there is more than one way to represent this information by using XML. You could also structure it like this:

```
<Person Forename="John" Surname="Sharp" Age="42" />
```

There are many other variations possible as well. How does an application know how to format data so that another application can read it correctly? The answer is that both applications have to agree on a layout. This layout is referred to as the XML schema for the data. Now, this is neither the time nor the place to become embroiled in a discussion of how XML schemas work. Just accept that an application can use an XML schema to convey information about how the data it is emitting is structured, and the application receiving the data can use this schema to help parse the data and make sense of it.

So, by adopting XML and schemas as a common data format, applications running on different computers can at least understand the data that they are using.

> **More Info**   If you want to know more about XML schemas and how they work, visit the World Wide Web Consortium (W3C) Web site at *http://www.w3.org*.

Sending and Receiving Web Service Requests

Using XML and XML schemas to format data enables Web services and users' (or client) applications to pass data back and forth in an unambiguous manner. However, client applications and Web services still need to agree on a protocol when sending and receiving requests. Additionally, a client application needs to be able to know what messages it can send to a Web service and what responses it can expect to receive.

To curtail another long story, Web services and client applications communicate with each other by using the Simple Object Access Protocol, or SOAP. The SOAP specification defines a number of things. The most important are the following:

- The format of a SOAP message
- How data should be encoded
- How to send messages
- How to handle replies to these messages

A Web service can advertise the messages that a client application can send it, and the responses the client application will receive, by publishing a Web Services Description Language (WSDL) document. A WSDL document is a piece of XML that conforms to a standard XML schema and that describes the messages the Web service can accept and the structure of the responses it will send back. A client application can use this information to determine how to communicate with the Web service.

> **More Info**   If you want detailed information about SOAP, visit the World Wide Web Consortium page at *http://www.w3.org/TR/soap*. If you want further information about WSDL, visit the page at *http://www.w3.org/TR/wsdl*.

Handling Security and Privacy in a Global Environment

Security is concerned with identifying users and services and then authorizing their access to resources. In a distributed environment, maintaining security is vitally important. In an isolated, non-networked, desktop environment, you could physically secure a PC to prevent an unauthorized user from typing on its keyboard or viewing its screen. When you connect computers together over a network, this is no longer sufficient; you now have to ensure that users accessing shared resources, data, and components running on a computer over a network have the appropriate access rights. Companies developing operating systems, such as Microsoft with Windows, incorporate many security features into their own platforms. Typically, these features include maintaining a list of users and the credentials that they use to identify these users, such as their passwords. These solutions can work well in an environment where it is possible to maintain such a list, such as within a single organization, but clearly it is not feasible to record identity and credential information for all computers and users accessing your services across the World Wide Web if you wish to make your services available outside of your enterprise.

A lot of research has been performed in understanding the challenges of maintaining security in a global environment, and many solutions have been proposed. To communicate in a secure manner, Web services and client applications need to agree on the form of security that they will use and how they will identify and verify each other. The Organization for the Advancement of Structured Information Standards (OASIS) is a consortium of organizations that have proposed a number of standard mechanisms for implementing security, such as using username/password pairs, X509 certificates, and Kerberos tokens. If you are creating Web services that provide access to privileged information, you should consider using one of these mechanisms to authenticate users.

> **More Info**   For detailed information about the OASIS security standards, visit the OASIS Web Service Security site at *http://www.oasis-open.org/committees/ tc_home.php?wg_abbrev=wss*.

Privacy is closely related to security, and equally important, especially when you start to communicate with services on the World Wide Web. You don't want other users to be able to intercept and read the messages flowing between your applications and Web services. To this end, Web services and client applications must also agree on a mechanism to ensure the privacy of their conversations. Typically, this means encrypting the messages that they exchange. As with security, there are several mechanisms available for encrypting messages, the most common of which relies on using public and private keys.

> **More Info**   For a good overview and introduction to public key cryptography, visit the Wikipedia Web site at *http://en.wikipedia.org/wiki/Public-key_cryptography*.

Incorporating security and privacy into a Web service and client application can be a non-trivial task. To make life easier for developers building Web services using the Microsoft .NET Framework, Microsoft introduced the Web Services Enhancements (WSE) package. WSE is a fully supported add-on to Microsoft Visual Studio, designed to help you create Web services that retain compatibility with the evolving Web service standards. It provides you with wizards and other tools that you can use to generate much of the code necessary to help protect Web services and client applications and can simplify the configuration and deployment of Web services.

The Purpose of Windows Communication Foundation

So, by using Visual Studio, the .NET Framework, and WSE, you can quickly build Web services and client applications that can communicate and interoperate with Web services and client applications running on other operating systems. So why do we need WCF? Well, as you have already seen, Web services are just one technology that you can use to create distributed applications for Windows. Others already mentioned include Enterprise Services and .NET Framework Remoting. Another example is Microsoft Message Queue (MSMQ). If you are building a distributed application for Windows, which technology should you use, and how difficult would it be to switch later if you need to? The purpose of WCF is to provide a unified programming model for many of these technologies, enabling you to build applications that are as independent as possible from the underlying mechanism being used to connect services and applications together (note that WCF applies as much to services operating in non-Web environments as it does to the World Wide Web). It is actually very difficult, if not impossible, to completely divorce the programmatic structure of an application or service from its communications infrastructure, but WCF lets you come very close to achieving this aim much of the time. Additionally, using WCF enables you to maintain backwards compatibility with many of the preceding technologies. For example, a WCF client application can easily communicate with a Web service that you created by using WSE.

To summarize, if you are considering building distributed applications and services for Microsoft Windows, you should use WCF.

Building a WCF Service

Visual Studio 2005 provides the ideal environment for building WCF services and applications. The Visual Studio Development Tools for the .NET Framework 3.0 include a project template that you can use for creating a WCF service. You will use this template to create a simple service that exposes methods for querying and maintaining information stored in a database. The database used is the sample *AdventureWorks* database. The Introduction to this book contains instructions for installing this database. The AdventureWorks company manufactures bicycles and accessories. The database contains details of the products that they sell, sales information, details of customers, and employee data. In the exercises in this chapter, you will build a WCF service that provides operations enabling a user to:

■ List the products sold by AdventureWorks

■ Obtain the details of a specific product

■ Query the current stock level of a product

■ Modify the stock level of a product

Figure 1-1 shows the tables in the *AdventureWorks* database used by the exercises in this chapter, and how these tables are related.

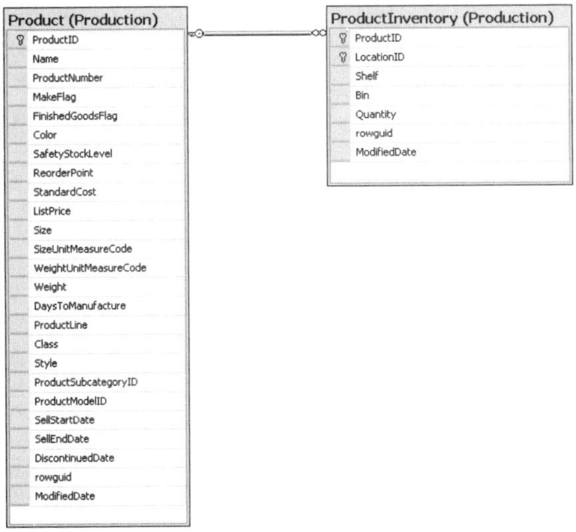

Figure 1-1   Tables holding product information in the *AdventureWorks* database.

To simplify the code that you need to write to access the database, but also to ensure that exercises are as realistic as possible, you will make use of the Data Access Application Block (DAAB). This is part of the Microsoft Enterprise Library. The purpose of the Enterprise Library is to simplify enterprise application development by providing a library of classes that you can use for performing the common tasks frequently required by professional applications. The DAAB contains classes that enable you to query and maintain information stored in a database. You can use the DAAB to write generic code that is independent of the underlying database technology—the DAAB hides the specific details of the database by using an application configuration file. Therefore, before using the DAAB in an application, you must create a configuration file for the application, which is what you will do first.

> **More Info**   For additional information about using the Enterprise Library, please visit the Microsoft Patterns and Practices Web site at *http://msdn.microsoft.com/practices/guidetype/ AppBlocks/default.asp*.

Preliminary exercise—Configure the Data Access Application Block

1. On the Windows Start menu, point to All Programs, point to Microsoft Patterns & Practices, point to Enterprise Library, and then click Enterprise Library Configuration.

2. In the Enterprise Configuration console, in the File menu, click New Application.

   The Application Configuration node appears in the tree view in the left pane of the console.

3. Right-click the Application Configuration node, point to New, and then click Data Access Application Block.

   The Data Access Application Block node and several child nodes appear in the tree-view in the left pane of the console.

4. In the tree-view in the left pane, select the Connection String node. In the right pane, change the *Name* property to *AdventureWorksConnection*. This is the name that you will use to refer to the connection in your applications. Verify that the *ProviderName* property is set to *System.Data.SqlClient*—this is the provider used to connect to Microsoft SQL Server.

5. In the tree view in the left pane, select the Database node. In the right pane, change the *Value* property to *AdventureWorks*. This is the name of the sample database.

> **Important**   Be sure to change the Value property and not the Name property.

![Enterprise Library Configuration window screenshot showing the configuration tree with Enterprise Library Configuration, Application Configuration, Data Access Application Block, Connection Strings, AdventureWorksConnection, Database, Server, Integrated Security, and Custom Provider Mappings nodes. The General pane shows Name: Database and Value: AdventureWorks.]

6. In the tree view in the left pane, select the Server node. In the right-hand pane, change the *Value* property to the name of the SQL Server instance you are using.

> **Tip**   If you are using a local instance of SQL Server 2005 Express Edition, you can leave the *Value* property of the Server node at its default setting.

7. In the tree view in the left pane, select the Integrated Security node. In the right pane, verify that the *Value* property is set to *SSPI*.

> **Note**   If you are not using integrated security, you will need to change this value and specify a username and password when you access SQL Server. However, it is highly recommended that you use integrated security when connecting to SQL Server.

8. In the Action menu, click Validate. Verify that no messages are reported in the Configuration Errors pane at the bottom of the console.

9. In the File menu, click Save Application. Save the application configuration file as Web.config in your C:\Documents and Settings*YourName*\My Documents\ folder. Replace *YourName* in this path with your Windows user name.

10. Close the Enterprise Library Configuration console.

Use the .NET Framework 3.0 and Visual Studio 2005 to create a WCF service project

1. Start Visual Studio 2005.

2. On the File menu, point to New and then click Project.

3. In the New Project dialog box, expand the Visual C# node in the Project types tree, and then click NET Framework 3.0.

4. In the Templates pane, select the WCF Service Library template.

Visual Studio 2005 actually provides two templates for creating a WCF service; the WCF Service Library template that you are using here, and the WCF Service template that is available when you create a new Web site (because of the similarity in the names, I will refer to this one as the WCF Service Web site template to avoid confusion). If you are creating a WCF service that is always going to be deployed by using IIS, then you could use the WCF Service Web site template. In the case of the service you are about to build, although you will initially deploy it to IIS, you will reuse it in a variety of other scenarios, so you will create it by using the WCF Service Library template. It is also instructive to understand the tasks involved in deploying a WCF service to IIS in case you ever need to perform them yourself, and using the WCF Service Library template gives you this opportunity!

You will get some practice at using the WCF Service Web site template in Chapter 5, "Protecting a WCF Service over the Internet."

5. In the Name field, type **ProductsService**.

6. In the Location field, type **C:\Documents and Settings\YourName\My Documents\Microsoft Press\WCF Step By Step\Chapter 1** if you are using Windows XP, or **C:\Users\YourName\Documents\Mirosoft Press\WCF Step By Step\Chapter 1** if you are using Windows Vista. To save space throughout the rest of this book, I will simply refer to the path "C:\Documents and Settings\YourName\My Documents" or "C:\Users\YourName\Documents as your "\My Documents" folder.

7. Ensure that the Create directory for solution check box is selected, and then click OK. Visual Studio 2005 creates the new project.

> **Note** From here on, I will assume that you understand how to create a new project by using Visual Studio 2005, and so I will simply ask you to create a new project, although I will specify the template and any specific project names you should use.

8. Using Solution Explorer, rename the Class1.cs file as ProductsService.cs.

9. In the Project menu, click Add Reference. In the Add Reference dialog box, click the Browse tab, and add references to the following assemblies required by the DAAB. You can find these assemblies in the C:\Program Files\Microsoft Enterprise Library\bin folder:

   ❑ *Microsoft.Practices.EnterpriseLibrary.Data.dll*

   ❑ *Microsoft.Practices.EnterpriseLibrary.Common.dll*

   ❑ *Microsoft.Practices.ObjectBuilder.dll*

10. In the code view window displaying ProductsService.cs, add the following statements to the top of the file:

    ```
    using Microsoft.Practices.EnterpriseLibrary.Data;
    using System.Data;
    ```

11. In the Project menu, click Add Existing Item. In the Add Existing Item dialog box, move to your \My Documents folder, and add the Web.config file that you created earlier.

> **Tip** Select *All Files* in the *Files of type* list box to see the Web.config file listed in the dialog box.

At this point, it is worth examining the code and comments that the WCF Service template contains. At the top of the ProductsService.cs file, apart from the statements you have just added, you will find the usual *using* statements referencing the *System, System.Collections.Generic*, and *System.Text* namespaces, followed by two additional statements referencing the System.Service-Model and System.Runtime.Serialization namespaces, as shown in Figure 1-2.

The System.ServiceModel namespace contains the classes used by WCF for defining services and their operations. You will see many of the classes and types in this namespace as you progress through this book. WCF uses the classes in the System.Runtime.Serialization namespace to convert objects into a stream of data for transmitting over the network (a process known as *serialization*) and to convert a stream of data received from the network back into objects (*deserialization*). You will learn a little about how WCF serializes and deserializes objects later in this chapter and look at serialization and deserialization in more depth as you progress through this book. In Solution Explorer, in the References folder, you will see references to the *System.ServiceModel* and *System.Runtime.Serialization* assemblies, which contain the code that implement the classes in these namespaces. You should also notice a reference to the *System.IdentityModel* assembly. This assembly contains namespaces and types that you can use to manage security and identity information, helping to protect a WCF service. You will learn more about security and protecting services in Chapter 4, "Protecting an Enterprise WCF Service," and Chapter 5.

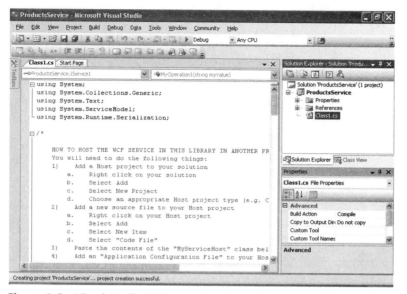

Figure 1-2   Visual Studio 2005, showing the code generated for a WCF service project.

Returning to the code view window displaying the *ProductsService.cs* class, you will find instructions on how to write an application that can host a WCF service. Feel free to read these instructions, but we will cover this process in more depth in Chapter 2, "Hosting a WCF Service." Below these instructions are more comments describing the structure of a WCF service. Again, feel free to examine these comments, but we are going to cover these concepts in detail, and expand upon them considerably, in the exercises throughout this book. Finally, towards the end of the file, you will see that the template defines a namespace for the ProductsService WCF service and includes some sample code for this service.

Defining Contracts

The structure of a WCF service enables you to adopt a "contract-first" approach to development. When performing contract-first development, you define the interfaces, or *contracts*, that the service will implement and then build a service that conforms to these contracts. This is not a new technique; COM developers have been using a very similar strategy for the last decade or so. The point behind using contract-first development is that it enables you to concentrate on the design of your service. If necessary, it can quickly be reviewed to ensure that it does not introduce any dependencies on specific hardware or software before you perform too much development; remember that in many cases client applications might not be built using WCF, or even be running on Windows.

In the following exercises, you will define the data and service contracts for the ProductsService WCF service. The data contract specifies the details of products that the WCF service can pass to operations. The service contract defines the operations that the WCF service will implement.

Define the data contract for the WCF service

1. Comment out the sample code and namespace in the ProductsService.cs file, as you are going to write your own code.

2. Add the following namespace to the end of the file:

```
namespace Products
{
}
```

3. Add the *Product* class shown below to the *Products* namespace:

```
// Data contract describing the details of a product
[DataContract]
public class Product
{
    [DataMember]
    public string Name;

    [DataMember]
    public string ProductNumber;

    [DataMember]
    public string Color;

    [DataMember]
    public decimal ListPrice;
}
```

The *DataContract* attribute identifies the class as defining a type that can be serialized and deserialized as an XML stream by WCF. All types that you pass to WCF operations or return from WCF operations must be serializable by WCF. You can apply the *Data-Contract* attribute to classes, structures, and enumerations.

You mark each member of the type with the *DataMember* attribute; any members not tagged in this way will not be serialized.

> **Note** You can use any other types that already have a data contract defined for them as the types of data members inside a data contract. You can also use any serializable type. This includes types such as string, int, and decimal, as well as many of the more complex types such as the *Collection* classes.

Define the service contract for the WCF service

1. Add the *IProductsService* interface shown below to the *Products* namespace, underneath the *Product* class:

```
// Service contract describing the operations provided by the WCF service
[ServiceContract]
public interface IProductsService
{
    // Get the product number of every product
```

```
[OperationContract]
List<string> ListProducts();

// Get the details of a single product
[OperationContract]
Product GetProduct(string productNumber);

// Get the current stock level for a product
[OperationContract]
int CurrentStockLevel(string productNumber);

// Change the stock level for a product
[OperationContract]
bool ChangeStockLevel(string productNumber, int newStockLevel, string shelf, int bin);
}
```

Note that a service contract should be defined by using an interface rather than a class, as this enables you to separate the definition of the contract from its implementation. You use the *ServiceContract* attribute to mark the interface as a service contract (the WCF runtime relies on the interface being tagged with this attribute when it is generating metadata for client applications that wish to use this service). Each method that you want to expose should be tagged with the *OperationContract* attribute. It is also worth noting that you can use generic types, such as List<>, as parameters or return values in a WCF service contract. As long as the types you use are serializable by WCF, that is all that matters. You will learn much more about service contracts as you proceed through this book.

Implementing the Service

Now that you have specified the structure of the data passed to the WCF service by using a data contract and defined the shape of the WCF service by using a service contract, the next step is to write the code that actually implements the service contract. As with any interface, you must implement every method defined by the service contract in the WCF service. Note that if you define additional methods in the WCF service that are not in the service contract, then these methods will not be visible to client applications using the service.

Implement the WCF service

1. Add the following class to the *Products* namespace, underneath the IProductService service contract:

   ```
   // WCF service class that implements the service contract
   public class ProductsServiceImpl : IProductsService
   {
   }
   ```

   Notice that a class that provides a WCF service should indicate that it implements a service contract, in this case, IProductService, by using standard C# inheritance notation.

2. Add the ListProducts method to the *ProductsServiceImpl* class:

```
public List<string> ListProducts()
{
    // Read the configuration information for connecting to
    // the AdventureWorks database
    Database dbAdventureWorks =
        DatabaseFactory.CreateDatabase("AdventureWorksConnection");

    // Retrieve the details of all products by using a DataReader
    string queryString = @"SELECT ProductNumber
                             FROM Production.Product";
    IDataReader productsReader =
        dbAdventureWorks.ExecuteReader(CommandType.Text, queryString);

    // Create and populate a list of products
    List<string> productsList = new List<string>();
    while (productsReader.Read())
    {
        string productNumber = productsReader.GetString(0);
        productsList.Add(productNumber);
    }

    //Return the list of products
    return productsList;
}
```

> **Tip** This code is available in the file ListProducts.txt in the Microsoft Press\WCF Step By Step\Chapter 1 folder under your \My Documents folder.

This code uses the DatabaseFactory.CreateDatabase method of the DAAB to obtain the connection parameters referenced by the AdventureWorksConnection settings that you defined earlier. The ExecuteReader method uses this information to connect to the database and perform its query. When the ListProduct method completes, the DAAB automatically disconnects from the database.

The code invokes the ExecuteReader method of the DAAB Database object to run a SQL query that returns a list of product numbers from the database. The data is returned as a *DataReader* object. The code then iterates through this list, retrieving each product number and storing them in a generic *List<string>* collection. The ListProducts method returns this *List<string>* object when the method completes.

> **Important** For the sake of clarity, this method does not include any exception handling. In the real world, you should check for exceptions and handle them accordingly. For more information, see Chapter 3, "Making Applications and Services Robust."

3. Add the GetProduct method to the *ProductsServiceImpl* class:

```
public Product GetProduct(string productNumber)
{
    Database dbAdventureWorks =
        DatabaseFactory.CreateDatabase("AdventureWorksConnection");
```

```
// Retrieve the details of the selected product by using a DataReader
string queryString = @"SELECT ProductNumber, Name, Color, ListPrice
                       FROM Production.Product
                       WHERE ProductNumber = '" + productNumber + "'";
IDataReader productsReader =
    dbAdventureWorks.ExecuteReader(CommandType.Text, queryString);

// Create and populate a product
Product product = new Product();
if (productsReader.Read())
{
    product.ProductNumber = productsReader.GetString(0);
    product.Name = productsReader.GetString(1);
    if (productsReader.IsDBNull(2))
    {
        product.Color = "N/A";
    }
    else
    {
        product.Color = productsReader.GetString(2);
    }
    product.ListPrice = productsReader.GetDecimal(3);
}

//Return the product
return product;
}
```

> **Tip** This code is available in the file GetProduct.txt in the Microsoft Press\WCF Step
> By Step\Chapter 1 folder under your \My Documents folder.

This method uses a technique very similar to that of the ListProducts method to connect to the database and retrieve the details of the specified product. The important point to pick up from this method is that it returns a *Product* object—you defined this type by using a data contract in the previous exercise.

4. Add the CurrentStockLevel method to the *ProductsServiceImpl* class:

```
public int CurrentStockLevel(string productNumber)
{
    Database dbAdventureWorks =
        DatabaseFactory.CreateDatabase("AdventureWorksConnection");

    // Obtain the current stock level of the selected product
    // The stock level can be found by summing the quantity of the product
    // available in all bins in the ProductInventory table
    // The ProductID value has to be retrieved from the Product table
    string queryString = @"SELECT SUM(Quantity)
                        FROM Production.ProductInventory
                        WHERE ProductID =
                            (SELECT ProductID
                             FROM Production.Product
```

```
                          WHERE ProductNumber = '" + productNumber +
                "')";
    int stockLevel =
        (int)dbAdventureWorks.ExecuteScalar(CommandType.Text, queryString);

    //Return the current stock level
    return stockLevel;
}
```

> **Tip**   This code is available in the file CurrentStockLevel.txt in the Microsoft Press\WCF Step By Step\Chapter 1 folder under your \My Documents folder.

Products are stored in one or more numbered bins in the warehouse, and each bin is on a named shelf. This method sums the current volume of the specified product held in all the bins on all the shelves where it is stored.

5. Add the ChangeStockLevel method to the *ProductsServiceImpl* class:

```
public bool ChangeStockLevel(string productNumber, int newStockLevel, string shelf, in
t bin)
{
    Database dbAdventureWorks =
        DatabaseFactory.CreateDatabase("AdventureWorksConnection");

    // Modify the current stock level of the selected product
    // The ProductID value has to be retrieved from the Product table
    string updateString = @"UPDATE Production.ProductInventory
                    SET Quantity = Quantity + " + newStockLevel +
                    "WHERE Shelf = '" + shelf + "'" +
                    "AND Bin = " + bin +
                    @"AND ProductID =
                        (SELECT ProductID
                         FROM Production.Product
                         WHERE ProductNumber = '" + productNumber +
                "')";
    int numRowsChanged =
     (int)dbAdventureWorks.ExecuteNonQuery(CommandType.Text, updateString);

    // If no rows were updated, return false to indicate that the input
    // parameters did not identify a valid product and location
    // Otherwise return true to indicate success
    return (numRowsChanged != 0);
}
```

> **Tip**   This code is available in the file ChangeStockLevel.txt in the Microsoft Press\WCF Step By Step\Chapter 1 folder under your \My Documents folder.

This method updates the quantity in stock for the specified product, in the specified bin, on the specified shelf. If this product is not actually located in this bin and shelf, the method returns false to indicate a possible user error (the user has probably just specified a wrong bin and shelf combination), otherwise it returns true.

> **Important** If you are an experienced database developer, you will probably be about to e-mail me telling me that using string concatenation to build SQL queries is bad practice. This approach renders your service vulnerable to SQL Injection attacks. However, this is intentional, and you will address this issue in Chapter 6, "Maintaining Data Contracts and Service Contracts," so for the time being, grit your teeth and bear with me.
>
> On the other hand, if this *is* the sort of code that you usually write when accessing a database, and have never heard of a SQL Injection attack, then pay special attention when you reach Chapter 6.

6. Build the project, and correct any syntax errors if necessary.

Configuring, Deploying, and Testing the WCF Service

You must host a WCF service in an application in order to run it and make it accessible to clients. You have several options available for hosting a WCF service, including creating a custom host application, building a Windows service application, and using IIS. In the following exercises, you will configure the ProductsService WCF service as a Web service hosted by IIS. You will then verify that you have configured and deployed it correctly by performing a simple test with Internet Explorer.

> **Note** As mentioned earlier, if you use the WCF Service Web site template for building a WCF service, then the service will automatically be deployed to IIS (or the Visual Studio Development Web Server, depending on the options that you select). The exercises in this section give you a feel for some of the tasks that Visual Studio 2005 performs when using this template, and how it varies from using the WCF Service Library template.

IIS expects the assemblies containing the code for Web services and Web applications to be located in the bin folder of the Web site. Therefore, to configure a WCF service as a Web service that can be hosted by IIS, you must ensure that the project assemblies are built in the bin folder of the project rather than the bin\Debug or bin\Release folders. You must also add a service definition file. This is a file that specifies the name of the class that IIS will execute, and the name of the assembly holding this class. Finally, you must edit the Web.config file and add endpoint information for the Web service. IIS uses this information to specify binding information for the Web service indicating how a client should communicate with the service, and the contract that the Web service implements.

Configure the WCF service

1. On the Project menu, click ProductsService properties to display the Property pages for the project.

2. Click the Build tab. In the Output section of the page, change the Output path property to bin.

3. On the File menu, click Save All.

4. On the Project menu, click Add New Item.

5. In the Add New Item dialog box, select the Text File template. Change the name of the file to ProductsService.svc, and then click Add. This is the service definition file for the Web service.

> **Important**   The service definition file must have the same name as the Web service, and have the .svc suffix.

6. Add the following code to the ProductsService.svc file displayed in the code view window:

```
<%@ServiceHost Service="Products.ProductsServiceImpl" %>
<%@Assembly Name="ProductsService" %>
```

The *Service* attribute of the ServiceHost directive specifies the namespace (*Products*) and the class (*ProductsServiceImpl*) that implements the service. The Assembly directive specifies the name of the assembly (*ProductsService*) containing this namespace and class.

7. Edit the Web.config file for the project. Currently, this file just contains a <Configuration> section containing the information generated by the Enterprise Library Configuration tool for connecting to the database. Edit the file, and add the following sections shown in bold:

```
<?xml version="1.0" encoding="utf-8" ?>
<configuration>
  <configSections>
      <section name="dataConfiguration" type="Microsoft.Practices.EnterpriseLibrary.
Data.Configuration.DatabaseSettings, Microsoft.Practices.EnterpriseLibrary.Data, Versi
on=2.0.0.0, Culture=neutral, PublicKeyToken=null" />
  </configSections>
  <dataConfiguration defaultDatabase="AdventureWorksConnection" />
  <connectionStrings>
      <add name="AdventureWorksConnection" connectionString="Database=
AdventureWorks;Server=(local)\SQLEXPRESS;Integrated Security=SSPI;"
          providerName="System.Data.SqlClient" />
  </connectionStrings>   <system.serviceModel>
    <services>
      <service name="Products.ProductsServiceImpl">
        <endpoint address=""
                binding="basicHttpBinding"
                contract="Products.IProductsService" />
      </service>
    </services>
  </system.serviceModel>
</configuration>
```

The <serviceModel> section of the Web.config file contains the configuration information for a WCF Web service. The <services> section contains the details for each service implemented. The name attribute of the *<service>* element specifies the namespace and class that implement the service..

The *<endpoint>* element provides the details of the service that client applications require in order to communicate with the service. An endpoint comprises three pieces of information: an address, a binding, and a contract. The address is the location that the application hosting the service uses to advertise the service. In the case of IIS, the *address* element actually is ignored as IIS will use a URL containing the name of the virtual directory holding the service and the name of the .svc file as the endpoint (in this case, *http:/ /localhost/ProductsService/ProductsService.svc*). The *binding* element specifies items such as the transport mechanism used to access the Web service, and the protocol to use, amongst other items. You can specify one of a number of standard bindings built into WCF that implement pre-configured binding information. In this case, the service uses the basicHttpBinding binding, which is compatible with many existing Web service client applications built using technologies other than WCF. You will learn much more about bindings as you progress through this book. Finally, the *contract* element indicates the contract that the service implements.

8. Build the solution.

You can now deploy the service to IIS by creating a virtual folder. You must also ensure that the account used to run the code for the Web service, the local ASPNET account on your computer by default, has sufficient rights to access the contents of this folder.

> **Note** Windows Vista and Windows XP use different versions of IIS, with different user interfaces. There are two versions of the next exercise. Please follow the instructions appropriate to your operating system.

Deploy the WCF service to IIS (Windows Vista only)

1. In the Windows Control Panel, click System and Maintenance, click Administrative Tools, and then double-click Internet Information Services (IIS) Manager.

   The Internet Information Services (IIS) Manager starts.

2. In the Internet Information Services (IIS) Manager, expand the node corresponding to your computer in the tree-view, and then expand Web sites.

3. Right-click Default Web Site, and then click Add Application.

   The Add Application dialog box appears.

4. In the Add Application dialog box, in the Alias text box type ProductsService.

5. Click the browse button (with the ellipses "...") adjacent to the Physical path text box. In the Browse for Folder dialog box, select the folder Microsoft Press\WCF Step By Step\Chapter 1\ProductsService\ProductsService under your \My Documents folder, click then click OK.

6. In the Add Application dialog box, click OK.

   The ProductsService Web application should appear under the Default Web site node in the Internet Information Services (IIS) Manager.

7. Close the Internet Information Services (IIS) Manager.

Deploy the WCF service to IIS (Windows XP only)

1. On the Windows Start menu, click Run.

2. In the Run dialog box, type **inetmgr**, and then click OK.

   The Internet Information Services console starts.

3. In the Internet Information Services console, expand the node corresponding to your computer in the tree-view, and then expand Web sites.

4. Right-click Default Web Site, point to New, and then click Virtual Directory.

   The Virtual Directory Creation Wizard starts.

5. In the Welcome to the Virtual Directory Creation Wizard page, click Next.

6. In the Virtual Directory Alias page, type ProductsService, and then click Next.

7. In the Web Site Content Directory page, click Browse, select the folder Microsoft Press\WCF Step By Step\Chapter 1\ProductsService\ProductsService under your \My Documents folder, click OK, and then click Next.

8. In the Access Permissions page, accept the default values, and then click Next.

9. In the You have successfully completed the Virtual Directory Creation Wizard page, click Finish.

   The ProductsService virtual directory should appear under the Default Web site node in the Internet Information Services console:

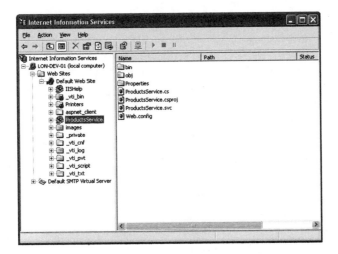

10. Close the Internet Information Services console.

You can now verify that you have correctly configured and deployed the service. The simplest way to check this is to use Internet Explorer to browse to the Web service.

Test the WCF service deployment

1. On the Windows Start menu, click Internet Explorer.

2. In the Address bar, type the address **http://localhost/ProductsService/ ProductsService.svc**, and then click Go.

   You should see a page like this:

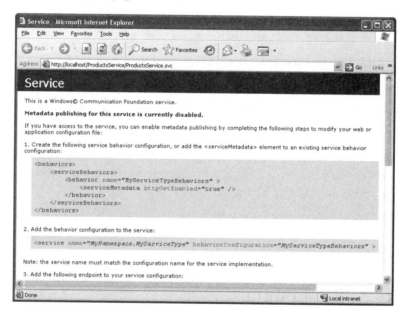

   Client applications require access to the metadata of a service so that they can determine the operations the service implements. For security reasons, WCF disables metadata publishing from services. You can obtain metadata information directly from the assembly holding the service contract, but this approach might not always be convenient. For example, if you are building a client application running on a computer that is different from that hosting the service, you might not have access to the service contract assembly. In the following steps, you will enable metadata publishing for the service. This will enable developers to obtain the metadata for the service by querying the service.

3. Return to Visual Studio 2005, and edit the Web.config file for the ProductsService project. Make the changes shown in bold to the <system.serviceModel> section this file, and then save your changes:

```
<system.serviceModel>
  <services>
    <service name="Products.ProductsServiceImpl"
```

```
              behaviorConfiguration="ProductsBehavior">
        <endpoint address=""
                  binding="basicHttpBinding"
                  contract="Products.IProductsService" />
    </service>
  </services>
  <behaviors>
    <serviceBehaviors>
      <behavior name="ProductsBehavior">
        <serviceMetadata httpGetEnabled="true" />
      </behavior>
    </serviceBehaviors>
  </behaviors>
</system.serviceModel>
```

These changes add a *behavior* called ProductsBehavior to the service. A service behavior extends the functionality of a service (you will learn a lot more about behaviors throughout this book). The definition of the ProductsBehavior behavior enables metadata publishing by setting the *httpGetEnabled* attribute of the *<serviceMetadata>* element to true.

4. Return to Internet Explorer and click Go again. The service will now display a different page:

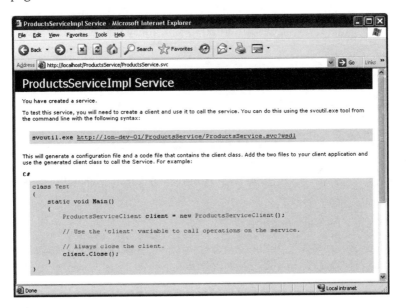

This page describes how you can obtain the metadata describing the service and use this information to help build a client application.

5. In the address bar, change the address to **http://localhost/ProductsService/ ProductsService.svc?wsdl**, and then click Go:

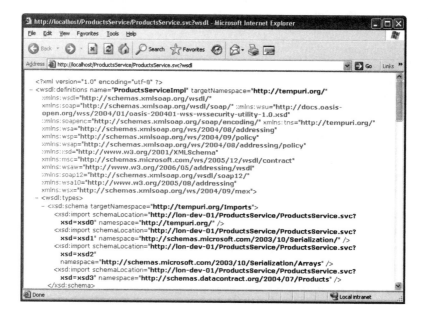

The service displays a page containing the metadata description of the service. You can see that this is XML. Visual Studio 2005 can query the service and use this information to generate a proxy class when building a WCF client application.

6. Close Internet Explorer.

Building a WCF Client

You can use the tools provided by WCF and Visual Studio 2005 to build a simple client application to test the WCF service. In the following exercises, you will build a console client application that invokes each of the operations defined by the service, and verify that the service operates as expected.

Build a console client application

1. In Visual Studio 2005, in Solution Explorer, right-click the ProductsService solution, point to Add, and then click New Project.

2. In the Add New Project window, select the Windows project type, click the Console Application template, set the name of the project to ProductsClient, and save it in the default folder for the solution. Click OK.

3. Make sure you have selected the ProductsClient project in Solution Explorer. On the Project menu, click Add Reference, and add a reference to the *System.ServiceModel* assembly.

4. On the Project menu, click Add Service Reference. In the Add Service Reference dialog box, type **http://localhost/ProductsService/ProductsService.svc?wsdl** for the service URL, type **ProductsService** for the service reference name, and then click OK.

This action queries the ProductsService service, retrieves the metadata, and generates a proxy class using this metadata. The client can use this *proxy* class to invoke the operations exposed by the ProductsService service. You can view the code for the *proxy* class by expanding the Service References folder in Solution Explorer, expanding the ProductsService.map folder, and double-clicking the ProductsService.cs file. Be careful not to change any of the code in this file.

5. In Solution Explorer, double-click the app.config file for the ProductsClient project to display this file in the code view window. This is the WCF client configuration file, and it was generated at the same time as the *proxy* class. It contains the settings the client uses to connect to the WCF service. Examine the <client> section towards the bottom of the file:

```
<client>
    <endpoint address="http://lon-dev-01/ProductsService/ProductsService.svc"
            binding="basicHttpBinding" bindingConfiguration=
```

```
"BasicHttpBinding_IProductsService"
            contract="ProductsClient.ProductsService.IProductsService"
            name="BasicHttpBinding_IProductsService" />
</client>
```

> **Note** Your file will contain the name of your computer in the endpoint address, rather than lon-dev-01.

The endpoint mirrors that of the ProductsService service, specifying the URL of the service, and the same binding and contract information. The main difference is the addition of the *name* attribute, enabling you to refer to the endpoint in your code (which you will do later in this exercise). Also, you can see that the file customizes the settings used by the basicHttpBinding binding. If you scroll back through the file, you can see the definition of this customized binding. Many of the predefined bindings available with WCF have a number of optional parameters that you can modify in this way. Do not change anything in this file.

6. Display the Program.cs file for the ProductsClient project in the code view window. Add the following statements to the top of the file:

```
using System.ServiceModel;
using ProductsClient.ProductsService;
```

You should always add a reference to the System.ServiceModel assembly and namespace to a WCF client application, as they provide the methods needed to communicate with a WCF service. The ProductsClient.ProductsService namespace contains the proxy class for the ProductsService WCF service.

7. In the Main method, add the following statements:

```
// Create a proxy object and connect to the service
ProductsServiceClient proxy =
    new ProductsServiceClient("BasicHttpBinding_IProductsService");
```

The *ProductsServiceClient* class is the name of the proxy type generated earlier. This code creates a new instance of the proxy and connects to the ProductsService service. The parameter to the constructor, BasicHttpBinding_IProductsService, specifies the name of the endpoint in the app.config file to which the client will connect.

8. Add the following code to the Main method:

```
// Test the operations in the service

// Obtain a list of all products
Console.WriteLine("Test 1: List all products");
string[] productNumbers = proxy.ListProducts();
foreach (string productNumber in productNumbers)
{
    Console.WriteLine("Number: " + productNumber);
}
Console.WriteLine();
```

This block of code tests the ListProducts method. This method should return an array of strings containing the product number of every product in the database. The foreach statement iterates through the list and displays them.

9. Add the following code to the Main method:

```
// Fetch the details for a specific product
Console.WriteLine("Test 2: Display the details of a product");
Product product = proxy.GetProduct("WB-H098");
Console.WriteLine("Number: " + product.ProductNumber);
Console.WriteLine("Name: " + product.Name);
Console.WriteLine("Color: " + product.Color);
Console.WriteLine("Price: " + product.ListPrice);
Console.WriteLine();
```

This section of code tests the GetProduct method. The GetProduct method returns the details for the specified product (in this case, product WB-H098) as a Product object. Remember that the definition of the Product type was specified in a data contract for the WCF service. The code defining this type in the client application was generated from the metadata for the service and can be found in the ProductsService.cs file, in the ProductsService.map folder, under Service References in Solution Explorer.

10. Add the following code to the Main method:

```
// Query the stock level of this product
Console.WriteLine("Test 3: Display the stock level of a product");
int numInStock = proxy.CurrentStockLevel("WB-H098");
Console.WriteLine("Current stock level: " + numInStock);
Console.WriteLine();
```

This block of code tests the CurrentStockLevel method. The value returned should be the total number of product WB-H098 held in the warehouse (the stock might be held in several bins, located on several shelves).

11. Add the following code to the Main method:

```
// Modify the stock level of this product
Console.WriteLine("Test 4: Modify the stock level of a product");
if (proxy.ChangeStockLevel("WB-H098", 100, "N/A", 0))
{
    numInStock = proxy.CurrentStockLevel("WB-H098");
    Console.WriteLine("Stock changed. Current stock level: " + numInStock);
}
else
{
    Console.WriteLine("Stock level update failed");
}
Console.WriteLine();
```

This code tests the ChangeStockLevel method. Product WB-H098 is located on shelf "N/A," in bin 0, and this code adds another 100 to the volume in stock. The code then calls the CurrentStockLevel method again, which should return the new stock level for this product.

12. Complete the Main method by adding the following code:

```
// Disconnect from the service
proxy.Close();
Console.WriteLine("Press ENTER to finish");
Console.ReadLine();
```

You disconnect from a service by calling the Close method of the proxy. You should not attempt to call further methods by using the proxy without connecting again.

13. Save the project, and build the solution.

The final step is to run the client application and verify that the service operates as expected.

Run the client application

1. In Solution Explorer, right-click the ProductsClient project, and then click Set as Startup Project.

2. On the Debug menu, click Start Without Debugging.

A console window opens. A list of product numbers should appear first, followed by the details of product WB-H098 (a water bottle), the current stock level (252), and the stock level after adding another 100 (352):

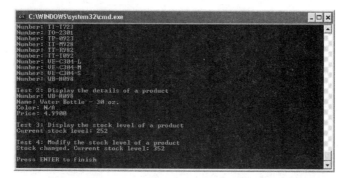

3. Press Enter to terminate the program and return to Visual Studio 2005.

Service-Oriented Architectures and Windows Communication Foundation

You have seen how, by using WCF, you can quickly build services that you can integrate into enterprise solutions. Apart from writing entirely new functionality, you can use WCF to implement services that wrap existing applications, and connect them together in ways that were previously difficult to achieve. WCF can act as the "glue" for combining applications and components together. Additionally, WCF can make use of standard protocols, data formats, and communications mechanisms, enabling interoperability with services developed by using other technologies. WCF is an ideal platform for implementing a Service-Oriented Architecture, or SOA.

An SOA consists of a set of resources on a network that are made available as independent services, and that can be accessed without requiring any knowledge of how they are implemented. You can combine the services in an SOA to create an enterprise application. I don't want to go into the full theory of SOA, but the main benefits are that it enables you to create complex solutions that are independent of any specific platform and location. This means that you can quickly replace or upgrade a service or move a service to a different site (possibly running on faster hardware), and as long as the service exposes the same interfaces as before, you can continue to use it without needing to modify any code. However, SOA is not a magic wand that will instantly solve all of your distributed application architecture problems. To successfully design and implement an SOA, you should be aware of what has become known as the "Four Tenets of Service Orientation." These are:

1. Boundaries are explicit. Applications and services communicate by sending messages to each other. You should not make any assumptions about how a service processes a request or how a client application handles any response to a request. Following this principle can help to remove dependencies between services and client applications. Additionally, sending and receiving messages has an associated cost in terms of communications. You should design the operations that services implement with this in mind, and ensure that clients call services only when necessary.

2. Services are autonomous. If you are building an application based on services, you might not have control over every service you are using, especially Web services hosted outside of your organization. The location of a Web service might change, or a service might be temporarily taken off-line for maintenance or other reasons. You should design your solutions to be loosely coupled, so that they can tolerate these changes and continue running even if one or more services are unavailable.

3. Services share schemas and contracts, not classes or types. Services publish information about the operations that they implement and the structure of the data that they expect to send and receive. Clients use this information when communicating with the service. You should design contracts and schemas to define the interfaces that your services expose. This can reduce the dependencies that clients have on a particular version of your services. Services can change and evolve over time, and a new version of a service might appear superseding a previous version. If a service is updated, it should maintain compatibility with existing clients by continuing to implement existing contracts and send messages that conform to existing schemas. If you need to modify a service and provide additional functionality, you can add contracts and schemas that extend the original capabilities of the service while retaining the existing contracts and schemas. Older client applications should continue to work unchanged.

4. Compatibility is based on policy. The schemas and contracts exposed by a service define the "shape" of the service but not the nonfunctional requirements that a client attempting to access the service must fulfill. For example, a service might have security requirements that state that clients must connect to it in a particular manner and send and receive messages by encrypting data in a specific way. This is an example of policy. The

policy requirements of a service cannot be specified by using contracts and should not require additional coding on the part of the client or the service—these requirements might change over time and so should be decoupled from the implementation of the service and clients. You should design services so that their policy requirements are independent of any implementation, and you should enforce clients to abide by any policies required by the service. Additionally, all services and client applications must agree on how to specify this policy information (typically by using some sort of configuration file). This is the purpose of the WS-Policy framework, published by the World Wide Web Consortium, and widely adopted by Web service developers.

> **More Info**   For further information about the WS-Policy framework, visit the World Wide Web Consortium Web site at *http://www.w3.org/Submission/WS-Policy/*.

This sounds like a lot to have to think about when creating services, but WCF has been designed with these principles in mind. As you progress through the rest of this book, you will meet many of the features WCF provides to help you build services that conform to SOA best practice.

Summary

This chapter has introduced you to WCF. You have learned the purpose of WCF and seen how to use it to create a simple Web service by adopting a contract-first approach to design. You have deployed the WCF Web service to IIS and seen how to create a client application that can access the service. Finally, you have learned the basic principles of SOA and should understand that using WCF can help you to build services for an SOA quickly and easily.

Chapter 2
Hosting a WCF Service

After completing this chapter, you will be able to:

- Describe how a WCF service runs.

- Explain the different ways you can host a WCF service.

- Build a Windows Presentation Foundation application and a Windows service that host a WCF service.

- Describe the different bindings available for communicating with a WCF service.

- Use multiple bindings with a WCF service.

In the previous chapter, you saw how to create a WCF service, and how to deploy a WCF service to IIS and access it from a client application. This chapter describes in more detail how a WCF service works and explains some of the other options you have for hosting a WCF service. In this chapter, you will build and configure host applications that process service requests and control the state of a WCF service. You will also learn more about how bindings work in WCF, and how the WCF runtime uses bindings to implement the nonfunctional features of a service.

How Does a WCF Service Work?

Functionally, a WCF service is just an object that exposes a set of operations that client applications can invoke. When building a service, you describe the operations for a service by using a service contract and then create a class that implements this contract. To execute the service, you have to provide a runtime environment for this object and then make the object available to client applications. The runtime environment for an object implementing a service is provided by a *host* application. You have already seen that you can use IIS to provide such a runtime environment. You can also create your own application to act as a host.

A host application has to perform a number of tasks, including:

- Starting and stopping the service

- Listening for requests from a client application and directing them to the service

- Sending any responses from the service back to the client applications

To understand more about how a host application works, it is helpful to look in more detail at service endpoints and the way in which the WCF runtime uses the binding information specified in endpoints to enable client applications to connect to the service.

Service Endpoints

A host application makes a service available to client applications by providing an endpoint to which clients can send requests. An endpoint contains three pieces of information:

1. The address of the service. The form of a service address depends on several factors, including the transport protocol being used. Different transport mechanisms use different address spaces. For example, in Chapter 1, "Introducing Windows Communication Foundation," you deployed a service to IIS using the address *http://localhost/ProductsService/ProductsService.svc*. This address specifies the virtual directory and the service definition (.svc) file. If you build your own custom host application, you can use a different transport mechanism, and you must specify an address that is appropriate to your chosen transport mechanism.

2. The binding supported by the service. The binding for a service describes how a client can connect to the service and the format of the data expected by the service. A binding can include the following information:

   ❑ The transport protocol. This must conform to the requirements of the service address. For example, if you are using IIS to host the service, you should specify the HTTP or HTTPS transport protocol. WCF also has built-in support for the TCP protocol, named-pipes, and message queues. You will see examples of addresses specified by using some of these transport schemes later in this chapter.

   ❑ The encoding format of messages. In many cases, request and response messages will be transmitted in XML format, encoded as ordinary text. However, in some cases you might need to transmit data using a binary encoding, especially if you are transmitting images or handling streams. You will learn more about using an appropriate encoding for messages in Chapter 12, "Implementing a WCF Service for Good Performance."

   ❑ The security requirements of the service. You can implement security at the transport level and at the message level, although different transport protocols have their own limitations and requirements. You will learn more about specifying the security requirements for a service in Chapter 4, "Protecting an Enterprise WCF Service," and in Chapter 5, "Protecting a WCF Service over the Internet."

   ❑ The transactional requirements of the service. A service typically provides access to one or more resources. Client applications update these resources by sending requests to the service. If a client makes multiple requests of a service that result in multiple updates, it can be important to ensure that *all* of these updates are made permanent. In the event of a failure, the service should undo *all* of these updates. This is the definition of a transaction. You will learn more bout building WCF services that support transactions in Chapter 8, "Supporting Transactions."

   ❑ The reliability of communications with the service. Clients usually connect to services across a network. Networks are notoriously unreliable and can fail at any time. If a client application is performing a conversation (an ordered exchange of several messages) with a service, information about the reliability of the service is important. For example, the service should try and ensure that it receives *all* messages sent by the client and receives them in the order that the client sent them. A service can ensure the integrity of conversations by implementing a reliable messaging protocol. You will learn more about reliable messaging in Chapter 9, "Implementing Reliable Sessions."

  3. The contract implemented by the service. A WCF service contract is an interface stored in a .NET Framework assembly and annotated with the *[ServiceContract]* attribute. The service contract describes the operations implemented by the service by tagging them with the *[OperationContract]* attribute. Any data passed to and from operations must be serializable. A service can define data contracts describing the structure of complex data and how this data should be serialized. The service can publish the description of its service contract, which a client application can use to ascertain the operations that the service implements and send messages that are correctly formatted.

Processing a Client Request

A service can respond to requests from multiple client applications simultaneously. To achieve this feat, the application hosting the service must be able to accept multiple incoming requests and direct service responses back to the appropriate client. Additionally, the host application must ensure that messages being sent between the client and service conform to the security, reliability, and transactional requirements of the binding being used. Fortunately, you don't have to write this functionality yourself. The WCF runtime environment provides a collection of *channel* objects that can perform this processing for you.

A channel is responsible for handling one aspect of message processing, as specified by the bindings of a service. For example, a transport channel manages communications by using a specific transport protocol, and a transaction channel controls the transactional integrity of a conversation. The WCF runtime provides built-in channels for each of the supported transport protocols. The WCF runtime also provides channels that handle the different ways that WCF can encode data, manage security, implement reliability, and perform transactions. The WCF runtime composes channels into a channel stack. All messages passing between the client and the service go through each channel in the channel stack. Each channel in the channel stack transforms the message in some way, and the output from one channel is passed as input to the next. The channel stack operates in two directions—messages received from clients across the network proceed up the channel stack to the service, and response messages sent back from the service traverse the channel stack in the opposite direction back to the network and then to the client. If a channel cannot process a message, it reports an error, an error message is sent back to the client, and the message is not processed any further.

> **Note**   There is an order to the channels in the channel stack. A transport channel always resides at the bottom of the stack and is the first channel to receive data from the network. On top of the transport channel will be an encoding channel. These two channels are mandatory. The remaining channels in a stack are optional.

When you start a service running, the WCF runtime uses the endpoint information specified as part of the service configuration and creates a *listener* object for each address specified for the service. When an incoming request is received, the WCF runtime constructs a channel stack by using the bindings specified for the address and routes the incoming data from the client through the stack. If a message successfully traverses all the channels in the channel stack, the transformed request is passed to an instance of the service for processing.

> **Note**   The channel model used by WCF makes the WCF framework very flexible. If you need to add a new transport protocol or implement an additional piece of functionality, you can write your own channel to perform the processing required and link it into the channel stack by adding it to the binding description of the service. However, this task is beyond the scope of this book.

The WCF runtime creates an *InstanceContext* object to control the interaction between the channel stack and the service instance. You can modify the way in which the WCF runtime instantiates the service through the *InstanceContext* object by specifying the *[ServiceBehavior]* attribute of the class implementing the service contract. The *ServiceBehavior* attribute has a property called *InstanceContextMode*, which can take the values shown in Table 2-1.

Table 2-1   InstanceContextMode Values

Value	Description
InstanceContextMode.PerCall	A new instance of the service will be created every time a client calls an operation. When the call completes, the service instance is recycled.
InstanceContextMode.PerSession	If the service implements sessions, a new instance of the service will be created at the start of the session and recycled when the session completes. A client can call the service several times during a session. However, the service instance cannot be used across more than one session. For more information about using sessions, see Chapter 7, "Maintaining State and Sequencing Operations."
InstanceContextMode.Single	Only one instance of the service is created and is shared by all clients and all sessions. The instance is created when the first client attempts to access it.

You can specify the *InstanceContextMode* property for a service like this:

```
[ServiceBehavior (InstanceContextMode=InstanceContextMode.PerSession)]
public class ProductsServiceImpl : IProductsService
{
  ...
}
```

A WCF client application can communicate with a WCF service by using a proxy class. You can generate this proxy class by using Visual Studio 2005 (as you did in Chapter 1) or by using the svcutil utility from the command line. This proxy class implements a channel stack on the client side. You configure this channel stack in the same way that you do for a service, by using bindings. All responses received from a service pass through the channels in this stack. To communicate successfully, the client and the service should use an equivalent channel stack containing a compatible set of bindings.

Hosting a WCF Service in a User Application

Apart from using an IIS Web service to host a WCF service, you have at least three further options. You can create an ordinary application that the user runs to start and stop the WCF service, or you can host the WCF service in a Windows service so that the WCF service is available as long as Windows is running. The third option, if you are using IIS version 7.0, is to use Windows Activation Services, or WAS. Using WAS, you can configure and host a WCF service without needing to run the World Wide Web Publishing Service. However, IIS 7.0 is not available for Windows XP, and we will not consider using WAS any further in this book.

> **More Info**   For detailed information about IIS 7.0, visit the IIS 7.0 Feature Reference Web site at *http://technet2.microsoft.com/WindowsServer/en/Library/582b556d-d404-4150-aa07-c5c0c750b6c81033.mspx?mfr=true*.

Using the ServiceHost Class

The discussion so far in this chapter has described the tasks that a host application for a WCF service must perform. You can achieve most of these tasks by using the *ServiceHost* class, available in the *System.ServiceModel* namespace. A *ServiceHost* object can instantiate a service object from an assembly holding the service class, configure the endpoints of the service by using bindings provided in a configuration file or in code, apply any security settings required by the service, and create listener objects for each address that you specify.

When you create a *ServiceHost* object, you specify the type of the class implementing the service. You can specify the addresses that the *ServiceHost* object should listen to for requests, like this:

```
ServiceHost productsServiceHost = new
    ServiceHost(typeof(ProductsServiceImpl),
    new Uri("http://localhost:8000/ProductsService/ProductsService.svc"),
    new Uri("tcp.net://localhost:8080/TcpProductsService");
```

This example uses the ProductsService service that you created in Chapter 1, and specifies two addresses: the first uses the HTTP transport, and the second uses TCP. Strictly speaking, the addresses that you specify in the ServiceHost constructor are *base addresses*. A base address is just the initial part of the address. If you provide an application configuration file that contains further address information, this information will be combined with the base addresses you specify here to generate the real addresses. For example, if you use the following code to instantiate the *ServiceHost* object:

```
ServiceHost productsServiceHost = new
    ServiceHost(typeof(ProductsServiceImpl),
    new Uri("http://localhost:8000/ProductsService"));
```

and the application configuration contains an endpoint definition like this:

```
<endpoint address="ProductsService.svc" binding="basicHttpBinding" name="ProductsServiceHttp
Endpoint" contract="Products.IProductsService" />
```

the WCF runtime will combine the two elements together to generate an address of "http://localhost:8000/ProductsService/ProductsService.svc." This is a very powerful feature that enables an administrator to direct a service to use a particular address on a specified site, but that also provides the developer with full control over the selection of the site hosting the service.

If you omit the base address information in the ServiceHost constructor, like this:

```
ServiceHost productsServiceHost = new
    ServiceHost(typeof(ProductsServiceImpl));
```

the WCF runtime will just use the address information specified in the application configuration file, and automatically listen for requests on all configured endpoints. This gives the administrator complete control over the addresses and transports used by the service. For convenience, in the examples in this book, you will adopt this approach and specify the complete address information in the application configuration file wherever possible. However, when building your own enterprise applications, you might prefer to provide the base addresses for service endpoints programmatically.

Note   There is one minor side effect of specifying complete addresses in the application configuration file; if you are building a host application and you wish to enable metadata publishing, you must provide the URL for the service to use to publish its metadata in the *HttpGetUrl* or *HttpsGetUrl* properties of the *serviceMetadata* element of the service behavior.

After you have created the *ServiceHost* object, you can start listening for requests by using the Open method, like this:

```
productsServiceHost.Open();
```

Opening a *ServiceHost* object causes the WCF runtime to examine the binding configuration for each endpoint of the service and start listening on each endpoint address. Opening a service can take some time. An overloaded version of the Open method is available that takes a *TimeSpan* object and that throws an exception if the Open method does not complete within the specified time. Additionally, the *ServiceHost* class supports the .NET Framework asynchronous mode of operations through the BeginOpen and EndOpen methods implementing the IAsynResult design pattern.

> **More Info** The IAsyncResult design pattern is commonly used throughout the .NET Framework, and is not peculiar to WCF. For details, see the topic "Asynchronous Programming Design Patterns" in the .NET Framework Developer's guide, available in the Microsoft Visual Studio 2005 Documentation, and also online at *http://msdn2.microsoft.com/en-us/library/ms228969.aspx*.

You stop a service by calling the Close method of the *ServiceHost* object. The Close method stops the WCF runtime listening for more requests and gracefully shuts the service down; any work in progress is allowed to complete. As with the Open method, you can close a service asynchronously by using the BeginClose and EndClose methods.

The *ServiceHost* class also provides events that you can use to track the state of a *ServiceHost* object. Table 2-2 summarizes these events.

Table 2-2 ServiceHost Events

Event	Description
Opening	The *ServiceHost* object is opening the service and is processing the binding information for each endpoint so that it can start listening.
Opened	The *ServiceHost* object has successfully opened the service, which is now ready to accept client requests.
Closing	The *ServiceHost* is executing the close method and waiting for all current service requests to complete processing.
Closed	The service has shut down. No listeners are active, and clients cannot send requests.
Faulted	The service has encountered an unrecoverable error. You can examine the *ServiceHost* object to try and determine the cause of the fault, but clients can no longer use the service. You must close the service and open it again before clients can connect.

Building a Windows Presentation Foundation Application to Host a WCF Service

Let's look at how to use the *ServiceHost* class to host a WCF application inside an ordinary application. You should have the .NET Framework 3.0 and the Microsoft Visual Studio Development Tools for .NET Framework 3.0 installed on your computer, so it makes sense to build a Windows Presentation Foundation (WPF) application.

Create a new Windows application to host the WCF service

1. Using Visual Studio 2005, create a new project. Select the NET Framework 3.0 project types under Visual C#, and use the Windows Application (WPF) template. Name the project ProductsServiceHost and save it in the Microsoft Press\WCF Step By Step\Chapter 2 folder under your \My Projects folder.

2. In Solution Explorer, rename the Window1.xaml file as HostController.xaml.

3. Open the App.xaml file. In the pane displaying the XAML description of the form, change the *StartupUri* attribute of the *Application* element to *HostController.xaml*, as shown in bold below:

```
<Application x:Class="ProductsServiceHost.App"
    xmlns="http://schemas.microsoft.com/winfx/2006/xaml/presentation"
    xmlns:x="http://schemas.microsoft.com/winfx/2006/xaml"
    StartupUri="HostController.xaml"
    >
    <Application.Resources>

    </Application.Resources>
</Application>
```

4. Open the HostController.xaml file. In the pane displaying the XAML description of the form, change the class name to *ProductsServiceHost.HostController*, and add the code highlighted in bold below to the form:

```
<Window x:Class="ProductsServiceHost.HostController"
    xmlns="http://schemas.microsoft.com/winfx/2006/xaml/presentation"
    xmlns:x="http://schemas.microsoft.com/winfx/2006/xaml"
    Title="ProductsServiceHost" Height="300" Width="300"
    >
    <Grid>
        <Button Height="23" HorizontalAlignment="Left" Margin="51,60,0,0" Name="start"
VerticalAlignment="Top" Width="75" Click="onStartClick">Start</Button>
        <Button Height="23" HorizontalAlignment="Right" Margin="0,60,56,0" Name="stop"
VerticalAlignment="Top" Width="75" IsEnabled="False" Click="onStopClick">Stop</Button>
        <Label Height="23" HorizontalAlignment="Left" Margin="51.37,0,0,108" Name=
"label1" VerticalAlignment="Bottom" Width="87.63">Service Status:</Label>
        <TextBox IsReadOnly="True" Margin="133,0,59,107" Name="status" Text="Service
Stopped" Height="26" VerticalAlignment="Bottom"></TextBox>
    </Grid>
</Window>
```

This code in the <Window> element changes the class reference to refer to the new name of the form.

The code in the <Grid> element adds two buttons, a label, and a text box to the form. The two buttons will enable a user to start and stop the WCF service, and the label and text box display a message indicating the current state of the WCF service (running or stopped). If you examine the *Click* attribute of the Start button, you can see that it invokes a method called onClickStart. Similarly, the *Click* attribute of the Stop button invokes a method called onClickStop. You will write the code that implements these methods in the next exercise.

5. Click the Design tab to refresh the display of the ProductsServiceHost form. Verify that your form looks like the following image:

The Stop button is initially disabled. You will write code to enable it when the service has started.

6. In Solution Explorer, expand the HostController.xaml node and double-click the file HostController.xaml.cs . The C# code behind the form is displayed in the code view window. Change all occurrences of Window1 in this file to HostController, to match the class named in the XAML description of the form, as shown below:

```csharp
namespace ProductsServiceHost
{
    /// <summary>
    /// Interaction logic for HostController.xaml
    /// </summary>

    public partial class HostController : Window
    {
        public HostController()
        {
            InitializeComponent();
        }
    }
}
```

You have now created a simple form that will act as the user interface for the service host. The next step is to add the code that actually starts and stops the service.

Add logic to start and stop the WCF service

1. In the ProductsServiceHost project, expand the References folder in Solution Explorer. Notice that the project already contains a reference for the *System.ServiceModel* assembly required by WCF applications and services.

2. Add a reference to the *ProductsService.dll* assembly, located in the Microsoft Press\WCF Step By Step\Chapter 2\ProductsService\ folder under your \My Projects folder. This assembly contains the code that defines the service contract and implements the ProductsService service. It is a copy of the assembly you created in Chapter 1.

3. In the code view window displaying the C# code behind the HostController form, add the following *using* statements to the list at the top of the file:

```
using System.ServiceModel;
using Products;
```

4. Add the following variable to the *HostController* class:

```
private ServiceHost productsServiceHost;
```

You will use this variable to control the ProductsService service.

5. In the *HostController* class, add the following method immediately after the HostController() constructor:

```
void onStartClick(object sender, EventArgs e)
{
    productsServiceHost = new ServiceHost(typeof(ProductsServiceImpl));
    productsServiceHost.Open();
    stop.IsEnabled = true;
    start.IsEnabled = false;
    status.Text = "Service Running";
}
```

This method is called when the user clicks the Start button on the form. The first line creates a new *ServiceHost* object. The parameter to the ServiceHost constructor is the type that implements the data contract for the service. The *ServiceHost* object will retrieve the endpoint containing the binding information containing the address from the application configuration file. The second line of this method starts the service host listening to this endpoint by calling the Open method. The remaining statements in this method enable the Stop button on the form, disable the Start button, and modify the status displayed on the form.

6. Add the following method to the *HostController* class:

```
void onStopClick(object sender, EventArgs e)
{
    productsServiceHost.Close();
    stop.IsEnabled = false;
```

```
    start.IsEnabled = true;
    status.Text = "Service Stopped";
}
```

This method is called when the user clicks the Stop button on the form. The Close method of the *ServiceHost* object stops it listening for more requests. The other state-ments re-enable the Start button, disable the Stop button, and update the service status displayed on the form.

7. Build the solution.

The final step is to provide a configuration file that specifies the binding information for the WCF service. You can reuse the existing configuration file from the original Web service, and rename it as an application configuration file.

Configure the Windows host application

1. In the Project menu, click Add Existing Item. Move to the Microsoft Press\WCF Step By Step\Chapter 2\Config\ folder under your \My Documents folder, and select the Web.config file. This is a copy of the Web.config file you used for the ProductsService Web service in Chapter 1.

> **Tip** By default, the Add Existing Item dialog box for a C# project only displays files with a .cs suffix. To display configuration file, select *All Files* in the *Files of type* drop-down list box.

2. In Solution Explorer, rename the Web.config file as App.config.

3. Open the App.config file, and add the address shown below in bold to the endpoint:

```
...
<system.serviceModel>
    <services>
      <service behaviorConfiguration="ProductsBehavior"
              name="Products.ProductsServiceImpl">
        <endpoint
          address="http://localhost:8000/ProductsService/ProductsService.svc"
          binding="basicHttpBinding"
          contract="Products.IProductsService" />
      </service>
      ...
    </services>
</system.serviceModel>
```

The address used here specifies port 8000. The default port for the HTTP protocol (port 80) is used by IIS. Attempting to create a new *ServiceHost* object listening to an address on port 80 will result in an exception unless you stop IIS first.

Also notice that the address still appears to reference the ProductsService.svc service def-inition file. However, you have not added this file to the service host application. In fact, a service definition file is only really required by IIS, and is optional if you are creating your own custom host application, as the information required to identify the assembly containing the class that implements the service is specified in the ServiceHost constructor. The address that you specify following the scheme, machine, and port ("ProductsService/ProductsService.svc" in this example) is really just a logical identifier that the WCF service uses to advertise the service to clients, and to which clients can connect. As long as it is valid syntax for a Web URL this part of the address can be almost anything. For consistency, when using the http scheme, it is worthwhile retaining the service definition file element as part of the address in case you revert back to using IIS to host the service.

> **Note**   This only applies to endpoints that use the HTTP and HTTPS transports. If you use a different mechanism, such as TCP, avoid referencing what looks like a filename in addresses.

4. Build the solution again. This action will generate the ProductsService.exe.config configuration file from the App.config file.

You can reuse the client application that you created for testing the ProductsService Web service in Chapter 1 (a copy is supplied for this exercise) with one small change—you must modify the address of the service in the application configuration file.

Test the Windows host application

1. In Solution Explorer, right-click the ProductsServiceHost solution, point to Add, and then click Existing Project.

2. Move to the Microsoft Press\WCF Step By Step\Chapter 2\ProductsClient\ folder under your \My Documents folder, and select the ProductsClient project file.

3. In the ProductsClient project in Solution Explorer, right-click the App.config file and click Edit WCF Configuration.

   The WCF Service Configuration Editor starts. This editor provides a graphical means of editing a configuration file for a WCF service and client application. You can still edit the configuration file manually if you prefer, but using this tool can reduce the scope for many of the common configuration errors.

4. In the WCF Service Configuration Editor, in the tree view in the Configuration pane in the left pane, select the BasicHttpBinding_IProductsService endpoint in the Endpoints folder under the Client folder. It should look like this, although the name of your computer in the Address field will probably be different:

5. In the Client Endpoint pane on the right side of the window, change the *Address* property to *http://localhost:8000/ProductsService/ProductsService.svc*.

> **Note**   Remember that this is a URL, or a logical address. Unlike the IIS implementation, there is not actually a physical file called ProductService.svc in this version of the ProductsService service. The service host just happens to be listening on an endpoint with an address that looks like a filename.

6. On the File menu, click Save, and then exit the WCF Service Configuration Editor.

> **Note**   When you return to Visual Studio 2005, if you had the App.config file open in a code view window, Visual Studio 2005 will detect that the contents of the file have changed and alert you with a message box displaying, "The file has been modified outside the source editor. Do you want to reload it?" Click Yes, otherwise you risk losing the changes you have made by using the WCF Service Configuration Editor.

7. In Solution Explorer, double-click the Program.cs file in the ProductsClient project. Add the statements shown in bold to the Main method of the *Program* class:

```
static void Main(string[] args)
{
    Console.WriteLine("Press ENTER when the service has started");
    Console.ReadLine();
    // Create a proxy object and connect to the service
    ProductsServiceClient proxy = new
        ProductsServiceClient("BasicHttpBinding_IProductsService");
    ...
}
```

These statements wait for the user to press the Enter key before creating the proxy object that connects to the service. This will give you time to start the service running.

8. Build the solution.

9. In Solution Explorer, right-click the ProductsServiceHost solution, and then click Set StartUp Projects.

10. In the Property Pages dialog box, click Multiple startup projects, set the Action for the ProductsClient and the ProductsServiceHost projects to Start, and then click OK.

11. On the Debug menu, click Start Without Debugging to start both projects running.

12. In the ProductsServiceHost form, click Start, and wait for the Service Status text box to change to Service Running.

13. In the console window running the ProductsClient application, press Enter. The application should run exactly as before, displaying a list of product numbers, displaying the details of product WB-H098, and then displaying and updating the stock level for this product.

14. Press Enter again to close the ProductsClient application. Close the ProductsServiceHost form.

Reconfiguring the Service to Use Multiple Endpoints

The HTTP protocol is a good choice to use as a transport for connecting to Web services. However, when accessing a service deployed within an organization, the TCP protocol can prove to be more efficient. If you want to maintain connectivity and network performance inside and outside an organization, you should consider providing multiple endpoints: one for external clients accessing the service by using HTTP, and another for internal clients accessing the service by using TCP. This is what you will do in the next set of exercises.

Add a TCP endpoint to the WCF service

1. In Solution Explorer, in the ProductsServiceHost project, right-click the App.config file for the ProductsServiceHost project, and then click Edit WCF Configuration.

2. In the WCF Service Configuration Editor, in the Configuration pane, expand the Products.ProductServiceImpl folder in the Services folder, and then expand the Endpoints folder. The existing endpoint is listed, with the name (Empty Name).

3. Click the (Empty Name) endpoint. In the Service Endpoint pane, set the *Name* property to *ProductsServiceHttpEndpoint*.

4. In the Configuration pane, right-click the Endpoints folder, and then click New Service Endpoint.

5. In the Service Endpoint pane, set the properties of the endpoint using the values in the following table:

Property	Value
Name	ProductsServiceTcpEndpoint
Address	net.tcp://localhost:8080/TcpProductsService
Binding	netTcpBinding
Contract	Products.IProductsService

> **Tip**   If you click the ellipses button in the *Contract* field, you can search for the assembly containing the contract by using the Contract Type Browser. When you select an assembly, the Contract Type Browser will display all the contracts available in the assembly.

6. Save the updated configuration, and then exit the WCF Service Configuration Editor.

7. Examine the App.config file by opening it in the code view window. Notice that the new endpoint has been added to the service, as follows:

```
<services>
      <service behaviorConfiguration="ProductsBehavior" name="Products.ProductsService
Impl">
          <endpoint address="" binding="basicHttpBinding" name="ProductsServiceHttpEndpo
int" contract="Products.IProductsService" />
          <endpoint address="net.tcp://localhost:8080/TcpProductsService"
binding="netTcpBinding" bindingConfiguration="" name="ProductsServiceTcpEndpoint"
contract="Products.IProductsService" />
      </service>
</services>
```

When the host application instantiates the *ServiceHost* object, it automatically creates an endpoint for each entry in the configuration file.

Reconfigure the client to connect to the TCP endpoint

1. In Solution Explorer, edit the app.config file for the ProductsClient project by using the WCF Service Configuration Editor.

2. In the WCF Service Configuration Editor, in the Client folder, right-click the Endpoints folder, and then click New Client Endpoint.

3. In the Client Endpoint pane, set the properties of the endpoint using the values in the following table:

Property	Value
Name	NetTcpBinding_IProductsService
Address	net.tcp://localhost:8080/TcpProductsService

Property	Value
Binding	netTcpBinding
Contract	ProductsClient.ProductsService.IProductsService

> **Note**   The type defining the contract is part of the proxy code generated for the client in Chapter 1. This type was compiled into the client executable assembly, *ProductsClient.exe*, located in the bin\Debug folder underneath the client project folder.

4. Save the client configuration file and exit the WCF Service Configuration Editor.

5. Examine the app.config file by opening it in the code view window. Notice that the new endpoint has been added to the client, as follows:

```
<client>
    <endpoint
        address="http://localhost:8000/ProductsService/ProductsService.svc"
        binding="basicHttpBinding"
        bindingConfiguration="BasicHttpBinding_IProductsService"
        contract="ProductsClient.ProductsService.IProductsService"
        name="BasicHttpBinding_IProductsService" />
    <endpoint
        address="net.tcp://localhost:8080/TcpProductsService"
        binding="netTcpBinding" bindingConfiguration=""
        contract="ProductsClient.ProductsService.IProductsService"
        name="NetTcpBinding_IProductsService" />
</client>
```

6. Edit the Program.cs file in the ProductsClient project. In the Main method, modify the statement that instantiates the proxy object to use the TCP endpoint, as follows:

```
// Create a proxy object and connect to the service
ProductsServiceClient proxy = new
    ProductsServiceClient("NetTcpBinding_IProductsService");
```

7. Build the solution.

Test the new endpoint

1. On the Debug menu, click Start Without Debugging to start both projects running.

2. In the ProductsServiceHost form, click Start, and wait for the Service Status text box to change to Service Running.

> **Note**   If you are running Windows Firewall, a Windows Security Alert will appear. In the alert, click Unblock to allow the service to open the TCP port.

3. In the console window running the ProductsClient application, press Enter. The application should run exactly as before. This time, however, the client is connecting to the service by using the TCP protocol.

4. Press Enter again to close the ProductsClient application. Close the ProductsServiceHost form.

Understanding Bindings

By now, you should appreciate that bindings are an important part of the framework provided by WCF. A binding consists of one or more binding elements. A binding element handles one particular non-functional aspect of a service, such as whether it supports transactions or how the service implements security. You compose binding elements together in various combinations to create a binding. Every binding should have a single binding element describing the transport protocol, and a binding should also contain a binding element that handles message encoding. You can add further binding elements to provide or enforce further features in a service. A binding element corresponds to a channel. Remember that when a host opens a service, the WCF runtime uses each binding element in the binding to create the channel stack. A client also creates channel stack when it connects to the service by opening a proxy object. To ensure that a client application can communicate successfully with a service, it should use a binding that provides binding elements that match those implemented by the service.

The WCF Predefined Bindings

The WCF library contains a number of classes in the *System.ServiceModel.Channels* namespace that implement binding elements. Examples include the *BinaryMessageEncodingBinaryElement* class that performs binary encoding and decoding for XML messages, the AsymmetricSecurityBindingElement class that enables you to enforce security by performing asymmetric encryption, the *HttpsTransportBindingElement* that uses the HTTPS transport protocol for transmitting messages, and the *ReliableSessionBindingElement* that you can use to implement reliable messaging. Most binding elements also provide properties that enable you to modify the way in which the binding elements work. For example, the *AsymmetricSecurityBindingElement* class has a property called *DefaultAlgorithmSuite* that you can use to specify the message encryption algorithm to use. WCF also enables you to define your own custom binding elements if none of the predefined binding elements meets your requirements. (Creating custom binding elements is beyond the scope of this book.)

The composability of binding elements into bindings provides a great deal of flexibility, but clearly not all combinations of binding elements make sense. Additionally, if you are building solutions for a global environment, it is worth remembering that not all client applications and services in a distributed solution will necessarily have been developed by using WCF; you should use bindings that are interoperable with services and applications developed by using other technologies.

The WS-* Specifications

As described in Chapter 1, many specifications and protocols have been defined, aimed at ensuring interoperability between Web services. Examples include the WS-Security specification defining how Web services can communicate in a secure manner, WS-Transactions for specifying how to implement transactions across a disparate collection of Web services, and WS-ReliableMessaging that describes a protocol that allows messages to be delivered reliably between distributed applications in the presence of software component, system, or network failures. Collectively, these specifications are known as the WS-* specifications. To ensure interoperability, you should create Web services that conform to these specifications.

The designers of WCF have provided a selection of predefined bindings in the WCF library, in the *System.ServiceModel* namespace. You have already used two of them: BasicHttpBinding and NetTcpBinding. Some of these bindings are aimed at clients and services primarily running on the Windows platform, but others (mainly the Web services bindings) are compatible with the WS-* specifications and the WS-I Basic Profile 1.1. Table 2-3 describes the bindings available in the WCF library:

Table 2-3   WCF Predefined Bindings

Binding	Description
BasicHttpBinding	This binding conforms to the WS-I Basic Profile 1.1. It can use the HTTP and HTTPS transport protocols and encodes messages as XML text. Use this binding to maintain compatibility with client applications previously developed to access ASMX-based Web services.
WSHttpBinding	This binding conforms to the WS-* specifications that support distributed transactions, and secure, reliable sessions. It supports the HTTP and HTTPS transport protocols. Messages can be encoded as XML text or by using the Message Transmission Optimization Mechanism (MTOM). MTOM is an efficient encoding mechanism for transporting messages that contain binary data. You will learn more about MTOM in Chapter 12.
WSDualHttpBinding	This binding is similar to WSHttpBinding, but it is suitable for handling duplex communications. Duplex messaging enables a client and service to perform two-way communication without requiring any form of synchronization (the more common pattern of communication is the request/reply model where a client sends a request and waits for a reply from the service). You will learn more about using duplex messaging in Chapter 14, "Using a Callback Contract to Publish and Subscribe to Events." Using this binding, messages can be encoded as XML Text or by using MTOM. However, this binding only supports the HTTP transport protocol, not HTTPS.

Table 2-3   WCF Predefined Bindings

Binding	Description
WSFederationBinding	This binding supports the WS-Federation specification. This specification enables Web services operating in different security realms to agree on a common mechanism for identifying users. A collection of cooperating Web services acting in this way is called a *federation*. An end-user that successfully connects any member of the federation has effectively logged into all of the members. WS-Federation defines several models for providing federated security, based on the WS-Trust, WS-Security, and WS-SecureConversation specifications. You will learn more about federation in Chapter 15, "Managing Identity with WIndows Card-Space."
NetTcpBinding	This binding uses the TCP transport protocol to transmit messages using a binary encoding. It offers higher performance than the bindings based on the HTTP protocols but less interoperability. It supports transactions, reliable sessions, and secure communications. It is ideally suited for use in a local area network, and between computers using the Windows operating system.
NetPeerTcpBinding	This binding supports peer-to-peer communications between applications using the TCP protocol. This binding supports secure communications and reliable, ordered delivery of messages. Messages are transmitted by using a binary encoding. Using peer-to-peer communications is outside the scope of this book, but for more information see the "Peer to Peer Networking" section in the Windows SDK Documentation.
NetNamedPipeBinding	This binding uses named pipes to implement high-performance communication between processes running on the same computer. This binding supports secure, reliable sessions and transactions. You cannot use this binding to connect to a service across a network.
NetMsmqBinding	This binding uses Microsoft Message Queue (MSMQ) as the transport to transmit messages between a client application and service both implemented by using WCF. This binding enables temporal isolation; messages are stored in a message queue, so the client and the service do not both have to be running at the same time. This binding supports secure, reliable sessions and transactions. Messages use a binary encoding.
MsmqIntegrationBinding	This binding enables you to build a WCF application that sends or receives messages from an MSMQ message queue. It is intended for use with existing applications that use MSMQ message queues (the NetMsmqBinding binding uses MSMQ as a transport between a WCF client and service).

The WS-I Basic Profile

When you implement a Web service, you should endeavor to maintain interoperability with other Web services, regardless of the technology you are using. When you create a Web service, you make use of a number of technical standards, such as XML, WSDL, SOAP, and WS-Security. Each of these specifications is a standard in its own right. New versions of these standards are continually emerging and will inevitably become adopted in the future. This poses a challenge. For example, if you create a Web service that exposes its interface by using WSDL 2, and a client application is using WSDL 1.1, will the client application still work? If you factor in the possibility that various applications could potentially support different versions, or subsets of the various standards, then interoperability, which is one of the most important value propositions of Web services, becomes difficult to achieve. This is where the WS-I Basic Profile comes in.

WS-I, or the Web Services Interoperability organization, defines a specific list of standards, versions, and additional rules that Web services and their clients should adopt to maintain interoperability. WS-I groups these items together into what is referred to as a *profile*. The current WS-I profile is called the WS-I Basic Profile 1.1. Web services that conform to the WS-I Basic Profile 1.1 should automatically be compatible with client applications and other Web services that also conform to the WS-I Basic Profile 1.1, regardless of how the Web services and client applications are implemented or the technologies used.

For a full list of the standards in WS-I Basic Profile 1.1, see the WS-I Basic Profile page at *http://www.ws-i.org/Profiles/BasicProfile-1.1-2004-08-24.html*.

Configuring Bindings

You can programmatically instantiate a binding and use it to create an endpoint for a service by using the AddServiceEndpoint method of the *ServiceHost* class. Similarly, you can write code to add a binding in a client application (you will see examples of these in Chapter 10, "Programmatically Controlling the Configuration and Communications"). However, as you have already seen, it is common to use a configuration file to specify the binding configuration information for a client and service. You can also set the properties for a binding in this way. As an example, examine the app.config file for the ProductsClient application:

```xml
<?xml version="1.0" encoding="utf-8" ?>
<configuration>
    <system.serviceModel>
        <bindings>
            <basicHttpBinding>
                <binding
                    name="BasicHttpBinding_IProductsService"
                    closeTimeout="00:01:00"
                    openTimeout="00:01:00"
```

```
                    receiveTimeout="00:10:00"
                    sendTimeout="00:01:00"
                    allowCookies="false"
                    bypassProxyOnLocal="false"
                    hostNameComparisonMode="StrongWildcard"
                    maxBufferSize="65536"
                    maxBufferPoolSize="524288"
                    maxReceivedMessageSize="65536"
                    messageEncoding="Text"
                    textEncoding="utf-8"
                    transferMode="Buffered"
                    useDefaultWebProxy="true">
                    <readerQuotas maxDepth="32"
                        maxStringContentLength="8192"
                        maxArrayLength="16384"
                        maxBytesPerRead="4096"
                        maxNameTableCharCount="16384" />
                    <security mode="None">
                        <transport
                            clientCredentialType="None"
                            proxyCredentialType="None"
                            realm="" />
                        <message
                            clientCredentialType="UserName"
                            algorithmSuite="Default" />
                    </security>
                </binding>
            </basicHttpBinding>
        </bindings>
        <client>
            <endpoint
                address="http://lon-dev-01/ProductsService/ProductsService.svc"
                binding="basicHttpBinding"
                bindingConfiguration="BasicHttpBinding_IProductsService"
                contract="ProductsClient.ProductsService.IProductsService"
                name="BasicHttpBinding_IProductsService" />
        </client>
    </system.serviceModel>
</configuration>
```

To recap from earlier, the <client> section specifies the endpoints for the client application. Each endpoint indicates the binding to use. The <bindings> section of the configuration file sets the properties of each binding—this section is optional if you are happy to use the default values for a binding. The example shown above explicitly sets the value for every property of the basicHttpBinding used by the client endpoint. You can find a full list of the properties for each binding in the "Bindings" section of the "Windows Communication Foundation Configuration Schema" topic in the Windows SDK Documentation provided with the Windows SDK.

Hosting a WCF Service in a Windows Service

Hosting a WCF Service in a user application relies on the user starting and stopping the service and not logging off. A better solution is to host a WCF service in a Windows service. This way, you can configure the Windows service to run automatically when Windows starts, but an administrator can still stop and restart the service if required.

> **Important**   The exercises in this section require that you have Administrator access to your computer. If you do not have this level of access, you will not be able to install, start, and stop Windows services.

In the exercises in this section, you will create a Windows service to act as a host for the ProductsService service. This service will limit requests only to client applications running on the same computer, and so you will configure it to use the named pipe transport listening to a fixed address.

> **More Info**   The exercises in this section assume you are familiar with how Windows services function, and that you understand how to use Windows Service Visual Studio template to create a new service. Windows services are distinct from WCF services, and a detailed discussion of how they work is outside the scope of this book. For further information about creating Windows services see the "Windows Service Applications" section in the Visual Studio 2005 Help documentation.

Create a new Windows service to host a WCF service

1. Using Visual Studio 2005, create a new project. Select the Windows project types, and use the Windows Service template. Name the project WindowsProductsService and save it in the Microsoft Press\WCF Step By Step\Chapter 2 folder under your \My Projects folder.

2. Using Solution Explorer, change the name of the Service1.cs to ServiceHostController.cs.

3. Add a reference to the *System.ServiceModel* assembly.

4. Add a reference to the *ProductsService.dll* assembly, located in the Microsoft Press\WCF Step By Step\Chapter 2\ProductsService folder under your \My Projects folder.

5. In the Project menu, click Add Existing Item and add the Web.config file located in the Microsoft Press\WCF Step By Step\Chapter 2\Config folder under your \My Projects folder to the project.

6. Rename the Web.config file as App.config.

7. Edit the App.config file and remove the <system.serviceModel> section. The file should look like this:

```xml
<?xml version="1.0" encoding="utf-8" ?>
<configuration>
  <configSections>
      <section name="dataConfiguration" type="Microsoft.Practices.EnterpriseLibrary.
Data.Configuration.DatabaseSettings, Microsoft.Practices.EnterpriseLibrary.Data,
Version=2.0.0.0, Culture=neutral, PublicKeyToken=null" />
  </configSections>
  <dataConfiguration defaultDatabase="AdventureWorksConnection" />
  <connectionStrings>
      <add name="AdventureWorksConnection" connectionString="Database=AdventureWorks
;Server=(local)\SQLEXPRESS;Integrated Security=SSPI;"
          providerName="System.Data.SqlClient" />
  </connectionStrings>
</configuration>
```

In the earlier exercises, you provided a URI and used the configuration file to associate the URI with a binding. You have just removed this configuration information. In the next exercise, you will bind the service to an endpoint by using code; the Windows service will use a named pipe for its endpoint because you want to restrict access to local client applications only.

Add logic to start and stop the Windows service

1. Open the ServiceHostController.cs file. In the design view window, click the link to switch to the code view.

2. In the code view window, add the following *using* statements to the list at the top of the file:

```
using System.ServiceModel;
using Products;
```

3. Add the following variable to the *ServiceHostController* class:

```
private ServiceHost productsServiceHost;
```

You will use this variable to control the ProductsService service.

4. Add the following statements shown in bold to the ServiceHostController constructor:

```
public ServiceHostController()
{
    InitializeComponent();
     // The name of the service that appears in the Registry
    this.ServiceName = "Products Service";
    // Allow an administrator to stop (and restart) the service
    this.CanStop = true;
    // Report Start and Stop events to the Windows event log
    this.AutoLog = true;
}
```

5. Add the code shown in bold to the OnStart method of the *ServiceHostController* class, replacing the TODO comment in this method:

```
protected override void OnStart(string[] args)
{    productsServiceHost = new ServiceHost(typeof(ProductsServiceImpl));
}
```

This statement creates a new instance of the ProductsService service, but remember that the App.config file does not specify an address or binding. You will supply the endpoint information for the service in the next step.

6. Add the statements shown below in bold to the OnStart method, after creating the *productsServiceHost* object:

```
protected override void OnStart(string[] args)
{
    productsServiceHost = new ServiceHost(typeof(ProductsServiceImpl));
    NetNamedPipeBinding binding = new NetNamedPipeBinding();
    productsServiceHost.AddServiceEndpoint(typeof(IProductsService),
        binding, "net.pipe://localhost/ProductsServicePipe");
    productsServiceHost.Open();
}
```

The first statement creates a *NetNamedPipeBinding* object. The second statement creates a new endpoint using this binding. It associates the binding with the "//localhost/ProductsServicePipe" named pipe and specifies that the service listening to the pipe implements the IProductsService service contract. The code then opens the service and waits for clients to connect.

7. Add the code shown in bold to the OnStop method of the *ServiceHostController* class, replacing the TODO comment in this method:

```
protected override void OnStop()
{    productsServiceHost.Close();
}
```

This statement closes the service when the service is shut down. Remember that WCF closes services gracefully, so the Close method can take some time to perform.

In the next exercise, you will add an installer for the Windows service. You will configure the service to run using the LocalSystem account. If you want to select a different account, ensure that the account you specify has access to the tables in the *AdventureWorks* database.

Create the service installer

1. In Solution Explorer, double-click the ServiceHostController.cs file to display the class in the design view window.

2. Right-click the design view, and then click Add Installer.

   The service installer is created and displays the serviceProcessInstaller1 and serviceInstaller1 components in the design view window.

3. Click the serviceInstaller1 component. In the Properties window, set the *ServiceName* property to *ProductsService*, and set the *StartType* property to *Automatic*.

4. In the design view window, click the serviceProcessInstaller1 component. In the Properties window, set the *Account* property to *LocalSystem*.

5. Build the solution.

The next stage is to install the service and start it running.

Install the Windows service

1. On the Windows Start menu, point to All Programs, point to Microsoft Visual Studio 2005, point to Visual Studio Tools, and then click Visual Studio 2005 Command Prompt.

2. In the Visual Studio 2005 Command Prompt window, move to the folder Microsoft Press\WCF Step By Step\Chapter 2\WindowsProductService\WindowsProductService\bin\Debug under your \My Documents folder.

3. Run the following command to install the WindowsProductsService service:

   ```
   installutil WindowsProductsService.exe
   ```

   The installutil utility outputs messages indicating the progress of the installation process. Verify that the service is installed successfully, without reporting any errors.

4. Using the Windows Control Panel, click Performance and Maintenance, click Administrative Tools, and double-click the Services applet.

> **Note**   If you are using Windows Vista, use click System and Maintenance in the Control Panel rather than Performance and Maintenance.

In the Services window, verify that the ProductsService service is present and configured using the property values specified by the service installer:

5. Start the service.

In the final exercise, you will use another copy of the ProductsClient application to test the Windows service. You will reconfigure the ProductsClient application to connect to the Windows service and verify that the service functions correctly.

Test the Windows service

1. Return to Visual Studio editing the WindowsProductsService solution. Add the ProductsClient project in the Microsoft Press\WCF Step By Step\Chapter 2\ProductsClient\ folder under your \My Documents folder, to the WindowsProductsService solution.

2. Edit the app.config file for the ProductsClient project by using the WCF Service Configuration Editor. In the Client folder, right-click the Endpoints node, and then click New Client Endpoint. Add a new client endpoint with the following property values:

Property	Value
Name	NetNamedPipeBinding_IProductsService
Address	net.pipe://localhost/ProductsServicePipe
Binding	netNamedPipeBinding
Contract	ProductsClient.ProductsService.IProductsService

3. Save the client configuration file and exit the WCF Service Configuration Editor.

4. Edit the Program.cs file. In the Main method, modify the statement that instantiates the proxy object to use the named pipe endpoint, as follows:

```
// Create a proxy object and connect to the service
ProductsServiceClient proxy = new
    ProductsServiceClient("NetNamedPipeBinding_IProductsService");
```

5. Build the solution.

6. In Solution Explorer, right-click the ProductsClient project and then click Set as StartUp Project.

7. On the Debug menu, click Start Without Debugging to start the client application running. Press Enter in the client console window.

   The ProductsClient application should run exactly as before. This time, however, the client is communicating with the WCF service running in the Windows service by using a named pipe.

8. Press Enter to close the ProductsClient application.

9. Return to the Services applet and stop the ProductsService service.

If you want to verify that the client application uses the Windows service and not some other instance of the ProductsService service that might be running (such as the Web service), try running the client after stopping the Windows service. It should fail with an EndpointNotFoundException stating that there is no endpoint listening at the address *net.pipe://localhost/ProductsServicePipe*.

Tip   You can uninstall the WindowsProductsService service by executing the command *installutil /u WindowsProductsService.exe* in a Visual Studio 2005 Command Prompt Window, in the bin\Debug folder for the WindowsProductsService project.

Summary

This chapter has shown you how to create an application that hosts a WCF service. You have seen the different types of application that you can use for this purpose, and you have built a WPF application and a Windows service. You have also learned a lot more about how WCF uses bindings to specify the transport protocol, encoding mechanism, and other non-functional aspects of a service such as reliability, security, and support for transactions. You have been introduced to the predefined bindings available in the WCF library. You have learned how to add multiple bindings to a service by using multiple endpoints. You have seen how to specify binding information by using a configuration file and how to specify a binding and endpoint for a service by using code.

Chapter 3
Making Applications and Services Robust

After completing this chapter, you will be able to:

- Explain how the WCF runtime can convert common language runtime exceptions into SOAP fault messages to transmit exception information from a WCF service.

- Use the *FaultContract* attribute in a service to define strongly-typed exceptions as SOAP faults.

- Catch and handle SOAP faults in a client application.

- Describe how to configure a WCF service to propagate information about unanticipated exceptions to client applications for debugging purposes.

- Describe how to detect the Faulted state in a WCF service host application and how to recover from this state.

- Explain how to detect and log unrecognized messages sent to a service.

Detecting and handling exceptions is an important part of any professional application. In a complex desktop application, many different situations can raise an exception, ranging from events such as unexpected or malformed user input, and programming errors, to failure of one or more hardware components in the computer running the application. In a distributed environment, the scope for exceptions is far greater, due to the nature of networks, and the fact that, in some cases, neither the application nor the development or administrative staff have control over how the network functions or its maintenance (Who is responsible for making sure that the Internet works?). If you factor in the possibility that your application might also access services written by some third party, who may modify or replace the service with a newer version (possibly untested!), or who may decide to remove the service altogether, then you might begin to wonder whether your distributed applications will ever be able to work reliably.

In this chapter, you will learn about how to handle exceptions in client applications and services developed by using WCF. You will learn how to specify the exceptions that a WCF service can raise and how to propagate information about exceptions from a WCF service to a WCF client. You will also learn about the states that a service can be in, how to determine when a host application switches from one state to another, and how to recover a service that has failed. Finally, you will see how to detect unrecognized messages sent to a service by client applications.

CLR Exceptions and SOAP Faults

A WCF service is a managed application that runs by using the .NET Framework common language runtime, or CLR. One important feature of the CLR is the protection that it provides when an error occurs; the CLR can detect many system-level errors and raise an exception if it detects any of them. A managed application can endeavor to catch these exceptions and either attempt some form of recovery or at least fail in a graceful manner, reporting the reason for the exception and providing information that can help a developer to understand the cause of the exception and take steps to rectify the situation in the future.

CLR exceptions are specific to the .NET Framework. WCF is intended to build client applications and services that are interoperable with other environments. For example, a Java client application would not understand the format of a CLR exception raised by a WCF service or how to handle it. Part of the SOAP specification describes how to format and send errors in SOAP messages, by using SOAP faults. The SOAP specification includes a schema for formatting SOAP faults as XML text and encapsulating them in a SOAP message. A SOAP fault must specify an error code and a text description of the fault (called the "reason"), and it can include other optional pieces of information. Interoperable services built by using the WCF should convert .NET Framework exceptions into SOAP faults and follow the SOAP specification for reporting these faults to client applications.

> **More Info**   For a detailed description of the format and contents of a SOAP fault, see the World Wide Web Consortium Web site *at http://www.w3.org/TR/soap12-part1/#soapfault.*

Throwing and Catching a SOAP Fault

The WCF library provides the *FaultException* class in the *System.ServiceModel* namespace. If a WCF service throws a *FaultException* object, the WCF runtime generates a SOAP fault message that is sent back to the client application.

In the first set of exercises in this chapter, you will add code to the WCF ProductsService service that detects selected problems when accessing the *AdventureWorks* database and uses the *FaultException* class to report these issues back to the client application.

Add code to the WCF service to throw a SOAP fault

1. Using Visual Studio 2005, open the solution file ProductsServiceFault.sln located in the Microsoft Press\WCF Step By Step\Chapter 3\ProductsServiceFault folder under your \My Documents folder.

   This solution contains three projects: a copy of the ProductsService service that you created in Chapter 1, "Introducing Windows Communication Foundation," a copy of the ProductsServiceHost application that acts as a host for this service that you created in Chapter 2, "Hosting a WCF Service," and a copy of the ProductsClient application that connects to the service, also from Chapter 2.

2. In the ProductsService project, open the file ProductsService.cs to display the code for the service in the code view window.

3. Locate the ListProducts method in the *ProductsServiceImpl* class. You should recall from Chapter 1, that this method uses the Data Access Application Block to connect to the *AdventureWorks* database and retrieve the product number of every product in the Production.Product table. The product numbers are stored in a list, which is returned to the client application.

4. Modify the statement that reads the configuration information for connecting to the database and trap any exceptions that can occur when connecting to the database, like this (shown in bold):

```
// Read the configuration information for connecting to the AdventureWorks database
Database dbAdventureWorks;
try
{
    dbAdventureWorks =
        DatabaseFactory.CreateDatabase("AdventureWorksConnection");
}
catch(Exception e)
{
    throw new FaultException(
    "Exception reading configuration information for the
AdventureWorks database: " +
        e.Message, new FaultCode("CreateDatabase"));
}
// Retrieve the details of all products by using a DataReader
...
```

If an exception occurs, this code creates a new *System.ServiceModel.FaultException* object with the details of the exception and throws it. The operation will stop running and will instead generate a SOAP fault, which is sent back to the client. The *FaultCode* object identifies the fault. The constructor used in this example simply specifies a name for the fault code.

> **Note** If you don't create a *FaultCode* object, the WCF runtime will automatically generate a FaultCode object itself, with the name *"Sender"* and add it to the SOAP fault sent back to the client.

5. Modify the statements that retrieve the details of products by using a *DataReader* object, as follows:

```
...
// Retrieve the details of all products by using a DataReader
IDataReader productsReader;
try
{
    string queryString = @"SELECT ProductNumber
                            FROM Production.Product";
    productsReader =
        dbAdventureWorks.ExecuteReader(CommandType.Text, queryString);
```

```
    }
    catch (Exception e)
    {
        throw new FaultException(
            "Exception querying the AdventureWorks database: " +
            e.Message, new FaultCode("ExecuteReader"));
    }
    // Create and populate a list of products
    ...
```

If an exception occurs while running the ExecuteReader method, the service generates a SOAP fault containing the corresponding message and fault code.

6. Modify the statements that create and populate the list of products, as shown below:

```
    ...
    // Create and populate a list of products
    List<string> productsList = new List<string>(); try
    {
        while (productsReader.Read())
        {
            string productNumber = productsReader.GetString(0);
            productsList.Add(productNumber);
        }
    }
    catch (Exception e)
    {
        throw new FaultException("Exception reading product numbers: " +
            e.Message, new FaultCode("Read/GetString"));
    }
    //Return the list of products
    return productsList;
```

Again, if an exception occurs in this block of code, the service generates a SOAP fault and returns it to the client.

Add code to the WCF client application to catch a SOAP fault

1. In the ProductsClient project, open the file Program.cs to display the code for the client application in the code view window.

2. In the Main method, add a *try/catch* block around the code that tests the operations in the WCF service, as shown below in bold:

```
    ...
    // Test the operations in the service try
    {
        // Obtain a list of all products
        ...
        // Fetch the details for a specific product
        ...
        // Query the stock level of this product
        ...
        // Modify the stock level of this product
```

```
    // Disconnect from the service
    proxy.Close(); }
catch (FaultException e)
{
    Console.WriteLine("{0}: {1}", e.Code.Name, e.Reason);
}
Console.WriteLine("Press ENTER to finish");
Console.ReadLine();
...
```

If any of the operations generate a SOAP fault, the WCF runtime on the client creates a *FaultException* object. The catch handler for the *FaultException* object displays the fault code and reason.

Test the FaultException handler

1. In the ProductsServiceHost project, edit the App.config file. The <connectionStrings> section of this file contains the information used by the DAAB to connect to the *AdventureWorks* database.

2. In the <*add*> element of the <connectionStrings> section, change the *connectionString* attribute to refer to the *Junk* database, as follows (do not change any other parts of the *connectString* attribute):

```
<connectionStrings>
    <add name=... connectionString="Database=Junk;..." providerName=... />
</connectionStrings>
```

3. Build and run the solution.

    The ProductsServiceHost form and the ProductsClient console should both start.

4. In the ProductsServiceHost form, click Start.

    If a Windows Security Alert message box appears, click Unblock. (The ProductsService-Host application uses TCP port 8000 as the address for the WCF service.)

5. When the service status in the ProductsServiceHost form displays "Service Running," press Enter in the ProductsClient console.

    After a short delay, the ProductsClient console reports an exception when performing test 1 (your message might vary if you are attempting to connect to the database as a different user):

The ProductsService service failed when attempting to fetch the product numbers from the *Junk* database by running the ExecuteReader method—the SOAP fault code is "ExecuteReader."

6. Press Enter to close the ProductsClient console.

7. Click Stop in the ProductsServiceHost form, and then close the form.

8. In the App.config file for the ProductsServiceHost application, change the database back to *AdventureWorks* in the *connectionString* attribute.

9. In the *<add>* element of the *<connectionStrings>* section, change the *name* attribute to *namex*, like this:

```
<connectionStrings>
    <add namex="AdventureWorksConnection" … />
</connectionStrings>
```

10. Build and run the solution again.

11. In the ProductsServiceHost form, click Start.

12. When the service status in the ProductsServiceHost form displays "Service Running," press Enter in the ProductsClient console.

   The ProductsClient console reports a different exception when performing test 1:

This time, the ProductsService service failed when reading the configuration file by running the CreateDatabase method—the SOAP fault code is "CreateDatabase." The CreateDatabase method expected to find the *name* attribute but instead found *namex*, which it did not understand.

13. Press Enter to close the ProductsClient console.

14. Click Stop in the ProductsServiceHost form and then close the form.

> **Note**   Do not change the *namex* attribute back to *name* just yet.

Using Strongly-Typed Faults

Throwing a FaultException is very simple but is actually not as useful as it first appears. A client application has to examine the *FaultException* object that it catches in order to determine the cause of the error, so it is not very easy to predict what exceptions could possibly occur when invoking a WCF service. All a developer can really do is write a very generalized catch handler with very limited scope for recovering from specific exceptions. It is analogous to using the System.Exception type to throw and handle exceptions in regular .NET Framework applications. A better solution is to use strongly typed SOAP faults.

In Chapter 1, you saw that a service contract for a WCF service contains a series of operation contracts defining the methods, or operations, that the service implements. A service contract can additionally include information about any faults that might occur when executing an operation. If an operation in a WCF service detects an exception, it can generate a specific SOAP fault message that it can send back to the client application. The SOAP fault message should contain sufficient detail to enable the user, or an administrator, to understand the reason for the exception and if possible take any necessary corrective action. A client application can use the fault information in the service contract to anticipate faults and provide specific handlers that can catch and process each different fault. These are strongly typed faults.

You specify the possible faults that can occur by using *FaultContract* attributes in a service contract. This is what you will do in the next set of exercises.

> **Note**   You can only apply the *FaultContract* attribute to operations that return a response. You cannot use them with one-way operations. You will learn more about one-way operations in Chapter 11, "Implementing OneWay and Asynchronous Operation."

Use the FaultContract attribute to specify the SOAP faults an operation can throw

1. In the ProductsServiceFault solution, in the ProductsService project, open the ProductsService.cs file.

2. In the ProductsServics.cs file, add the following classes:

```
// Classes for passing fault information back to client applications
[DataContract]
public class ConfigFault
{
    [DataMember]
    public string ConfigOperation;

    [DataMember]
    public string ConfigReason;

    [DataMember]
    public string ConfigMessage;
}

[DataContract]
public class DatabaseFault
{
    [DataMember]
    public string DbOperation;

    [DataMember]
    public string DbReason;

    [DataMember]
    public string DbMessage;
}
```

These classes define types that you will use for passing the details of SOAP faults as exceptions from a service back to a client. Note that, although both classes have a similar shape, you can pass almost any type of information in a SOAP fault; the key point is that the type and its members must be serializable. These two classes use the *DataContract* and *DataMember* attributes to specify how they should be serialized.

3. Locate the *IProductsService* interface.

   This interface defines the service contract for the ProductsService.

4. In the *IProductsService* interface, modify the definition of the ListProducts operation as follows:

```
[ServiceContract]
public interface IProductsService
{
    // Get the product number of every product
    [FaultContract(typeof(ConfigFault))]
    [FaultContract(typeof(DatabaseFault))]
    [OperationContract]
    List<string> ListProducts();
    …
}
```

The *FaultContract* attributes indicate that the ListProducts method can generate SOAP faults, which a client application should be prepared to handle. The type parameter to the *FaultContract* attribute specifies the information that the SOAP fault will contain. In this case, the ListProducts operation can generate two types of SOAP faults: one based on the ConfigFault type, and the other based on the DatabaseFault type.

Add code to the WCF service to throw strongly typed faults

1. In the ProductsServices.cs file, locate the ListProducts method in the *ProductsServiceImpl* class.

2. Replace the code in the first *catch* block, as follows:

```
catch(Exception e)
{
    ConfigFault cf = new ConfigFault();
    cf.ConfigOperation = "CreateDatabase";
    cf.ConfigReason = "Exception reading configuration information for the
AdventureWorks database.";
    cf.ConfigMessage = e.Message;
    throw new FaultException<ConfigFault>(cf);
}
```

This block creates and populates a *ConfigFault* object with the details of the exception. The *throw* statement creates a new *FaultException* object based on this *ConfigFault* object. Note that in this case, the code makes use of the generic *FaultException* class; the type parameter specifies a serializable type with the type-specific details of the exception. At runtime, WCF uses the information in this object to create a SOAP fault message. The FaultException constructor is overloaded, and you can optionally specify a reason message and a fault code, as well as the *ConfigFault* object.

3. Replace the code in the second *catch* block, as follows:

```
catch (Exception e)
{
    DatabaseFault df = new DatabaseFault();
    df.DbOperation = "ExecuteReader";
    df.DbReason = "Exception querying the AdventureWorks database.";
    df.DbMessage = e.Message;
    throw new FaultException<DatabaseFault>(df);
}
```

This block of code is similar to the previous *catch* handler, except that it creates a *DatabaseFault* object and throws a FaultException based on this object. The rationale behind using a different type for the exception is that the kinds of exceptions that could arise when accessing a database are fundamentally different from the exceptions that could occur when reading configuration information. Although not shown in this example, the information returned by a database access exception could be quite different from the information returned by a configuration exception.

4. Replace the code in the third *catch* block, as follows:

```
catch (Exception e)
{
    DatabaseFault df = new DatabaseFault();
    df.DbOperation = "Read/GetString";
    df.DbReason = "Exception reading product numbers.";
```

```
    df.DbMessage = e.Message;
    throw new FaultException<DatabaseFault>(df);
}
```

This *catch* handler also uses the DatabaseFault type because the exceptions that could occur in the corresponding *try* block are most likely to arise from the Read method (fetching the next row of data from the database) or from the GetString method (extracting the data from the current row).

5. Build the solution.

You can now modify the client application to handle the exceptions thrown by the service. However, first you must regenerate the proxy class that the client uses to communicate with the service.

Regenerate the proxy class for the WCF client application

1. Open a Visual Studio 2005 Command Prompt window and move to the folder \Microsoft Press\WCF Step By Step\Chapter 3\ProductsServiceFault\ProductsService\bin folder under your \My Documents folder.

2. Run the following command:

```
svcutil ProductsService.dll
```

This command runs the svcutil utility to extract the definition of the ProductsService and the other types from the assembly. It generates the following files:

❑ Products.xsd. This is an XML schema file that describe the structure of the Config-Fault, Databasefault, and Products types. The svcutil utility uses the information specified in the data contracts for these types to generate this file. Part of this file, displaying the ConfigFault type, is shown below:

```
...
<xs:complexType name="ConfigFault">
  <xs:sequence>
    <xs:element minOccurs="0" name="ConfigMessage" nillable="true" type=
"xs:string" />
    <xs:element minOccurs="0" name="ConfigOperation" nillable="true" type=
"xs:string" />
    <xs:element minOccurs="0" name="ConfigReason" nillable="true" type=
"xs:string" />
  </xs:sequence>
</xs:complexType>
<xs:element name="ConfigFault" nillable="true" type="tns:ConfigFault" />
<xs:complexType name="DatabaseFault">
 <xs:sequence>
   <xs:element minOccurs="0" name="DbMessage" nillable="true" type="xs:string" />
   <xs:element minOccurs="0" name="DbOperation" nillable="true" type=
"xs:string" />
   <xs:element minOccurs="0" name="DbReason" nillable="true" type="xs:string" />
 </xs:sequence>
```

```
</xs:complexType>
...
```

❑ Tempuri.org.xsd. This is another XML schema file. This schema describes the messages that a client can send to, or receive from, the ProductsService service. You will
see later (in the WSDL file for the service), that each operation in the service is
defined by a pair of messages: the first message in the pair specifies the message
that the client must send to invoke the operation, and the second message specifies the response sent back by the service. This file references the data contract in
the Products.xsd file to obtain the description of the Products type used by
response message of the GetProduct operation. Part of this file, defining the messages for the ListProducts and GetProduct operations, is shown below:

```
...
<xs:element name="ListProducts">
  <xs:complexType>
    <xs:sequence />
  </xs:complexType>
</xs:element>
<xs:element name="ListProductsResponse">
  <xs:complexType>
    <xs:sequence>
      <xs:element minOccurs="0" name="ListProductsResult" nillable="true" xmlns:q
1="http://schemas.microsoft.com/2003/10/Serialization/
Arrays" type="q1:ArrayOfstring" />
    </xs:sequence>
  </xs:complexType>
</xs:element>
<xs:element name="GetProduct">
  <xs:complexType>
    <xs:sequence>
      <xs:element minOccurs="0" name="productNumber" nillable="true" type="xs:str
ing" />
    </xs:sequence>
  </xs:complexType>
</xs:element>
<xs:element name="GetProductResponse">
  <xs:complexType>
    <xs:sequence>
      <xs:element minOccurs="0" name="GetProductResult" nillable="true" xmlns:q2=
"http://schemas.datacontract.org/2004/07/Products" type="q2:Product" />
    </xs:sequence>
  </xs:complexType>
</xs:element>
...
```

Note The name of this file and the namespace of the types in this file are dictated by
the *ServiceContract* attribute of the interface implemented by the service. The name
Tempuri.org is the default namespace. You can change it by specifying the Namespace
parameter in the *ServiceContract* attribute, like this:

```
[ServiceContract (Namespace="Adventure-Works.com")]
```

❑ Schemas.microsoft.com.2003.10.Serialization.Arrays.xsd. This file is another XML schema that describes how to represent an array of strings in a SOAP message. The ListProducts operation references this information in the ListProductsResponse message. The value returned by the ListProducts operation is a list of product numbers. Product numbers are held as strings, and the .NET Framework generic List<> type is serialized as an array when transmitted as part of a SOAP message.

❑ Schemas.microsoft.com.2003.10.Serialization.xsd. This XML schema file describes how to represent the primitive types (such as float, int, decimal, and string) in a SOAP message, as well as some other built-in types frequently used when sending SOAP messages.

❑ Tempuri.org.wsdl. This file contains the WSDL description of the service, describing how the messages and data contracts are used to implement the operations that a client application can invoke. It references the XML schema files to define the data and messages that implement operations. Notice that the definition of the ListProducts operation includes the two fault messages that you defined earlier:

```
...
<wsdl:operation name="ListProducts">
        <wsdl:input wsaw:Action="http://tempuri.org/IProductsService/
ListProducts" message="tns:IProductsService_ListProducts_InputMessage" />
        <wsdl:output wsaw:Action="http://tempuri.org/IProductsService/
ListProductsResponse" message="tns:IProductsService_ListProducts_OutputMessage" /
>
        <wsdl:fault wsaw:Action="http://tempuri.org/IProductsService/
ListProductsConfigFaultFault" name="ConfigFaultFault" message=
"tns:IProductsService_ListProducts_ConfigFaultFault_FaultMessage" />
        <wsdl:fault wsaw:Action="http://tempuri.org/IProductsService/
ListProductsDatabaseFaultFault" name="DatabaseFaultFault" message=
"tns:IProductsService_ListProducts_DatabaseFaultFault_FaultMessage" />
</wsdl:operation>
...
```

3. You can use the WSDL file and the XML schemas to generate the proxy class. In the Visual Studio 2005 Command Prompt window, run the following command:

```
svcutil /namespace:*,ProductsClient.ProductsService tempuri.org.wsdl *.xsd
```

This command runs the svcutil utility again, but this time it uses the information in the WSDL file and all the schema files (*.xsd) to generate a C# source file containing a class that can act as a proxy object for the service. The namespace parameter specifies the *C#* namespace generated for the class (the namespace shown here has been selected to be the same as that generated by Visual Studio 2005 in the exercises in Chapter 1, to minimize the changes required to the client application). The svcutil utility creates two files:

❑ Products.cs. This is the source code for the proxy class.

❑ Output.config. This is an example application configuration file that the client application could use to configure the proxy to communicate with the service. By default, the configuration file generates an endpoint definition with the basicHttp-Binding binding.

> **Note**   You can also use the svcutil utility to generate a proxy directly from a Web service endpoint rather than generating the metadata from an assembly. This is what Visual Studio 2005 does when you use the Add Service Reference command in the Project menu.

4. In Visual Studio 2005, in the ProductsClient project, delete the Service References folder and its contents.

5. In the Project menu, click Add Existing Item, and add the file Products.cs that you have just created, from the Microsoft Press\WCF Step By Step\Chapter 3\ProductsService-Fault\ProductsService\bin folder, located under your \My Documents folder.

Add code to the WCF client application to catch a strongly typed fault

1. In the ProductsClient project, open the Program.cs file to display it in the code view window.

2. Add the following *catch* handlers shown in bold after the *try* block in the Main method (leave the existing FaultException handler in place as well):

```
catch(FaultException<ConfigFault> cf)
{
    Console.WriteLine("ConfigFault {0}: {1}\n{2}",
        cf.Detail.ConfigOperation, cf.Detail.ConfigMessage,
        cf.Detail.ConfigReason);
}
catch (FaultException<DatabaseFault> df)
{
    Console.WriteLine("DatabaseFault {0}: {1}\n{2}", df.Detail.DbOperation,
        df.Detail.DbMessage, df.Detail.DbReason);
}
catch (FaultException e)
{
    Console.WriteLine("{0}: {1}", e.Code.Name, e.Reason);
}
```

These two handlers catch the ConfigFault and DatabaseFault exceptions. Notice that the fields containing the exception information that are populated by the ProductsService (*ConfigOperation*, *ConfigMessage*, *ConfigReason*, *DbOperation*, *DbMessage*, and *DbReason*) are located in the *Detail* field of the exception object.

> **Important**   You must place these two exception handlers before the non-generic FaultException handler. The non-generic handler would attempt to catch these exceptions if it occurred first, and the compiler would not let you build the solution.

3. Build and run the solution without debugging.

4. When the ProductsServiceHost form appears, click Start to run the service.

5. When the service has started, in the client application console window press Enter.

   The application configuration file for the service host application still contains the attribute *namex* rather than *name* in the <add> element of the <connectionStrings> section. The service throws a ConfigException, which is serialized as a SOAP fault. The client application catches this fault and displays the details.

6. Press Enter to close the client application. Stop the service and close the ProductsServiceHost form.

7. Edit the App.config file for the ProductsServiceHost project. Set the *namex* attribute in the <add> element in the <connectString> section back to *name*, and save the file.

8. Edit the ProductsService.cs file in the ProductsService project. In the ListProducts method in the *ProductsServiceImpl* class, modify the statement that reads the product number from the *productsReader* data reader object to try and extract the information from column 1 rather than column 0, as follows:

```
while (productsReader.Read())
{
    string productNumber = productsReader.GetString(1);
    productsList.Add(productNumber);
}
```

9. Build and run the solution without debugging.

10. When the ProductsServiceHost form appears, click Start to run the service.

11. When the service has started, in the client application console window press Enter.

   The application configuration file for the service host application is now correct, but the code that you just modified attempts to access the second column in the data reader object, when the query only returns a single column. This "mistake" causes the service to generate a SOAP fault containing a DatabaseException with details of the Read/GetString failure.

12. Press Enter to close the client application. Stop the service and close the ProductsServiceHost form.

13. Edit the ProductsService.cs file in the ProductsService project. In the ListProducts method in the *ProductsServiceImpl* class, correct the statement that reads the product number from the *productsReader* data reader object to extract the information from column 0, as follows:

```
while (productsReader.Read())
{
    string productNumber = productsReader.GetString(0);
    productsList.Add(productNumber);
}
```

14. Build and run the solution without debugging.

15. In the ProductsServiceHost form, start the service. Press Enter in the client application console window. Verify that the code now runs without any exceptions. Close the client console window and the ProductsServiceHost form when you have finished.

Reporting Unanticipated Exceptions

Specifying the possible exceptions that a service can throw when performing an operation is an important part of the contract for a service. If you use strongly typed exceptions, you must specify every exception that an operation can throw in the service contract. If a service throws a strongly typed exception that is not specified in the service contract, the details of the exception are not propagated to the client—the exception does not form part of the WSDL description of the operation used to generate the client proxy. There will inevitably be situations where it is difficult to anticipate the exceptions that an operation could throw. In these cases, you should catch the exception in the service, and if you need to send it to the client, raise an ordinary (non-generic) FaultException as you did in the first set of exercises in this chapter.

While you are developing a WCF service, it can be useful to send information about all exceptions that occur in the service, anticipated or not, to the client application for debugging purposes. You will see how you can achieve this in the next set of exercises.

Modify the WCF service to throw an unanticipated exception

1. In the ProductsServiceFault solution, in the ProductsService project, edit the ProductsService.cs file.

2. Add the following statement as the first line of code in the ListProducts method in the *IProductsImpl* class:

```
public List<string> ListProducts()
{
    int i = 0, j = 0, k = i / j;
    ...
```

This statement will generate a DivideByZeroException. Note that the method does not trap this exception, and it is not mentioned in the service contract.

3. Build and run the solution without debugging.

4. In the ProductsServiceHost form, click Start. In the client application console window, press Enter to connect to the service and invoke the ListProducts operation.

The service throws the DivideByZero exception. However, the details of the exception are not forwarded to the client application. Instead, the WCF runtime generates a very nondescript SOAP fault that is caught by the *DefaultException* handler in the client:

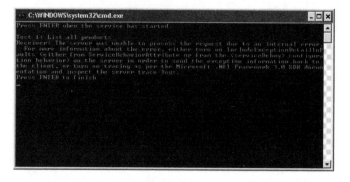

This lack of detail is actually a security feature. If the service provided a complete description of the exception to the client, then, depending on the information provided, a malicious user could glean potentially useful information about the structure of the service and its internal workings.

5. Close the client console window. Stop the service, and close the ProductsServiceHost form.

In the next exercise you will configure the host server to provide detailed information about unanticipated exceptions.

Configure the WCF service to send details of exceptions

1. In the ProductsServiceHost project, edit the App.config file.

2. In the <serviceBehaviors> section of the App.config file, remove the <serviceMetadataBehavior> element from the <behavior> section and replace it with the <serviceDebug> behavior, like this:

```
<behaviors>
  <serviceBehaviors>
    <behavior name="ProductsBehavior">
      <serviceDebug includeExceptionDetailInFaults="true"/>
    </behavior>
  </serviceBehaviors>
</behaviors>
```

Setting the *includeExceptionDetailInFaults* attribute to true causes WCF to transmit the full details of exceptions when it generates SOAP faults for unanticipated errors.

3. Build and run the solution with debugging.

4. In the ProductsServiceHost form, click Start. In the client application console window, press Enter.

The service throws the DivideByZero exception. This time, the client is sent specific information about the exception and reports it:

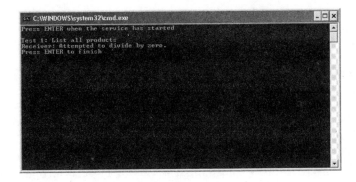

5. Close the client console window. Stop the service, and close the ProductsServiceHost form.

6. In the ProductsService project, edit the ProductsService.cs file.

7. In the ListProducts method, remove the line of code that causes the DivideByZeroException.

8. In the App.config file for the ProductsServiceHost project, set the *includeExceptionDetailInFauts* attribute of the <serviceDebug> element to false.

9. Build and run the solution without debugging.

10. In the ProductsServiceHost form, start the service. Press Enter in the client application console window. Verify that the code runs without any exceptions. Close the client console window and the ProductsServiceHost form when you have finished.

The previous exercise used the application configuration file to specify the serviceDebug behavior for the service. You can perform the same task by using the *ServiceBehavior* attribute of the class that implements the service, like this:

```
[ServiceBehavior(IncludeExceptionDetailInFaults=true)]
public class ProductsServiceImpl : IProductsService
{
    ...
}
```

However, it is recommended that you enable this behavior only by using the application configuration file. There are a couple of good reasons for this:

■ You can turn the behavior on and off in the configuration file without rebuilding the application. You should not deploy an application to a production environment with this behavior enabled, and it is very easy to forget that you have enabled this behavior if you use the *ServiceBehavior* attribute in code.

■ If you enable this behavior in code, you *cannot* disable it by using the application configuration file. Rather more confusingly, if you disable this behavior in code, you *can* enable it in the application configuration file. The general rule is that if the IncludeExceptionDetailInFaults behavior is enabled either in code or in the application configuration file, it will work. It has to be disabled in both places to turn it off. Keep life simple by only specifying this behavior in one place—the application configuration file.

Managing Exceptions in Service Host Applications

In Chapter 2, you saw how to create a host application for a WCF service and use this application to control the lifecycle of the service. A service host application uses a *ServiceHost* object to instantiate and manage a WCF service. The *ServiceHost* class implements a finite-state machine. A *ServiceHost* object can be in one of a small number of states, and there are well-defined rules that determine how the WCF runtime transitions a *ServiceHost* object from one state to another. Some of these transitions occur as the result of specific method calls, while others are caused by exceptions in the service, in the communications infrastructure, or in the objects implementing the channel stack. A service host application should be prepared to handle these transitions and attempt recovery to ensure that the service is available whenever possible.

ServiceHost States and Transitions

When you instantiate a *ServiceHost* object, it starts in the **Created** state. In this state, you can configure the object; you can use the AddServiceEndpoint method to cause the *ServiceHost* object to listen for requests on a particular endpoint for example. A *ServiceHost* object in this state is not ready to accept requests from client applications.

You start a *ServiceHost* object listening for requests by using the Open method (or the BeginOpen method if you are using the asynchronous programming model). The *ServiceHost* object moves to the **Opening** state while it creates the channel stacks specified by the bindings for each endpoint and starts the service. If an exception occurs at this point, the object transitions to the **Faulted** state. If the *ServiceHost* object successfully opens the communication channels for the service, it moves to the **Opened** state. Only in this state can the object accept requests from client applications and direct them to the service.

You stop a *ServiceHost* object listening for client requests by using the Close (or BeginClose) method. The *ServiceHost* object enters the **Closing** state. Currently running requests are allowed to complete, but clients can no longer send new requests to the service. When all outstanding requests have finished, the *ServiceHost* object moves to the **Closed** state. You can also stop a service by using the Abort method. This method closes the service immediately without waiting for the service to finish processing client requests. Stopping or aborting the service disposes the service object hosted by the *ServiceHost* object and reclaims any resources it was using. To start the service, you must recreate the *ServiceHost* object with a new instance of the service and then execute the Open method to reconstruct the channel stacks and start listening for requests again.

A *ServiceHost* object enters the **Faulted** state either when it fails to open correctly or if it detects an unrecoverable error in a channel used by the *ServiceHost* object to communicate with clients (for example, if some sort of protocol error occurs). When a *ServiceHost* object is in the **Faulted** state, you can examine the properties of the object to try and ascertain the cause of the failure, but you cannot send requests to the service. To recover the service, you should use the Abort method to close the service, recreate the *ServiceHost* object, and then execute the Open method again. Figure 3-1 summarizes the state transitions for a *ServiceHost* object, and the methods and conditions that cause the object to move between states.

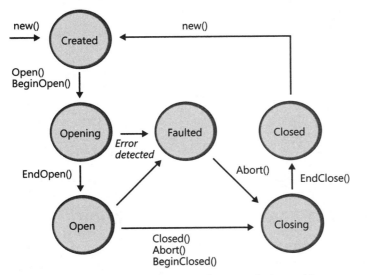

Figure 3-1   State transition diagram for a *ServiceHost* object.

> **Tip**   You can determine the current state of a *ServiceHost* object by examining the value of its *State* property.

Handling Faults in a Host Application

When a *ServiceHost* object moves from one state to another, it can trigger an event. These events were described in Table 2-2 in Chapter 2. From an error-handling perspective, the most important of these is the *Faulted* event, which occurs when a *ServiceHost* object enters the **Faulted** state. You should subscribe to this event, and provide a method that attempts to determine the cause, and then abort and restart the service, like this:

```
// ServiceHost object for hosting a WCF service
ServiceHost productsServiceHost;
productsServiceHost = new ServiceHost(…);
…
// Subscribe to the Faulted event of the productsServiceHost object
productsServiceHost.Faulted += new EventHandler(faultHandler);
…
// FaultHandler method
// Runs when productsServiceHost enters the Faulted state
void faultHandler(object sender, EventArgs e)
{
    // Examine the properties of the productsServiceHost object
```

```
    // and log the reasons for the fault
    ...
    // Abort the service
    productsServiceHost.Abort();

    // Recreate the ServiceHost object
    productsServiceHost = new ServiceHost(...);

    // Start the service
    productsServiceHost.Open();
}
```

> **Note**   You can use the Close method rather than Abort in the *fault* handler, but a service in the **Faulted** state will not be able to continue processing requests. Using the Abort method to close the service can reduce the time required in the FaultHandler method to restart the service.

Handling Unexpected Messages in a Host Application

One other exceptional circumstance that can arise in a host application is an unexpected message from a client. Client applications built using the WCF library typically communicate with the service by using a proxy object, generated by using the svcutil utility. The proxy object provides a strongly typed interface to the service that specifies the operations the client can request (and therefore the messages that the client sends). It is unlikely that a WCF client using correctly generated proxy object will send an unexpected message. However, remember that a WCF service is simply a service that accepts SOAP messages, and developers building client applications can use whatever means they see fit for sending these messages. Developers building Java client applications will typically use Java-specific tools and libraries for constructing and sending SOAP messages. WCF also provides a low-level mechanism that enables developers to open a channel to a service, create SOAP messages, and then send them to the service, as shown in this fragment of code:

```
// Create a binding and endpoint to communicate with the ProductsService
BasicHttpBinding binding = new BasicHttpBinding();
EndpointAddress address = new EndpointAddress(
    "http://localhost:8000/ProductsService/ProductsService.svc");
ChannelFactory<IRequestChannel> factory = new
    ChannelFactory<IRequestChannel>(binding, address);

// Connect to the ProductsService service
IRequestChannel channel = factory.CreateChannel();
channel.Open();

// Send a ListProducts request to the service
Message request = Message.CreateMessage(MessageVersion.Soap11,
    "http://tempuri.org/IProductsService/ListProducts");
Message reply = channel.Request(request);
```

```
// Process the reply
// (should be a SOAP message with a list of product numbers)
...
// Release resources and close the connection
reply.Close();
channel.Close();
factory.Close();
```

Don't worry too much about the details of this block of code—you will learn more about using *Message* and *Channel* objects in Chapter 10, "Programmatically Controlling the Configuration and Communications." The key statement is the line that creates the message sent to the ProductsService service:

```
Message request = Message.CreateMessage(MessageVersion.Soap11,
    "http://tempuri.org/IProductsService/ListProducts");
```

The second parameter to the CreateMessage method specifies the action that identifies the message sent to the service. If you recall the earlier discussion in this chapter describing the use of the svcutil utility to generate the client proxy, one of the files generated contained the WSDL description of the service. The WSDL description includes the definitions of each of the operations exposed by the service, and the messages that an application sends to invoke these operations. Here is part of the WSDL describing the ListProducts operation:

```
<wsdl:operation name="ListProducts">
        <wsdl:input wsaw:Action="http://tempuri.org/IProductsService/
ListProducts" message="tns:IProductsService_ListProducts_InputMessage" />
    ...
</wsdl:operation>
```

When the service receives a message identified by the action *http://tempuri.org/ IProductsService/ListProducts*, it performs the ListProducts operation. If a client application sends a message specifying an action that the service does not recognize, the service host application raises the *UnknownMessageReceived* event. The host application can catch this event and record the unrecognized message, like this:

```
// ServiceHost object for hosting a WCF service
ServiceHost productsServiceHost;
productsServiceHost = new ServiceHost(...);
...
// Subscribe to the UnknownMessageReceived event of the
// productsServiceHost object
productsServiceHost.UnknownMessageReceived += new
    EventHandler<UnknownMessageReceivedEventArgs>(unknownMessage);
...
// UnknownMessageReceived event handler
void unknownMessage(object sender, UnknownMessageReceivedEventArgs e)
{
    // Log the unknown message
    ...
    // Display a message to the administrator
    MessageBox.Show("A client attempted to send the message " +
```

```
            e.Message.Headers.Action;
}
```

There could be a perfectly innocent explanation for a client sending a message such as this, or it could be part of a more concerted attack by a malicious user trying to probe a service and gather information about the operations it supports; remember that by default, WCF Web services do not publish their metadata, so an attacker might not have access to the WSDL description of a service.

One other possibility is that a WCF client application is using an out-of-date proxy object for sending messages to the service. If a developer modifies the service contract for a WCF service, she might change the messages that the service sends and receives. If any client applications that use the service are not updated, they might send messages that the service no longer understands. Therefore, if you update a service, you should ensure that you retain backwards compatibility with existing clients. The same issues can arise with data contracts. You will learn more about how to update data contracts for a WCF service safely in Chapter 6, "Maintaining Data Contracts and Service Contracts."

Summary

In this chapter, you have seen how to use *FaultException* classes to send information about exceptions back to client applications as SOAP faults. You have seen how to use the *FaultContract* attribute to specify the faults that a service can send and how to catch these faults in a client application. You have also learned how to propagate information about unanticipated exceptions from a service to a client for debugging purposes. You should understand how to make a service host application robust by tracking the states of a service, recovering from faults, and handling unexpected messages sent by client applications.

Chapter 4
Protecting an Enterprise WCF Service

After completing this chapter, you will be able to:

- Describe the different aspects of security that you should consider when implementing a WCF service.

- Explain how to provide privacy and integrity of messages at the message level and at the transport level when communicating between a client application and a WCF service.

- Explain how to configure a WCF service to authenticate users when running in a Windows environment and how a client application can provide a user's credentials to a WCF service for authentication.

- Describe how to define and use roles to authorize access to operations in a WCF service.

- Summarize how a WCF service can use impersonation to provide fine-grained access control over resources to authorized users.

Security is a fundamentally important aspect of any system, especially when a system comprises distributed applications and services. Security is also a very broad topic. For this reason, you are going to consider how to implement security in several different scenarios, spread across three chapters. This chapter concentrates on managing security within a single organization. In this environment, there is usually an inherent degree of trust between the computers running client applications and those hosting services. Users running applications are frequently members of the same, well-defined security domain. Services have access to the information in this security domain and can use it to authenticate users directly. In Chapter 5, "Protecting a WCF Service over the Internet," you will look at how to enforce security when client applications and services run in different security domains separated by an insecure network, where it is not possible, or even desirable, to directly authenticate users. In Chapter 15, "Managing Identity with Windows CardSpace," you will see how to implement an identity meta-system to help authenticate users in a federated environment.

What Is Security?

Security is concerned with protecting users running client applications, services, and the messages that pass between them. Security encompasses a range of issues. The most common aspects of security that most developers are familiar with include user authentication, where a user attempts to prove their identity, and authorization, where a service decides which resources a user can access based on their identity. However, in a distributed environment, security has many other facets. These include:

■ Maintaining confidentiality of communications between a client application and a service. It is possible for applications to eavesdrop on the data being transmitted across the network. For example, take a look at the number of software and hardware network analyzers available—many administrators use them for tracking connectivity and bandwidth problems in a network, but an unscrupulous user could also track the packets passing over the network for malicious purposes. The information in these packets could include private financial data or confidential personal information that should not be common knowledge even to other members of the same organization. Typically, you achieve confidentiality by encrypting messages.

■ Preventing tampering or corruption of messages. In an environment where message confidentiality is assured, it is still possible for a malicious user to intercept messages and corrupt them before sending them to their final destination. You can use techniques such as message hashing to generate a digital signature for the file, which a service can use to help detect corrupt or modified messages.

■ Ensuring verifiable delivery of messages. Even if a malicious user cannot decipher intercepted messages, the possibility of interception means that messages could either be diverted and not delivered at all or delivered repeatedly (known as a "replay attack"). Several schemes are available that can help detect replay attacks, including using a time-stamp within a message (if the timestamp is outside reasonable limits when the service receives the message, it can discard it) and assigning unique identifiers to messages (if the service receives two messages with the same identifier, then it knows that there is a problem!). Similarly, using a reliable message protocol can help to ensure that messages are either delivered to the destination within a reasonable time or that the sender will be alerted if they are not. You will learn more about reliable messaging in Chapter 9, "Implementing Reliable Sessions."

■ Preventing impersonation of services. Although not so common inside an enterprise as it is when using the Internet, it is possible for one service to impersonate another to obtain confidential data from a user. This phenomenon is sometimes known as "spoofing." The user running the client application thinks they are communicating with the real service but are actually sending their details and other information to an entirely different service that happens to respond in a similar manner. This means that it can be as important for a client application to authenticate the service and verify that it is genuine as it is for a service to authenticate the user running the client application. You will look at how you can implement this form of two-way authentication by using certificates in Chapter 5.

It is worth remembering that there is no such thing as absolute security. Hackers and fraudsters can invariably devise new and interesting ways to intercept, compromise, or otherwise disrupt the message flow. The important point is to be aware of the threats and have a plan for introducing countermeasures that can reduce their effects. Fortunately, WCF provides a highly extensible model that can adapt and evolve to meet many current security issues and (hopefully) counter new threats as they appear. The WCF implementation of security is also relatively unobtrusive. By careful design and configuration, you can separate many of the security-related aspects of a client application and service from the business logic, enabling you to modify or extend the security of your system without requiring that you rewrite large chunks of code.

Authentication and Authorization in a Windows Environment

To authenticate a user, a service must provide a means of enabling a user to identify herself and then prove that identity. Inside a single organization, it is common to maintain a single database of users and their means of identification. In a Windows environment, this typically means using *Active Directory*. In a single organization, it is not unreasonable to expect that all services and client applications have access to the same *Active Directory* database, and this database defines the security domain for the system. A service can be configured to use information held in the *Active Directory* database to authenticate users. When the user runs an application that accesses the service, the application can prompt the user for their username and password and transmit this information to the service. The service can query *Active Directory* to verify that the username is valid and the password is correct.

> **Note**   Many of the discussions on this chapter that refer to *Active Directory* also apply to Windows computers that are not actually part of a domain but that maintain their own local users and groups database. The exercises in this chapter have been tested on a stand-alone computer running Microsoft Windows XP and Windows Vista.
>
> In a Windows domain, a service can also identify users by using the Kerberos protocol, and a WCF client application can verify the identity of a service by using the same protocol. However, Kerberos is only available if you have access to a Windows Server domain controller. This chapter does not describe how to configure a WCF service and client application to perform Kerberos authentication. For a brief summary of how Kerberos authentication works, see the Kerberos V5 Authentication page on the Microsoft Web site at *http://technet2.microsoft.com/WindowsServer/f/?en/library /d55683e8-1258-4555-93cb-77138d33beab1033.mspx.*

This approach works regardless of where the user is actually running the client application; it could be executing on a computer in the user's bedroom connecting to the service across an Intranet link, for example. However, a user located in the office might already be logged on to an organization's security domain, so prompting them for the username and password again becomes cumbersome (why should they need to keep on logging in?). Fortunately, the Windows operating system provides support for this very common scenario. When a user successfully logs in to a security domain, the details of the user's credentials are cached in the user's login process. When the user runs an application that requires authentication with a service, Windows can provide these details to the application, which can then forward them to the service. This mechanism is known as Windows Integrated Security.

> **Note** In a very large organization, the security domain might span several *Active Directory* databases managed independently by administrators in different parts of the organization. It is possible to configure trust relationships between these separate domains, effectively presenting them as a single security domain.

After a service has verified the identity of the user running the client application, it must then determine whether the user has the appropriate authority to invoke the specified operations. Typically, administrators assign users to roles, and the service developer can indicate which roles are allowed to access which operations. WCF can utilize .NET Framework declarative security to associate roles with operations. WCF can use a *role provider* to determine to which roles a user belongs. The .NET Framework provides three role providers that you can use for storing role information. These role providers are:

- Windows Token Role Provider, which uses roles based on Active Directory groups.

- SQL Role Provider, which uses roles stored in a SQL Server database.

- Authorization Store Role Provider, which uses roles defined by using the Microsoft Authorization Manager tool. This tool enables you to store role information in Active Directory or in XML files.

> **More Info** For detailed information on using Microsoft Authorization Manager to define and implement roles, see the Authorization Manager page on the Microsoft Web site at *http:/ /technet2.microsoft.com/WindowsServer/en/library/1b4de9c6-4df9-4b5a-83e9- fb8d497723781033.mspx?mfr=true.*

In this chapter, you will use the Windows Token Role Provider. This provider is ideal for use inside an enterprise that uses Windows Integrated Security for authentication. In Chapter 5, you will see how to use the SQL Role Provider as this is more suited to Internet-based services.

Transport and Message Level Security

User identity information has to be transported from a client application to a service. This information is critical, and so it should be transmitted in as secure a manner as possible. This normally means encrypting these details. Additionally, after the user has been authenticated, the contents of messages passing between the client application and service might also require some form of encryption, depending on the sensitivity of the information in these messages. There are many ways that client applications and services can achieve this aim, but the important point is that the client applications and the service must agree on the mechanism that they use, and they must be able to decrypt messages sent by the other. Various standardization efforts have led to the use of public/private key cryptography being used to this effect.

> **More Info**   For a good introduction to public key cryptography, visit the Understanding
> Public Key Cryptography page on the Microsoft Web site at *http://www.microsoft.com/technet/*
> *prodtechnol/exchange/guides/E2k3MsgSecGuide/6e75927b-bec3-475b-bf09-*
> *764c8ffc7027.mspx?mfr=true.*

When building Web services, you can perform authentication and encryption at two points
when sending and receiving messages: at the transport level and at the message level.

Transport Level Security

Transport level authentication is typically implemented at the operating system level before
the application or service receiving the message even knows that there is a message to receive!
A service can specify the type of credentials it requires, but it is the operating system's responsibility to ensure that the correct credentials are provided and to validate them.

Many communications protocols can encrypt and decrypt data as it is sent and received. The
most common example of such a protocol is HTTPS, which uses a technology called the
Secure Sockets Layer (SSL) to encrypt and decrypt data by using keys provided in certificates.
When a client application connects to a service by using the HTTPS protocol, the underlying
transport infrastructure for the client application and service can negotiate over the degree of
encryption to perform and exchange a certificate containing keys that they can use to encrypt
and decrypt messages. Because all of this happens at the transport level, it is transparent to
the client application and service; all they have to do is specify that they will communicate
using the HTTPS protocol. However, an administrator has to install and configure the appropriate certificates for the service host application. Unsurprisingly, you can also use transport
level security with the TCP protocol (SSL is itself based on TCP). Named pipes also support
transport level security.

> **More Info**   In this chapter, you will configure HTTPS for use with a self-hosted WCF ser-
> vice. If you are hosting a WCF service in IIS, the configuration process is a little different. You
> will learn more about configuring HTTPS with IIS in Chapter 5.

Message Level Security

Authentication at the message level is the responsibility of the service. The credentials of the
user are included in messages sent to the service, and the service has to verify that they are
valid. Additionally, message level privacy and integrity is also the responsibility of the client
application and service—they encrypt and decrypt messages themselves using an agreed
encryption algorithm and a negotiated set of encryption keys. Standards such as the WS-Security specification from OASIS describe the message level security schemes that many Web services implementations have adopted, and by following the recommendations of WS-Security
you can help to ensure the interoperability of your client applications and services with those
developed by using technologies other than WCF.

Transport level security has the advantage over message level security that it can often rely on hardware support and can be very efficient—encrypting and decrypting data can be a resource-intensive process, so anything that improves performance is very welcome. Additionally, transport level authentication checks are enforced before the client application actually starts sending application level messages, so performing authentication at this level detects authentication failures more quickly and with less network overhead. The primary disadvantage of transport level security is that it operates on a point-to-point basis; by the time the service receives a message, it has already been decrypted by the underlying transport mechanism. In a situation where a service should simply forward a message on to another service rather than process it, it has full access to the message contents. The service could modify the message or extract confidential information before forwarding it. Using message level encryption can help to mitigate this problem. Message level security provides end-to-end encryption. A client application and the service acting as the final destination can agree on an encryption key and an encryption algorithm to use for messages. When a message arrives at the intermediate service, it is still encrypted. If the intermediate service does not have access to the encryption key or has no knowledge of the selected encryption algorithm, it cannot easily decrypt the message.

Implementing message level security sounds like it could add quite a lot of work to the development effort required for building a service. However, WCF greatly simplifies matters and reduces the development effort required by incorporating much of the code required as part of the standard bindings you can specify when configuring an endpoint for a service. All you need to do is set the properties of your selected binding appropriately (you will see several examples throughout this chapter).

Implementing Security in a Windows Domain

In the following exercises, you will see how to use transport and message level security in some common scenarios that can arise within a single organization. Because it is easier to demonstrate and explain things this way around, you will start by learning how to implement message confidentiality by encrypting messages. You will then see how to authenticate users running in a Windows environment, and finally, how to use the Windows Token Role provider to authorize access to operations.

Protecting a TCP Service at the Message Level

Message encryption is a very common requirement of most distributed systems; so much so that the majority of the standard bindings available in the WCF library encrypt messages by default. For example, the NetTcpBinding binding automatically encrypts data at the transport level if you have configured SSL over TCP. The NetTcpBinding binding also supports encryption at the message level, giving you a greater degree of control over the encryption algorithm used and without requiring you to configure SSL. You will use message level security to implement message encryption in the first exercise.

Enable message level encryption for the NetTcpBinding binding for the WCF service

1. Using Visual Studio 2005, open the solution file ProductsService.sln located in the Microsoft Press\WCF Step By Step\Chapter 4\ProductsService folder under your \My Documents folder.

   This solution contains three projects: the ProductsService service, the ProductsService-Host application, and the ProductsClient. These projects are configured to catch and handle SOAP faults, as described in Chapter 3, "Making Applications and Services Robust."

2. Expand the ProductsServiceHost project in Solution Explorer, right-click the App.config file, and then click Edit WCF Configuration.

3. In the WCF Service Configuration Editor, right-click the Bindings folder and then click New Binding Configuration.

4. In the Create a New Binding dialog box, select the netTcpBinding binding type and then click OK.

   The WCF Service Configuration Editor generates a binding configuration with the default settings for the NetTcpBinding binding.

5. In the right pane of the WCF Service Configuration Editor, change the *Name* property of the binding to *ProductsServiceTcpBindingConfig*.

6. Click the Security tab.

7. Change the *Mode* property to *Message*. Change the *AlgorithmSuite* property to *Basic128*. Leave the *MessageClientCredentialType* property set to Windows.

   These settings cause the binding to use message level security. Users will be expected to provide a valid Windows username and password, and all messages will be encrypted by using the Advanced Encryption Standard (AES) 128-bit algorithm. This is a widely used algorithm that is relatively quick to perform but should provide sufficient privacy for messages inside an organization (if you are sending messages across a public wide area network such as the Internet, you might prefer to use Basic256, which is the default value).

> **Note**   If you set the Mode to None, then the binding will not encrypt data and any settings you specify for transport or message level security will be ignored. The Transport mode selects transport level security (SSL) rather than message level security, and the TransportWithMessageCredential mode uses message level security to provide the identity of the user for authorization purposes, while performing encryption at the transport level. Transport level encryption is usually more efficient than message level encryption, although it requires more configuration on the part of the administrator.

8. In the left pane of the WCF Service Configuration Editor, expand the Products.Prod-uctsServiceImpl service in the Services folder, expand the Endpoints folder, and then click the ProductsServiceTcpBinding endpoint.

9. In the right pane, set the *BindingConfiguration* property to *ProductsServiceTcpBindingConfig.*

    This action associates the binding configuration with the binding. All messages sent by using the ProductsServiceTcpBinding will use message level security and will be encrypted.

10. Save the configuration, and then exit the WCF Service Configuration Editor.

11. In Visual Studio 2005, open the file App.config in the ProductsServiceHost project. In the <system.serviceModel> section, you should see the new binding configuration, and the reference to this configuration in the ProductsServiceTcpBinding endpoint, as follows:

```
...
<system.serviceModel>
  <bindings>
    <netTcpBinding>
      <binding name="ProductsServiceTcpBindingConfig">
        <security mode="Message">
          <message algorithmSuite="Basic128" />
        </security>
      </binding>
    </netTcpBinding>
  </bindings>
  <services>
    <service behaviorConfiguration="ProductsBehavior"
             name="Products.ProductsServiceImpl">
      ...
      <endpoint binding="netTcpBinding"
        bindingConfiguration="ProductsServiceTcpBindingConfig"
        name="ProductsServiceTcpBinding" contract="Products.IProductsService" />
    </service>
  </services>
  ...
</system.serviceModel>
```

    Be careful not to change anything in this file. Close the App.config file when you have finished examining it.

The service will expect clients that connect to the endpoint for this binding to use the same message level security settings. You will configure the client next.

Enable message level encryption for the NetTcpBinding binding for the WCF client

1. In the ProductsClient project, edit the app.config file by using the WCF Service Config-uration Editor.

2. In the WCF Service Configuration Editor, right-click the Bindings folder and then click New Binding Configuration.

> **Note**   The client configuration file already contains a binding configuration for the basicHttpBinding that was generated in Chapter 1, "Introducing Windows Communication Foundation." Be careful not to modify this binding configuration by mistake!

3. In the Create a New Binding dialog box, select the netTcpBinding binding type and then click OK.

4. In the right pane of the WCF Service Configuration Editor, change the *Name* property of the binding to *ProductsClientTcpBindingConfig*.

5. Click the Security tab.

6. Change the Mode property to Message. Change the *AlgorithmSuite* property to *Basic128*. Leave the MessageClientCredentialType property set to *Windows*.

> **Note**   If you select a different algorithm suite for the client and server, they will not be able to decipher each other's communications. This will result in a runtime exception in the channel stack. If you are curious about this, try setting the *AlgorithmSuite* to *TripleDes* (for example) and examine the exception that occurs when you run the solution later.

7. In the left pane of the WCF Service Configuration Editor, click the NetTcpBinding_IProductsService node in the Endpoints folder, under the Client folder.

8. In the right pane, set the BindingConfiguration property to *ProductsClientTcpBinding Config*.

9. Save the configuration, and then exit the WCF Service Configuration Editor.

10. Start the solution without debugging.

11. In the ProductsServiceHost form, click Start. If a Windows Security Alert dialog box appears, click Unblock to allow the service to access the TCP port.

12. In the client console window, press Enter. Verify that the client application runs exactly as before.

13. Press Enter to close the client console window. Stop the service and close the ProductsServiceHost form.

This exercise has shown you how easy it is to configure a WCF service and client application to secure messages by performing encryption, but how do you actually *know* that the messages have been encrypted? To answer this question, you can enable message tracing and then examine the messages as they flow in and out of the service.

Configure message tracing for the WCF service

1. In Visual Studio 2005, edit the App.config file for the ProductsServiceHost project by using the WCF Service Configuration Editor.

2. In the WCF Service Configuration Editor, expand the Diagnostics folder and then click Message Logging.

3. In the right pane displaying the message logging settings, set the following properties to *True*:

   ❑ LogEntireMessage

   ❑ *LogMessagesAtServiceLevel*

   ❑ *LogMessagesAtTransportLevel*

   The *LogEntireMessage* property specifies whether the trace output should include the body of messages sent and received. Setting this property to *True* includes the body of the message. The default value, *False*, only traces the message header. Setting the *LogMessagesAtServiceLevel* property to *True* traces messages as they are presented to the service and as they are output from the service. If you are using message level security, this trace will show the unencrypted messages after they have been received and decrypted at the message level (for incoming messages) or before they are encrypted (for outgoing messages). Setting the *LogMessagesAtTransportLevel* property to *True* traces messages as they are sent to or received from the transport level. If you are using message level security, the messages traced at this point will be encrypted, although if you are using transport level security messages will already have been decrypted (for incoming messages) or not yet encrypted (for outgoing messages) at this point.

   > **Important**   Tracing at the message level records messages in their unencrypted form. You should ensure that you protect the trace files that are generated and only let authorized users examine this data.

4. In the left pane, right-click the Sources folder and then click New Source.

   All tracing information for WCF is received from one or more trace sources. In this case, you will use the MessageLogging source, which traces messages. You can also use other sources. For example, the ServiceModel source traces events that occur in a service, such as tracking when a service starts listening, receives requests, and sends responses.

5. In the right pane, set the *Name* property to System.*ServiceModel.MessageLogging*. Set the *Trace level* property to *Verbose*.

6. In the left pane, right-click the Listeners folder, and then click New Listener.

   A listener object is responsible for receiving data from the trace sources, formatting and filtering them, and then sending them to a destination.

7. In the right pane, set the *Name* property to *MessageLog*.

8. In the *InitData* property, click the ellipses button. In the Save Log As dialog box, move to the Microsoft Press\WCF Step By Step\Chapter 4 folder under your \My Documents folder. Set the file name to Products.svclog, and then click Save.

   The *InitData* property specifies the name of the file that the listener will use for saving trace data. When tracing starts, if this file does not exist, the listener will create it; otherwise, it will append trace information to the end of any existing data in the file.

9. In the *TraceOutputOptions* property, click the dropdown arrow. Clear all items in the list. The trace output options are useful if you are tracing messages for multiple client applications and you need to be able to correlate the different request and response messages. In this example, you will be running a single client application, so this additional information is not really necessary.

10. Verify that the *TypeName* property is set to *System.Diagnostics.XmlWriter.TraceListener*. The listener can output data in several formats. However, you will be using another tool called the Service Trace Viewer to examine the trace output, and this tool expects the data to be in XML format.

11. Click Add at the bottom of the right pane. In the Add Tracing Source dialog box, select the System.ServiceModel.MessageLogging source, and then click OK.

12. Save the configuration, and then exit the WCF Service Configuration Editor.

Run the WCF client and service and examine the trace output

1. Start the solution without debugging.

2. In the ProductsServiceHost form, click Start.

3. In the client console window, press Enter. Verify that the client application still runs correctly.

4. Press Enter to close the client console window. Stop the service and close the ProductsServiceHost form.

5. On the Windows Start menu, point to All Programs, point to Microsoft Windows SDK, point to Tools, and then click Service Trace Viewer.

6. In the Service Trace Viewer, on the File menu, click Add.

7. In the Open dialog box, move to the Microsoft Press\WCF Step By Step\Chapter 4\ProductsService folder under your \My Documents folder, select the file Products.svclog, and then click Open.

8. In the Service Trace Viewer, in the left pane, click the Message tab. You will see a list of messages sent and received by the service, identified by their *Action* values.

> **Tip**   Expand the *Action* column in this pane to see more of the name for each action.

At the top of this list are a number of messages in the *http://schemas.xmlsoap.org/ws/2005/02/trust* namespace. These messages are concerned with sending and verifying the user's identity, and negotiating the encryption mechanism and encryption keys that the client application and WCF service will use for sending and receiving messages. These messages are followed by the application messages received and sent by the WCF service, identified by the *http://tempuri.org* namespace.

9. Click the first message with the action *http://tempuri.org/IProductsService/ListProducts*. Note that each action occurs twice. This is because you traced each message twice: once at the message level and once at the transport level.

10. In the lower right pane, click the Message tab. The window will display the entire SOAP message. This is the version of the message passed from the transport level to the message level. The message has a rather lengthy SOAP header, which you can examine at your leisure. The interesting part is the SOAP body, at the end of the message. This is the encrypted ListProducts request received from the client application. The *<e:Cipher-Value>* element contains the data for the request, as highlighted in the following image:

11. In the left pane, click the second message with the action *http://tempuri.org/IProductsService/ListProducts*. In the right pane, scroll to the end of the Message window. This is the unencrypted version of the message passed from the message level to the service:

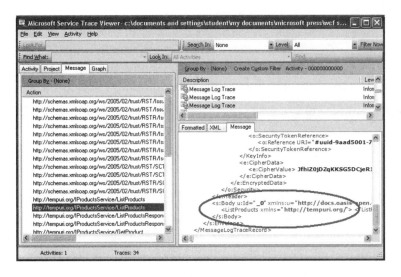

12. In the left pane, click the first message with the action *http://tempuri.org/IProductsSer-vice/ListProductsResponse*. In the right pane, examine the message body in the Message window. You can see that this is an unencrypted message containing the list of products returned in response to the ListProducts request. This message is the output from the service to the message level and so has not yet been encrypted.

13. In the left pane, click the second message with the action *http://tempuri.org /IProductsService/ListProductsResponse*. In the right pane, scroll to the bottom of the Message window and examine the message body. This time you can see that this is the encrypted response sent by the message level to the transport level for transmission back to the client.

14. Examine the other messages. When you have finished, close the Service Trace Viewer.

Protecting an HTTP Service at the Transport Level

If you recall, the ProductsServiceHost application exposes two endpoints for clients to connect to: one based on the TCP protocol and the other using HTTP. The HTTP endpoint is configured to use the BasicHttpBinding binding. The BasicHttpBinding binding conforms to the WS-BasicProfile 1.1 specification and is intended for use with existing legacy Web services and clients. It is fully interoperable with ASP.NET Web services. By default, this binding provides minimal security; it does not support message level encryption or authentication, for example. To implement message confidentiality and remain interoperable with ASP.NET Web services, you should use transport level security. This requires you to configure HTTPS.

Note   The BasicHttpBinding binding also supports message level security. Ordinary ASP.NET Web services and client applications do not implement the WS-Security specification, and so will not be able to communicate with a service that implements message level security. However, Microsoft Web Services Enhancements (WSE) does support WS-Security,

> so Web services that you create by using WSE can communicate with a WCF service through an endpoint based on the BasicHttpBinding binding by using message level security.

Specify transport level security for the BasicHttpBinding binding for the WCF service

1. In Visual Studio 2005, in the ProductsServiceHost project in Solution Explorer, edit the App.config file by using the WCF Service Configuration Editor.

2. In the WCF Service Configuration Editor, right-click the Bindings folder and then click New Binding Configuration.

3. In the Create a New Binding dialog box, select the basicHttpBinding binding type and then click OK.

4. In the right pane of the WCF Service Configuration Editor, change the *Name* property of the binding to *ProductsServiceBasicHttpBindingConfig*.

5. Click the Security tab. Set the Mode to Transport.

   In this mode, message security is provided by using HTTPS. You must configure SSL for the service by using a certificate. The client authenticates the service by using the service's SSL certificate. The service authenticates the client by using the mechanism specified by the *TransportClientCredentialType* property. The default value of *None* does not provide any authentication—you will examine some of the other values you can specify for this property later in this chapter.

6. In the left pane of the WCF Service Configuration Editor, expand the ProductsServicesImpl service in the Services folder, expand the Endpoints folder, and then click the ProductsServiceHttpEndpoint endpoint.

7. In the right pane, set the *BindingConfiguration* property to *ProductsServiceBasicHttpBindingConfig*.

8. HTTP Web services that implement transport level security *must* specify the https scheme, so change the *Address* property as follows:

   `https://localhost:8000/ProductsService/ProductsService.svc`

9. Save the configuration, and exit the WCF Service Configuration Editor.

10. Rebuild the ProductsServiceHost project.

The next step is to reconfigure and modify the client to connect to the service by using the endpoint corresponding to the BasicHttpBinding binding.

Specify transport level security for the BasicHttpBinding binding for the WCF client

1. In the ProductsClient project, edit the app.config file by using the WCF Service Configuration Editor.

2. In the WCF Service Configuration Editor, expand the Bindings folder and then click the BasicHttpBinding_IProductsService binding.

3. In the right pane of the WCF Service Configuration Editor, change the *Name* property of the binding to *ProductsClientBasicHttpBindingConfig*. (This is to make the name of the binding consistent with the other bindings you have created. The original binding name was generated by the svcutil utility back in Chapter 1.)

4. Click the Security tab. Change the Mode to Transport.

5. In the left pane of the WCF Service Configuration Editor, click the BasicHttpBinding_IProductsService endpoint in the Endpoints folder, under the Client folder.

6. In the right pane, change the address to use the https scheme as shown below, and verify that the *BindingConfiguration* property has changed to *ProductsClientBasicHttpBindingConfig*:

    https://localhost:8000/ProductsService/ProductsService.svc

7. Save the configuration, and then exit the WCF Service Configuration Editor.

8. In Visual Studio 2005, in Solution Explorer, open the Program.cs file for the ProductsClient project.

9. In the Main method, update the statement that creates the proxy object to connect to the WCF service by using the endpoint named BasicHttpBinding_IProductsService:

    ```
    ProductsServiceClient proxy = new ProductsServiceClient("BasicHttpBinding_
    IProductsService");
    ```

10. Rebuild the ProductsClient project.

    If you try and run the client and service at this point, the client will fail with a CommunicationException, like this:

    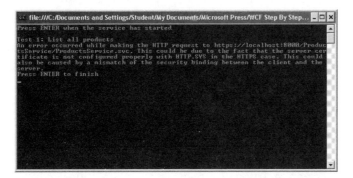

This error occurs because you have not yet configured transport security for the HTTPS protocol. In the next exercise, you will create a certificate for the WCF service, and configure SSL for the service by using the httpcfg utility.

Configure the WCF HTTP endpoint with an SSL certificate

1. On the Windows Start menu, point to All Programs, point to Microsoft Windows SDK, and then click CMD Shell.

   A command prompt window opens, with an environment configured for running the Windows SDK tools.

2. In the command prompt window, type the following command:

   ```
   makecert -sr LocalMachine -ss My -n CN=HTTPS-Server -sky exchange -sk HTTPS-Key
   ```

   The makecert utility is a useful tool for creating test certificates that you can use for development purposes. The command shown here creates a certificate that is stored in the Personal certificates store for the LocalMachine account. For detailed information about the options for the makecert utility, see the Windows SDK Documentation installed with the Windows SDK.

> **Important**   Certificates that you create by using the makecert utility should not be used in a production environment as they are not certified by a verifiable certification authority. Remember that the service sends this certificate to the client to prove its identity. The client must be able to trust that this certificate was created by a reliable source that can verify the veracity of the service. When deploying a production service, you should obtain your certificates from recognized certification authority, such as VeriSign or Thawte. Alternatively, you can use Windows Certificate Services, which enables an enterprise to generate its own certificates.

To use the httpcfg utility to configure SSL for the service, you need to find the thumbprint of the certificate. The thumbprint is a hexadecimal string that uniquely identifies the certificate. You can obtain this information by using the Certificates Microsoft Management Console snap-in.

3. In the command prompt window, type the following command:

   ```
   mmc
   ```

   This command starts the Microsoft Management Console, displaying the default Console Root window.

4. In the File menu, click Add/Remove Snap-In.

5. In the Add/Remove Snap-In dialog box, click Add.

6. In the Add Standalone Snap-In dialog box, select the Certificates snap-in and then click Add.

7. In the Certificates Snap-In dialog box, select Computer account and then click Next.

8. In the Select Computer dialog box, select Local computer and then click Finish.

9. In the Add Standalone Snap-In dialog box, click Close.

10. In the Add/Remove Snap-In dialog box, click OK.

11. In the Console Root window, expand the Certificates node, expand the Personal folder, and then click the Certificates folder. The HTTPS-Server certificate that you created by using the makecert utility should be displayed:

12. Double-click the HTTPS-Server certificate.

13. In the Certificate window, click the Details tab. Scroll to the bottom of the window displaying the details of the certificate. Click the *Thumbprint* property, and make a note of the hexadecimal string displayed in the lower window:

> **Tip**   You might find it useful to simply select the text in the lower window and copy it to the Windows clipboard.

14. Click OK, close the Microsoft Management Console window, and return to the command prompt window.

15. In the command prompt window, type the command shown below. Replace the hexadecimal string following the *–h* flag with the digits from the certificate thumbprint (remove all spaces from the thumbprint string first):

```
httpcfg set ssl -i 0.0.0.0:8000 -h c390e7a4491cf97b96729167bf50186a4b68e052
```

If this command is successful, it should report the message "HttpSetServiceConfiguration completed with 0."

> **Note**   Be very careful to specify the correct thumbprint. If you type an invalid thumbprint, the command still succeeds, but the client will not be able to communicate with the service as the thumbprint does not refer to a valid certificate.

This command binds the certificate with the thumbprint indicated with the *–h* flag to the port indicated by the *–i* flag. The port is specified as the IP address of the computer followed by the port. Specifying an IP address of 0.0.0.0 denotes the local computer.

> **Note**   Under Windows Vista, use the netsh command to configure SSL rather than httpcfg., like this: netsh http add sslcert ipport=0.0.0.0:8000 certhash= c390e7a4491cf97b96729167bf50186a4b68e052 appid={00112233-4455-6677-8899- AABBCCDDEEFF}. The certhash parameter specifies the thumbprint. The appid parameter is a GUID that identifies this binding of the certificate to the port; you can use any unique GUID.

> **Warning**   When a client application receives a certificate from a server, the WCF runtime attempts to ascertain that the certificate is valid and that the authority that issued it is trusted. The WCF runtime will fail this check when using the certificate that you have just installed. The following exercise shows how to force the WCF runtime to override this check and allow this certificate to be used. You should *never* do this in a production environment! The code is provided as-is, and without further explanation (it is not the author's work—it was written by developers at Microsoft and is included in one of the WCF technology samples provided with the Windows SDK). In the real world, you should go out and buy a valid certificate.

Add code to the WCF client to override certificate validation checking

1. In Visual Studio 2005, edit the Program.cs file for the ProductsClient project.

2. Add the following *using* statements to the list at the top of the file:

```
using System.Security.Crytography.X509Certificates;
using System.Net;
```

3. Add the following class to the *ProductsClient* namespace, underneath the *Program* class:

> **Note**   The code for this class is available in the PermissiveCertificatePolicy.cs file in the Chapter 4 folder, if you don't want to type it in manually.

```
// WARNING: This code is only needed for test certificates such as those
// created by makecert. It is not recommended for production code.
class PermissiveCertificatePolicy
{
    string subjectName;
    static PermissiveCertificatePolicy currentPolicy;
    PermissiveCertificatePolicy(string subjectName)
    {
        this.subjectName = subjectName;
        ServicePointManager.ServerCertificateValidationCallback +=
            new System.Net.Security.RemoteCertificateValidationCallback
            (RemoteCertValidate);
    }

    public static void Enact(string subjectName)
    {
        currentPolicy = new PermissiveCertificatePolicy(subjectName);
    }

    bool RemoteCertValidate(object sender, X509Certificate cert,
            X509Chain chain, System.Net.Security.SslPolicyErrors error)
    {
        if (cert.Subject == subjectName)
        {
            return true;
        }

        return false;
    }
}
```

4. Add the following statement shown in bold to the Main method of the *Program* class, immediately before creating the proxy object:

```
…
PermissiveCertificatePolicy.Enact("CN=HTTPS-Server");
ProductServiceClient proxy = new ProductServiceClient(…);
…
```

Run the WCF client and service

1. Start the solution without debugging.

2. In the ProductsServiceHost form, click Start.

3. In the client console window, press Enter. Verify that the client application runs correctly.

4. Press Enter to close the client console window. Stop the service and close the ProductsServiceHost form.

Protecting an HTTP Service at the Message Level

You can configure the BasicHttpBinding binding to provide message level security by selecting the Message security mode for the binding. In this mode, the service uses SOAP message level security to encrypt the message. The service must have a certificate installed, and the client uses the public key from the service's certificate to perform the encryption. The service can send the certificate containing its public key at the start of the message exchange, or an administrator can install the service certificate on the client computer before the client application (in which case you must specify how to locate the service certificate in the client certificate store by adding a service behavior using the *<serviceCredentials>* element to the client configuration file). You will learn more about this in Chapter 5. Additionally, the only authentication mechanism supported by a WCF service that uses this mode requires that the client application identifies itself with a certificate—you cannot use authentication mechanisms such as Windows Integrated Security with this mode.

One other option is to use the TransportWithMessageCredential security mode. This is a hybrid combination of message level and transport level security. The service uses the HTTPS protocol and a certificate to provide message integrity and confidentiality. Client authentication is handled at the message level by using SOAP message security, and the client application can provide a username and password to identify the user. You will learn more about this security mode in Chapter 5.

If you really want to implement message level security for a WCF service with the minimum of fuss and configuration, you can opt to use the WSHttpBinding binding. The WSHttpBinding binding conforms to the current WS-* specifications and follows the WS-Security specification for encrypting messages and authenticating users by default. The following exercises demonstrate how to use the WSHttpBinding binding to implement message level security over HTTP.

Configure the WCF service to use the WSHttpBinding binding

1. In Visual Studio 2005, edit the App.config file for the ProductsServiceHost project by using the WCF Service Configuration Editor.

2. In the left pane, expand the Products.ProductsServiceImpl node under the Services folder, right-click Endpoints, and then click New Service Endpoint.

3. In the right pane, set the properties of the endpoint to the values in the following table. Leave all other properties with their default value:

Property	Value
Name	ProductsServiceWSHttpEndpoint
Address	http://localhost:8010/ProductsService/ProductsService.svc
Binding	wsHttpBinding
Contract	Products.IProductsService

Notice that the scheme used for the address of this endpoint is http, and not https.

4. Save the changes, and exit the WCF Service Configuration Editor.

5. Rebuild the ProductsServiceHost project.

Configure the WCF client to use the WSHttpBinding binding

1. Edit the app.config file for the ProductsClient project by using the WCF Service Configuration Editor.

2. In the left pane, right-click Endpoints in the Client folder, and then click New Client Endpoint.

3. In the right pane, set the properties of the endpoint to the values in the following table:

Property	Value
Name	WSHttpBinding_IProductsService
Address	http://localhost:8010/ProductsService/ProductsService.svc
Binding	wsHttpBinding
Contract	ProductsClient.ProductsService.IProductsService

4. Save the changes, and exit the WCF Service Configuration Editor.

5. In Visual Studio 2005, edit the Program.cs file in the ProductsClient project. In the Main method, change the code that creates the proxy object to use the new binding, as follows:

```
ProductsServiceClient proxy = new
    ProductsServiceClient("WSHttpBinding_IProductsService");
```

6. Rebuild the ProductsClient project.

Run the WCF client and service and examine the trace output

1. Using Windows Explorer, delete the existing trace file Products.svclog in the Microsoft Press\WCF Step By Step\Chapter 4\ProductsService folder under your \My Documents folder.

2. In Visual Studio 2005, start the solution without debugging.

3. In the ProductsServiceHost form, click Start. In the client console window, press Enter. Verify that the client application still runs correctly. Press Enter to close the client console window. Stop the service and close the ProductsServiceHost form.

4. Start the Service Trace Viewer tool, and open the Products.svclog file.

5. In the Service Trace Viewer, in the left pane, click the Message tab.

6. Click the first message with the action *http://tempuri.org/IProductsService/ListProducts*. In the lower right pane, click the Message tab. You can see that the message has been encrypted—the body element of the message contains encrypted data.

7. In the left pane, click the second message with the action *http://tempuri.org/IProductsService/ListProducts*. In the right pane, scroll to the end of the Message window. This is the unencrypted version of the message passed from the message level to the service.

8. Examine the two ListProductsResponse messages. As with the NetTcpBinding example earlier in this chapter, you can see the encrypted version of the message being output by the service to the message level and the encrypted version of the message passing from the message level to the transport level.

9. Close the Service Trace Viewer.

The WSHttpBinding binding uses the 256-bit version of the AES encryption algorithm to encrypt data by default. You can select a different algorithm by creating a binding behavior and specifying the algorithm to use in the *AlgorithmSuite* property of the behavior, as you did when configuring message level security for the NetTcpBinding binding earlier in this chapter.

Authenticating Windows Users

So far, you have seen how to configure the NetTcpBinding, BasicHttpBinding, and WSHttpBinding bindings to support confidentiality and privacy by encrypting messages. However, transporting messages securely is only useful if a service can verify the identity of the user running the client application. In the exercises that follow, you will look at how a service can authenticate a user when the client application and service are both running within the same Windows domain. In Chapter 5, you will see how to perform authentication when a client and service are located in different, possibly non-Windows, security domains.

You will start by adding code to the ProductsService service that displays the name of the user calling the ListProducts operation. You will then be able to see the effect that the authentication options available in WCF have on the identity passed from a client application to a service.

> **Note** You can configure authentication to be largely transparent to the WCF service. You will see in the exercises in this section that most of the actual authentication process is performed by the WCF runtime executing the service. All the service needs to do is specify the type of authentication it requires.

Display the name of the user calling an operation in the WCF service

1. In Visual Studio 2005, add a reference to the *System.Windows.Forms* assembly to the ProductsService project.

2. Open the ProductsService.cs file.

This file contains the code that implements the operations for the ProductsService service.

3. Add the following *using* statements to the list at the top of the file:

```
using System.Threading;
using System.Windows.Forms;
```

4. Locate the ListProducts method in the *ProductsServiceImpl* class. Add the following statements as the first two lines of the method:

```
string userName = Thread.CurrentPrincipal.Identity.Name;
MessageBox.Show("Username is " + userName,
            "ProductsService Authentication");
```

The first statement retrieves the name of the Windows user that the current thread is running on behalf of. The second statement displays the username in a message box.

5. Edit the Program.cs file in the ProductsClient project. In the Main method, change the code that creates the proxy object to use the BasicHttpBinding binding, as follows:

```
ProductsServiceClient proxy = new
    ProductsServiceClient("BasicHttpBinding_IProductsService");
```

6. Start the solution without debugging.

7. In the ProductsServiceHost form, click Start. In the client console window, press Enter.

A message box appears, displaying the user name sent by the client application. The user name will appear to be missing. This is not an error. By default, the BasicHttpBinding binding does not send authentication information about users. All messages are sent as the anonymous user.

8. Click OK, and verify that the client application still runs correctly.

9. Press Enter to close the client console window. Stop the service and close the ProductsServiceHost form.

In the next set of exercises, you will revisit the BasicHttpBinding binding and implement user authentication. Many of the authentication options available for this binding apply to other bindings as well.

Configure the BasicHttpBinding binding for the WCF service to use Basic authentication

1. Edit the App.config file in the ProductsServiceHost project by using the WCF Service Configuration Editor.

2. In the left pane, expand the Bindings folder and click the ProductsServiceBasicHttp-BindingConfig node.

3. In the right pane, click the Security tab.

   Notice that the *TransportClientCredentialType* property is currently set to *None*, so the service is not expecting client applications to provide authentication information about users, and anyone who can connect to the service can send it messages and invoke operations.

4. Set the *TransportClientCredentialType* property to *Basic*.

   When using Basic authentication, the client application must provide a username and password, which is transmitted to the service. The WCF runtime executing the service can use this information to authenticate the user running the client application, and if the user is valid, it will provide the identity of the user to the service.

5. Save the configuration, and close the WCF Service Configuration Editor.

6. Start the solution.

7. In the ProductsServiceHost form, click Start. In the client console window, press Enter.

   The client fails with a MessageSecurityException exception, "The HTTP request is unauthorized with client authentication scheme 'Anonymous'... ." The WCF runtime for the service was expecting the client application to provide a username and password, which it has not done.

8. Close the client console window, stop the service, and close the ProductsServiceHost form.

Modify the WCF client to supply the user credentials to the service

1. In Visual Studio 2005, edit the app.config file in the ProductsClient project by using the WCF Service Configuration Editor.

2. In the left pane, expand the Bindings folder and click the ProductsClientBasicHttpBind-ingConfig node.

3. In the right pane, click the Security tab.

4. Set the *TransportClientCredentialType* property to *Basic*.

5. Save the configuration, and close the WCF Service Configuration Editor.

6. Edit the Program.cs file in the ProductsClient project.

7. In the Main method, add the following statements shown in bold immediately after the code that creates the proxy object. Replace LON-DEV-01 with the name of your domain or computer (if you are not currently a member of a domain), replace Student with your username, and replace Pa$$w0rd with your password:

```
ProductsServiceClient proxy = new
    ProductsServiceClient("BasicHttpBinding_IProductsService");
```

```
proxy.ClientCredentials.UserName.UserName = "LON-DEV-01\\Student";
proxy.ClientCredentials.UserName.Password = "Pa$$w0rd";
```

The *ClientCredentials* property of a WCF proxy object provides a mechanism for a client application to provide the credentials to send to the service. The *UserName* property of *ClientCredentials* can hold a username and password. Other properties are available, such as *ClientCertificate*, which enable you to supply different types of credentials information as required by the service configuration.

> **Warning**   This code is for illustrative purposes in this exercise only. In a production application, you should prompt the user for their name and password. You should never hard-code these details into an application.

8. Start the solution without debugging.

9. In the ProductsServiceHost form, click Start. In the client console window, press Enter.

   A message box appears, displaying the user name sent by the client application. This time, the user name appears as expected, verifying that the operation is executing with the credentials of the user.

   > **ProductsService Authentication** ☒
   >
   > Username is LON-DEV-01\Student
   >
   > [OK]

10. Click OK, and verify that the client application still runs correctly.

11. Press Enter to close the client console window. Stop the service and close the ProductsServiceHost form.

Using Basic authentication, you can provide the username and password of the user, and the WCF runtime executing the service will check that these credentials are valid. If you provide an invalid username of password, the WCF runtime will reject the request and the client will receive another MessageSecurityException exception with the message "The HTTP request was forbidden... ."

Basic authentication is a good solution if the user running the client application is not currently logged into the security domain used by the service.

> **Note**   You can also configure the NetTCPBinding and WSHttpBinding bindings at the message level to require Username authentication. This is very similar to Basic authentication at the transport level as far as client application is concerned, although somewhat different as far as the service is concerned, as it takes responsibility for authenticating the user itself (typically using a custom database of usernames and passwords). However, usernames and passwords are not encrypted at the message level, so WCF insists that the underlying transport provide encryption to prevent the credential details being transmitted across an open network as clear text.

If the user is logged in to the domain, then you can make use of Windows Integrated Security to provide the user's credentials automatically, rather than prompting the user for them again (or worse still, hard-coding them in your application!).

Configure the BasicHttpBinding binding for the WCF service and client to use Windows authentication

1. Edit the App.config file in the ProductsServiceHost project by using the WCF Service Configuration Editor.

2. In the left pane, expand the Bindings folder, and click the ProductsServiceBasicHttp-BindingConfig node.

3. In the right pane, click the Security tab.

4. Set the *TransportClientCredentialType* property to Windows.

5. Save the configuration and close the WCF Service Configuration Editor.

6. In Visual Studio 2005, edit the app.config file in the ProductsClient project by using the WCF Service Configuration Editor.

7. Repeat the process in steps 2 through 5, above and set the *TransportClientCredentialType* property of the ProductsClientBasicHttpBindingConfig binding configuration to Windows.

8. Save the configuration, and close the WCF Service Configuration Editor.

9. Edit the Program.cs file in the ProductsClient project.

10. In the Main method, comment out the two statements that add the username and password to the *ClientCredentials* property of the proxy object.

11. Start the solution without debugging.

12. In the ProductsServiceHost form, click Start. In the client console window, press Enter.

    The message box appears displaying your Windows username, which was sent by the client application. However, rather than you having to supply the username and password, the WCF runtime executing the client application picked this information up from the user's process automatically.

> **Note**   If you omitted to comment out the lines that populated the *ClientCredentials* object, the solution still works; the credentials provided are simply ignored. However, note the *ClientCredentials* property has a Windows property that you can use to provide a domain, username, and password to the service if you want the service to run as a different Windows user. Any values that you specify in the *Windows* property override those retrieved from the user's login process. The usual warnings about hard-coding usernames and password in your code still apply:

```
proxy.ClientCredentials.Windows.ClientCredential.Domain = "LON-DEV-01";
proxy.ClientCredentials.Windows.ClientCredential.UserName = "Administrator";
proxy.ClientCredentials.Windows.ClientCredential.Password = "P@ssw0rd";
```

13. Click OK in the message box, and verify that the client application still runs correctly.

14. Press Enter to close the client console window. Stop the service and close the ProductsServiceHost form.

When you use Windows Integrated Security, usernames and passwords are not transmitted as clear text. You can use Windows Integrated Security at the message level with the NetTCPBinding and WSHttpBinding bindings without needing to implement encryption at the transport level.

Examine the authentication mechanism used by the NetTcpBinding binding

1. Edit the App.config file in the ProductsServiceHost project by using the WCF Service Configuration Editor.

2. In the left pane, expand the Bindings folder, and click the ProductsServiceBasicTcpBindingConfig node.

3. In the right pane, click the Security tab.

4. Verify that the *MessageClientCredentialType* property is set to Windows.

   You have been using Windows Integrated Security without realizing it in earlier exercises!

> **Note**   The WSHttpBinding binding also defaults to using Windows Integrated Security.

5. Close the WCF Service Configuration Editor without saving changes.

6. Edit the Program.cs file for the ProductsClient project and modify the statement that creates the proxy object to use the NetTcpBinding binding, as follows:

```
ProductsServiceClient proxy = new
    ProductsServiceClient("NetTcpBinding_IProductsService");
```

7. Start the solution without debugging.

8. In the ProductsServiceHost form, click Start. In the client console window, press Enter.

   The familiar message box appears, displaying your Windows user name, proving that the NetTcpBinding automatically picks up your identity from Windows.

9. Click OK, and allow the client application to finish. Press Enter to close the client console window. Stop the service and close the ProductsServiceHost form.

Authorizing Users

After a service has established the identity of the user, it can then determine whether the service should perform the requested operations for the user. Different operations in a service could be considered more privileged than others. For example, in the ProductsService service, you might wish to let any staff who work in the warehouse query the product information in the *AdventureWorks* database but limit access to operations such as ChangeStockLevel, which modify data, to staff members who are stock controllers. WCF can use the features of the .NET Framework to enable a developer to specify which users and roles have the authority to request operations. You can perform this task declaratively (by using attributes) or imperatively (by adding code to the operations).

The authorization mechanism used by WCF requires access to a database defining users and the roles that they can fulfill. If you are performing authentication by using Active Directory, it makes sense to use the *Active Directory* database to hold the roles for each user as well. Therefore, the first step is to ensure that the WCF service is configured to retrieve roles from Active Directory by using the Windows Token Role Provider.

Configure the WCF service to use the Windows Token Role Provider

1. Edit the App.config file in the ProductsServiceHost project by using the WCF Service Configuration Editor.

2. In the left pane, expand the Advanced folder, expand the Service Behaviors folder and then click the ProductsBehavior node.

    The ProductsBehavior behavior currently contains the *serviceDebug* element. You added this behavior to the service in Chapter 3.

3. In the right pane, click Add.

4. In the Adding Behavior Element Extension Sections dialog box, select serviceAuthorization and then click Add.

    The serviceAuthorization behavior is added to the list of behaviors.

5. In the left pane, click serviceAuthorization under the ProductsBehavior node.

6. In the right pane, verify that the *PrincipalPermissionMode* property is set to *UseWindowsGroups*.

    By default, WCF uses the Windows Token Role Provider to authenticate users, so you don't actually need to change anything. However, you can configure the *serviceBehavior* element to specify a different role provider, such as the SQL Role Provider or the Authorization Store Role Provider mentioned earlier in this chapter. (You will configure the service to use the SQL Role Provider in Chapter 5.)

7. Save the configuration and close the WCF Service Configuration Editor.

The next step is to define the roles that can request the operations in the WCF service. When using the Windows Token Role Provider, Active Directory groups correspond to roles, so you define groups in the *Active Directory* database and add users to these groups.

> **Note**   The following exercise assumes you do not have access to the *Active Directory* database for your organization, so it uses the Windows local users and groups database instead. The principles are the same, however.

Create groups for warehouse staff and stock controller staff

1. On the Windows Start menu, right-click My Computer, and then click Manage.

    The Computer Management console appears.

2. In the Computer Management console, under the System Tools node, expand the Local Users and Groups node, right-click the Groups folder, and then click New Group.

3. In the New Group dialog box, enter WarehouseStaff for the Group name, and then click Create.

4. Still in the New Group dialog box, enter StockControllers for the Group name, and then click Create.

5. Click Close to close the New Group dialog box.

    The two new groups should appear in the list of groups in right pane of the Computer Management console.

6. In the left pane of the Computer Management console, right-click the Users folder and then click New User.

7. In the New User dialog box, use the values in the following table to set the properties of the user and then click Create.

Property	Value
User name	Fred
Password	Pa$$w0rd
Confirm password	Pa$$w0rd
User must change password at next logon	Unchecked

8. Add another user by specifying the values in the following table, and then click Create again.

Property	Value
User name	Bert
Password	Pa$$w0rd

Property	Value
Confirm password	Pa$$w0rd
User must change password at next logon	Unchecked

9. Click Close the close the New User dialog box.

10. In the left pane of the Computer Management console, click the Users folder.

    The two new users should appear in the list in the right pane of the Computer Management console.

11. In the right pane of the Computer Management console, right-click Bert and then click Properties.

12. In the Bert Properties dialog box, click the Member Of tab and then click Add.

13. In the Select Groups dialog box, type WarehouseStaff in the text box and then click OK.

    Bert is added to the WarehouseStaff group.

14. In the Bert Properties dialog box, click OK.

15. In the right pane of the Computer Management console, right-click Fred and then click Properties.

16. In the Fred Properties dialog box, click the Member Of tab and then click Add.

17. In the Select Groups dialog box, type WarehouseStaff in the text box and then click OK.

18. Click Add again. In the Select Groups dialog box, type StockControllers in the text box and then click OK.

    Fred is added to the WarehouseStaff and StockControllers groups—he has two roles.

19. In the Fred Properties dialog box, click OK.

20. Close the Computer Management console.

You can now use the groups you have just defined to specify the roles that can request each of the operations in the ProductsService service. To show how to specify authorization declaratively and imperatively, you will use attributes to specify the role for the operations that simply query the *AdventureWorks* database, but you will write code to specify the role that can modify the database.

Specify the roles for the WCF service operations

1. In Visual Studio 2005, open the ProductsService.cs file in the ProductsService project.

2. Add the following *using* statements to the list at the top of the file:

```
using System.Security;
using System.Security.Permissions;
using System.Security.Principal;
```

3. Locate the ListProducts method in the *ProductsServiceImpl* class. Add the following attribute, shown in bold, to this method:

```
[PrincipalPermission(SecurityAction.Demand, Role="WarehouseStaff")]
public List<string> ListProducts()
{
    ...
}
```

The *PrincipalPermission* attribute specifies the authorization requirements of the method. In this case, the SecurityAction.Demand parameter indicates that the method requires that the user meet the criteria specified by the following parameters. The Role parameter indicates that the user must be a member of the WarehouseStaff role.

You can identify specific users by using the optional Name parameter. However, if you specify Name and Role, then the user must match both criteria to be granted access (if the user is not a member of the specified role, they will not be allowed to execute the method). If you require users to be granted access to the method if they have a specific name *or* are a member of a specific group, you can use the *PrincipalPermission* attribute twice, like this:

```
[PrincipalPermission(SecurityAction.Demand, Role="WarehouseStaff")]
// LON-DEV-01\Student is not a member of the WarehouseStaff group
[PrincipalPermission(SecurityAction.Demand, Name="LON-DEV-01\\Student")]
public List<string> ListProducts()
{
    ...
}
```

You can also specify SecurityAction.Deny as the first parameter to the *PrincipalPermission* attribute. If you do this, the specified users and roles will be explicitly denied access to the method.

4. Apply the *PrincipalPermission* attribute with the WarehouseStaff group to the GetProduct and CurrentStockLevel methods, as shown in bold below:

```
[PrincipalPermission(SecurityAction.Demand, Role="WarehouseStaff")]
public Product GetProduct(string ProductNumber)
{
    ...
}
```

```
[PrincipalPermission(SecurityAction.Demand, Role="WarehouseStaff")]
public int GetStockLevel(string ProductNumber)
{
    ...
}
```

5. Locate the ChangeStockLevel method. Add the following code, shown in bold, to the start of this method:

```
public bool ChangeStockLevel(...)
{
```

```
// Determine whether the user is a member of the StockControllers role
WindowsPrincipal user = new WindowsPrincipal(
        (WindowsIdentity)Thread.CurrentPrincipal.Identity);
if (!(user.IsInRole("StockControllers")))
{
    // If the user is not in the StockControllers role,
    // throw a SecurityException
    throw new SecurityException("Access denied");
}    …
}
```

The first statement retrieves the identity information for the user and uses it to create a *WindowsPrincipal* object. Note that the identity returned by the current thread must be cast to a *WindowsIdentity* object. A *WindowsPrincipal* object is a representation of the user. It exposes the IsInRole method that this code uses to determine whether the user is a member of the StockControllers role. The IsInRole method returns *true* if the user is a member of the role, *false* otherwise. If the user is not a member of the role, the code throws a SecurityException exception with the message "Access Denied."

> **Warning**   It is tempting to provide more detail in the SecurityException exception. This practice is not recommended, as it could provide an attacker with useful information that they might be able to use to try and infiltrate your system. Keep the exception message bland!

Test the authorization for the WCF service

1. Start the solution without debugging.

2. In the ProductsServiceHost form, click Start. In the client console window, press Enter.

   Assuming you are not currently logged in to Windows as Fred or Bert, the client application stops and reports the message "Access is denied" when attempting to invoke the ListProducts operation. This is because the authenticated Windows account for the client application must be a member of the WarehouseStaff role:

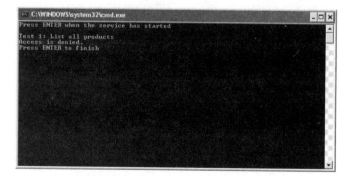

3. Press Enter to close the client console window, and then stop the service and close the ProductsServiceHost form.

4. In the ProductsClient project in Solution Explorer, open the Program.cs file.

5. In the Main method, add the following statements shown in bold immediately after the statement that creates the proxy object. Replace the value "*LON-DEV-01*" specified in the *Domain* property with the name of your computer:

```
ProductsServiceClient proxy = new
    ProductsServiceClient("NetTcpBinding_IProductsService");
proxy.ClientCredentials.Windows.ClientCredential.Domain = "LON-DEV-01";
proxy.ClientCredentials.Windows.ClientCredential.UserName = "Bert";
proxy.ClientCredentials.Windows.ClientCredential.Password = "Pa$$w0rd";
```

These statements explicitly set the Windows credentials for the user to those of Bert. The WCF runtime on the client will send these credentials to the service, rather than using those in the user's login process.

6. Start the solution again, without debugging.

7. In the ProductsServiceHost form, click Start. In the client console window, press Enter.

This time, Bert is a member of the WarehouseStaff role and is granted access to the List-Products, GetProduct, and CurrentStockLevel operations.

8. When the ListProducts method runs, it displays the message box confirming that the identity of the authenticated user is Bert. Click OK to continue execution. The first three tests run successfully, but when the client application attempts to perform test 4, which requires invoking the ChangeStockLevel operation, Bert has not been granted access to this method, and so the test fails with the "Access is denied" message:

9. Press Enter to close the client console window, and then stop the service and close the ProductsServiceHost form.

10. Return to the Program.cs file in the code view window.

11. In the Main method, change the Windows username of the user to Fred, like this:

```
proxy.ClientCredentials.Windows.ClientCredential.Domain = "LON-DEV-01";
proxy.ClientCredentials.Windows.ClientCredential.UserName = "Fred";
proxy.ClientCredentials.Windows.ClientCredential.Password = "Pa$$w0rd";
```

12. Build and start the solution again without debugging.

13. In the ProductsServiceHost form, click Start. In the client console window, press Enter.

    Fred is a member of the WarehouseStaff role and the StockControllers role, and so he is able to invoke all the operations in the ProductsService service.

14. When the ListProducts method displays the message box with the name of the authenticated user, verify that the username is Fred and then click OK.

15. The client application performs all four tests successfully. Press Enter to close the client console window, and then stop the service and close the ProductsServiceHost form.

Using Impersonation to Access Resources

Authenticating a user establishes the identity of the user to the WCF service, which can then perform authorization checks to verify that the user should be allowed to perform the requested operation. The method that implements the operation might require access to resources on the computer running the WCF service. By default, the service will attempt to gain access to these resources by using its own credentials. For example, when a method in the ProductsService service connects to the *AdventureWorks* database, it does so as the account running the service. When using Windows authentication, it is possible to specify that the WCF service should access resources by using the authenticated identity of the user instead. So, if Fred has been granted access to the *AdventureWorks* database, the WCF service can connect to SQL Server as Fred and will have access to all the database resources to which Fred has been granted access. If the user connects as Bert, the WCF service might be able to use a different set of resources in the database, depending on Bert's access rights. The same principle applies to other resources, such as files, folders, and network shares. Using impersonation gives an administrator fine-grained control over the ability of a WCF service to read or write possibly sensitive information and can provide an additional degree of security—just because the user can connect to the WCF service, they might not be able to perform operations that retrieve or modify confidential data unless the administrator has explicitly granted the user access to this data.

You can enable impersonation for an operation by setting the *Impersonation* property of the *OperationBehavior* attribute, like this (shown in bold):

```
[PrincipalPermission(SecurityAction.Demand, Role="WarehouseStaff")]
[OperationBehavior(Impersonation=ImpersonationLevel.Required)]
public List<string> ListProducts
{
    ...
}
```

Specifying the value *ImpersonationLevel.Required* enforces impersonation. The client application must also agree to this requirement and specify the level of impersonation that the WCF service application can use (you will see how to do this shortly). You can also specify the *ImpersonationLevel.Allowed*, which enables the WCF service to impersonate the user if the client application permits, but executes as the identity running the service application if not, and *ImpersonationLevel.NotAllowed*, which disables impersonation.

If you need to specify an impersonation level setting for all operations, you can set the *ImpersonateCallerForAllOperations* attribute of the *<serviceBehavior>* element of the service behavior to *true* in the service configuration file, as shown in bold below:

```xml
<?xml version="1.0" encoding="utf-8" ?>
<configuration>
  ...
  <system.serviceModel>
    ...
    <services>
      <service behaviorConfiguration="ProductsBehavior" name="Products.ProductsServiceImpl">
        ...
    </services>
    <behaviors>
      <serviceBehaviors>
        <behavior name="ProductsBehavior">
          <serviceAuthorization principalPermissionMode="UseWindowsGroups"
            impersonateCallerForAllOperations="false" />
        </behavior>
      </serviceBehaviors>
    </behaviors>
  </system.serviceModel>
</configuration>
```

You configure the client application to indicate the level of impersonation that the service can use by defining a behavior for the endpoint and specifying the *AllowedImpersonationLevel* property. The following fragments of a client configuration file highlight the pertinent elements:

```xml
<?xml version="1.0" encoding="utf-8" ?>
<configuration>
  <system.serviceModel>
    <behaviors>
      <endpointBehaviors>
        <behavior name="ImpersonationBehavior">
          <clientCredentials>
            <windows allowedImpersonationLevel="Impersonation" />
            ...
          </clientCredentials>
        </behavior>
      </endpointBehaviors>
    </behaviors>
    ...
    <client>
      ...
      <endpoint
        address="http://localhost:8010/ProductsService/ProductsService.svc"
        behaviorConfiguration="ImpersonationBehavior"
        binding="wsHttpBinding"
```

```
        contract="ProductsClient.ProductsService.IProductsService"
        name="WSHttpBinding_IProductsService" />
    </client>
  </system.serviceModel>
</configuration>
```

You can specify one of the following values for the *AllowedImpersonationLevel* property:

- *Impersonate.* The service can use the user's identity when accessing local resources on the computer hosting the service. However, the service cannot access resources on remote computers.

- *Delegation.* The service can use the user's identity when accessing local resources on the computer hosting the service and on remote computers. The service can pass the identity of the user on to remote services, which may authenticate the user and perform operations impersonating this user.

- *Identify.* The service can use the user's credentials to authenticate the user and authorize access to operations but cannot impersonate the user.

- *Anonymous.* The service does not use the user's identity to authenticate the user but can use the user's credentials to perform access checks against resources accessed by the service. This setting is only valid for transport mechanisms such as named pipes that connect a client application to a service executing on the same computer. If the service is running on a remote computer, the setting is handled in the same way as the "Identify" option.

- *None.* The service does not attempt to impersonate the user.

Summary

In this chapter, you have seen how to use the features of WCF bindings to control the degree of protection afforded to a WCF service. You have seen how to configure encryption for messages flowing between a client application and a service, at the message level and at the transport level. You have learned how to specify the authentication mode for a binding and how to pass Windows credentials from a client application to a WCF service. You have also learned how to authorize access to operations for authenticated users and how to provide access to resources based on a user's authenticated identity by using impersonation.

Chapter 5
Protecting a WCF Service over the Internet

After completing this chapter, you will be able to:

- Describe how to configure and use the SQL Membership Provider and the SQL Role Provider for ASP.NET to store and query user identity and role information for a WCF service.
- Explain how to configure a WCF service to authenticate users by using certificates.
- Describe how to use certificates to authenticate a WCF service to a client application.

Managing client application and WCF service security inside an organization requires some thought, but WCF provides bindings and behaviors that you can use to simplify many of the tasks associated with protecting communications. Together with the authentication and authorization features included with the .NET Framework 3.0, you can help to ensure that clients and services transmit messages in a confidential manner and have a reasonable degree of confidence that only authorized users are submitting requests to services. However, bear in mind that an organization's internal network is a relatively benign environment because of its inherent privacy—hackers might be able to penetrate your network, but this is an exceptional circumstance rather than the norm. As long as your system and network administrators maintain the security of the organization's infrastructure, you can assume a certain degree of trust between client applications and services. Features such as message encryption, authentication, and authorization are important, but they can operate at the relatively unobtrusive level described in Chapter 4 "Protecting an Enterprise WCF Service."

When you start connecting client applications and services across a public network such as the Internet, you can no longer make any assumptions about the trustworthiness of client applications, services, or the communications passing between them. For example, how does a client application verify that the service it is sending messages to is the real service and not some nefarious spoof that happens to have supplanted the real service or that is simply intercepting and logging messages before forwarding them on to the real service? How does a service know that the user running the client application is who he or she says she is? How does a service distinguish genuine requests sent by an authenticated client application from those generated by some program written by an attacker attempting to probe the service by sending it messages and seeing whether the service responds with any error information that displays any potential security weaknesses? The Internet is a potentially hostile environment, and you must treat all communications passing over it with the utmost suspicion. In this chapter, you will examine some techniques that you can use to help protect client applications, services, and the information transmitted between them.

Authenticating Users and Services in an Internet Environment

Maintaining information about all users that can legitimately access a service and their credentials typically requires some form of database. In a Windows environment, Active Directory provides just such a database, and a WCF service can use Windows Integrated Security to help authenticate users that are part of the same Windows domain as the service. When client applications connect to the service across the Internet, this approach is not always feasible; a client application will probably not be running using the same security domain as the service (it might not even be a Windows application). In this environment, you can use several alternative approaches for maintaining a list of authenticated users for a WCF service. For example, you can employ the SQL Membership Provider to store a list of users and their credentials in a SQL Server database, together with the SQL Role Provider to associate users with roles. Alternatively, you can use the Authorization Store Role Provider to record users and roles in XML files. In the exercises in this chapter, you will make use of the SQL Membership Provider and SQL Role Provider.

> **Important**   Chapter 4 described how to use impersonation to enable a service to access resources. Impersonation requires that the service can identify the user as a Windows account in its local security domain, so it is not available when alternative authentication mechanisms such as the SQL Membership Provider are used.

Authenticating and Authorizing Users by Using the SQL Membership Provider and the SQL Role Provider

To make a WCF service available across the Internet, you would typically host it by using Microsoft Internet Information Services (IIS) as described in Chapter 1, "Introducing Windows Communication Foundation." Hosting a WCF service in this way enables you to use the ASP.NET Web Site Administration Tool to easily create a SQL Server database containing the security information for the service and manage users and roles. You can then configure the WCF service to use the SQL Membership Provider to authenticate users, and the SQL Role Provider to retrieve role information for authorizing users. This is what you will do in the following set of exercises.

> **Note**   The procedure for creating a Web site that uses transport security based on SSL differs between Windows XP and Windows Vista. The exercises in this section call out the differences, so make sure you follow the appropriate steps for the operating system you are using.

The first exercise only applies to Windows Vista.

Configure IIS7 bindings (Windows Vista only)

1. In the Windows Control Panel, click System and Maintenance, click Administrative Tools, and then double-click Internet Information Services (IIS) Manager.

2. In the Internet Information Services (IIS) Manager, in the left pane, expand the node that corresponds to your computer, expand Web Sites, right-click Default Web Site, and then click Edit Bindings.

3. In the Web Site Bindings dialog box, if https is *not* configured, click Add. In the Add Web Site Binding dialog box, set Type to https, set the SSL certificate to HTTPS-Server, and then click OK.

4. In the Web Site Bindings dialog box, click Close.

5. Leave the Internet Information Services (IIS) Manager open.

The next exercise applies to Windows Vista and Windows XP.

Create an ASP.NET Web site to host the WCF service

1. Using Visual Studio 2005, create a new Web site.

2. In the New Web Site dialog box, select the WCF Service template. Set the Location to HTTP, set the language to Visual C#, and then click Browse.

3. In the Choose Location dialog box, click Local IIS. In the right pane, click Default Web Site, and then click the Create New Virtual Directory icon in the top right corner of the dialog box.

4. In the New Virtual Directory dialog box, enter InternetProductsService for the Alias name. Click Browse adjacent to the Folder text box.

5. In the Browse For Folder dialog box, move to the Microsoft Press\WCF Step By Step\Chapter 5 folder under your \My Documents folder. Click the Create New Folder icon in the toolbar.

6. In the New Folder dialog box, enter the name InternetProductsService and then click OK.

7. In the Browse For Folder dialog box, click Open.

8. In the New Virtual Directory dialog box, click OK.

9. In the Choose Location dialog box, click the InternetProductsService folder in the Default Web Site node. Check the Use Secure Sockets Layer check box at the bottom of the dialog box, and then click Open.

10. In the New Web Site dialog box, verify that the address for the new Web site is *https:// localhost/InternetProductsService* and then click OK.

The InternetProductsService Web site is configured to listen for requests by using the HTTPS protocol. This is good practice when building Web sites for hosting Web services that will be accessed from the Internet as it provides a much greater degree of privacy than using unencrypted communications.

> **Note**   You can still perform message level encryption as well if you need to provide end-to-end security rather than point-to-point. However, remember that encryption is a necessarily expensive operation. Encrypting at two levels will impact performance. Transport level encryption tends to be much faster than message level.encryption. So, if performance is a limiting factor and you have to make a choice, then go for transport level security.

Although you have specified that the Web site requires clients to connect by using HTTPS, you still need to perform some additional configuration of IIS. In particular, you must install a certificate that the IIS service and client applications can use for encrypting messages.

> **Important**   In the following exercise, you will use the same test certificate that you created in Chapter 4. It is worth emphasizing again that, in a production environment, you should procure a real certificate from a reputable certification authority.

The next exercise has two versions; one for Windows Vista and one for Windows XP.

Configure the IIS Web site to support HTTPS communications (Windows Vista only)

1. Return to the Internet Information Services (IIS) Manager.

2. In the left pane, right-click the Default Web Site folder, and then click Refresh.

3. Click the InternetProductsService node in the Default Web Site folder and make sure the main panel in the console displays the Web Site in Features View (If the main panel is displaying the folders App_Code, and Add_Data, and the files Service.svc and Web.config, it is in Content View; right-click the InternetProductsService node, and click Switch to Features View.)

4. In the IIS area in the main panel, double-click SSL Settings.

5. In the SSL Settings pane, check Require SSL, but leave all the other properties at their default values.

6. In the right pane, click Apply.

7. In the Internet Information Services (IIS) Manager navigation bar, click Back. In the main panel, double-click Authentication.

8. In the Authentication pane, click Basic Authentication. In the right pane, click Enable.

9. Close the Internet Information Services (IIS) Manager.

Configure the IIS Web site to support HTTPS communications (Windows XP only)

1. On the Windows Start menu, click Run.

2. In the Run dialog box, type **inetmgr** and then click OK.

   The Internet Information Services console starts.

3. In the Internet Information Services console, expand the node corresponding to your computer in the tree view and then expand Web sites.

4. Right-click the Default Web Site node, and then click Properties.

5. In the *Default Web Site* Properties dialog box, click the Directory Security tab.

6. In the Directory Security page, under Secure communications, click Server Certificate.

   The Web Server Certificate Wizard starts.

7. In the Welcome to the Web Server Certificate Wizard page, click Next.

8. In the Server Certificate page, select Assign an existing certificate and then click Next.

9. In the Available Certificates page, select the HTTPS-Server certificate and then click Next.

10. In the Certificate Summary page, click Next.

11. In the Completing the Web Server Certificate Wizard page, click Finish.

12. In the *Default Web Site* Properties dialog box, click OK.

13. In the Internet Information Services console, expand the Default Web Site node, right-click the InternetProductsService node, and then click Properties.

14. In the InternetProductsService Properties dialog box, click the Directory Security tab.

15. In the Directory Security page, under Secure communications, click Edit.

16. In the Secure Communications dialog box, check Require secure channel (SSL), but leave other properties at their default value, as shown below, and then click OK.

17. In the Directory Security page, under Anonymous access and authentication control, click Edit.

18. In the Authentication Methods dialog box, clear the Integrated Windows authentication check box and select the Basic authentication check box. When the Internet Service Manager message box appears warning that site should use HTTPS, click Yes. Click OK.

19. In the InternetProductsService Properties dialog box, click OK.

20. Close the Internet Information Services console.

The remaining exercises apply to Windows Vista and Windows XP.

Import the code for the WCF service into the IIS Web site

1. Return to Visual Studio displaying the InternetProductsService solution.

2. In Solution Explorer, expand the App_Code folder and delete the file Service.cs.

    The Service.cs file contains code for a sample WCF Web service. You will not need this file, although you are welcome to look at it before removing it.

3. In Solution Explorer, right-click the App_Code folder and then click Add Existing Item.

4. In the Add Existing Item dialog box, move to the Microsoft Press\WCF Step By Step\Chapter 5\ProductsService folder under your \My Documents folder, select the ProductsService.cs file, and then click Add.

    The ProductsService.cs file contains the code for the ProductsService service. This is almost the same code that you used in Chapter 4 (the statements that display the user identity in the ListProducts method have been removed as you should not attempt to display an interactive message box from a WCF service hosted by IIS).

5. In Solution Explorer, rename the Service.svc file as ProductsService.svc.

6. Double-click the ProductsService.svc file to display the service definition file in the code view window. Modify this file as shown in bold below:

    ```
    <% @ServiceHost Language=C# Debug="true" Service="Products.ProductsServiceImpl" CodeBehind="~/App_Code/ProductsService.cs"%>
    ```

7. In Solution Explorer, delete the Web.config file.

8. In the Website menu, click Add Existing Item. In the Add Existing Item dialog box, move to the Microsoft Press\WCF Step By Step\Chapter 5\ProductsService folder under your \My Documents folder, select the App.config file, and then click Add.

    This is the configuration file used by the WCF host application in Chapter 4. You must rename this file as Web.config for the Web service to recognize it properly.

9. Using Solution Explorer, rename the App.config file as Web.config.

10. Edit the Web.config file by using the WCF Service Configuration Editor.

11. In the WCF Service Configuration Editor, in the Services folder, expand the Products.ProductsServiceImpl node, expand the EndPoints folder, and delete the ProductsServiceTcpBinding endpoint and the ProductsServiceHttpEndpoint endpoint.

    This version of the WCF service is only going to be accessed by client applications using the HTTPS protocol over the wsHttpBinding binding to connect from the Internet.

> **Important**   It is good practice to remove any endpoints that a service is not going to use. They could expose unexpected vulnerabilities if an attacker manages to penetrate the network security of your organization.

12. In the left pane, expand the Bindings folder. Delete both binding configurations located in this folder.

    These binding configurations are for the basicHttpBinding and netTcpBinding bindings that you have just removed.

13. Right-click the Binding folder and then click New Binding Configuration. In the Create a New Binding dialog box, select wsHttpBinding and then click OK.

14. In the right pane, set the *Name* property of the binding to *ProductsServiceWSHttpBindingConfig*.

15. Click the Security tab. Set the *Mode* property of the binding to *TransportWithMessageCredential*, set the *MessageClientCredentialType* property to *UserName*, and set the *TransportClientCredentialType* to *None*.

    The host Web site is configured to use the HTTPS protocol, so the WCF service must be configured to support transport level security. The TransportWithMessageCredential mode uses HTTPS at the transport level to protect messages traversing the network and uses the server certificate to authenticate with the client. The user's credentials are authenticated by using message level security—this is the level at which the SQL Role Provider operates.

16. In the left pane, select the ProductsServiceWSHttpEndpoint endpoint in the Endpoints folder under the Products.ProductsServiceImpl node. In the right pane, set the *BindingConfiguration* property to *ProductsServiceWSHttpBindingConfig*.

> **Note**   IIS is hosting this service, so you can leave the *Address* property blank. The address IIS will use is a combination of the URL of the WCF service and the name of the service definition file, in this case, https://localhost/InternetProductsService/ProductsService.svc.

17. In the left pane, expand the Advanced folder, expand the Service Behaviors folder, right-click the ProductsBehavior node, and then click Add Service Behavior Element Extension.

18. In the Adding Behavior Element Extension Sections dialog box, select serviceMetadata and then click Add.

19. Click the serviceMetadata node under ProductsBehavior. In the right pane, set the *HttpsGetEnabled* property to *True* but leave the *HttpGetEnabled* property set to *False*.

20. Save the changes, and exit the WCF Service Configuration Editor.

21. In Visual Studio 2005, in the Website menu, click Add Reference. In the Add Reference dialog box, click the Browse tab and add a reference to the *Microsoft.Practices.EnterpriseLibrary.Data.dll* assembly in the C:\Program Files\Microsoft Enterprise Library\bin folder.

> **Note**   This action automatically adds references to the *Microsoft.Practices EnterpriseLibrary.Common.dll* and *Microsoft.Practices.ObjectBuilder.dll* assemblies as these are referenced by the *Microsoft.Practices.EnterpriseLibrary.Data.dll* assembly.

22. Start Internet Explorer and go to the Web site https://localhost/InternetProductsService/ProductsService.svc. Depending on how you have configured Internet Explorer on your computer, you might be prompted with a Security Alert message box. If so, click OK to acknowledge the message.

> **Note**   Windows Vista displays an error page with the message "There is a problem with this website's security certificate." This is because the certificate you used for configuring SSL was not issued by a recognized trusted certificate authority. If this was a commercial Web site, you should choose not to view it. However, in this case the Web site is perfectly safe, so click the link "Continue to this website (not recommended)."

If another Security Alert message box appears, click Yes to accept the security certificate of the Web site.

Internet Explorer opens the page *https://localhost/InternetProductsService/ProductsService.svc*, as shown in the following image:

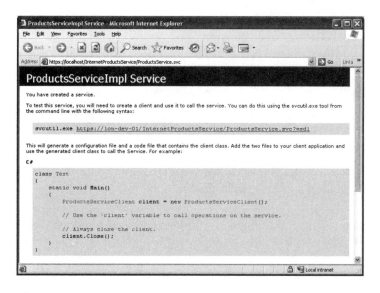

23. Close Internet Explorer.

Now that you have deployed, configured, and tested the WCF service by using IIS, you can use the ASP.NET Administration Tool to define the users and roles that will be permitted to access the service. To keep things simple, you will create roles (WarehouseStaff and StockControllers) and users (Fred and Bert) that mimic those you created by using Windows in Chapter 4.

Define users and roles for the WCF service

1. In Visual Studio 2005, in the Website menu, click ASP.NET Configuration.

    The ASP.NET Web Site Administration Tool starts. This is actually another Web application that runs using the ASP.NET Development Server (a stand-alone Web server installed with Visual Studio 2005, and separate from IIS):

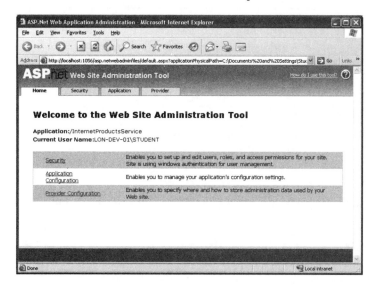

This tool provides pages enabling you to add and manage users for your Web site, specify Web application settings that you want to be stored in the application configuration file (not WCF settings), and indicate how security information such as user names and passwords are stored. By default, the ASP.NET Web Site Administration Tool stores security information in a local SQL Server database called ASPNETDB.MDF that it creates in the App_Data folder of your Web site.

2. Click the Security tab.

The Security page appears. You can use this page to manager users, specify the authentication mechanism that the Web site uses, define roles for users, and specify access rules for controlling access to the Web site.

> **Note**   The first time you click the Security link there will be a delay before the page is displayed. This is because the tool creates the *ASPNETDB.MDF* database at this point.

3. In the Users section of the page, click the Select authentication type link.

A new page appears asking how users will access your Web site. You have two options available:

❑ From the Internet. This option enables you to define users and roles in the SQL Server database. Users accessing your application must provide an identity that maps to a valid user.

> **Note**   The explanation given for the From the internet option on the page assumes you are building an ASP.NET Web site rather than a WCF Web service, which is why it describes using forms-based authentication. A client application connecting to a WCF service can provide the user's credentials by populating the *ClientCredentials* property of the proxy object being used to send requests to the WCF service.

❑ From a local network. This option is selected by default. This option configures the Web site to use Windows authentication; all users must be members of a Windows domain that your Web site can access.

4. Click From the internet, and then click Done.

You return to the Security page.

5. In the Users section, notice that the number of existing users that can access your Web site is currently zero. Click the Create user link.

The Create User page appears.

6. In the Create User page, add a new user with the values shown in the following table:

Prompt	Response
User name	Bert
Password	Pa$$w0rd
Confirm password	Pa$$w0rd
E-mail	Bert@Adventure-Works.com
Security Question	What was the name of your first pet
Security Answer	Tiddles

Note   You must supply values for all fields in this screen. The *E-mail*, *Security Question*, and *Security Answer* fields can be used by the ASP.NET PasswordRecovery control to recover or reset a user's password. Detailed discussion of the PasswordRecovery control is outside the scope of this book.

7. Ensure that the Active User box is checked and then click Create User.

   The message "Complete. Your account has been successfully created." appears in a new page.

8. Click Continue. The Create User page reappears, enabling you to add further users. Add another user using the information shown in the following table:

Prompt	Response
User name	Fred
Password	Pa$$w0rd

Prompt	Response
Confirm password	Pa$$w0rd
E-mail	Fred@Adventure-Works.com
Security Question	What was the name of your first pet
Security Answer	Rover

9. Ensure that the Active User box is checked, and then click Create User.

10. Click Back to return to the Security page. Verify that the number of existing users is now set to 2.

11. In the Roles section of the page, click the Enable roles link.

12. When roles have been enabled, click the Create or Manage roles link.

    The Create New Role page appears.

13. In the New role name text box, type WarehouseStaff and then click Add Role.

    The new role appears on the page, together with links enabling you to add and remove users to or from this role.

14. Click the Manage link.

    Another page appears, enabling you to specify the users that are members of this role. You can search for users or list users whose names begin with a specific letter and then add them to the role. Click the All link to display all users.

15. Check the User Is In Role box for Bert and Fred, as shown in the following image:

16. Wait for the page to be redisplayed, and then click Back.

> **Important**   If you click Back before the page is redisplayed, the users might not be added to the roles correctly.

17. In Create New Role page, in the New role name text box, type StockControllers and then click Add Role.

18. Click the Manage link for the StockControllers role. Add Fred to the StockControllers role, wait for the page to be redisplayed, and then click Back.

19. Close the Internet Explorer window displaying the ASP.NET Web Site Administration tool.

> **Note**   The ASP.NET Web Site Administration Tool modifies the Web.config file of the Web service. When you return to Visual Studio, if you have the Web.config file open for editing in the code view window, you will be alerted that the file has been modified. In the message box, click Yes to reload the file.

The next step is to modify the behavior of the WCF service to perform authorization by using the users and roles defined in the SQL Server database rather than by using Windows users and groups.

Configure the WCF service to use the SQL Role Provider and the SQL Membership Provider

1. In Visual Studio 2005, in Solution Explorer, right-click the Web.config file and then click Edit WCF Configuration.

2. In the WCF Service Configuration Editor, expand the Advanced folder, expand the Service Behaviors folder, and then expand the ProductsBehavior node.

3. Click the serviceAuthorization node under the ProductsBehavior node.In the right pane, set the *PrincipalPermissionMode* property to *UseAspNetRoles* and type **AspNetSqlRoleProvider** for the *RoleProviderName* property.

   The RoleProviderName property identifies a particular configuration for the identity role provider that will be used to map users to roles. The value *"AspNetSqlRoleProvider"* is actually defined in the Machine.config file and specifies the version of the SQL Role Provider to use to authorize users, together with information, about how to connect to the database holding the user and role information.

4. In the left pane, right-click the ProductsBehavior node and then click Add Service Behavior Element Extension. In the Adding Behavior Element Extension Sections dialog box, select serviceCredentials and then click Add.

5. In the left pane, click the serviceCredentials node. In the right pane, set the *UserName-PasswordValidationMode* property to *MembershipProvider* and type

AspNetSqlMembershipProvider for the *MembershipProviderName* property. The membership provider is responsible for authenticating users based on their names and passwords stored in the SQL Server database. The value *"AspNetSqlMembershipProvider"* is defined in the Machine.config file.

> **Note**   Try not to get too confused by the role provider and the membership provider. WCF uses the membership provider for authenticating users, and it uses the role provider for authorizing users' access to resources after they have been authenticated.

6. Save the configuration, and then exit the WCF Service Configuration Editor.

You can now test the WCF service by using the client application developed in the previous chapters. First, you must make some changes so that the client application connects to the WCF service by using the correct binding and address.

Modify the WCF client application to connect to the updated WCF service

1. In Visual Studio, in Solution Explorer, right-click the InternetProductsService solution, point to Add, and then click Existing Project.

2. In the Add Existing Project dialog box, move to the Microsoft Press\WCF Step By Step\Chapter 5\ProductsClient folder under your \My Documents folder, select the ProductsClient.csproj project file, and then click Open.

3. Use the WCF Service Configuration Editor to open the app.config file for the ProductsClient project.

4. In the WCF Service Configuration Editor, right-click the Bindings folder and then click the New Binding Configuration. In the Create a New Binding dialog box, select wsHttpBinding and then click OK.

5. In the right pane, set the *Name* property to *ProductsClientWSHttpBindingConfig*.

6. Click the Security tab, set the *Mode* property to *TransportWithMessageCredential* and set the *MessageClientCredentialType* property to *UserName*.

7. In the left pane, in the Endpoints folder under the Client folder, select the WSHttpBinding_IProductsService endpoint.

8. In the right pane, change the *Address* property to *https://localhost/InternetProducts Service/ProductsService.svc* and set the *BindingConfiguration* property to *Products ClientWSHttpBindingConfig*.

9. Save the configuration and then exit the WCF Service Configuration Editor.

10. In Solution Explorer, open the Program.cs file in the ProductsClient project. In the code view window, in the Main method of the Program class, change the statement that creates the proxy to refer to the WSHttpBinding_IProductsService endpoint, like this:

```
ProductsServiceClient proxy =
    new ProductsServiceClient("WSHttpBinding_IProductsService");
```

11. Replace the three statements that set the *Domain*, *UserName*, and *Password* properties of the *ClientCredentials.Windows.ClientCredential* property of the proxy object with the following statements:

```
proxy.ClientCredentials.UserName.UserName = "Bert";
proxy.ClientCredentials.UserName.Password = "Pa$$w0rd";
```

The client application uses message level authentication to send the user's credentials to the WCF service. You specify the credentials to send by using the *ClientCredentials.UserName* property of the proxy object.

> **Important** To reiterate the point made in Chapter 4, this code is for illustrative purposes in this exercise only. You should never hard-code usernames and password directly into an application.

Test the WCF service

1. In Solution Explorer, right-click the ProductsClient project and then click Set as Startup Project.

2. Start the solution without debugging. When the client console window appears, press Enter to connect to the service.

   The first three tests should run successfully, but the final test fails with the error shown in the following image:

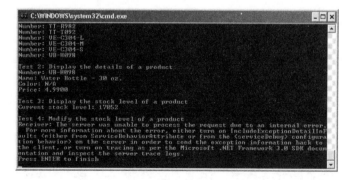

The *PrincipalPermission* attributes implementing security demands for the first three methods automatically use the currently configured role provider. In Chapter 4, they used the Windows Token Role Provider and authorized users based on their Windows identity. In these exercises, they are using the SQL Role Provider. The problem is that the method executed by test 4 does not use the *PrincipalPermission* attribute—the authorization check is performed by using code. In particular, the following statement attempts to retrieve the identity of the user assuming it was a Windows principal, which it no longer is:

```
WindowsPrincipal user = new WindowsPrincipal(
    (WindowsIdentity)Thread.CurrentPrincipal.Identity);
```

Press Enter and return to Visual Studio 2005.

3. Edit the ProductsService.cs file in the App_Code folder of the WCF service project. Locate the ChangeStockLevel method, and modify the two lines of code that create the user variable and test this variable to determine whether the user is a member of the StockControllers role, as shown in bold below:

```
// Determine whether the user is a member of the StockControllers role
IIdentity user = ServiceSecurityContext.Current.PrimaryIdentity;
if (!(System.Web.Security.Roles.IsUserInRole(user.Name,
    "StockControllers"))) {
    ...
```

The *ServiceSecurityContext* class contains information about the current security context for the WCF operation being performed. This security context information includes the identity if the user requesting the operation, which is available in the *Current.PrimaryIdentity* property. You can use the name held in this identity object to determine the whether the user is a member of a specific role by using the IsInRole method of the *System.Web.Security.Roles* class. The *Roles* class accesses the data in the currently configured role provider for the WCF service to perform its work.

4. Start the solution without debugging. Press Enter when the client application window appears. This time, test 4 fails with the error "Access is denied." This is because Bert is not a member of the StockControllers role.

5. Press Enter again to close the application.

6. Edit the Program.cs file in the ProductsClient project. Change the username sent to the WCF service through the proxy as follows:

```
proxy.ClientCredentials.UserName.UserName = "Fred";
```

7. Start the solution without debugging. Press Enter when the client application window appears. Fred is a member of the WarehouseStaff and StockControllers role, and all tests should run successfully.

8. Press Enter to close the application.

Authenticating and Authorizing Users by Using Certificates

Using a username and password to identify a user provides a degree of security, but you are probably all too familiar with the shortcomings of many implementations that follow this approach. It is very easy to disclose a password (possibly unwittingly) to another user. Many people use passwords that are easy for them to remember, and typically passwords are often short, or easily guessed (how many times have you used "password," or "1234," or something equally insecure?). Even your mother's maiden name, suitably scrambled, is not that secure—this information is frequently available in the public domain, which is why it is nonsense for banks to use this as a piece of information to identity yourself whenever you need to contact them (I will get off my security hobbyhorse now).

Using a public key infrastructure (PKI) can help to overcome some of the shortcomings of passwords. PKI provides a mechanism both for encrypting messages and for authenticating them.

PKI is based on pairs of keys (a key is a long sequence of random numbers): a public key that you can use to encrypt messages, and a private key that you can use to decrypt them again. These keys should be unique. If you want to communicate with a third party, you can send them a copy of your public key. The third party can encrypt their messages using this key and transmit them to you. You can decrypt these messages using your private key. The theory is that only your private key can decrypt a message encrypted by using your public key, so it does not matter if someone else intercepts the message because they will not be able to read it. In practice, it is possible to decrypt messages even if you don't have the private key, but it takes a lot of effort, and the longer the key, the more time and effort it takes—use keys with 128 bits or more.

Public and private keys can also work the other way around. If you encrypt a message with your private key, anyone with the public key can decrypt it. This does not sound too useful until you consider that this provides a convenient mechanism for verifying the source of a message. If a third party receives an encrypted message that purports to come from you, but that it cannot decrypt by using the public key that you provided, then the chances are that this message was actually from someone else pretending to be you (only you can send messages that can be decrypted by using your public key). The third party should probably discard the message in this case.

Where do you get keys? Well, you can request a pair of keys in a certificate from a certification authority, or CA. The CA will perform various checks to ensure that you are whom you actually say you are, and if they are satisfied, they will issue you with a certificate containing a public key and a private key (you usually have to pay for this service). The certificate also contains other bits of identity information about you and about the CA itself.

When you wish to communicate with a third party, you can send them a message that includes a hash (a calculated summary, a bit like a checksum but more complicated) of the message contents encrypted with your private key—this is referred to as your signature. You can arrange for a copy of your certificate, minus your private key, to be installed in the certificate store on the third-party computer as an out-of-band operation by the administrator at that end or attach a copy of your certificate, minus the private key, with the message when you send it. When the third party examines your certificate, it can verify that it was issued by a recognized and trusted CA, and that it has not been revoked before continuing (a certificate can be withdrawn if the service no longer wishes to trust the client, and the service can maintain a list of withdrawn certificates in its certificate revocation list). If the third party does not recognize or trust the CA, they can simply reject the message. Assuming that the third party does trust the CA, it can use the public key from your certificate to decrypt the signature and verify the unencrypted hash against the message (the third party generates its own hash of the message contents using the same algorithm that you did and compares his hash to yours). If this is successful, the third party will then have a reasonable degree of assurance that the message was sent by you. It can also be very confident that the message has not been corrupted or otherwise tampered with as it passed across the network. The third party can use the identity information from your certificate to determine your level of authorization and process your request if you have the appropriate authority.

A service can also use a certificate to authenticate itself to a client application, reducing the likelihood of the client connecting to a spoof service.

> **Note**   This discussion has been primarily concerned with signing messages for authentication purposes. You can use certificates to encrypt messages as well but the process is slightly more complex. When a client application wants to send an encrypted and signed message to a service, it first signs the message by using its own private key and then encrypts the complete, signed message by using the service's public key. The service decrypts the signed message using its private key and then authenticates the message by using the client application's public key.
>
> If the service sends an encrypted and signed response back to the client, the process is reversed; the service signs the message with its private key and encrypts the message with the client application's public key. The client application decrypts the signed message with its private key and uses the service's public key to authenticate the message.
>
> You can see that communications that require the use of certificates include a complex protocol involving an initial exchange of certificates and keys. However, the additional security that using certificates provides makes this overhead very worthwhile.

You should always obtain the certificates that you use to identify yourself and secure your communications from a reputable certification authority that is trusted by you and those parties with whom you wish to communicate. And you should never ever disclose your own personal private key!

In the exercises in this section, you will see how you can use certificates to sign messages and authenticate users to a WCF service application.

Modify the WCF service to require client applications to authenticate by using certificates

1. Using Visual Studio 2005, edit the Web.config file for the WCF service project by using the WCF Service Configuration Editor.

2. In the WCF Service Configuration Editor, expand the Bindings folder and then click the ProductsServiceWSHttpBindingConfig binding configuration.

3. In the right pane, click the Security tab. Change the *MessageClientCredentialType* property to *Certificate*.

    The WCF service now requires that client applications supply a certificate to authenticate users. The *NegotiateServiceCredential* property on this page specifies how the client application sends the certificate to the WCF service. If this property is set to *True* (the default value), the WCF service expects the client application to include its certificate with the messages that it sends (actually, a series of initial messages occur while the client and WCF service exchange certificates). If this property is set to *False*, the administrator for the WCF service must install the client certificate manually in the Trusted People certificate store of the computer running the service. Set this property to False, as you will manually install the client certificates in a later step.

4. In the left pane, expand the Advanced folder, expand the Service Behaviors folder, expand the ProductsBehavior behavior, expand the serviceCredentials node, and then click the clientCertificate node.

The *CertificateValidationMode* property in the upper part of this page enables you to specify the how the WCF service verifies the trustworthiness of client certificates. It can have the following values:

- ❑ *ChainTrust* (the default). The service will verify that the CA that issued the certificate is valid and can be trusted—the CA must either have a certificate that is stored in the Trusted Root Certification Authorities store on the service's computer, or have a certificate that was issued by another CA that is recorded in the Trusted Root Certification Authorities store, or have a certificate that was issued by a CA that has a certificate that was issued by another CA recorded in Trusted Root Certification Authorities store, and so on. The service will navigate its way up the chain of CA certificates until it either finds a trusted CA or reaches the end of the chain. If the service fails to establish that the chain ends in a trusted CA, then the client certificate is not trusted, and it is rejected.

- ❑ *PeerTrust*. The service searches the Trusted People store for the client certificate. If the service finds a matching certificate, the client is trusted. If not, the client request is rejected.

- ❑ *PeerOrChainTrust*. The service deems that the client certificate is valid if it is in the Trusted People store, or it can verify that the certificate was issued by a trusted CA by using the ChainTrust mechanism described above.

- ❑ *Custom*. The services uses a class that implements your own custom certificate validation process. You specify the class that implements the custom validation by using the CustomeCertificateValidatorType property.

- ❑ *None*. The service does not attempt to verify the client certificate and just accepts it as valid.

By default, the service will look in stores in the LocalMachine store location when validating certificates. This is useful if you are hosting the WCF service in IIS. If you are creating a self-hosted service running by using a specific user account, you can configure the WCF service to look in the CurrentUser store location instead by changing the *TrustedStoreLocation* property.

The *RevocationMode* property specifies whether the service should also check to see whether the client certificate has been revoked (the client is no longer trusted). The service can query its online revocation list (Online), its cached revocation list (Offline), or not bother checking (NoCheck).

5. In the right pane, set the *CertificateValidationMode* property to *PeerTrust*.

> **Important** In the following exercises you will be using test certificates generated by using the makecert utility to identify users. These certificates do not have a trusted CA. To enable the WCF service to be able to use these certificates, you can either disable validation checking (which is very dangerous and never recommended) or arrange for the certificates to be placed in the Trusted People store, which is what you have specified here.

6. Save the configuration, and close the WCF Service Configuration Editor.

You can now configure the client application to send a certificate to the WCF service.

Modify the WCF client application to authenticate with the WCF service by using a certificate

1. Edit the app.config file for the ProductsClient project by using the WCF Service Configuration Editor.

2. Expand the Bindings folder, and then click the ProductsClientWSHttpBindingConfig binding configuration.

3. In the right pane, click the Security tab. Set the *MessageClientCredentialType* property to *Certificate*, and set the NegotiateServiceCredential property to *False*.

4. Save the configuration, and close the WCF Service Configuration Editor.

You can now create certificates for the two test users, Bert and Fred, and then modify the client application to send a certificate that identifies the user to the WCF service.

Create certificates to identify the test users

1. On the Windows Start menu, point to All Programs, point to Microsoft Windows SDK, and then click CMD Shell.

2. In the command prompt window, type the following command:

```
makecert -sr CurrentUser -ss My -n CN=Bert -sky exchange
```

This command creates a certificate with the subject "Bert," and places it in the Personal store of the currently logged on user.

3. In the command prompt window, type the following command:

```
makecert -sr CurrentUser -ss My -n CN=Fred -sky exchange
```

This command creates another certificate with the subject "Fred."

The certificates for Bert and Fred are in the Personal certificate store of the current user. The WCF service requires the administrator to install a copy of these certificates into the Trusted People store of the local computer. In the next exercise, you will export a copy of the personal certificates to a pair of files and then import the certificates to the Trusted People store for the local computer.

Note   The certmgr command that you use in the following exercise provides options enabling you to copy a certificate directly from one store to another in a single command. However, in the real world you would more likely export a certificate to a file, transport the file (in a secure manner) to the computer hosting the service, and then import the certificate into the certificate store. This is the approach used in the following exercise.

Export the users' certificates, and import them into the server's certificate store

1. In the command prompt window, type the following command:

    ```
    certmgr -put -c -n Bert -r CurrentUser -s My bert.cer
    ```

    This command retrieves a copy of Bert's certificate from the Personal store (My) for the current user and creates a file called Bert.cer. This file contains a copy of the certificate including its public key, but NOT the private key.

2. Type the following command:

    ```
    certmgr -add bert.cer -c -r LocalMachine -s TrustedPeople
    ```

    This command imports the certificate into the Trusted People store for the local computer.

3. Type the following commands to export Fred's certificate and import it into the Trusted People store for the local computer:

    ```
    certmgr -put -c -n Fred -r CurrentUser -s My fred.cer
    certmgr -add fred.cer -c -r LocalMachine -s TrustedPeople
    ```

4. Close the command prompt window.

Update the WCF client application to send a certificate to the WCF service

1. In Visual Studio 2005, open the Program.cs file in the ProductsClient project to display it in the code view window.

2. In the Main method of the *Program* class, replace the two statements that set the *User-Name* and *Password* properties of the *ClientCredentials.UserName* property of the proxy object with the following statement:

    ```
    proxy.ClientCredentials.ClientCertificate.SetCertificate(
        StoreLocation.CurrentUser, StoreName.My,
        X509FindType.FindBySubjectName, "Bert");
    ```

    This statement retrieves Bert's certificate from the Personal store of the current user and adds it to the credentials sent to the WCF service.

3. Start the solution without debugging. In the client console window, press Enter.

The first test fails with the message "Access is denied." The WCF service has authenticated the client certificate (you would get a different exception if the authentication had failed), but the service is still attempting to authorize users based on the information stored in the SQL Server database used by the SQL Role Provider.

4. Press Enter to close the client console window.

You need to modify the definitions of the users and roles in the SQL Server database to map user identities retrieved from user's certificates to roles. But first, you need to understand the identifiers that the WCF service uses when clients authenticate by using certificates.

Investigate the identities of users authenticated by using certificates

1. Open the ProductsService.cs file in the App_Code folder in the WCF service project.

2. Comment out the *PrincipalPermission* attribute for the ListProducts method in the *ProductsServiceImpl* class. Add the statements shown in bold to the start of the method:

```
//[PrincipalPermission(SecurityAction.Demand, Role="WarehouseStaff")]
public List<string> ListProducts()
{
  string userName = ServiceSecurityContext.Current.PrimaryIdentity.Name;
  List<string> tempList = new List<string>();
  tempList.Add(userName);
  return tempList;
  ...
}
```

The *Current.PrimaryIdentity.Name* property of the *ServiceSecurityContext* object contains the name of the currently authenticated user. This code returns a list of one string, containing the user's name.

> **Note** Using an existing operation in the WCF service means that you don't need to regenerate the proxy for the client. Visual Studio will generate a warning, "Unreachable code detected," for the remaining code in the method. You can ignore this warning, as you will remove the statements you have just added when you have finished with them.

3. Start the solution without debugging. In the client console window, press Enter. Test 1 now succeeds and displays the identity of the user, as shown below:

The authenticated user name consists of two parts: the subject name, and the thumbprint of the certificate. The thumbprint uniquely identifies the certificate (multiple certificates can have the same subject name), so yours will probably be different from the one shown here. This is the information that you need to store in the SQL Server database, so make a note of the thumbprint.

4. Press Enter to close the client console window.

Update the user information in the SQL Server database

1. In Visual Studio 2005, select the WCF service project in Solution Explorer. In the Website menu, click ASP.NET Configuration to run the ASP.NET Web Site Administration Tool.

2. In the ASP.NET Web Site Administration Tool, click the Security tab and then click the Create user link.

3. On the Create User page, set the *User Name* field to the value displayed by the client application in the previous exercise. Include the subject name prefixed with "CN=," followed by a semicolon, a space, and the thumbprint of the certificate.

    Fill in the remaining fields with dummy values (the ASP.NET Web Site Administration Tool insists that you fill in all fields), and select the WarehouseStaff role. Click Create User when you have finished:

4. Click Continue. Leave the ASP.NET Web Site Administration Tool running (you will need it again shortly) and return to Visual Studio 2005.

5. Run the solution again without debugging. In the client console window, press Enter.

    Test 1 still displays the user name, but tests 2 and 3 now succeed. The user has been identified as a member of the WarehouseStaff role, although test 4 still fails because the user is not a member of the StockControllers role.

6. Press Enter to close the client console window.

7. In Visual Studio 2005, return to the Program.cs file in the ProductsClient project.

8. In the Main method of the *Program* class, change the statement that sets the client credentials to use Fred's certificate:

```
proxy.ClientCredentials.ClientCertificate.SetCertificate(
    StoreLocation.CurrentUser, StoreName.My,
    X509FindType.FindBySubjectName, "Fred");
```

9. Start the solution without debugging. In the client console window, press Enter. Make a note of the user name and thumbprint displayed by the first test. Test 2 fails, as you have not yet added the new credentials for Fred to the SQL Server database.

10. Press Enter to close the client console window.

11. Return to the ASP.NET Web Site Administration Tool. Add another user with the subject "CN=Fred" and the appropriate thumbprint. Make this user a member of the StockControllers and WarehouseStaff roles.

12. When the user has been created, close the ASP.NET Web Site Administration Tool.

13. In Visual Studio 2005, return to the ProductsService.cs file containing the code for the WCF service.

14. Uncomment the *PrincipalPermission* attribute for the ListProducts method, and comment out the four lines of code you added earlier, returning the method to its original state (more or less):

```
[PrincipalPermission(SecurityAction.Demand, Role="WarehouseStaff")]
public List<string> ListProducts()
{   // string userName = ServiceSecurityContext.Current.PrimaryIdentity.Name;   //
  List<string> tempList = new List<string>();   // tempList.Add(username);
  // return tempList;

  //Read the configuration information...
  Database dbAdventureWorks;
  ... }
```

15. Run the solution again without debugging. In the client console window, press Enter.

    All four tests should execute successfully.

16. Press Enter to close the client console window.

You have seen how to use certificates to authenticate users, and how to authenticate users identified by certificates. Note that IIS also enables you to map client certificates to Windows accounts if you prefer not to use the SQL Role Provider. For more information, see the Enabling Client Certificates in IIS 6.0 page, on the Microsoft Technet Web site at *http://technet2.microsoft.com/WindowsServer/en/Library/19cd478b-9a61-43a8-b288-67afa1a343b41033.mspx.*

There is one further feature worth mentioning at this point. The client application currently hard-codes the details and location of the user's certificate. This is almost as bad a practice as hard-coding usernames and passwords. However, it is also a little unreasonable to expect users to know the details of their certificates, so prompting them for this information is not a feasible alternative. In addition, an administrator might not actually *want* the user to know too much about their certificates; this information could be dangerous in the hands of a naive user. An alternative approach is for an administrator to put the details of the certificate in the application configuration file for the client. You can define a client endpoint behavior that contains the client credentials, and reference this behavior from the endpoint. The code below highlights the relevant fragments from a client application configuration file (you can, of course, create this behavior and attach it to the endpoint by using the WCF Service Configuration Editor):

```xml
<?xml version="1.0" encoding="utf-8" ?>
<configuration>
  <system.serviceModel>
    <behaviors>
      <endpointBehaviors>
        <behavior name="ClientCertificateBehavior">
          <clientCredentials>
              <clientCertificate findValue="Fred"
                          x509FindType="FindBySubjectName"
                          storeLocation="CurrentUser" storeName="My" />
          </clientCredentials>
        </behavior>
      </endpointBehaviors>
    </behaviors>
    <bindings>
      <wsHttpBinding>
        <binding name="ProductsClientWSHttpBindingConfig">
          <security mode="TransportWithMessageCredential">
            <transport clientCredentialType="None"
                        proxyCredentialType="None" />
            <message clientCredentialType="Certificate" />
          </security>
        </binding>
      </wsHttpBinding>
    </bindings>
    <client>
      <endpoint
        address="https://localhost/InternetProductsService/ProductsService.svc"

        behaviorConfiguration="ClientCertificateBehavior"
        binding="wsHttpBinding"
        bindingConfiguration="ProductsClientWSHttpBindingConfig"
        contract="ProductsClient.ProductsService.IProductsService"
        name="WSHttpBinding_IProductsService" />
    </client>
  </system.serviceModel>
</configuration>
```

Authenticating a Service by Using a Certificate

Using the HTTPS protocol with a service gives a client application a reasonable degree of confidence that communications with the service are secure. The service sends the client a certificate with a key that the client application uses for encrypting communications, and the client application verifies that the certificate sent by the service has originated from a trusted CA. However, HTTPS is primarily concerned with the confidentiality of communications. Authentication for the purpose of establishing an SSL session is not the same as performing message authentication, which can verify the identity of the message sender. The client application frequently assumes that it is sending messages in a secure manner to a specific, trusted service, but is this assumption always valid? The client might actually be securely exchanging messages with a totally different, spoof service—it is not unknown for hackers to infiltrate DNS servers and arrange for messages addressed to one server to be rerouted elsewhere. To alleviate concerns of this type, you can implement message level security with mutual authentication in place of using transport level security.

The protocol and mechanism used for authenticating a service to a client is very similar to that used by the service to authenticate a client. The service signs the messages it sends to the client application by using its private key. The client application uses a public key from a copy of the service's certificate held in its own certificate store to decode and verify the signature. If the decoding fails, the service's signature is not recognized (it is possibly a different service pretending to be the real service), and the client can reject the message from the service. All communications are also encrypted, as described when using message level security in Chapter 4.

In the following exercises, you will create another ASP.NET Web site to host a copy of the WCF service that implements message level security. You will then configure a certificate for the WCF service that the client application will use to authenticate the WCF service. The first exercise has different versions for Windows Vista and for Windows XP.

Create an ASP.NET Web site to host the WCF service that will implement message level security (Windows Vista only)

1. Right-click the ASP.NET Development Server icon in the bottom right corner of the Windows toolbar, and then click Stop.

2. Using Windows Explorer, move to the Microsoft Press\WCF Step By Step\Chapter 5 folder under your \My Documents folder.

3. Create a copy of the InternetProductsService folder and rename it as MutualAuthenticationProductsService.

4. In the Windows Control Panel, click System and Maintenance, click Administrative Tools, and the double-click Internet Information Services (IIS) Manager.

5. In the Internet Information Services (IIS) Manager, in the left pane, expand the node that corresponds to your computer, expand Web Sites, right-click Default Web Site, and then click Add Application.

6. In the Add Application dialog box, enter MutualAuthenticationProductsService for the Alias, set the Physical path to the Microsoft Press\WCF Step By Step\Chapter 5\ MutualAuthenticationProductsService folder under your \My Documents folder, and then click OK.

7. Close the Internet Information Services (IIS) Manager.

Create an ASP.NET Web site to host the WCF service that will implement message level security (Windows XP)

1. Right-click the ASP.NET Development Server icon in the bottom right corner of the Windows toolbar, and then click Stop.

2. Using Windows Explorer, move to the Microsoft Press\WCF Step By Step\Chapter 5 folder under your \My Documents folder.

3. Create a copy of the InternetProductsService folder and rename it as MutualAuthenticationProductsService.

4. On the Windows Start menu, click Run. In the Run dialog box, type **inetmgr** and then click OK.

   The Internet Information Services console opens.

5. In the Internet Information Service console, expand the node that corresponds to your computer, expand Web sites, right-click Default Web Site, point to New, and then click Virtual Directory.

   The Virtual Directory Creation Wizard appears.

6. In the Welcome to the Virtual Directory Creation Wizard page, click Next.

7. In the Virtual Directory Alias page, type MutualAuthenticationProductsService, and then click Next.

8. In the Web Site Content Directory page, click Browse, select the folder Microsoft Press\WCF Step By Step\Chapter 5\MutualAuthenticationProductsService under your \My Documents folder, click OK, and then click Next.

9. In the Access Permissions page, accept the default values, and then click Next.

10. In the You have successfully completed the Virtual Directory Creation Wizard page, click Finish.

    The MutualAuthenicationProductsService virtual directory should appear under the Default Web site node in the Internet Information Services console.

11. Close the Internet Information Services console.

The remaining exercises apply to Windows Vista and Windows XP.

Configure the WCF service to authenticate itself to client applications

1. On the Windows Start menu, point to All Programs, point to Microsoft Windows SDK, and then click CMD Shell.

2. In the command prompt window, type the following command:

```
makecert -sr LocalMachine -ss My -n CN=localhost -sky exchange
```

This command creates a certificate with the subject "localhost," and places it in the Personal store of the local computer. The subject name for a service certificate should match the name of host computer in the URL that the client application uses to connect to the service.

If you are hosting a WCF service by using IIS, as you are in this exercise, you must grant the ASPNET account read access to the certificate by using the procedure in the next step. If you are using a self-hosted service, then the following step is not necessary, depending upon the authority of the account you use to execute the self-hosted service.

3. Type the following command:

```
findprivatekey My LocalMachine -n CN=localhost -a
```

The output from this command is the name of a private key file associated with the local host certificate in the certificate store. It should look something like this (the hexadecimal UUID identifying the certificate will be different on your computer):

```
C:\Documents and Settings\All Users\Application Data\Microsoft\Crypto\RSA\MachineKeys\
7b90a71bfc56f2582e916a51aed6df9a_9e8a4e8d-4db3-4431-b652-45fbf9358c29
```

This is the file that you need to grant read access on for the ASPNET account.

4. Type the following command (replacing the UUID of the certificate with your own value):

```
cacls "C:\Documents and Settings\All Users\Application Data\Microsoft\Crypto\RSA\
MachineKeys\7b90a71bfc56f2582e916a51aed6df9a_9e8a4e8d-4db3-4431-b652-45fbf9358c29" /
E /G ASPNET:R
```

> **Note** Windows Vista runs Web applications by using the Network Service account rather than ASPNET. If you are using Windows Vista, replace ASPNET in this command with NETWORKSERVICE.

5. Type the following command to stop and restart IIS:

```
iisreset
```

Leave the command prompt window open, as you will need it later.

6. In Visual Studio 2005, in the Solution Explorer, right-click the InternetProductsService solution, point to Add, and then click Existing Web Site.

7. In the Add Existing Web Site dialog box, ensure that Local IIS is selected, click the MutualAuthenticationProductsService site, clear the Use Secure Sockets Layer check box, and then click Open.

8. Edit the Web.config file of the MutualAuthenticationProductsService Web site by using the WCF Service Configuration Editor.

9. In the WCF Service Configuration Editor, in the left pane, expand the Bindings folder and click the ProductsServiceWSHttpBindingConfig binding configuration.

10. In the right pane, click the Security tab. Set the *Mode* property to *Message*.

11. In the left pane, expand the Advanced folder, expand the Service Behaviors folder, expand the ProductsBehavior node, expand the serviceCredentials node, and then click the serviceCertificate node.

12. In the right pane, set the *FindValue* property to *localhost* and set the *X509FindType* property to *FindBySubjectName*. Verify that the *StoreLocation* property is set to *LocalMachine* and that the *StoreName* property is set to *My*.

13. Save the configuration, and close the WCF Service Configuration Editor.

You have now enabled the WCF service to authenticate itself to client applications by signing messages with its certificate. In the real world, the administrator for the computer hosting the WCF service would export this certificate and then distribute it to all computers running the client application. The next exercise simulates this process.

Export the WCF service certificate and import it into the client certificate store

1. Return to the command prompt window and type the following command:

```
certmgr -put -c -n localhost -r LocalMachine -s My localhost.cer
```

This command retrieves a copy of the localhost certificate used by the WCF service to authenticate itself and creates a file called localhost.cer. Remember that this file contains a copy of the certificate including its public key but NOT the private key. The administrator can distribute this file to all client computers.

2. Type the following command:

```
certmgr -add localhost.cer -c -r CurrentUser -s My
```

This command imports the certificate into the certificate store for the current user. This is typically what an administrator would do to make the certificate available to the client application.

Leave the command prompt window open.

You can now configure the client application to authenticate the WCF service by using the localhost certificate in the CurrentUser certificate store.

Configure the WCF client application to authenticate the WCF service

1. In Visual Studio 2005, edit the app.config file of the ProductsClient project by using the WCF Service Configuration Editor.

2. In the Client Configuration Editor, in the Endpoints folder under the Client folder, click the WSHttpBinding_IProductsService node.

3. In the right pane, change the *Address* property to *http://localhost/MutualAuthentication-ProductsService/ProductsService.svc*. This is the address of the WCF service. Notice that it uses the HTTP protocol, and not HTTPS.

4. In the left pane, expand the Bindings folder and then select the ProductsClientWSHttp-BindingConfig binding configuration.

5. In the right pane, click the Security tab. Set the *Mode* property to *Message*.

6. In the left pane, expand the Advanced folder, right-click the Endpoint Behaviors node, and then click New Endpoint Behavior Configuration.

7. In the right pane, enter *AuthenticationBehavior* for the *Name* property and then click Add.

8. In the Adding Behavior Element Extension Sections dialog box, select clientCredentials and then click Add.

9. In the left pane, expand the clientCredentials node, expand the serviceCertificate node, and then click the defaultCertificate node.

10. In the right pane, enter localhost for the *FindValue* property and set the *X509FindType* property to *FindBySubjectName*.

11. Return to the WSHttpBinding_IProductsService endpoint in the Endpoints folder under the Client folder. Set the *BehaviorConfiguration* property to *AuthenticationBehavior*.

12. Save the configuration, and close the WCF Service Configuration Editor.

13. Edit the Program.cs file for the ProductsClient application. In the Main method, comment out the code the overrides the validity check of the certificate exported by the HTTPS implementation of the WCF service—this statement is not required by this version of the client:

    ```
    // PermissiveCertificatePolicy.Enact("CN=HTTPS-Server");
    ```

Verify that the client application authenticates the WCF service

1. Start the solution without debugging. In the client console window, press Enter.

    The client application should complete all four tests successfully.

> **Tip**   If the client application fails with a message stating that the service could not be activated, check to make sure that you provided the correct endpoint address for the service in the configuration file and that you have granted read permission over the correct certificate file to the ASPNET account.

2. Press Enter to close the client console window.

3. Return to the command prompt window, and type the following command:

```
certmgr -del -c -n localhost -r LocalMachine -s My
```

   This command removes the localhost certificate from the LocalMachine certificate store.

4. Type the following command:

```
makecert -sr LocalMachine -ss My -n CN=localhost -sky exchange
```

   This command creates another certificate with the same subject name as before. When you run the WCF service, it will find this certificate and present it to the client application.

5. Restart IIS by running the following command:

```
iisreset
```

   When IIS has restarted, close the command prompt window.

6. Return to Visual Studio 2005 and start the solution without debugging. In the client console window, press Enter.

   The client application should now fail with a MessageSecurityException "An unsecured or incorrectly secured fault was received from the other party... ."

   The private key in the localhost certificate used by the WCF service to sign messages has changed, so the client cannot use the public key in its copy of the localhost certificate to verify the signature of the messages sent by the WCF service. This situation is analogous to a rogue version of the WCF service being placed at the same address as the real service and highlights the benefits of authenticating a service in a client application.

> **Important**   The only way the rogue service can imitate the real WCF service is if it has access to the same private key as the real WCF service. This shows once again the importance of keeping your private keys private.

7. Press Enter to close the client console window.

Summary

In this chapter, you have seen how to authenticate and authorize users and services when they are running in different Windows domains across the Internet. You have learned how to configure the SQL Membership Provider to authenticate users against credentials held in a SQL Server database, and the SQL Role Provider to specify the roles that a user has for authorization purposes. You also should understand how client applications and services can use certificates to authenticate each other and explain how they can use public and private keys to help protect the privacy of communications in a potentially hostile network environment.

Chapter 6
Maintaining Service Contracts and Data Contracts

After completing this chapter, you will be able to:

- Describe how to protect the individual operations in a service contract.
- Explain which changes to a service require client applications to be updated.
- Implement different versions of a service contract in a service.
- Modify a data contract and explain which changes will break existing client applications.
- Describe how WCF can generate default values for missing items in a data contract.

In Chapter 1, "Introducing Windows Communication Foundation," you learned that one of the fundamental tenets of Service Oriented Architectures (SOA) is that services share schemas and contracts, not classes or types. When you define a service, you specify the operations that it supports by defining a service contract. The service contract describes each operation, together with its parameters, and any return types. A WCF service can publish its service contract definition, and a developer can use this information to build client applications that communicate with the service. In a WCF environment, a developer uses the svcutil utility to generate a proxy class for the client from the WSDL description of the service. The client uses this proxy to communicate with the service.

The service contract is only one part of the story, however. The operations in a service contract can take parameters and return values. Client applications must provide data formatted in a manner that the service expects. Many of the primitive types in the .NET Framework have predefined formats, but more complex data types such as classes, structures, and enumerations require the service to specify how client applications should package this information up in messages that it sends to the service and the format for any information sent by the service back to client applications. You encapsulate this information in data contracts. Each complex data type used by a service should have a corresponding data contract. The service publishes this information together with the service contract, and the definitions of each complex type are included in the proxy code generated by the svcutil utility.

You should be able to see how service contracts and data contracts are fundamental parts of a service. If a client application does not understand the set of operations that a service exposes or the type of data used by these services, then it will have severe trouble communicating with the service.

Modifying a Service Contract

A service contract is an interface that the WCF tools and infrastructure can convert into a WSDL document, listing the operations for a service as a series of SOAP messages and message responses. You provide an implementation of these methods in a class in the service. When a service executes, the WCF runtime creates a channel stack by using the bindings specified in the service configuration file and listens for client requests in the form of one of these messages. The WCF runtime then converts each SOAP message sent by a client application into a method call and invokes the corresponding method in an instance of the class implementing the service (you will learn how and when the WCF runtime actually creates this instance in Chapter 7, "Maintaining State and Sequencing Operations"). Any data returned by the method is converted back into a SOAP response message and is sent back through the channel stack for transmission to the client application.

You can draw two conclusions from the preceding discussion:

1. The service contract does not depend on the communication mechanism that the service uses to send and receive messages. The communications mechanism is governed by the channel stack constructed from the binding information specified in the service configuration file. You can change the network protocol or address of a service without modifying the code in the service or in any client applications that access the service (although client applications must use compatible endpoints in their configuration files). To a large extent, the security requirements of a service are also independent of the service contract, although there are exceptions, as you will see in this chapter.

2. Client applications wishing to communicate with the service must be able to construct the appropriate SOAP messages. These messages depend on the service contract; if the service contract changes, then the client must be provided with an up-to-date version, otherwise, it runs the risk of sending messages that the service does not understand or that are formatted incorrectly. Alternatively, if the response messages returned by a service change, a client application might not be able to handle them correctly.

You will examine what this means from a practical perspective in the exercises in this section.

Selectively Protecting Operations

The previous two chapters have shown how to protect the messages passing between client applications and services. However, the techniques shown have concentrated on using bindings and behaviors of a service to protect the service as a whole. By modifying the service contract, you can specify different security requirements for operations in the same service.

> **Note**   Protecting a service by modifying binding and behavior information is an example of the fourth tenet of SOA—compatibility is based on policy. You can protect a service in a variety of ways without modifying the service contract, as long as the client applications and service follow compatible security policies. Selectively protecting an operation *is* a change to the service contract because now the protection mechanism becomes tightly coupled to the operation, rather than being a policy attribute of the service.

Specify the security requirements for operations in the WCF service

1. Using Visual Studio 2005, open the solution file ProductsService.sln located in the Microsoft Press\WCF Step By Step\Chapter 6\ProductsService folder under your \My Documents folder.

   This solution contains an amended copy of the ProductsClient, ProductsService, and ProductsServiceHost projects from Chapter 4, "Protecting an Enterprise WCF Service" (the service does not display a message box showing the identity of the user, and the client application contains an additional exception handler).

2. Edit the ProductsService.cs file in the ProductsService project, and locate the *IProductsService* interface that defines the service contract.

3. In the *IProductsService* interface, amend the *OperationContract* attribute for the ListProducts and GetProduct methods as shown in bold below:

```
[ServiceContract]
public interface IProductsService
{
    // Get the product number of every product
    ...
    [OperationContract(ProtectionLevel =
                    System.Net.Security.ProtectionLevel.EncryptAndSign)]
    List<string> ListProducts();

    // Get the details of a single product
    [OperationContract(ProtectionLevel =
                    System.Net.Security.ProtectionLevel.EncryptAndSign)]
    Product GetProduct(string productNumber);
    ...
}
```

   The *ProtectionLevel* property of the *OperationContract* attribute specifies how messages invoking this operation, and output by this operation, are protected. In this case, calls to the *ListProducts* and *GetProduct* operations must be signed by the client and encrypted by using a key negotiated with the service. This requires that the security mode of the binding used by the client and service specified message level authentication and that the client and service specify the same value for the *AlgorithmSuite* property (go back and look at Chapter 4 if you need to refresh your memory about these properties). In fact, this is the default protection level for operations when you configure message level security.

4. Modify the *OperationContract* attribute for the CurrentStockLevel and ChangeStockLevel methods as shown in bold below:

```
[ServiceContract]
public interface IProductsService
{
    …

    // Get the current stock level for a product
    [OperationContract(ProtectionLevel =
                       System.Net.Security.ProtectionLevel.Sign)]
    int CurrentStockLevel(string productNumber);

    // Change the stock level for a product
    [OperationContract(ProtectionLevel =
                       System.Net.Security.ProtectionLevel.Sign)]
    bool ChangeStockLevel(string productNumber, int newStockLevel,
                          string shelf, int bin);
}
```

Calls to theses operations must be signed, but not encrypted. The protection level specified here overrides the message level security configured for the binding. You can also specify a value of *System.Net.Security.ProtectionLevel.Sign* if you don't want to sign messages either, although you should use this setting with caution as it has obvious security implications.

5. Edit the app.config file in the ProductsClient project by using the WCF Service Configuration Editor.

6. In the WCF Service Configuration Editor, expand the Bindings folder and then select the ProductsClientTcpBindingConfig binding configuration. In the right pane, click the Security tab. Verify that the *Mode* property is set to *Message*, the *AlgorithmSuite* property is set to *Basic128*, and the *MessageClientCredentialType* property is set to *Windows*.

> **Note** For simplicity, these exercises assume that the client application and WCF service operate in the same Windows domain. If you are running in an Internet environment, you can change the MessageClientCredentialType to UserName or Certificate, as described in Chapter 5, "Protecting a WCF Service over the Internet."

7. Save any changes you have made to the app.config file, and then close the WCF Service Configuration Editor.

8. Edit the App.config file in the ProductsServiceHost project by using the WCF Service Configuration Editor. Follow the procedure in Step 6 to verify that the security settings for the ProductsServiceTcpBindingConfig binding configuration match those of the client application.

9. In the left pane, expand the Diagnostics folder and then click the Message Logging node. In the right pane, set the *LogMessagesAtServiceLevel* property to *False* but ensure that the *LogMessagesAtTransportLevel* property is set to *True*.

You will use the Service Trace Viewer to examine the messages sent between the client application and the service. To minimize the logging overhead, the WCF runtime will only trace messages as they flow in and out of the transport level. At this level, you will be able to see the effects of the message level security applied by the binding and the service contract—logging at the service (message) level will only show unencrypted messages as they are received and sent by the service.

10. In the left pane, expand the Listeners folder, and then click the MessageLog node. Set the *InitData* property to the Products.svclog file in the Microsoft Press\WCF Step By Step\Chapter 6 folder under your \My Documents folder.

11. Save the changes, and exit the Service Configuration Editor.

Test the modified service

1. Start the solution without debugging. In the ProductsServiceHost form, click Start (if a Windows Security Alert message box appears, click Unblock to allow the service to open the TCP port it uses for listening for client requests). In the client console window, press Enter.

    Tests 1 and 2 complete successfully because the binding implements a policy of encryption and signing, and this automatically meets the requirements of the operation contract for the ListProducts and GetProduct operations. However, test 3 raises the exception, "The primary signature must be encrypted" because the *CurrentStockLevel* operation specifies only signing in the operation contract, but the binding is also encrypting information. The problem is that you have modified the service contract, but you have not updated the corresponding code in the client application; the proxy used by the client application is still expecting to send signed and encrypted messages to the service for tests 3 and 4.

2. Press Enter to close the client console window. In the ProductsServiceHost form, click Stop and then close the form.

3. In Visual Studio 2005, open the Products.cs file in the ProductsClient project.

    This file contains the code for the proxy that you generated by using the svcutil tool in Chapter 3 ,"Making Applications and Services Robust." You now have two choices: you can regenerate the proxy again or you can modify the code in this file to incorporate the changes required. Under normal circumstances, it would be advisable to regenerate the proxy, but in this case it is more informative for you to modify the code so that you can see the changes required in the proxy code.

4. Scroll through the Products.cs file to locate the definition of the *IProductsService* interface (this should be somewhere around line 228).

    You should be able to recognize the methods in this interface as they correspond very closely to the methods in the service contract. The return type of the ListProducts method is slightly different—it is an array of strings rather than a generic list, and the *OperationContract* and *FaultContract* attributes for each operation include *Action* and *ReplyAction* properties identifying the names of the SOAP messages that the WCF runtime uses when communicating with the WCF service.

5. Modify the *OperationContract* attribute for the CurrentStockLevel and ChangeStockLevel methods as shown in bold below (do not modify the *Action* and *ReplyAction* properties):

```
[System.ServiceModel.OperationContractAttribute(ProtectionLevel=System.Net.Security.
ProtectionLevel.Sign, Action= …)]
int CurrentStockLevel(string productNumber);

[System.ServiceModel.OperationContractAttribute(ProtectionLevel = System.Net.Security.
ProtectionLevel.Sign, Action = …)]
bool ChangeStockLevel(string productNumber, int newStockLevel, string shelf, int bin);
```

6. Using Windows Explorer, delete the Products.svclog file in the Microsoft Press\WCF Step By Step\Chapter 6 folder under your \My Documents folder.

7. In Visual Studio 2005, start the solution without debugging. In the ProductsServiceHost form, click Start. In the client console window, press Enter.

   All tests should now complete successfully.

8. Press Enter to close the client console window. In the ProductsServiceHost form, click Stop and then close the form.

9. Start the Service Trace Viewer (in the Microsoft Windows SDK, Tools program group).

10. In the Service Trace Viewer, open the Products.svclog file in the Microsoft Press\WCF Step By Step\Chapter 6 folder under your \My Documents folder.

11. In the left pane, click the Message tab. You should see six messages concerned with negotiating the encryption keys used by the client and service; these messages have an Action in the *http://schemas.xmlsoap.org* namespace. Following these are ten messages corresponding to the messages received by the service, and the responses sent back to the client application with an Action in the *http://tempuri.org* namespace. There are two further messages at the end, again with an Action in the *http://schemas.xmlsoap.org* namespace.

> **Tip** Expand the Action column in the left pane to see more of the name for each action.

12. Click the message with the Action *http://tempuri.org/IProductsService/ListProducts*. In the lower right pane, click the Formatted tab and scroll to the bottom of the pane to display the Envelope Information section (if the Envelope Section is not visible, expand the Message Log area in this pane). In the Parameters box, note that the Method used to send the data is e:EncryptedData, and that the parameter sent by the client application has been encrypted, as highlighted in the following image:

13. In the left pane, click the message with the Action *http://tempuri.org/IProductsService/ ListProductsResponse*. In the lower-right pane, verify that this response message is also encrypted. Follow the same procedure to examine the *http://tempuri.org/IProductsSer- vice/GetProduct* and *http://tempuri.org/IProductsService/GetProductResponse* messages and verify that they are also encrypted.

14. In the left pane, click the *http://tempuri.org/IProductsService/ChangeStockLevel* message. In the lower right pane, you should observe that the Method is CurrentStockLevel and that the parameter is an unencrypted product number:

15. In the left pane, click the *http://tempuri.org/IProductsService/ChangeStockLevelResponse* message. This message should also be unencrypted. Examine the *http://tempuri.org/ IProductsService/ChangeStockLevel* and *http://tempuri.org/IProductsService/ChangeStock-LevelResponse* messages. These messages should be unencrypted as well.

16. In the File menu, click Close All. Leave the Service Trace Viewer open.

Versioning a Service

Change happens. It is almost inevitable that a widely used service will evolve as circumstances and business process change. In many cases, these changes will manifest themselves as modifications to the code that implements the operations in a service. However, it is also possible that the definitions of operations might need to change as well; you might need to add new operations, retire old or redundant operations, or change the parameters and return types of existing operations. Clearly, these modifications require updating the service contract. However, client applications depend on the service contract to specify the messages that the service receives and the responses it sends. If the service contract changes, what happens to clients that used the previous version of the contract? Will they still work or do you need to go and visit every client installation and update the code? Do you actually know where to locate every client? If client applications connect across the Internet, there could be a large number of them located anywhere in the world.

You can see that modifying a service is not a task that you should undertake lightly and, as far as possible, you should take steps to ensure that existing clients will continue to function without requiring to be updated. To this end, it helps to understand what actually happens when you change a service or a service contract and the strategies that you can follow to minimize any detrimental impact of these changes. The following exercises illustrate some common scenarios.

Add a method to the WCF service and amend the business logic of operations

1. Using Visual Studio 2005, edit the ProductsService.cs file in the ProductsService project.

2. Add the following method to the *ProductsServiceImpl* class:

```
public bool IsPotentialSqlInjectionAttack(string data)
{
    // Check to see whether the data contains a rogue character
    // or the string "--", or the string "/*"
    char[] rogueChars = { ';', '\'', '\\', '"', '=', '%', '_', '*' };
    if ((data.IndexOfAny(rogueChars) != -1) ||
        data.Contains("--") || data.Contains("/*"))
        return true;
    else
        return false;
}
```

> **Note**   A copy of this code is supplied in the PotentialSqlInjectionAttack.txt file, in the Microsoft Press\WCF Step By Step\Chapter 6 folder under your \My Documents folder.

The Adventure-Works organization has recently conducted a security audit of some of their applications. The auditors have identified the ProductsService service as being prone to a SQL injection attack. This method checks a string for characters and substrings that are typically used by an attacker, returning *true* if the string is suspect and *false* if the string seems safe.

> **More Info**   For a description of what a SQL injection attack is and how dangerous it can be, see the SQL Injection topic in SQL Server Books Online, also available at *http://msdn2.microsoft.com/en-us/library/ms161953.aspx*. The solution shown here is quite primitive, but gives you an idea of what you need to do to protect your service. Alternative strategies exist, such as using SQL parameters, to provide the data values to the SQL statement.

3. Add the statements shown below in bold to the start of the GetProduct method, before the code that connects to the database:

```
public Product GetProduct(string productNumber)
{
    // Check for potential SQL Injection attack
    if (IsPotentialSqlInjectionAttack(productNumber))
    {
        return new Product();
    }
    // Connect to the AdventureWorks database
    ...
}
```

If the productNumber provided by the user contains characters that are commonly used by a SQL Injection attack, the method simply returns an empty product, otherwise, it operates as before.

> **Important**   Do not return an error message in this situation. An attacker could use this information to determine that you are explicitly checking for SQL injection attacks and attempt to probe further. Returning a value that contains no meaningful data provides no further information to the attacker. Additionally, although not shown in this example, you should also log this message, and record the identity of the user sending the message.

4. Add the following statements to the start of the CurrentStockLevel method:

```
public int CurrentStockLevel(string productNumber)
{
    // Check for potential SQL Injection attack
    if (IsPotentialSqlInjectionAttack(productNumber))
    {
```

```
        return 0;
    }
    // Connect to the AdventureWorks database
    …
}
```

If the user provides a suspect product number, the method returns a stock level of zero.

5. Add the statements shown below to the start of the ChangeStockLevel method:

```
public bool ChangeStockLevel(string productNumber, int newStockLevel,
                             string shelf, int bin)
{
    // Check for potential SQL Injection attack
    if (IsPotentialSqlInjectionAttack(productNumber) ||
        IsPotentialSqlInjectionAttack(shelf))
    {
        return false;
    }    …
}
```

This time you need to check two string parameters. The method returns *false* and does not update the database if either string is suspicious.

6. Start the solution without debugging. In the ProductsServiceHost form, click Start In the client console window, press Enter.

All tests should execute successfully.

7. Press Enter to close the client console window. In the ProductsServiceHost form, click Stop and then close the form.

8. In Visual Studio 2005, edit the Program.cs file in the ProductsClient project. In the Main method, locate the statement that invokes the GetProduct operation and change the parameter that the client sends to this operation, like this:

```
Product product =
    proxy.GetProduct("WB-H098'; DELETE FROM Production.Product --");
```

This rather sneaky piece of code passes a string that contains a valid product number but also contains an SQL DELETE statement that maliciously attempts to delete all products from the *AdventureWorks* database. Although this would most likely fail (even without the code that checks for an SQL injection attack) because of the referential integrity checking performed by SQL Server, it is still a loophole you would probably rather not leave exposed.

9. Start the solution without debugging. In the ProductsServiceHost form, click Start In the client console window, press Enter.

Tests 1, 2, and 4 perform successfully, but the output from test 2 displays an "empty" product—all the fields are either blank or zero:

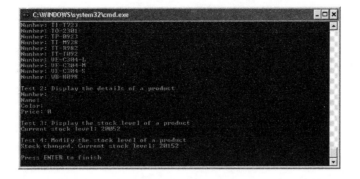

10. Press Enter to close the client console window. In the ProductsServiceHost form, click Stop and then close the form.

11. Edit the Program.cs file in the ProductsClient project, and change the line that calls the GetProduct method back to its original state:

```
Product product = proxy.GetProduct("WB-H098");
```

Although the service has changed and a new public method has been added, the service contract has not been updated. The IsPotentialSqlInjectionAttack method is not accessible to client applications, which can continue to access the service exactly as before. This is an example of a nonbreaking change to a service.

Add a parameter to an existing operation in the service contract

1. Using Visual Studio 2005, edit the ProductsService.cs file in the ProductsService project.

2. Locate the definition of the IProductsService interface. Add a parameter to the ListProducts method, as follows:

```
List<string> ListProducts(string match)
```

The Adventure-Works organization has dramatically increased the number of products that they manufacture. The original ListProducts method returns a list comprising thousands of rows. It has therefore been decided to modify this operation to enable the user to constrain the list of products returned to be those whose name matches a string specified by the user.

3. In the *ProductsServiceImpl* class, update the definition of the ListProducts method:

```
public List<string> ListProducts(string match)
```

4. Add the following statements to the start of the method, before the code that reads the configuration information for connecting to the database:

```
// Check for potential SQL Injection attack
if (IsPotentialSqlInjectionAttack(match))
{
    return new List<string>();
}
```

5. Change the SQL statement that retrieves the product numbers from the database as shown in bold below:

```
// Retrieve the details of all products by using a DataReader
IDataReader productsReader;
try
{
    string queryString = @"SELECT ProductNumber
                           FROM Production.Product
                           WHERE Name LIKE '%" + match + "%'";
    productsReader = dbAdventureWorks.ExecuteReader(CommandType.Text, queryString);
}
```

6. Start the solution without debugging. In the ProductsServiceHost form, click Start In the client console window, press Enter

Test 1 fails, reporting an internal error:

7. Press Enter to close the client console window. In the ProductsServiceHost form, click Stop and then close the form.

The problem now is that the client application is attempting to invoke a version of an operation that the service no longer implements (the SOAP message expected by the service includes a parameter that the client has not supplied). This is a breaking change, and presents an issue that you must address. You will see how in the following exercises.

Add a new operation to the WCF service

1. Using Visual Studio 2005, edit the ProductsService.cs file in the ProductsService project.

2. In the *IProductsService* interface, remove the parameter from the ListProducts method and add another version of the ListProducts method, called ListSelectedProducts, that includes this parameter to the interface, as follows:

```
// Get the product number of every product
[FaultContract(typeof(ConfigFault))]
[FaultContract(typeof(DatabaseFault))]
[OperationContract(ProtectionLevel=
                System.Net.Security.ProtectionLevel.EncryptAndSign)]
List<string> ListProducts();  // Get the product number of selected products
```

```
[FaultContract(typeof(ConfigFault))]
[FaultContract(typeof(DatabaseFault))]
[OperationContract(ProtectionLevel =
                System.Net.Security.ProtectionLevel.EncryptAndSign)]
List<string> ListSelectedProducts(string match);
```

> **Note**   C# permits you to have multiple methods in an interface and a class that have
> the same name as long as their signatures differ. This is called "overloading." So, in the-
> ory, you could create two versions of the same method, both called ListProducts, one
> which takes no parameters and the other which takes a single string parameter. How-
> ever, the SOAP standard does not allow a service to expose multiple operations that
> share the same name in the same service, so this approach would fail.
>
> Apart from giving the operations different names in the C# interface, an alternative
> approach is to use the *Name* property of the *OperationContract* attribute in the service
> contract, like this:
>
> ```
> [OperationContract(Name="ListSelectedProducts", …]
> List<string> ListProducts(string match);
> ```
>
> WCF uses this property to generate the names for the SOAP request and response
> messages. If you don't provide a value for the *Name* property, WCF uses the name of
> the method instead. You should also notice that the name of an operation in a service
> contract impacts the SOAP request and response messages, and changing the name of
> an operation is therefore a breaking change to the service contract.

3. In the *ProductsServiceImpl* class, change the name of the ListProducts method to ListSe-
    lectedProducts:

    ```
    [PrincipalPermission(SecurityAction.Demand, Role = "WarehouseStaff")]
    public List<string> ListSelectedProducts(string match)
    {
        …
    }
    ```

4. Add a new implementation of the original ListProducts method to the *ProductsServiceIm-
    ple* class, like this:

    ```
    [PrincipalPermission(SecurityAction.Demand, Role = "WarehouseStaff")]
    public List<string> ListProducts()
    {
        return ListSelectedProducts("");
    }
    ```

    The ListProducts method uses the ListSelectedProducts method, passing in an empty
    string as the parameter. The SQL SELECT statement in the ListSelectedProducts
    method will therefore return all products; the query criteria it generates will be "WHERE
    Name LIKE '%%'."

5. Start the solution without debugging. In the ProductsServiceHost form, click Start In the
    client console window, press Enter. All tests should now succeed.

6. Press Enter to close the client console window. In the ProductsServiceHost form, click
    Stop and then close the form.

Adding a new operation to a service contract is another nonbreaking change. New client applications can send messages corresponding to the new operation (you can generate a proxy that includes the new operation by using the svcutil utility if you are building a WCF client application). Existing client applications using the old version of the proxy still continue to function, but are not aware that the new operation exists.

There is still a potential issue, however. If you want new client applications to be able to call only the new operation (ListSelectedProducts) and not use the older operation (ListProducts), how can you hide this operation from them? The answer is to use multiple service contracts. Keep the existing service contract unchanged, and define a new service contract that includes the new version of the operation, but not the old version. The code fragments below show the existing contract (IProductsService), and the new one (IProductsServiceV2). The code fragments also show the recommended way of identifying and naming the different versions of a service contract by using the *Namespace* and *Name* properties of the *ServiceContract* attribute. By default, the service contract uses the namespace "*http://tempuri.org,*" and takes its name from the name of the interface (if you recall, when using the Service Trace Viewer to examine the messages sent to the ProductsService, you saw that they were all of the form "*http://tempuri.org/IProductsService/...*"). When defining a new version of a service contract, use the *Namespace* property to identify the version by including the date, but keep the *Name* property the same for each version. However, be warned that modifying the *Namespace* or *Name* properties of a service contract constitutes a breaking change as these items are used to help identify the SOAP messages sent between the client application and the service:

```
// Service contract describing the operations provided by the WCF service
[ServiceContract(Namespace="http://adventure-works.com/2006/07/04",
                 Name="ProductsService")]
public interface IProductsService
{
    // Get the product number of every product
    [FaultContract(typeof(ConfigFault))]
    [FaultContract(typeof(DatabaseFault))]
    [OperationContract(ProtectionLevel=
                       System.Net.Security.ProtectionLevel.EncryptAndSign)]
    List<string> ListProducts();

    // Get the details of a single product
    ...
}


// Version 2 of the service contract
[ServiceContract(Namespace="http://adventure-works.com/2006/08/31",
                 Name="ProductsService")]
public interface IProductsServiceV2
{
    // Get the product number of selected products
    [FaultContract(typeof(ConfigFault))]
    [FaultContract(typeof(DatabaseFault))]
    [OperationContract(ProtectionLevel =
```

```
                            System.Net.Security.ProtectionLevel.EncryptAndSign)]
    List<string> ListSelectedProducts(string match);

    // Get the details of a single product
    ...
}
```

The service implementation class, *ProductsServiceImpl*, should implement both of these inter-faces. The code for the methods common to both interfaces (GetProduct, CurrentStockLevel, and ChangeStockLevel) needs to be provided only once in this class:

```
public class ProductsServiceImpl : IProductsService, IProductsServiceV2
{
    // Implement ListProducts, ListSelectedProducts,
    // GetProduct, CurrentStockLevel, and ChangeStockLevel
    ...
}
```

Finally, create a separate set of endpoints for the new version of the service contract (one for each binding). You can use the WCF Service Configuration Editor, or edit the service configuration file by hand, to add an endpoint with the contract attribute set to *Products.IProductsServiceV2*:

```
<system.serviceModel>
    ...
    <services>
        <service behaviorConfiguration="..."
                name="Products.ProductsServiceImpl">
            ...
            <endpoint binding="..." bindingConfiguration="..."
                    name="..." contract="Products.IProductsServiceV2" />
        </service>
    </services>
</system.serviceModel>
```

Note   You can find a working implementation of the ProductsService service, and a client application, that provides these two versions of the service contract in the ProductsServiceV2 folder, located in the Microsoft Press\WCF Step By Step\Chapter 6 folder under My Documents. You will make use of this solution later in this chapter.

Making Breaking and Nonbreaking Changes to a Service Contract

Strictly speaking, you should consider a service contract to be immutable; any changes that you make to the contract are likely to affect client applications, which might no longer be able to communicate with the service correctly. In practice, you have seen that you can make some changes to a service contract without breaking the terms of this contract as far as a WCF client application is concerned. Table 6-1 summarizes some common changes that developers frequently make to service contracts and the effects that these changes can have on existing client applications.

Table 6-1 **Service Contract Changes**

Change	Effect
Adding a new operation	This is a nonbreaking change. Existing client applications are unaffected, but the new operation is not visible to WCF client applications connecting to the service by using a proxy generated from the WSDL description of the original service contract. Existing client applications that dynamically query services and construct messages can use the new operation. For more details, see Chapter 10, "Programmatically Controlling the Configuration and Communications."
Removing an operation	This is a breaking change. Existing client applications that invoke the operation will no longer function correctly, although client applications that do not use the operation remain unaffected.
Changing the name of an operation	This is a breaking change. Existing client applications that invoke the operation will no longer work, although client applications that do not use the operation remain unaffected. Note that the name of an operation defaults to the name of the method in the service contract. You can change the name of a method but retain the original name of the operation by using the *Name* property in the *OperationContract* attribute of the method, like this: [OperationContract (Name="ListProducts")] List<string> ListAllProducts(); This is good practice, as it removes any dependency between the service contract and the name of the physical method that implements the operation.
Changing the protection level of an operation	This is a breaking change. Existing client applications will not be able to invoke the operation.
Adding a parameter to an operation	This is a breaking change. Existing client applications will no longer be able to invoke the operation, as the SOAP messages they send will be incompatible with the SOAP messages expected by the service.
Reordering parameters in an operation	This is a breaking change. The results are not easily predictable (some existing client applications might continue to work).
Removing a parameter from an operation	This is a breaking change. As with reordering parameters, the results are not easily predictable.
Changing the types of parameters or the return type of an operation	This is a breaking change. Existing client applications might continue to function, but there is a significant risk that data in SOAP messages will be lost or misinterpreted. This includes applying or removing the *ref* and *out* modifiers to parameters, even if the underlying type does not change. For more information, see the section "Modifying a Data Contract" later in this chapter.

Table 6-1   Service Contract Changes

Change	Effect
Adding a FaultContract to an operation	This is a breaking change. Existing client applications can be sent fault messages that they will not be able to interpret correctly.
Removing a FaultContract from an operation	This is a nonbreaking change. Existing client applications will continue to function correctly, although any handlers for trapping the faults specified by this fault contract will be rendered obsolete.
Changing the *Name* or *Namespace* property of the *ServiceContract* attribute for a service contract	This is a breaking change. Existing client applications that use the previous name or namespace will no longer be able to send messages to the service.

Making breaking changes to a service contract requires you to update the client applications that use the service. If client applications use WCF proxies, you will need to regenerate these proxies. However, the recommended approach for modifying a service contract is to create a new version and to leave the existing version intact, as described in the previous section. This removes the requirement for you to update existing client applications, although they will not be able to use any new features of the service.

Modifying a Data Contract

The methods in a service contract can take parameters and return values. The data for these parameters and return values is included in the SOAP messages that pass between the client application and service. SOAP messages encode data values as tagged XML text. The WCF runtime uses the built-in XML serialization features of the .NET Framework to serialize and deserialize primitive .NET Framework data types, such as integers, real numbers, or even strings. For more complex structured types, the service must specify the exact format for the serialized representation; there could be several ways to depict the same structured data as XML. You define structured types by using data contracts. The WCF runtime can then use data contract serializer (an instance of the *DataContractSerializer* class) to serialize and deserialize these types.

Using a data contract, you can specify exactly how the service expects the data to be formatted as XML. The data contract is used by a data contract serializer in WCF client applications to describe how to serialize the data for parameters into XML, and by a data contract serializer in the service to deserialize the XML back into data values that it can process. Values returned by a service are similarly serialized as XML and transmitted back to the client application, which deserializes them.

Data Contract and Data Member Attributes

You saw in Chapter 1 how to define a simple data contract representing products in the *AdventureWorks* database. To remind you, this is what the data contract looks like:

```
// Data contract describing the details of a product
[DataContract]
public class Product
{
    [DataMember]
    public string Name;

    [DataMember]
    public string ProductNumber;

    [DataMember]
    public string Color;

    [DataMember]
    public decimal ListPrice;
}
```

Tagging a class with the *DataContract* attribute marks it as serializable by using the data contract serializer. The data contract serializer will serialize and deserialize each member of the class marked with the *DataMember* attribute. In the example shown here, the members of the class are .NET Framework primitive types, and the serializer uses its own built-in rules to convert these types into a form that can be included in an XML message, like this:

```
<GetProductResponse xmlns="http://adventure-works.com/2006/07/04">
  <GetProductResult
  xmlns:d4p1="http://schemas.datacontract.org/2004/07/Products"
  xmlns:i="http://www.w3.org/2001/XMLSchema-instance">
    <d4p1:Color>N/A</d4p1:Color>
    <d4p1:ListPrice>4.9900</d4p1:ListPrice>
    <d4p1:Name>Water Bottle - 30 oz.</d4p1:Name>
    <d4p1:ProductNumber>WB-H098</d4p1:ProductNumber>
  </GetProductResult>
</GetProductResponse>
```

If any of the members of a data contract are themselves structured types, they should also be marked with the *DataContract* attribute. The data contract serializer can then recursively apply its own serialization and deserialization process to these members.

The *DataContract* and *DataMember* attributes have optional properties that you can use to tailor the way in which the data contract serializer performs its work. You will investigate some of these properties in the exercises in this section.

Change the order of members in the Product data contract

1. Using Visual Studio 2005, open the solution file ProductsService.sln located in the Microsoft Press\WCF Step By Step\Chapter 6\ProductsServiceV2 folder under your \My Documents folder.

This solution contains the implementation of the ProductsService service providing two versions of the service contract, as described earlier. The client application still uses version 1 of the service contract.

2. Open the ProductsService.cs file in the ProductsService project and locate the *Product* class. Note that the order of the members of this class is *Name, ProductNumber, Color,* and *ListPrice*.

3. Using Windows Explorer, delete the Products.svclog file in the Microsoft Press\WCF Step By Step\Chapter 6 folder under your \My Documents folder.

4. In Visual Studio 2005, start the solution without debugging. In the ProductsServiceHost form, click Start. In the client console window, press Enter.

   All tests should run successfully.

5. Press Enter to close the client console window. In the ProductsServiceHost form, click Stop, and then close the form.

6. Return to the Service Trace Viewer, and open the Products.svclog file in the Microsoft Press\WCF Step By Step\Chapter 6 folder under your \My Documents folder.

7. In the left pane, click the Message tab. Click the fourth message in the *http://adventure-works.com/2006/07/04* namespace. This is the GetProductResponse message sent by the service to the client when replying to a GetProduct message.

> **Note**   The WCF service configuration file for this version of the solution enables tracing at the service level rather than the transport level. All messages are traced in their unencrypted format to make it easier for you to examine their contents.

8. In the lower right pane, click the Message tab. Scroll this pane to display the body of the SOAP message. Note that the order of the fields in this message is *Color, ListPrice, Name,* and *ProductNumber*. This sequence is different from the order of the members in the *Product* class.

   The data contract serializer serializes the members of a data contract in alphabetic order. Rather than let the names of members imply an order, it is recommended that you use the *Order* property of the *DataMember* attribute to explicitly specify the sequence of the members.

9. Close the Products.svclog trace file, but leave the Service Trace Viewer open.

10. Return to Visual Studio 2005 and edit the ProductsService.cs file in the ProductsService project. Amend the *DataMember* attributes of each member as shown below, in bold:

```
[DataContract]
public class Product
{
    [DataMember(Order=0)]
    public string Name;
```

```
    [DataMember(Order=1)]
    public string ProductNumber;

    [DataMember(Order=2)]
    public string Color;

    [DataMember(Order=3)]
    public decimal ListPrice;
}
```

The data contract serializer will serialize members of the *Product* class starting with the member with the lowest *Order* value. If two members have the same *Order* value, then they will be serialized in alphabetic order.

11. Using Windows Explorer, delete the Products.svclog file in the Microsoft Press\WCF Step By Step\Chapter 6 folder under your \My Documents folder.

12. In Visual Studio 2005, start the solution without debugging. In the ProductsServiceHost form, click Start. In the client console window, press Enter.

     All tests appear to run successfully. However, if you examine the output from test 2 displaying the details of a product more closely, you should see that the Color is blank and the Price is zero. Changing the order of members in a data contract is a breaking change (you will fix the client application later).

13. Press Enter to close the client console window. In the ProductsServiceHost form, click Stop and then close the form.

14. Return to the Service Trace Viewer, and open the Products.svclog file in the Microsoft Press\WCF Step By Step\Chapter 6 folder under your \My Documents folder.

15. In the left pane, click the Message tab. Click the fourth message in the *http://adventure-works.com/2006/07/04* namespace. In the lower right pane, click the Message tab. Note that the order of the fields in this message is now *Name*, *ProductNumber*, *Color*, and *ListPrice*. This sequence now matches the order of the members in the *Product* class. You can see that the service is emitting the data in the products contract in the correct sequence even though the client application is not receiving this data correctly.

16. Close the Products.svclog trace file, but leave the Service Trace Viewer open.

You need to regenerate the proxy for the client application to make things work properly. Before doing that though, it is worth also looking at how changing the names of data members also affects a data contract.

In a manner similar to the service contract, the data contract serializer uses the name of each data member to form the name of each serialized field. Consequently, changing the name of a data member is also a breaking change that requires updating client applications. Like the operations in a service contract, you can provide a logical name for data members that the data contract serializer will use in place of the physical name of the data members; the *Data-Member* attribute provides the *Name* property for this purpose. You can use this feature to rename the physical members of a data contract while keeping the logical names the same, like this:

```
[DataContract]
public class Product
{
    [DataMember(Order=0)]
    public string Name;   // Serializer uses physical name of member

    [DataMember(Order=1, Name="ProductNumber")]
    public string Number; // Field renamed. Serializer uses Name property
    ...
}
```

The *DataContract* attribute provides a *Namespace* property. By default, WCF uses the namespace "*http://schemas.datacontract.org/2004/07*" with the *.NET Framework* namespace containing the data contract appended to the end. In the ProductsService service, the Product data contract is a member of the *Products .NET Framework* namespace, so messages are serialized with the namespace "*http://schemas.datacontract.org/2004/07/Products*." You can override this behavior by specifying a value for the *Namespace* property of the *DataContract* attribute. This is good practice; you can include date information in the namespace to help identify a specific version of the data contract. If you update the data contract, then modify the namespace with the update date.

Change the namespace of the Product data contract

1. In Visual Studio 2005, edit the ProductsService.cs file in the ProductsService project.

2. Modify the *DataContract* attribute for the *Product* class as shown in bold below:

```
[DataContract (Namespace=
    "http://adventure-works.com/datacontract/2007/03/01/Product")]
public class Product
{
    ...
}
```

(For the purposes of this exercise, pretend that the current date is 1 March 2007.)

3. Using Windows Explorer, delete the Products.svclog file in the Microsoft Press\WCF Step By Step\Chapter 6 folder under your \My Documents folder.

4. In Visual Studio 2005, start the solution without debugging. In the ProductsServiceHost form, click Start. In the client console window, press Enter.

    All tests should run, but this time test 2 is also missing the product number and name (previously, only the color and price were omitted). Changing the namespace for a data contract is another example of a breaking change.

5. Press Enter to close the client console window. In the ProductsServiceHost form, click Stop and then close the form.

6. Return to the Service Trace Viewer, and open the Products.svclog file in the Microsoft Press\WCF Step By Step\Chapter 6 folder under your \My Documents folder.

7. In the left pane, click the Message tab. Click the fourth message in the *http://adventure-works.com/2006/07/04* namespace. In the lower right pane, click the Message tab. Verify that the namespace for the fields in the message body is new namespace; the *<GetProductResult>* element creates an alias for the namespace called "*d4p1*," and the fields in the message are prefixed with this alias.

8. Close the Products.svclog trace file, but leave the Service Trace Viewer open.

You can see that the ProductsService service is formatting messages as expected, although the client application is not currently processing them correctly. The next step is to regenerate the proxy for the client application. You will also take the opportunity to switch the client application to use version 2 of the ProductsService interface.

Regenerate the proxy class and update the WCF client application

1. Open a Visual Studio 2005 Command Prompt window and move to the folder \Microsoft Press\WCF Step By Step\Chapter 6\ProductsServiceV2\ProductsService\bin folder under your \My Documents folder.

2. Run the following command to generate the schema files and WSDL description file the ProductsService service:

```
svcutil ProductsService.dll
```

This command should generate the following files:

- ❑ adventure-works.com.2006.07.04.wsdl
- ❑ adventure-works.com.2006.08.31.wsdl
- ❑ adventure-works.com.2006.07.04.xsd
- ❑ adventure-works.com.2006.08.31.xsd
- ❑ schemas.microsoft.com.2003.10.Serialization.xsd
- ❑ schemas.microsoft.com.2003.10.Serialization.Arrays.xsd
- ❑ Products.xsd
- ❑ adventure-works.com.datacontract.2007.03.01.xsd

Notice that as the service now contains two service contracts, this command generates two WSDL description files with their corresponding schemas.

3. Run the following command to generate the proxy class from the WSDL description file for the version 2 interface (2006.08.31) and the schema files:

```
svcutil /namespace:*,ProductsClient.ProductsService adventure-
works.com.2006.08.31.wsdl *.xsd /out:ProductsV2.cs
```

> **Note**   If you need to generate a proxy for the version
> 1 interface (2006.07.04), then simply specify the appropriate WSDL file.

4. Leave the Visual Studio 2005 Command Prompt window open, and return to Visual Studio 2005.

5. In the ProductsClient project, delete the Products.cs file.

6. In the Project menu, click Add Existing Item. Move to the Microsoft Press\WCF Step By Step\Chapter 6\ProductsServiceV2\ProductsService\bin folder, located under your \My Documents folder, and add the file ProductsV2.cs.

7. The client application currently invokes the ListProducts operation. This operation is not available in version 2 of the ProductsService service. Edit the Program.cs file in the ProductsClient project. In the Main method, change the code that performs test 1 to call the ListSelectedProducts method, passing in a product name that matches all bicycle frames:

```
// Obtain a list of all bicycle frames
Console.WriteLine("Test 1: List all bicycle frames");
string[] productNumbers = proxy.ListSelectedProducts("Frame");
```

8. Start the solution without debugging. In the ProductsServiceHost form, click Start. In the client console window, press Enter.

All tests should run successfully, and test 2 should now display valid data for product WB-H098 (a 30-oz water bottle of indeterminate color that costs $4.99).

9. Press Enter to close the client console window. In the ProductsServiceHost form, click Stop and then close the form.

You can now see that you should carefully assess the impact of updating a data contract, as doing so can cause client applications to malfunction in ways that are not always apparent. The nature of SOAP serialization means that reorganized or misplaced fields end up being assigned default values, which are very easy to miss!

You can also add new members to a data contract. Under some circumstances, you can perform this task without breaking existing client applications.

> **Note**   Adding a member to a data contract changes the schema exported by WCF. Client applications use this schema to determine the format of the data they send and receive in SOAP message. Many client applications that use SOAP (including those built by using WCF, and ASP.NET Web services) will happily ignore additional fields in SOAP messages. However, a small number of client applications created by using other technologies can enable strict schema validation. If you have to support these types of client applications, you cannot add new fields to a data contract without updating those client applications as well. In these cases, you should adopt a data contract versioning strategy similar to that shown for versioning service contracts. For more information, see the topic, Best Practices: Data Contract Versioning in the Microsoft Windows SDK documentation, also available on the Microsoft Web site at *http://windowssdk.msdn.microsoft.com/en-us/library/ms733832.aspx*.

Add a new field to the Product data contract to examine how a client handles unexpected fields

1. Using Visual Studio 2005, edit the ProductsService.cs file in the ProductsService project.

2. Add the following member, shown in bold, to the end of the Product data contract:

```
public class Product
{
    ...

    [DataMember(Order=0)]
    public decimal StandardCost; }
```

The StandardCost in the Product table in the *AdventureWorks* database records the cost of the product to the Adventure Works organization. The difference between the value in the ListPrice column and this one is the profit that Adventure Works makes whenever it sells an item. Adding this member with the *Order* property set to zero causes it to be serialized as the second member of the data contract. The Name member, which also has the *Order* property set to zero, will be output first, as it comes alphabetically before StandardCost.

> **Note**   As mentioned earlier, I would not normally recommend that you rely on alpha-betical order to determine the sequence of members in a data contract, but in this case there is a reason for this approach; you will quickly be able to see what happens in a client application when an unexpected data member appears in the middle of a data contract.

3. Find the GetProduct method in the *ProductsServiceImpl* class. In this method, update the SQL statement that retrieves product information from the database, as follows:

```
// Retrieve the details of the selected product by using a DataReader
string queryString =
    @"SELECT ProductNumber, Name, Color, ListPrice, StandardCost
    FROM Production.Product
    WHERE ProductNumber = '" + productNumber + "'";
```

4. In the block of code belonging to the *if* statement that populates the product passed back to the client application, add the following statement to copy the value in the Stan-dardCost column to the *Product* object:

```
if (productsReader.Read())
{
    ...

    product.StandardCost = productsReader.GetDecimal(4); }
```

5. Using Windows Explorer, delete the Products.svclog file in the Microsoft Press\WCF Step By Step\Chapter 6 folder under your \My Documents folder.

6. In Visual Studio 2005, start the solution without debugging. In the ProductsServiceHost form, click Start. In the client console window, press Enter.

All tests should run successfully, including test 2, which completely ignores the new member of the data contract. Adding a new member in the middle of a data contract does not affect the client application at all.

7. Press Enter to close the client console window. In the ProductsServiceHost form, click Stop and then close the form.

8. Return to the Service Trace Viewer, and open the Products.svclog file in the Microsoft Press\WCF Step By Step\Chapter 6 folder under your \My Documents folder.

9. In the left pane, click the Message tab. Click the fourth message in the *http://adventure-works.com/2006/07/04* namespace. Remember that this is the GetProductResponse message sent by the service to the client when replying to a GetProduct message.

10. In the lower right pane, click the Message tab. Scroll this pane to display the body of the SOAP message. Notice that the *StandardCost* field appears between the *Name* and *ProductNumber* fields.

   The data contract serializer serializes every member of the data contract. The WCF client application is not expecting the *StandardCost* field, and as it does not perform strict schema validation, the client application simply ignores this extra field.

11. Close the Products.svclog trace file, and exit the Service Trace Viewer open.

12. Regenerate the proxy object for the client application:

   ❑ In the Visual Studio 2005 Command Prompt window, run the command:

   ```
   svcutil ProductsService.dll
   ```

   ❑ Run the command:

   ```
   svcutil /namespace:*,ProductsClient.ProductsService adventure-
   works.com.2006.08.31.wsdl *.xsd /out:ProductsV2.cs
   ```

13. Return to Visual Studio 2005. In the ProductsClient project, delete the ProductsV2.cs file and replace it with the new file located in the Microsoft Press\WCF Step By Step\Chapter 6\ProductsServiceV2\ProductsService\bin folder, located under your \My Documents folder.

14. Edit the Program.cs file in the ProductsClient project. In the Main method, add a statement after the code that performs test 2, to display the standard cost:

   ```
   Console.WriteLine("Price: " + product.ListPrice);
   Console.WriteLine("Standard Cost: " + product.StandardCost);
   Console.WriteLine();
   ```

15. Start the solution without debugging. In the ProductsServiceHost form, click Start. In the client console window, press Enter.

   All tests should run successfully, and test 2 should now include the standard cost ($1.8663).

16. Press Enter to close the client console window. In the ProductsServiceHost form, click Stop and then close the form.

While it is acceptable for a client application to discard a field sent by the service, this scenario can cause complications if the client application is later expected to send data to the service that includes this missing field. You will examine this scenario in the next exercise.

Add another operation to the WCF service for investigating data contract serialization

1. In Visual Studio 2005, edit the ProductsService.cs file in the ProductsService project.

2. Add the following operation to the IProductServiceV2 service contract:

    ```
    public interface IProductServiceV2
    {
        ...
        // Update the details of the specified product in the database
        [OperationContract]
        void UpdateProductDetails(Product product);
    }
    ```

    A client application will be able to use this operation to modify the details of a product in the database.

3. Add the implementation of the UpdateProductDetails method to the end of the *ProductsServiceImpl* class:

    ```
    public class ProductsServiceImpl : ...
    {
        ...
        public void UpdateProductDetails(Product product)
        {
            string msg = String.Format("Number: {0}\nName: {1}",
                product.ProductNumber, product.Name);
            System.Windows.Forms.MessageBox.Show(msg);
        }
    }
    ```

    This method displays the product number and name sent by the client application. In the real world, this method would also update the database with the information in the parameter passed to the method. To keep things straightforward, the logic to perform this task has been omitted.

4. Build the solution.

5. Regenerate the proxy object for the client application:

    ❑ In the Visual Studio 2005 Command Prompt window, run the command:

    ```
    svcutil ProductsService.dll
    ```

    ❑ Run the command:

    ```
    svcutil /namespace:*,ProductsClient.ProductsService adventure-
    works.com.2006.08.31.wsdl *.xsd /out:ProductsV2.cs
    ```

6. Return to Visual Studio 2005. In the ProductsClient project, delete the ProductsV2.cs file and replace it with the new file located in the Microsoft Press\WCF Step By

Step\Chapter 6\ProductsServiceV2\ProductsService\bin folder, located under your \My Documents folder.

7. Edit the Program.cs file in the ProductsClient project. In the Main method, add the following statements that test the new operation to the *try* block:

```
try
{
    …
    // Modify the details of this product
    Console.WriteLine("Test 5: Modify the details of a product");
    product.ProductNumber = "WB-H098";
    product.Name = "Water Bottle - 1 liter";
    proxy.UpdateProductDetails(product);
    Console.WriteLine("Request sent");
    Console.WriteLine();

    // Disconnect from the service
    proxy.Close();
}
```

8. Start the solution without debugging. In the ProductsServiceHost form, click Start. In the client console window, press Enter.

When test 5 runs, a message box appears displaying the product number and the new product name.

Click OK to close the message box.

9. Press Enter to close the client console window. In the ProductsServiceHost form, click Stop and then close the form.

The client application successfully sends a *Product* object to the WCF service using the definition from the data contract. But what happens if the client application uses a version of the data contract that has a missing field?

Add another field to the Product data contract and examine the default value

1. In Visual Studio 2005, edit the ProductsService.cs file in the ProductsService project and add the following member, shown in bold, to the end of the Product data contract:

```
public class Product
{
    …
    [DataMember(Order=4)]
    public bool FinishedGoodsFlag; }
```

The FinishedGoodsFlag in the Product table indicates whether the product is a complete item (such as a water bottle) or a component used to construct other parts (such as a chaining nut).

2. In the UpdateProductDetails method in the *ProductsServiceImpl* class, modify the statements that display the product details to include the FinishedGoodsFlag member:

```
public void UpdateProductDetails(Product product)
{
    string msg = String.Format("Number: {0}\nName: {1}\nFlag: {2}",
        product.ProductNumber, product.Name, product.FinishedGoodsFlag);
    System.Windows.Forms.MessageBox.Show(msg);
}
```

3. Start the solution without debugging. In the ProductsServiceHost form, click Start. In the client console window, press Enter.

   When test 5 runs, the message box displays the value *False* for the FinishedGoodsFlag. The client application is still using the old version of the Product data contract and did not populate this field—this is the default value for a Boolean field in a SOAP message.

   Click OK to close the message box.

4. Press Enter to close the client console window. In the ProductsServiceHost form, click Stop and then close the form.

As when changing the order of data members, you should be very mindful of existing client applications when adding a new member to a data contract. If the client application does not populate every field in a serialized object, WCF will use default values—*False* for Booleans, *0* for numerics, and *null* for objects. If these default values are unacceptable, you can customize the serialization and deserialization process by adding methods annotated with the *OnSerializing* and *OnDeserializing* attributes to the WCF service.

> **More Info**   The details of customizing the serialization process are beyond the scope of this book, but for more information, examine the topic Version Tolerant Serialization Callbacks in the Microsoft Windows SDK documentation, also available on the Microsoft Web site at *http://windowssdk.msdn.microsoft.com/en-us/library/ms733734.aspx*.

Data Contract Compatibility

If you need to version a data contract, you should do so in a manner that maintains compatibility with existing client applications. The *DataMember* attribute provides two properties that can assist you:

- *IsRequired*. If you set this property to *True*, then the SOAP message that the service receives must include a value in this data member. By default, the value of this property is *False*, and the WCF runtime will generate default values for any missing fields.

- *EmitDefaultValue*. If you set this property to *True*, the WCF runtime on the client will generate a default value for a data member if it is not included in the SOAP message sent by the client application. This property is *True* by default.

If you need to maintain strict conformance to a data contract in future versions of the service, you should set the *IsRequired* property of each data member in the data contract to *True* and set the *EmitDefaultValue* property to *False* when building *the first version of a service*. You should never make a data member mandatory (*IsRequired* set to *True*) in a new version of a data contract if it was previously optional (*IsRequired* set to *False*).

It is possible for a client application to request data conforming to a data contract from a service, modify that data, and then submit it back to the service, in a manner similar to calling the GetProduct method followed by the UpdateProductDetails method in the ProductsService example. If a client application uses the old version of a data contract that is missing one or more members, such as the FinishedGoodsFlag, what happens to this information when the client sends the data back to the service? The WCF runtime implements a technique called "Round-tripping" to ensure that data does not get lost.

Examine how the WCF runtime performs round-tripping

1. In Visual Studio 2005, edit the ProductsService.cs file in the ProductsService project.

2. In the GetProduct method in the *ProductsServiceImpl* class, add the statement shown in bold below to the end of the block belonging to the *if* statement that populates the *Product* object returned to the client application:

    ```
    if (productsReader.Read())
    {
        ...
        product.FinishedGoodsFlag = true;
    }
    ```

    Remember that the default value for Booleans is *false*.

3. Start the solution without debugging. In the ProductsServiceHost form, click Start. In the client console window, press Enter.

    When test 5 runs, the message box displays the value *True* for the FinishedGoodsFlag. This is the value originally provided by the service and which has been sent through the client application and back to the service. Although the client application does not know anything about this field, it has managed to preserve its value.

    Click OK to close the message box.

4. Press Enter to close the client console window. In the *ProductsServiceHost* form, click Stop and then close the form.

The WCF library performs round-tripping by using the IExtensibleDataObject interface. If you examine the code in the ProductsV2.cs file, you will see that the client proxy version of the *Product* class implements this interface. This interface defines a single property called *ExtensionData*, of type *ExtensionDataObject*. The *ExtensionData* property generated for the client proxy simply reads and writes data to a private field of type *ExtensionObjectData*, like this:

```
public partial class Product : object,
    System.Runtime.Serialization.IExtensibleDataObject
{
    private System.Runtime.Serialization.ExtensionDataObject
        extensionDataField;

    ...
    public System.Runtime.Serialization.ExtensionDataObject ExtensionData
```

```
    {
        get
        {
            return this.extensionDataField;
        }
        set
        {
            this.extensionDataField = value;
        }
    }
}
```

The *extensionDataField* field acts as a "bucket" for all undefined data items received by the client; rather than discarding them, the proxy automatically stores them in this field. When the client proxy transmits the *Product* object back to the service, it includes the data in this field. If you need to disable this feature (if you want to ensure strict schema compliance in client applications, for example), you can set the *IgnoreExtensionDataObject* property of the data contract serializer in the endpoint behavior to true for the endpoint that the client is using. You can perform this task by using the client application configuration file, like this:

```
<system.serviceModel>
    <behaviors>
        <endpointBehaviors>
            <behavior name="IgnoreBehavior">
                <dataContractSerializer ignoreExtensionDataObject="true" />
            </behavior>
        </endpointBehaviors>
    </behaviors>
    ...
    <client>
        <endpoint address="net.tcp://localhost:8080/TcpProductsService"
            behaviorConfiguration="IgnoreBehavior" ... />
    </client>
</system.serviceModel>
```

You can also disable extension data objects on the server-side by setting the *IgnoreExtensionDataObject* property of data contract serializer for a single service endpoint or for all server endpoints by adding a service behavior.

Data Contract Serialization and Security

Remember that a data contract provides a potential entry point for a malicious user to hack into your system—by attempting a SQL Injection attack, for example. You must design your data contracts to be resistant to misuse such as this.

Another common example is a "Denial of Service" attack. In this type of attack, a user invokes methods in your service by sending them vast quantities of data. Your service then spends much of its time simply trying to receive and read this data, and performance suffers accordingly. To avoid this type of attack, don't define data contracts that involve large, nested data structures, arrays, or collections of indeterminate length. If you must define data contracts that allow a user to send an array, collection, or nested data, then limit the size of the data they can send by using the *readerQuota* properties of the service bindings:

```
<system.serviceModel>
    <bindings>
        <netTcpBinding>
            <binding name="ProductsServiceTcpBindingConfig">
                <readerQuotas maxDepth="2" maxStringContentLength="1024"
                 maxArrayLength="1024" />
                ...
            </binding>
        </netTcpBinding>
    </bindings>
    <services>
        <service ...>
            <endpoint binding="netTcpBinding"
            bindingConfiguration="ProductsServiceTcpBindingConfig" .../>
            ...
        </service>
    </services>
</system.serviceModel>
```

The *readerQuotas* properties include:

- *MaxArrayLength*. This is the maximum length of any array, in bytes, that the user can send to the service.

- *MaxDepth*. If a data structure contains nested data structures, this value specifies the maximum level of nesting allowed.

- *MaxStringContentLength*. This is the maximum length of any string, in characters, that the user can send to the service.

If a client application attempts to send a message of a size that exceeds these parameters, WCF will abort the request. By default, these properties are set to zero, which turns off any restrictions on data length.

Summary

In this chapter, you have learned how WCF uses service and data contracts to define the operations that a service exposes to client applications and the information that client applications can send to, or receive from, these operations. You have seen why it is important to design service and data contracts carefully, and how to create new versions of service and data contracts while maintaining compatibility with existing client applications.

Chapter 7
Maintaining State and Sequencing Operations

After completing this chapter, you will be able to:

- Describe how WCF creates an instance of a service.

- Explain the different options available for creating service instances.

- Manage state information in a WCF service in a scalable manner.

- Fine-tune the way in which the WCF runtime manages service instances.

- Describe how to control the life cycle of a service instance.

In all the exercises that you have performed so far, the client application has invoked a series of operations in a WCF service. The order of these operations has been immaterial, and calling one operation before another has had no impact on the functionality of either; the operations are totally independent. In the real world, a Web service might require that operations be invoked in a particular sequence. For example, if you are implementing shopping cart functionality in a service, it does not make sense to allow a client application to perform a checkout operation to pay for goods before actually putting anything into the shopping cart.

The issue of sequencing operations should naturally lead you to consider the need to maintain state information between operations. Taking the shopping cart example, where should the data that describes the items in the shopping cart be held? You have at least two options:

- Maintain the shopping cart in the client application, pass the information that describes the shopping cart contents as a parameter to each operation, and return the updated shopping cart contents from the operation back to the client. This is a variation of the solution implemented by traditional Web applications (including ASP.NET Web applications) that used cookies stored on the user's computer to store information. It relieved the Web application of the burden of maintaining state information between client calls, but there was nothing to stop the client application directly modifying the data in the cookie or even inadvertently corrupting it in some manner. Additionally, cookies can be a security risk, so many Web browsers implement features to enable a user to disable their use, making it difficult to store state information on the user's computer. In a Web service environment (as opposed to a Web application and browser combination), a client application can maintain state information by using its own code rather than relying on cookies. However, this strategy ties the client application to the Web service and can result in a very tight coupling between the two, with all the inherent fragility and maintenance problems that this can cause.

- Maintain the shopping cart in the service. The first time the user running the client application attempts to add something to the shopping cart, the service creates a data structure to represent the items being added. As the user adds further items to the shopping cart, they are stored in this data structure. When the user wants to pay for the items in the shopping cart, the service can calculate the total, perform an exchange with the user through the client application to establish the payment method, and then arrange for dispatch of the items. In a WCF environment, all interactions between the client application and the service are performed by invoking well-defined operations specified by using a service contract. Additionally, the client application does not need to know how the service actually implements the shopping cart.

The second approach sounds the more promising of the two, but there are several issues that you must address when building a Web service to handle this scenario. In this chapter, you will investigate some of these issues, and see how you can resolve them.

Managing State in a WCF Service

It makes sense to look at how to manage and maintain state in a WCF service first and then return to the issue of sequencing operations later.

The exercises that you performed in previous chapters involved stateless operations. All the information required to perform an operation in the ProductsService service has been passed in as a series of parameters by the client application. When an operation has completed, the service "forgets" that the client ever invoked it! In the shopping cart scenario, the situation is different. You must maintain the shopping cart between operations. In the exercises in this section, you will learn that this approach requires a little thought and careful design.

Create the ShoppingCartService service

1. Using Visual Studio 2005, create a new project. Select the .NET Framework 3.0 project types under Visual C# and use the WCF Service Library template. Name the project ShoppingCartService and save it in the Microsoft Press\WCF Step By Step\Chapter 7 folder under your \My Projects folder.

2. In Solution Explorer, rename the Class1.cs file as ShoppingCartService.cs.

3. In the code view window displaying the ShoppingCartService.cs file, delete all the comments and code apart from the *using* statements at the top of the file.

4. In Solution Explorer, add references to the *Microsoft.Practices.EnterpriseLibrary.Data.dll*, *Microsoft.Practices.EnterpriseLibrary.Common.dll*, and *Microsoft.Practices.ObjectBuilder.dll* assemblies located in the C:\Program Files\Microsoft Enterprise Library\bin folder.

5. In the code view window displaying ShoppingCartService.cs, add the following *using* statements to the list at the top of the file:

```
using Microsoft.Practices.EnterpriseLibrary.Data;
using System.Data;
```

6. Add a namespace definition for the *ShoppingCartService* namespace to the file, underneath the *using* statements. The file should look like this:

```
using System;
using System.Collections.Generic;
using System.Text;
using System.ServiceModel;
using System.Runtime.Serialization;
using Microsoft.Practices.EnterpriseLibrary.Data;
using System.Data;
namespace ShoppingCartService
{
}
```

7. Add the following data structure shown in bold to the *ShoppingCartService* namespace:

```
namespace ShoppingCartService
{
    // Shopping cart item
    class ShoppingCartItem
    {
        public string ProductNumber;
        public string ProductName;
        public decimal Cost;
        public int Volume;
    }
}
```

This class defines the items that can be stored in the shopping cart. A shopping cart will contain a list of these items. Notice that this is not a data contract; this class is for internal use by the service. If a client application queries the contents of the shopping cart, the service will send it a simplified representation as a string. In this way, there should be no dependencies between the structure of the shopping cart and the client applications that manipulate them.

8. Add the following service contract to the *ShoppingCartService* namespace, after the *ShoppingCartItem* class:

```
namespace ShoppingCartService
{
    ...
    [ServiceContract(Namespace = "http://adventure-works.com/2007/03/01",
                     Name = "ShoppingCartService")]
    public interface IShoppingCartService
    {
        [OperationContract(Name="AddItemToCart")]
        bool AddItemToCart(string productNumber);

        [OperationContract(Name = "RemoveItemFromCart")]
        bool RemoveItemFromCart(string productNumber);

        [OperationContract(Name = "GetShoppingCart")]
        string GetShoppingCart();
```

```
        [OperationContract(Name = "Checkout")]
        bool Checkout();
    }
}
```

The client application will invoke the AddItemToCart and RemoveItemFromCart operations to manipulate the shopping cart. In the *AdventureWorks* database, items are identified by their product number. To add more than one instance of an item requires
invoking the AddItemToCart operation once for each instance. These operations return
true if they are successful, *false* otherwise.

The GetShoppingCart operation will return a string representation of the shopping cart
contents that the client application can display.

The client application will call the Checkout operation if the user wants to purchase the
goods in the shopping cart. Again, this operation returns *true* if it is successful, *false* otherwise.

> **Note** For the purposes of this example, assume that the user has an account with
> Adventure-Works, and so the Checkout operation simply arranges dispatch of the
> goods to the customer's address. The customer will be billed separately.

9. Add the following class to the *ShoppingCartService* namespace:

```
namespace ShoppingCartService
{
    ...

    public class ShoppingCartServiceImpl : IShoppingCartService
    {
    }
}
```

This class will implement the operations for the *IShoppingCartService* interface.

10. Add the shoppingCart variable shown below to the *ShoppingCartServiceImpl* class:

```
public class ShoppingCartServiceImpl : IShoppingCartService
{
    private List<ShoppingCartItem> shoppingCart =
        new List<ShoppingCartItem>();
}
```

This variable will hold the user's shopping cart, comprising a list of *ShoppingCartItem*
objects.

11. Add the private method shown below to the *ShoppingCartServiceImpl* class:

```
// Examine the shopping cart to determine whether an item with a
// specified product number has already been added.
// If so, return a reference to the item, otherwise return null
private ShoppingCartItem find(List<ShoppingCartItem> shoppingCart,
                             string productNumber)
{
```

```
foreach (ShoppingCartItem item in shoppingCart)
{
    if (string.Compare(item.ProductNumber, productNumber) == 0)
    {
        return item;
    }
}

return null;
}
```

This AddItemToCart and RemoveItemFromCart operations will make use of this utility method.

> **Note**   The code for this method is available in the file Find.txt located in the Chapter 7 folder.

12. Implement the AddToCart method in the *ShoppingCartServiceImpl* class, as shown below:

```
public bool AddItemToCart(string productNumber)
{
    // Note: For clarity, this method performs very limited security
    // checking and exception handling
    try
    {
        // Check to see whether the user has already added this
        // product to the shopping cart
        ShoppingCartItem item = find(shoppingCart, productNumber);

        // If so, increment the volume
        if (item != null)
        {
            item.Volume++;
            return true;
        }

        // Otherwise retrieve the details of the product from the database
        else
        {
            // Connect to the AdventureWorks database
            Database dbAdventureWorks =
                DatabaseFactory.CreateDatabase("AdventureWorksConnection");

            // Retrieve the details of the selected product
            string queryString = @"SELECT Name, ListPrice
                        FROM Production.Product
                        WHERE ProductNumber = '" + productNumber + "'";
            IDataReader productsReader =
             dbAdventureWorks.ExecuteReader(CommandType.Text, queryString);

            // Check to see whether the user has already added
            // this product to the shopping cart
            // Create and populate a new shopping cart item
```

```
        ShoppingCartItem newItem = new ShoppingCartItem();
        if (productsReader.Read())
        {
            newItem.ProductNumber = productNumber;
            newItem.ProductName = productsReader.GetString(0);
            newItem.Cost = productsReader.GetDecimal(1);
            newItem.Volume = 1;

            // Add the new item to the shopping cart
            shoppingCart.Add(newItem);

            // Indicate success
            return true;
        }
        else
        {
            // No such product in the database
            return false;
        }
    }
}
catch (Exception)
{
    // Indicate failure
    return false;
}
}
```

> **Note**   The code for this method is available in the file AddItemToCart.txt located in
> the Chapter 7 folder.

For clarity, this method does not perform any security checking (such as protecting
against SQL injection attacks) and exception handling is minimal. In a production
application, you should address these aspects robustly, as described in the preceding
chapters.

13. Add the RemoveItemFromCart method shown below to the *ShoppingCartServiceImpl*
    class:

```
public bool RemoveItemFromCart(string productNumber)
{
    // Determine whether the specified product has an
    // item in the shopping cart
    ShoppingCartItem item = find(shoppingCart, productNumber);

    // If so, then decrement the volume
    if (item != null)
    {
        item.Volume--;

        // If the volume is zero, remove the item from the shopping cart
        if (item.Volume == 0)
        {
            shoppingCart.Remove(item);
```

```
    }

    // Indicate success
    return true;
}

// No such item in the shopping cart
return false;
}
```

> **Note**   The code for this method is available in the file RemoveItemFromCart.txt located in the Chapter 7 folder.

14. Implement the GetShoppingCart method in the *ShoppingCartServiceImpl* class, as follows:

```
public string GetShoppingCart()
{
    // Create a string holding a formatted representation
    // of the shopping cart
    string formattedContent = "";
    decimal totalCost = 0;

    foreach (ShoppingCartItem item in shoppingCart)
    {
        string itemString = String.Format(
            "Number: {0}\tName: {1}\tCost: {2}\tVolume: {3}",
            item.ProductNumber, item.ProductName, item.Cost,
            item.Volume);
        totalCost += (item.Cost * item.Volume);
        formattedContent += itemString + "\n";
    }

    formattedContent += "\nTotalCost: " + totalCost;
    return formattedContent;
}
```

> **Note**   The code for this method is available in the file GetShoppingCart.txt located in the Chapter 7 folder.

This method generates a string describing the contents of the shopping cart. The string contains a line for each item, with the total cost of the items in the shopping cart at the end.

> **Note**   Although not shown in this method, you should format numeric values containing monetary items using the current locale.

15. Add the Checkout method to the *ShoppingCartServiceImpl* class, as follows:

```
public bool Checkout()
{
    // Not currently implemented - just return true
    return true;
}
```

This method is simply a placeholder. In a production system, this method would perform tasks such as arranging the dispatch of items, billing the user, and updating the database to reflect the changes in stock volume according to the user's order.

16. Build the solution.

You now need to build a host application for this service. You will use a simple console application for this purpose.

Create a host application for the ShoppingCartService service

1. Add a new project to the ShoppingCartService solution. Select the Windows project types under Visual C# and use the Console Application template. Name the project ShoppingCartHost and save it in the Microsoft Press\WCF Step By Step\Chapter 7\ShoppingCartService folder under your \My Projects folder.

> **Tip**   In the File menu, point to Add, and then click New Project to add a new project to a solution.

2. Add the App.config file located in the Microsoft Press\WCF Step By Step\Chapter 7\Config folder under your \My Projects folder to the ShoppingCartHost project.

   This configuration file currently just contains the definition of the connection string that the service uses for connecting to the *AdventureWorks* database.

> **Tip**   In the Project menu, click Add Existing item to add a file to a project. You will also need to select All Files (*.*) in the Files of type dropdown in the Add Existing Item dialog box to display the App.config file.

3. Edit the App.config file by using the WCF Service Configuration Editor. In the right pane, click Create a New Service.

   The New Service Element Wizard starts.

4. In the "What is the service type of your service?" page, click Browse. In the Type Browser window, move to the ShoppingCartService\ShoppingCartService\bin\Debug folder under the Chapter 7 folder, and double-click the *ShoppingCartService.dll* assembly. Select the ShoppingCartService.ShoppingCartServiceImpl type, and then click Open. In the "What is the service type of your service?" page, click Next.

5. In the "What service contract are you using?" page, select the ShoppingCartService.IShoppingCartService contract, and then click Next.

6. In the "What communications mode is your service using?" page, click HTTP, and then click Next.

7. In the "What method of interoperability do you want to use?" page, select Advanced Web Services interoperability, select Simplex communication, and then click Next.

8. In the "What is the address of your endpoint?" page, enter **http://localhost:9000 /ShoppingCartService/ShoppingCartService.svc** and then click Next.

9. In the "The wizard is ready to create a service configuration" page, click Finish.

    The wizard adds the service to the configuration file, and creates an endpoint definition for the service.

10. Save the configuration file, and then exit the WCF Service Configuration Editor. Allow Visual Studio 2005 to reload the updated App.config file. The <system.serviceModel> section should look like this:

```
<system.serviceModel>
  <services>
    <service name="ShoppingCartService.ShoppingCartServiceImpl">
      <endpoint address=
"http://localhost:9000/ShoppingCartService/ShopppingCartService.svc"
        binding="wsHttpBinding" bindingConfiguration="" contract="ShoppingCartService.
IShoppingCartService" />
    </service>
  </services>
</system.serviceModel>
```

11. In Solution Explorer, add a reference to the *System.ServiceModel* assembly and a reference to the ShoppingCartService project to the ShoppingCartHost project.

12. Edit the Program.cs file in the ShoppingCartHost project. Add the following *using* statement to the list at the top of the file:

```
using System.ServiceModel;
```

13. Add the statements shown below in bold to the Main method in the *Program* class:

```
class Program
{
    static void Main(string[] args)
    {
        ServiceHost host = new ServiceHost(
            typeof(ShoppingCartService.ShoppingCartServiceImpl));
        host.Open();
        Console.WriteLine("Service running");
        Console.WriteLine("Press ENTER to stop the service");
        Console.ReadLine();
        host.Close();
    }
}
```

    This code creates a new instance of the ShoppingCartService service, listening on the HTTP endpoint you specified in the configuration file.

The next task is to build a client application to test the ShoppingCartService service. You will create another Console application to do this.

Create a client application to test the ShoppingCartService service

1. Add another new project to the ShoppingCartService solution. Select the Windows project types under Visual C#, and select the Console Application template. Name the project ShoppingCartClient and save it in the Microsoft Press\WCF Step By Step\Chapter 7\ShoppingCartService folder under your \My Projects folder.

2. In the ShoppingCartClient project, add a reference to the *System.ServiceModel* assembly.

3. Generate a proxy class for the client application by using the following procedure:

   ❑ Open a Visual Studio 2005 Command Prompt window and move to the ShoppingCartService\ShoppingCartService\bin\Debug folder in the Microsoft Press\WCF Step By Step\Chapter 7 folder under your \My Projects folder

   ❑ In the Visual Studio 2005 Command Prompt window, run the command:

   ```
   svcutil ShoppingCartService.dll
   ```

   ❑ Run the command:

   ```
   svcutil /namespace:*,ShoppingCartClient.ShoppingCartService adventure-
   works.com.2007.03.01.wsdl *.xsd /out:ShoppingCartServiceProxy.cs
   ```

4. Return to Visual Studio 2005, and add the ShoppingCartServiceProxy.cs file in the ShoppingCartService\ShoppingCartService\bin\Debug folder to the ShoppingCartClient project.

> **Note** You can also use the *Add Service Reference* command in the Project menu to generate the proxy for an HTTP service and add it to the client project. However, the service must be running for Visual Studio 2005 to be able to do this, and the service must enable metadata publishing (by default, this feature is disabled). See Chapter 1, "Introducing Windows Communication Foundation," for details on how to do this.

5. Add a new application configuration file to the ShoppingCartClient project. Name this file App.config.

> **Tip** To add a new file to a project, on the Project menu, click Add New Item.

6. Edit the App.config file in the ShoppingCartClient project by using the WCF Service Configuration Editor. In the left pane, click the Client folder and then click Create a New Client in the right pane.

   The New Client Element Wizard starts.

7. In the "What method do you want to use to create the client?" page, select From service config. Click Browse by the Config file text box. In the Open dialog box, move to the

Chapter 7\ShoppingCartService\ShoppingCartHost folder, select the app.config file, and then click Open. In the "What method do you want to use to create the client?" page click Next.

8. In the "Which service endpoint do you want to connect to?" page, accept the default service endpoint and then click Next.

9. In the "What name do you want to use or the client configuration?" page, type **HttpBinding_ShoppingCartService** and then click Next.

10. In the "The wizard is ready to create a client configuration" page, click Finish.

    The wizard adds the client definition to the configuration file and creates an endpoint called HttpBinding_ShoppingCartService that the client application can use to connect to the ShoppingCartService service. However, the name of the type implementing the contract in the client proxy has a different name from that used by the service, so you must change the value added to the client configuration file.

11. Click the HttpBinding_ShoppingCartService endpoint in the left pane. In the right pane, set the *Contract* property to *ShoppingCartClient.ShoppingCartService.*ShoppingCartService (the type is ShoppingCartService in the *ShoppingCartClient.ShoppingCartService* namespace in the client proxy).

12. Save the configuration file, and exit the WCF Service Configuration Editor. Allow Visual Studio 2005 to reload the modified App.config file. The App.config file for the Shopping-CartClient application should look like this:

```xml
<?xml version="1.0" encoding="utf-8" ?>
<configuration>
  <system.serviceModel>
    <client>
      <endpoint address="http://localhost:9000/ShoppingCartService/
ShoppingCartService.svc"
          binding="wsHttpBinding" bindingConfiguration="" contract="ShoppingCartClient
.ShoppingCartService.ShoppingCartService"
          name="HttpBinding_ShoppingCartService">
        <identity>
          <certificateReference storeName="My" storeLocation="LocalMachine" x509Find
Type="FindSubjectDistinguishedName" />
        </identity>
      </endpoint>
    </client>
  </system.serviceModel>
</configuration>
```

    Remove the *<identity>* element, and its child *<certificateReference>* element from the configuration file. This version of the service does not use certificates.

13. In Visual Studio 2005, edit the Program.cs file in the ShoppingCartClient project. Add the following *using* statements to the list at the top of the file.

```
using System.ServiceModel;
using ShoppingCartClient.ShoppingCartService;
```

14. Add the statements below, shown in bold, to the Main method of the *Program* class:

```
static void Main(string[] args)
{
    Console.WriteLine("Press ENTER when the service has started");
    Console.ReadLine();
    try
    {
        // Connect to the ShoppingCartService service
        ShoppingCartServiceClient proxy =
        new ShoppingCartServiceClient("HttpBinding_ShoppingCartService");

        // Add two water bottles to the shopping cart
        proxy.AddItemToCart("WB-H098");
        proxy.AddItemToCart("WB-H098");
        // Add a mountain seat assembly to the shopping cart
        proxy.AddItemToCart("SA-M198");
        // Query the shopping cart and display the result
        string cartContents = proxy.GetShoppingCart();
        Console.WriteLine(cartContents);
        // Disconnect from the ShoppingCartService service
        proxy.Close();
    }
    catch (Exception e)
    {
        Console.WriteLine("Exception: {0}", e.Message);
    }
    Console.WriteLine("Press ENTER to finish");
    Console.ReadLine();
}
```

> **Note**   Complete code for the Main method is available in the file Main.txt located in the Chapter 7 folder.

The code in the *try* block creates a proxy object for communicating with the service. The application then adds three items to the shopping cart—two water bottles and a mountain seat assembly—before querying the current contents of the shopping cart and displaying the result.

15. In Solution Explorer, right-click the ShoppingCartService solution and then click Set StartUp Projects. In the right pane of the Solution 'ShoppingCartService' Property Pages dialog box, select Multiple startup projects, and set the *Action* property for the Shopping-CartClient and ShoppingCartHost projects to *Start*. Click OK.

16. Start the solution without debugging. In the client console window displaying the message "Press ENTER when the service has started," press Enter.

> **Note** If a Windows Security Alert message box appears, click Unblock to allow the service to use HTTP port 9000.

The client application adds the three items to the shopping cart and displays the result, as shown in the following image:

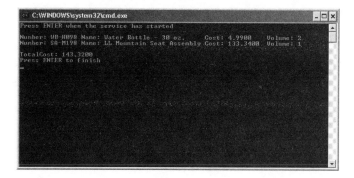

17.   Press Enter to close the client application console window. In the host application console window, press Enter to stop the service.

This technique for maintaining the shopping cart in the service appears to work well. But, this is one of those situations that should leave you feeling a little bit suspicious, as everything appears to be just a bit too easy!

Service Instance Context Modes

If you think for a minute about what is going on, the service creates an instance of the shopping cart when an instance of the service is itself created by the host; the shoppingCart variable is a private instance variable in the *ShoppingCartServiceImpl* class. What happens if two clients attempt to use the service simultaneously? The answer is that each client gets their own instance of the service, with its own instance of the shoppingCart variable. This is an important point. By default, the first time each client invokes an operation in a service, the host creates a new instance of the service just for that client. How long does the instance last? You can see from the shopping cart example that the instance hangs around between operation calls, otherwise it would not be able to maintain its state in an instance variable. The service instance is only destroyed after the client has closed the connection to the host (in true .NET Framework fashion, you do not know exactly how long the instance will hang around after the client application closes the connection because it depends on when the .NET Framework garbage collector decides it is time to reclaim memory). Now think what happens if you have 10 concurrent clients—you get 10 instances of the service. What if you have 10,000 concurrent clients? You get 10,000 instances of the service. If the client is an interactive application that runs for an indeterminate period while the user browses the product catalog and decides which items to buy, you had better be running the host application on a machine with plenty of memory!

Note If you are using the TCP, or named pipe transport, you can restrict the maximum number of concurrent sessions for a service by setting the *MaxConnections* property of the binding configuration. For these transports, the default limit is 10 connections. If you are using IIS to host a WCF service using the HTTP or HTTPS transports, you can configure IIS with the maximum number of concurrent connections it should allow—the details of how to do this are beyond the scope of this book, as it varies depending on which version of IIS you are using.

You can control the relationship between client applications and instances of a service by using the *InstanceContextMode* property of the *ServiceBehavior* attribute of the service. You specify this attribute when defining the class that implements the service contract, like this:

```
[ServiceBehavior(InstanceContextMode = InstanceContextMode.PerSession)]
public class ShoppingCartService : IShoppingCartService
{
    ...
}
```

The *InstanceContextMode* property can take one of the following three values: *InstanceMode.PerSession*, *InstanceMode.PerCall*, and *InstanceMode.Single*. The following sections describe these instance context modes.

The PerSession Instance Context Mode

The PerSession instance context mode specifies that the service instance is created when a client application first invokes an operation, and the instance remains active, responding to client requests, until the client application closes the connection, typically by calling the Close method on the proxy object. The time between invoking the first operation and closing the connection is referred to as the client application's "session," and the service instance is private to the session. Each time a client application creates a new session, it gets a new instance of the service. Two sessions cannot share a service instance when using this instance context mode, even if both sessions are created by the same instance of the client application.

It is possible for a client application to create multiple threads and then attempt to invoke operations in the same session simultaneously. By default, a service is single-threaded and will not process more than one request at a time. If a new request arrives while the service is still processing an earlier request, the WCF runtime causes the new request to wait for the earlier one to complete. The new request could possibly time-out while it is waiting to be handled. You can modify this behavior. The *ServiceBehavior* attribute has another property called *ConcurrencyMode*. You can set this property to specify how to process concurrent requests in the same session, like this:

```
[ServiceBehavior(..., ConcurrencyMode = ConcurrencyMode.Single)]
public class ShoppingCartService : IShoppingCartService
{
```

```
    ...
}
```

The default value for this property is *ConcurrencyMode.Single*, which causes the service to behave as just described. You can also set this property to *ConcurrencyMode.Multiple*, in which case the service instance is multithreaded and can accept simultaneous requests. However, setting the *Concurrency* property to this value does not make any guarantees about synchronization. You must take responsibility for ensuring that the code you write in the service is thread-safe.

> **Note**   There is a third mode called ConcurrencyMode.Reentrant. In this mode, the service instance is single-threaded, but allows the code in your service to call out to other services and applications, which can then subsequently call back into your service. However, this mode makes no guarantees about the state of data in your instance of the service. It is the responsibility of your code to ensure that the state of service instance remains consistent, and that the service doesn't accidentally deadlock itself.

The PerCall Instance Context Mode

The InstanceContextMode.PerCall instance context mode creates a new instance of the service every time the client application invokes an operation. The instance is destroyed when the operation completes. The advantage of this instance context mode is that it releases resources in the host between operations, greatly improving scalability. If you consider the situation with 10,000 concurrent users and the PerSession instance context mode, the main issue is that the host has to hold 10,000 instances of the service, even if 9,999 of them are not currently performing any operations because the users have gone to lunch without closing their copy of the client application and terminating their sessions. If you use the PerCall instance context mode instead, then the host will only need to hold an instance for the one active user.

The disadvantage of using this instance context mode is that maintaining state between operations is more challenging. You cannot retain information in instance variables in the service, so you must save any required state information in persistent storage, such as a disk file or database. It also complicates the design of operations, as a client application must identify itself so that the service can retrieve the appropriate state from storage (you will investigate one way of achieving this in an exercise later in this chapter).

You can see that the lifetime of a service instance depends on how long it takes the service to perform the requested operation, so keep your operations concise. You should be very careful if an operation creates additional threads, as the service instance will live on until all of these threads complete, even if the main thread has long-since returned any results to the client application; this can seriously affect scalability. You should also avoid registering callbacks in a service. Registering a callback does not block service completion, and the object calling back might find that the service instance has been reclaimed and recycled. The CLR traps this eventuality so it is not a security risk, but it is inconvenient to the object calling back as it will receive an exception.

The Single Instance Context Mode

The InstanceContextMode.Single instance context mode creates a new instance of the service the first time a client application invokes an operation and then uses this same instance to handle all subsequent requests from this client and *every other client that connects to the same service*. The instance is destroyed only when the host application shuts the service down. The main advantage of this instance context mode, apart from the reduced resource requirements, is that all users can easily share data. Arguably, this is also the principal disadvantage of this instance context mode!

The InstanceContextMode.Single instance context mode minimizes the resources used by the service at the cost of the same instance being expected to handle every single request. If you have 10,000 concurrent users, that could be a lot of requests. Also, if the service is single threaded (the *ConcurrencyMode* property of the *ServiceBehavior* attribute is set to *Concurrency-Mode.Single*), then expect many timeouts unless operations complete very quickly. Consequently, you should set the concurrency mode to ConcurrencyMode.Multiple and implement synchronization to ensure that all operations are thread-safe.

> **More Info** Detailed discussion of synchronization techniques in the .NET Framework is outside the scope of this book, but for more information see the topic "Synchronizing Data For Multithreading" in the Microsoft Windows SDK Documentation or on the Microsoft Web site at *http://msdn2.microsoft.com/en-us/library/z8chs7ft.aspx*.

In the next exercise, you will examine the effects of using the PerCall and Single instance context modes.

Investigate the InstanceContextMode property of the ServiceBehavior

1. In Visual Studio 2005, edit the ShoppingCartService.cs file in the ShoppingCartService project.

2. Add the *ServiceBehavior* attribute to the *ShoppingCartServiceImpl* class, with the *Instance-ContextMode* property set to *InstanceContextMode.PerCall*, as shown in bold below:

   ```
   [ServiceBehavior(InstanceContextMode = InstanceContextMode.PerCall)]
   public class ShoppingCartService : IShoppingCartService
   {
       ...
   }
   ```

3. Start the solution without debugging. In the ShoppingCartClient console window displaying the message "Press ENTER when the service has started," press Enter.

The client application adds the three items to the shopping cart as before, but the result displayed after retrieving the shopping cart from the service shows no items and a total cost of zero:

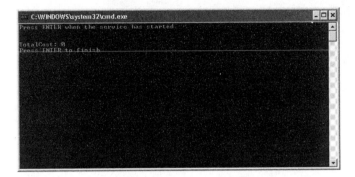

Every time the client application calls the service, it calls a new instance of the service. The shopping cart is destroyed every time an operation completes, so the string returned by the GetShoppingCart operation is a representation of an empty shopping cart.

4. Press Enter to close the client application console window. In the host application console window, press Enter to stop the service.

5. In Visual Studio 2005, change the *InstanceContextMode* property of the *ServiceBehavior* attribute of the ShoppingCartService to *InstanceContextMode.Single*, as follows:

```
[ServiceBehavior(InstanceContextMode = InstanceContextMode.Single)]
public class ShoppingCartService : IShoppingCartService
{
    ...
}
```

6. Start the solution without debugging. In the ShoppingCartClient console window press Enter.

    This time, the client application displays the shopping cart containing two water bottles and a mountain seat assembly. All appears to be well at first glance.

7. Press Enter to close the client application console window, but leave the host application running.

8. In Visual Studio 2005, right-click the ShoppingCartClient project, point to Debug, and click Start new instance.

    This action runs the client application again without restarting the service host application.

9. In the ShoppingCartClient console window press Enter.

    The shopping cart displayed by the client application now contains four water bottles and two mountain seat assemblies:

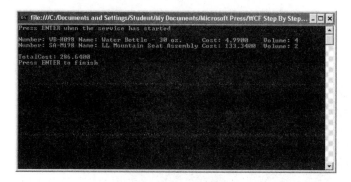

The second run of the client application used the same instance of the service as the first run, and the items were added to the same instance of the shopping cart.

10. Press Enter to close the client application console window. In the host application console window, press Enter to stop the service.

> **Tip** The PerSession instance context mode is the default when you use an endpoint that requires sessions. This is actually most of the time, unless you disable security (absolutely not recommended), or use the BasicHttpBinding binding, which does not support sessions when the service host defaults to using the PerCall instance context mode. This can be quite confusing, so it is better to always explicitly state the instance context mode your service requires by using the *ServiceBehavior* attribute.

Maintaining State with the PerCall Instance Context Mode

The exercises so far in this chapter have highlighted what happens when you change the instance context mode for a service. In the ShoppingCartService service, which instance context mode should you use? In a real-world environment, using a proper client application rather than the test code you have been working with, the user could spend a significant amount of time browsing for items of interest before adding them to their shopping cart. In this case, it makes sense to use the PerCall instance context mode. But you must provide a mechanism to store and recreate the shopping cart each time the client application invokes an operation. There are several ways you can achieve this, including generating an identifier for the shopping cart when the service first creates it, returning this identifier to the client application, and forcing the client to pass this identifier in to all subsequent operations as a parameter. This technique, and its variations, are frequently used, but suffer from many of the same security drawbacks as cookies as far as the service is concerned; it is possible for a client application to forge a shopping cart identifier and hijack another user's shopping cart.

An alternative strategy is to employ the user's own identity as a key for saving and retrieving state information. In a secure environment, this information is transmitted as part of the request anyway, and so it is transparent to client applications—for example, the wsHttpBinding binding uses Windows Integrated Security and transmits the user's credentials to the WCF service by default. You will make use of this information in the following exercise.

> **Note**   The same mechanism works even if you are using a non-Windows specific mechanism to identify users, such as certificates, and so is a valuable technique in an Internet security environment. The important thing is that you have a unique identifier for the user—it does not have to be a Windows username.

Manage state in the ShoppingCartService service

1. In Visual Studio 2005, edit the ShoppingCartService.cs file in the ShoppingCartService project.

2. Add the following *using* statements to the list at the top of the file:

```
using System.IO;
using System.Xml.Serialization;
```

You will use classes in these namespaces to serialize the user's shopping cart and save it in a text file.

3. Modify the definition of the *ShoppingCartItem* class; mark it with the *Serializable* attribute, and change its visibility to public, as shown in bold below:

```
[Serializable]
public class ShoppingCartItem
{
    ...
}
```

You can only serialize publicly accessible classes by using the XML serializer.

4. Add the saveShoppingCart method shown below to the *ShoppingCartServiceImpl* class:

```
// Save the shopping cart for the current user to a local XML
// file named after the user
private void saveShoppingCart()
{
    string userName = ServiceSecurityContext.Current.PrimaryIdentity.Name;
    foreach (char badChar in Path.GetInvalidFileNameChars())
    {
        userName = userName.Replace(badChar, '!');
    }
    string fileName = userName + ".xml";
    TextWriter writer = new StreamWriter(fileName);

    XmlSerializer ser = new XmlSerializer(typeof(List<ShoppingCartItem>));
    ser.Serialize(writer, shoppingCart);
    writer.Close();
}
```

> **Note** The code for this method is available in the file SaveShoppingCart.txt located in the Chapter 7 folder.

This private utility method retrieves the name of the user running the client application and creates a file name based on this username, with an ".xml" suffix. The username could include a domain name, with a separating "\" character. This character is not allowed in file names, so the code replaces any "\" characters, and any other characters in the username that are not allowed in filenames, with a "!" character.

> **Note** If you are using certificates rather than Window's usernames to identify users in an Internet environment, the file names will still be legal although they will look a little strange, as user identities in this scheme have the form "CN=*user*; FA097524718BD8765D6E4AA7654891245BCAD85."

The method then uses an *XmlSerializer* object to serialize the user's shopping cart to this file before closing the file and finishing.

> **Note** For clarity, this method does not perform any exception checking. In a production environment, you should be prepared to be more robust.

5. Add the restoreShoppingCart method shown here to the *ShoppingCartServiceImpl* class:

```
// Restore the shopping cart for the current user from the local XML
// file named after the user
private void restoreShoppingCart()
{
    string userName = ServiceSecurityContext.Current.PrimaryIdentity.Name;
    foreach (char badChar in Path.GetInvalidFileNameChars())
    {
        userName = userName.Replace(badChar, '!');
    }
    string fileName = userName + ".xml";

    if (File.Exists(fileName))
    {
        TextReader reader = new StreamReader(fileName);

        XmlSerializer ser =
            new XmlSerializer(typeof(List<ShoppingCartItem>));
        shoppingCart = (List<ShoppingCartItem>)ser.Deserialize(reader);
        reader.Close();
    }
}
```

> **Note** The code for this method is available in the file RestoreShoppingCart.txt located in the Chapter 7 folder.

This method uses the username to generate a file name using the same strategy as the saveShoppingCart method. If the file exists, this method opens the file and deserializes its contents into the shoppingCart variable before closing it. If there is no such file, the shoppingCart variable is left at its initial value of *null*.

> **Note** In a production environment, you should verify that the file contains a valid representation of a shopping cart before attempting to cast its contents and assign it to the shoppingCart variable.

6. In the AddItemToCart method, call the restoreShoppingCart method before examining the shopping cart, as follows:

```
public bool AddItemToCart(string productNumber)
{
    // Note: For clarity, this method performs very limited security
    // checking and exception handling
    try
    {
        // Check to see whether the user has already added this
        // product to the shopping cart          restoreShoppingCart();
        ShoppingCartItem item = find(shoppingCart, productNumber);
        ...
}
```

7. In the block of code that increments the volume field of an item, following the *if* statement, call the saveShoppingCart method to preserve its contents before returning:

```
if (item != null)
{
    item.Volume++;
    saveShoppingCart();
    return true;
}
```

8. In the block of code that adds a new item to the shopping cart, call the saveShopping-Cart method before returning:

```
if (productsReader.Read())
{
    ...
    // Add the new item to the shopping cart
    shoppingCart.Add(newItem);
    saveShoppingCart();

    // Indicate success
    return true;
}
```

There is no need to save the shopping cart whenever the method fails (returns *false*).

9. In the RemoveItemFromCart method, call the restoreShoppingCart method before examining the shopping cart, as follows:

```
public bool RemoveItemFromCart(string productNumber)
{
    // Determine whether the specified product has an
    // item in the shopping cart
    restoreShoppingCart();
    ShoppingCartItem item = find(shoppingCart, productNumber);
    ...
}
```

10. Save the shopping cart after successfully removing the specified item and before returning *true*:

```
// Indicate success
saveShoppingCart();
return true;
```

11. In the GetShoppingCart method, call the restoreShoppingCart method before iterating through the contents of the shopping cart, as follows:

```
public string GetShoppingCart()
{
    ...
    restoreShoppingCart();
    foreach (ShoppingCartItem item in shoppingCart)
    {
        ...
    }
}
```

12. Change the *InstanceContextMode* property of the *ServiceBehavior* attribute of the *ShoppingCartServiceImpl* class back to *InstanceContextMode.PerCall*:

```
[ServiceBehavior(InstanceContextMode = InstanceContextMode.PerCall)]
public class ShoppingCartServiceImpl : IShoppingCartService
{
    ...
}
```

Remember that this instance context mode releases the service instance at the end of each operation.

Test the state management feature of the ShoppingCartService service

1. Start the solution without debugging. In the ShoppingCartClient console window, press Enter.

   The client application adds the three items to the shopping cart and then displays the contents. The service saves and restores the shopping cart between operations.

2. Press Enter to close the client application console window. In the host application console window, press Enter to stop the service.

3. Start the solution again. In the client application console window, press Enter. This time, the client displays a shopping cart containing four water bottles and two mountain seat

assemblies. Because the state information is stored in an external file, it persists across service shutdown and restart.

> **Note**   As an additional exercise, you could add some code to the Checkout method to delete the shopping cart file for the user after they have paid for their goods.

4. Press Enter to close the client application console window. In the host application console window, press Enter to stop the service.

5. Using Windows Explorer, move to the Chapter 7\ShoppingCartService\Shopping-CartHost\bin\Debug folder. You should see an XML file in this folder called YourDomain!YourName.xml, where YourDomain is the name of your Windows XP computer, or the domain you are a member of, and YourName is your Windows username.

6. Open this file by using Notepad. It should look like this:

```xml
<?xml version="1.0" encoding="utf-8"?>
<ArrayOfShoppingCartItem xmlns:xsi="http://www.w3.org/2001/XMLSchema-
instance" xmlns:xsd="http://www.w3.org/2001/XMLSchema">
  <ShoppingCartItem>
    <ProductNumber>WB-H098</ProductNumber>
    <ProductName>Water Bottle - 30 oz.</ProductName>
    <Cost>4.9900</Cost>
    <Volume>4</Volume>
  </ShoppingCartItem>
  <ShoppingCartItem>
    <ProductNumber>SA-M198</ProductNumber>
    <ProductName>LL Mountain Seat Assembly</ProductName>
    <Cost>133.3400</Cost>
    <Volume>2</Volume>
  </ShoppingCartItem>
</ArrayOfShoppingCartItem>
```

Close Notepad and return to Visual Studio 2005.

7. Return to Visual Studio 2005, and edit the Program.cs file in the ShoppingCartClient project. Add the statements shown in bold below to the Main method, replacing LON-DEV-01 with the name of your domain or computer:

```csharp
...
// Connect to the ShoppingCartService service
ShoppingCartServiceClient proxy =
    new ShoppingCartServiceClient("HttpBinding_ShoppingCartService");

// Provide credentials to identify the user
proxy.ClientCredentials.Windows.ClientCredential.Domain = "LON-DEV-01";
proxy.ClientCredentials.Windows.ClientCredential.UserName = "Fred";
proxy.ClientCredentials.Windows.ClientCredential.Password = "Pa$$w0rd";

// Add two water bottles to the shopping cart
proxy.AddItemToCart("WB-H098");
...
```

You created the user Fred in Chapter 4, "Protecting an Enterprise WCF Service."

8. Start the solution without debugging. In the client application console window, press Enter. The client application displays a shopping cart containing only three items—this is Fred's shopping cart and not the one created earlier.

9. Press Enter to close the client application console window. In the host application console window, press Enter to stop the service.

10. In Windows Explorer, you should see another XML file in Chapter 7\ShoppingCartService\ShoppingCartHost\bin\Debug folder, called *YourDomain!*Fred.xml.

This solution implements an effective balance between resource use and responsiveness. Although a new service instance has to be created for every operation, and it takes time to restore and save session state, you do not need to retain a service instance in memory for every active client application, so the solution should scale effectively as more and more users access your service.

There are two other points worth making about the sample code in this exercise:

1. The restoreShoppingCart and saveShoppingCart methods are not currently thread-safe. This might not seem important as the ShoppingCartService uses the PerCall instance context mode and the single-threaded concurrency mode. However, if the same user (such as Fred) runs two concurrent instances of the client application, it will establish two concurrent instances of the service, which will both attempt to read and write the same file. The file access semantics of the .NET Framework class library prevents the two service instances from physically writing to the same file at the same time, but both service instances can still interfere with each other. Specifically, the saveShoppingCart method simply overwrites the XML file, so one instance of the service can obliterate any data saved by the other instance. In a production environment, you should take steps to prevent this situation from occurring, such as using some sort of locking scheme, or maybe using a database rather than a set of XML files.

2. The saveShoppingCart method creates human-readable XML files. In a production environment, you should arrange for these files to be stored in a secure location rather than the folder holding the service executables. For reasons of privacy, you don't want other users to be able to access these files or modify them.

Selectively Controlling Service Instance Deactivation

The service instance context mode determines the lifetime of service instances. This property is global across the service; you set it once for the service class, and the WCF runtime handles client application requests and directs them to an appropriate instance of the service (possibly creating a new instance of the service), irrespective of the operations that the client application actually invokes.

The WCF runtime enables you to selectively control when a service instance is deactivated, based on the operations being called. You can tag each method that implements an operation in a service with the *OperationBehavior* attribute. This attribute has a property called *ReleaseIn-*

stanceMode that you can use to modify the behavior of the service instance context mode. You use the *OperationBehavior* attribute like this:

```
[OperationBehavior(ReleaseInstanceMode = ReleaseInstanceMode.AfterCall)]
public bool Checkout()
{
    ...
}
```

The *ReleaseInstanceMode* property can take one of these values:

- *ReleaseInstanceMode.AfterCall*. When the operation completes, the WCF runtime will release the service instance for recycling. If the client invokes another operation, the WCF runtime will create a new service instance to handle the request.

- *ReleaseInstanceMode.BeforeCall*. If a service instance exists for the client application, the WCF runtime will release it for recycling and create a new one for handling the client application request.

- *ReleaseInstanceMode.BeforeAndAfterCall*. This is a combination of the previous two values; the WCF runtime creates a new service instance for handling the operation and releases the service instance for recycling when the operation completes.

- *ReleaseInstanceMode.None*. This is the default value. The service instance is managed according to the service instance context mode.

You should be aware that you can only use the *ReleaseInstanceMode* property to reduce the lifetime of a service instance, and you should understand the interplay between the *InstanceContextMode* property of the *ServiceBehavior* attribute and the *ReleaseInstanceMode* property of any *OperationBehavior* attributes adorning methods in the service class. For example, if you specify an *InstanceContextMode* value of *InstanceContextMode.PerCall* and a *ReleaseInstanceMode* value of *ReleaseInstanceMode.BeforeCall* for an operation, the WCF runtime will still release the service instance when the operation completes. The semantics of *InstanceContextMode.PerCall* cause the service to be released at the end of an operation, and the *ReleaseInstanceMode* property cannot force the WCF runtime to let the service instance live on. On the other hand, if you specify an *InstanceContextMode* value of *InstanceContextMode.Single* and a *ReleaseInstanceMode* value of *ReleaseInstanceMode.AfterCall* for an operation, the WCF runtime will release the service instance at the end of the operation, destroying any shared resources in the process (there are some threading issues that you should also consider as part of your design if the service is multi-threaded, in this case).

The *ReleaseInstanceMode* property of the OperationBehavior is most commonly used in conjunction with the PerSession instance context mode. If you need to create a service that uses PerSession instancing, you should carefully assess whether you actually need to hold a service instance for the entire duration of a session. For example, if you know that a client always invokes a particular operation or one of a set of operations at the end of a logical piece of work, you can consider setting the *ReleaseInstanceMode* property for the operation to *ReleaseInstanceMode.AfterCall.*

An alternative technique is to make use of some operation properties that you can use to control the sequence of operations in a session, which you will look at next.

Sequencing Operations in a WCF Service

When using the PerSession instance context mode, it is often useful to be able to control the order in which a client application invokes operations in a WCF service. Revisiting the ShoppingCartService service, suppose that you decide to use the PerSession instance context mode rather than PerCall. In this scenario, it might not make sense to allow the client application to remove an item from the shopping cart, query the contents of the shopping cart, or perform a checkout operation, if the user has not actually added any items to the shopping cart. Equally, it would be questionable practice to allow the user to add an item to the shopping cart after the user has already checked out and paid for the items in the cart. There is actually a simple sequence to the operations in the ShoppingCartService service, and the service should enforce this sequence:

1. Add an item to the shopping cart.

2. Add another item, remove an item, or query the contents of the shopping cart.

3. Check out and empty the shopping cart.

When you define an operation in a service contract, the *OperationContract* attribute provides two Boolean properties that you can use to control the order of operations and the consequent lifetime of the service instance:

■ *IsInitiating.* If you set this property to *true*, a client operation can invoke this operation to initiate a new session and create a new service instance. If a session already exists, then this property has no further effect. By default, this property is set to *true*. If you set this property to *false*, then a client application cannot invoke this operation until another operation has initiated the session and created a service instance. At least one operation in a service contract must have this property set to *true*.

■ *IsTerminating.* If you set this property to *true*, the WCF runtime will terminate the session and release the service instance when the operation completes. The client application must create a new connection to the service before invoking another operation, which must have the *IsInitiating* property set to true. The default value for this property is *false*. If no operations in a service contract specify a value of *true* for this property, the session remains active until the client application closes the connection to the service.

> **Note**   These properties are specific to WCF, and do not conform to any current WS-* standards. Using them can impact the interoperability of your service with client applications created by using other technologies.

The WCF runtime checks the values of these properties for consistency at runtime in conjunction with another property for the service contract called *SessionMode*. The *SessionMode* property of the service contract specifies whether the service supports reliable sessions. If you specify a value of *false* for the *IsInitiating* property of any operation, then you must set the *SessionMode* property of the service contract to *SessionMode.Required*, otherwise the WCF runtime will throw an exception. Similarly, you can only set the *IsTerminating* property to *true* if the *SessionMode* property of the service is set to *SessionMode.Required*.

> **More Info**   You will learn more about the *SessionMode* property of a service contract, and reliable sessions, in Chapter 9, "Implementing Reliable Sessions."

In the final set of exercises in this chapter, you will see how to apply the *IsInitiating* and *IsTerminating* properties of the *OperationBehavior* attribute.

Control the sequence of operations in the ShoppingCartService service

1. In Visual Studio 2005, edit the ShoppingCartService.cs file in theShoppingCartService project.

2. Add the *SessionMode* property to the *ServiceContract* attribute for the *IShoppingCartService* interface, as shown in bold below:

```
[ServiceContract(SessionMode = SessionMode.Required,
                 Namespace = "http://adventure-works.com/2007/03/01",
                 Name = "ShoppingCartService")]
public interface IShoppingCartService
{
    …
}
```

3. Modify the operations in the *IProductsService* interface by specifying which operations initiate a session and which operations cause a session to terminate, as follows:

```
public interface IShoppingCartService
{
    [OperationContract(Name="AddItemToCart", IsInitiating = true)]
    bool AddItemToCart(string productNumber);

    [OperationContract(Name = "RemoveItemFromCart", IsInitiating = false)]
    bool RemoveItemFromCart(string productNumber);

    [OperationContract(Name = "GetShoppingCart", IsInitiating = false)]
    string GetShoppingCart();

    [OperationContract(Name = "Checkout", IsInitiating = false,
```

```
                                                IsTerminating = true)]
        bool Checkout();
}
```

4. Change the *InstanceContextMode* property of the service to create a new instance of the service for each session:

```
[ServiceBehavior(InstanceContextMode = InstanceContextMode.PerSession)]
public class ShoppingCartServiceImpl : IShoppingCartService
{
    ...
}
```

5. In the AddItemToCart method, comment out the single statement that calls the restore-ShoppingCart method and the two statements that call the saveShoppingCart method.

   The service is using the PerSession instance context mode, so the session will maintain its own copy of the user's shopping cart in memory; these method calls are now unnecessary.

6. In the RemoveItemFromCart method, comment out the statement that calls the restore-ShoppingCart method and the statement that calls the saveShoppingCart method.

7. In the GetShoppingCart method, comment out the statement that calls the restoreShoppingCart method.

You can test the effects of these changes by modifying the client application.

Test the operation sequencing in the ShoppingCartService service

1. Edit the ShoppingCartServiceProxy.cs file in the ShoppingCartClient project. This is the proxy class that you generated earlier. You have modified the service contract, so you must update this class to reflect these changes. You can use the svcutil utility to generate a new version of the proxy, but the changes are quite small so it is easier to add them by hand:

   ❑ Modify the *ServiceContract* attribute for the *ShoppingCartService* interface and specify the *SessionMode* property:

   ```
   [System.ServiceModel.ServiceContractAttribute(SessionMode=System.ServiceModel.Ses
   sionMode.Required, Namespace="…", …)]
   ```

   ❑ Add the *IsInitiating* property to the *OperationContract* attribute of the AddItemTo-Cart, RemoveItemFromCart, and GetShoppingCart methods:

   ```
   [System.ServiceModel.OperationContractAttribute(IsInitiating = true, Action="…")]
   bool AddItemToCart(string productNumber);

   [System.ServiceModel.OperationContractAttribute(IsInitiating = false, Action="… "
   )] bool RemoveItemFromCart(string productNumber);

   [System.ServiceModel.OperationContractAttribute(IsInitiating = false, Action="…")
   ] string GetShoppingCart();
   ```

❑ Add the *IsInitiating* property and the *IsTerminating* property to the *OperationContract* attribute of the Checkout method:

```
[System.ServiceModel.OperationContractAttribute(IsInitiating = false,
IsTerminating = true, Action="...")]
bool Checkout();
```

2. Edit the Program.cs file in the ShoppingCartClient project. Add the statements shown below in bold between the code that displays the shopping cart and the code that closes the proxy:

```
...
// Query the shopping cart and display the result
string cartContents = proxy.GetShoppingCart();
Console.WriteLine(cartContents);

// Buy the goods in the shopping cart proxy.Checkout();
Console.WriteLine("Goods purchased");

// Go on another shopping expedition and buy more goods
// Add a road seat assembly to the shopping cart
proxy.AddItemToCart("SA-R127");

// Add a touring seat assembly to the shopping cart
proxy.AddItemToCart("SA-T872");

// Remove the road seat assembly
proxy.RemoveItemFromCart("SA-R127");

// Display the shopping basket
cartContents = proxy.GetShoppingCart();
Console.WriteLine(cartContents);

// Buy these goods as well proxy.Checkout();
Console.WriteLine("Goods purchased");

// Disconnect from the ShoppingCartService service
proxy.Close();
...
```

The first statement that invokes the Checkout operation terminates the session and destroys the shopping cart. The statements that follow therefore require a new session, with its own shopping cart.

3. Start the solution without debugging. In the ShoppingCartClient console window, press Enter.

The client application adds the three items to the shopping cart and outputs the contents. It then displays an error:

This demonstrates that the Checkout method successfully terminated the session. The service has closed the channel that the client application was using when the session finished. The client application must create a new channel before it can communicate with the service again.

4. Press Enter to close the client application console window. In the host application console window, press Enter to stop the service.

5. The simplest way to create a new connection is to rebuild the proxy. However, you must ensure that you provide the user's credentials again, as these will be lost when the new instance of the proxy is created.

   In Visual Studio 2005, add the following statements after the code that performs the Checkout operation in the Main method of the *Program* class in the ShoppingCartService project:

```
...
// Buy the goods in the shopping cart
proxy.Checkout();
Console.WriteLine("Goods purchased");

// Go an another shopping expedition and buy more goods
proxy = new ShoppingCartServiceClient("HttpBinding_ShoppingCartService");

// Provide credentials to identify the user
proxy.ClientCredentials.Windows.ClientCredential.Domain = "LON-DEV-01";
proxy.ClientCredentials.Windows.ClientCredential.UserName = "Fred";
proxy.ClientCredentials.Windows.ClientCredential.Password = "Pa$$w0rd";

// Add a road seat assembly to the shopping cart
proxy.AddItemToCart("SA-R127");
...
```

6. Start the solution again. In the ShoppingCartClient console window, press Enter.

   The client application successfully creates a second session after terminating the first. The second session has its own shopping cart:

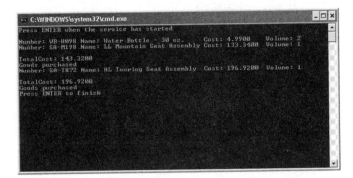

7. Press Enter to close the client application console window. In the host application console window, press Enter to stop the service.

As an additional exercise, you can test the effects of invoking the RemoveItemFromCart, GetShoppingCart, or Checkout operations without calling AddItemToCart first. These operations do not create a new session, and the client application should fail, with the exception shown in Figure 7-1.

Figure 7-1   Invoking operations in the wrong sequence.

Summary

In this chapter, you have seen the different options that the WCF runtime provides for creating an instance of a service. A service instance can exist for the duration of a single operation or for the entire session, until the client application closes the connection. In many cases, a service instance is private to a client, but WCF also supports singleton service instances that can be shared by multiple instances of a client. You have also seen how you can selectively control which operations create a new session and which operations close a session.

Chapter 8
Supporting Transactions

After completing this chapter, you will be able to:

- Describe the transaction management protocols available with WCF.
- Use transactions with WCF services and operations.
- Explain how to implement secure, distributed transactions by using the WS-AtomicTransaction protocol.
- Describe the impact that using transactions can have on the design of a WCF service.

A common requirement of most applications is the need to ensure internal consistency in the data that they manipulate. You can use transactions to help achieve this aim. A transaction is an atomic unit of work or a series of operations that should either all be performed or, if something unexpected happens, all be undone. The classic example of a transaction concerns the transfer of funds between two bank accounts, comprising the deduction of an amount of money from one account and an equivalent addition to the other account. If the addition operation fails, then the deduction operation must be undone, otherwise the money is lost (and the bank risks losing its trading license!). Traditionally, transactions were associated with database systems, but the semantics of transactions can be applied to any series of operations that involve making changes to data.

In a Web service environment, a transaction can span several services, possibly running on different computers within different organizations—this is a distributed transaction. In this environment, the underlying infrastructure must be able to guarantee consistency across a network and between potentially heterogeneous data stores. This is a complex task, bearing in mind the number of possible failure points in a network. This problem has been the subject of much research, and the commonly accepted standard mechanism for handling distributed transactions is the two-phase commit protocol. The OASIS organization has proposed the Web Services Atomic Transaction (WS-AtomicTransaction) specification describing a standard mechanism for handling transactions in a Web services infrastructure. The WS-AtomicTransaction specification defines the semantics of the two-phase commit protocol between Web services. Web services running on an infrastructure that conforms to the WS-AtomicTransaction specification should be interoperable with each other from a transactional perspective.

> **More Info**   For detailed information about the WS-AtomicTransaction specification, see the Web Services Atomic Transaction document on the Microsoft Web site at *http://msdn.microsoft.com/library/en-us/dnglobspec/html/ws-atomictransaction.pdf*.

The WS-AtomicTransaction specification is primarily useful when building Web services. However, WCF is not just concerned with Web services, and you can use it to build applications based on many other technologies, such as COM, MSMQ, and .NET Framework Remoting. Microsoft has provided their own transaction management features built into the current family of Microsoft Windows operating systems—Distributed Transaction Coordinator, or DTC, which uses its own optimized transaction protocol. Transactions based on the DTC transaction protocol are referred to as OLE transactions (OLE was the name of a technology that was the forerunner of COM). OLE transactions are ideal if you are building solutions based on Microsoft technologies.

The .NET Framework 3.0 provides a number of classes in the *System.Transactions* namespace. These classes provide an interface to the transaction management features of WCF, enabling you to develop code that is independent from the technology used to control the transactions that your code performs. In this chapter, you will see how to create a WCF service that supports transactions, and how to build client applications that can initiate and control them.

Using Transactions in the ShoppingCartService Service

The ShoppingCartService service currently enables users to add items to their shopping cart, but it does not perform many of the consistency checks that a production application should include. For example, the service always assumes that goods are in stock when adding them to the user's shopping cart and makes no attempt to update stock levels. You will rectify these shortcomings in the exercises in this section.

Implementing OLE Transactions

You will start by examining how to configure a WCF service to use transactions with a TCP endpoint. Endpoints established by using the TCP transport can incorporate OLE transactions.

Enable transactions in the ShoppingCartService service

1. Using Visual Studio 2005, open the solution file ShoppingCartService.sln located in the Microsoft Press\WCF Step By Step\Chapter 8\ShoppingCartService folder under your \My Documents folder.

   This solution contains a modified copy of the ShoppingCartService, and ShoppingCartServiceHost and ShoppingCartClient projects from Chapter 7, "Maintaining State and Sequencing Operations." The ShoppingCartHost project exposes a TCP endpoint rather than the HTTP endpoint that you configured in Chapter 7, and the ShoppingCartClient application has been simplified and modified to communicate using this TCP endpoint.

2. Add a reference to the *System.Transactions* assembly to the ShoppingCartService project. This assembly contains some of the classes and attributes required to manage transactions. Some other types and attributes you will use are in the *System.ServiceModel* assembly, which is already referenced by the ShoppingCartService project.

3. Edit the ShoppingCartService.cs file in the ShoppingCartService project.

4. Locate the *ServiceBehavior* attribute preceding the *ShoppingCartServiceImpl* class. Add the *TransactionIsolationLevel* property, shown in bold below, to this attribute:

```
[ServiceBehavior(InstanceContextMode = InstanceContextMode.PerSession,
TransactionIsolationLevel=System.Transactions.IsolationLevel.RepeatableRead)]
public class ShoppingCartServiceImpl : IShoppingCartService
{
    ...
}
```

The *TransactionIsolationLevel* property determines how the database management system (SQL Server in the exercises in this book) lets concurrent transactions overlap. In a typical system, you need to allow multiple concurrent users to access the database at the same time. However, this can lead to problems if two users try to modify the same data at the same time or one user tries to query data that another user is modifying. You must ensure that concurrent users cannot interfere adversely with each other—they must be isolated. Typically, whenever a user modifies, inserts, or deletes data during a transaction, the database management system locks the affected data until the transaction completes. If the transaction commits, the database management system makes the changes permanent. If an error occurs and the transaction rolls back, the database management system undoes the changes. The *TransactionIsolationLevel* property specifies how the locks taken out during a transaction when it modifies data affect other transactions attempting to access the same data. It can take one of several values. The most common ones are:

- ❑ *IsolationLevel.ReadUncommitted*. This isolation level enables the transaction to read data that another transaction has modified and locked but not yet committed. This isolation level provides the most concurrency, at the risk of the user being presented with "dirty" data that might change unexpectedly if the modifying transaction rolls back the changes rather than committing them.

- ❑ *IsolationLevel.ReadCommitted*. This isolation level prevents the transaction from reading data that another transaction has modified, but not yet committed. The reading transaction will be forced to wait until the modified data is unlocked. Although this isolation level prevents read access to dirty data, it does not guarantee consistency; if the transaction reads the same data twice, there is the possibility that another transaction might have modified the data in between reads, so the reading transaction would be presented with two different versions of the data.

- ❑ *IsolationLevel.RepeatableRead*. This isolation level is similar to the *ReadCommitted* isolation level but causes the transaction reading the data to lock it until the reading transaction finishes (the *ReadCommitted* isolation level does not cause a transaction to lock data that it reads). The transaction can then safely read the same data as many times as it wants and it cannot be changed by another transaction until this transaction has completed. This isolation level therefore provides more consistency, at the cost of reduced concurrency.

❑ *IsolationLevel.Serializable*. This isolation level takes the *RepeatableRead* isolation level one stage further. When using the *RepeatableRead* isolation level, data read by a transaction cannot change. However, it is possible for a transaction to execute the same query twice and obtain different results if another transaction inserts data that matches the query criteria: new rows suddenly appear. The *Serializable* isolation level prevents this inconsistency from occurring by restricting the rows that other concurrent transactions can add to the database. This isolation level provides the greatest degree of consistency, but the degree of concurrency can be significantly reduced.

Unless you have good reason to choose otherwise, use the *IsolationLevel.RepeatableRead* isolation level.

5. In the *ShoppingCartServiceImpl* class, add the following *OperationBehavior* attribute to the AddItemToCart method:

```
[OperationBehavior(TransactionScopeRequired=true,
                TransactionAutoComplete=false)]
public bool AddItemToCart(string productNumber)
{
    ...
}
```

You are going to modify the AddItemToCart method to check the level of stock for the selected product and modify the stock level if the product is available. The client application should only invoke this operation in the context of a transaction, to ensure that the changes can be undone if some sort of failure occurs. Setting the *TransactionScopeRequired* property of the *OperationBehavior* attribute to *true* forces the operation to execute as part of a transaction: either the client application must initiate the transaction (you will see how to do this shortly) or the WCF runtime will automatically create a new transaction when this operation runs.

The *TransactionAutoComplete* property specifies what happens to the transaction when the operation finishes. If you set this property to *true*, the transaction automatically commits and makes all its changes permanent. Setting this property to *false* keeps the transaction active; the changes are not committed yet. The default value for this property is *true*. In the case of the AddItemToCart method, you don't want to commit changes and finish the transaction until the user has checked out, so the code sets this property to *false*.

6. Add the *TransactionFlow* attribute shown below to definition of the AddItemToCart method *in the IShoppingCartService* **interface**, after the *OperationContract* attribute. Add the same attribute to the remaining methods in this interface, as shown in bold below:

```
public interface IShoppingCartInterface
{
```

```
[OperationContract(Name = "AddItemToCart", IsInitiating = true)]
[TransactionFlow(TransactionFlowOption.Mandatory)]
public bool AddItemToCart(string productNumber)

[OperationContract(Name = "RemoveItemFromCart", IsInitiating = false)]
[TransactionFlow(TransactionFlowOption.Mandatory)]
bool RemoveItemFromCart(string productNumber);

[OperationContract(Name = "GetShoppingCart", IsInitiating = false)]
[TransactionFlow(TransactionFlowOption.Mandatory)]
string GetShoppingCart();

[OperationContract(Name = "Checkout", IsInitiating = false,
                   IsTerminating = true)]
[TransactionFlow(TransactionFlowOption.Mandatory)]
bool Checkout();
}
```

The description of the *TransactionScopeRequired* property in the previous step mentioned that the WCF runtime automatically creates a new transaction when invoking an operation if necessary. In the shopping cart scenario, you want the client application to be responsible for creating its own transactions. You can enforce this rule by applying the *TransactionFlow* attribute to the operation contract. Specifying a parameter of *TransactionFlowOption.Mandatory* indicates that the client application must create a transaction before calling this operation and send the details of this transaction as part of the SOAP message header when invoking the operation. The other values you can specify are *TransactionFlowOption.Allowed*, which will use a transaction created by the client if one exists but the WCF runtime will create a new transaction if not, and *TransactionFlowOption.NotAllowed*, which will always cause the WCF runtime to disregard any client transaction and always create a new one.

The default value is *TransactionFlowOption.NotAllowed*.

7. You can now amend the code in the *ShoppingCartServiceImpl* class to check stock levels and update them in the database, safe in the knowledge that this functionality is protected by transactions—if anything should go wrong, the changes will be rolled back automatically.

    Add the decrementStock method, shown below, to the *ShoppingCartServiceImpl* class:

```
public bool decrementStock(string productNumber)
{
    // Update the first row for this product in the
    // ProductInventory table that has a quantity value
    // of greater than zero

    try
    {
        Database dbAdventureWorks =
            DatabaseFactory.CreateDatabase("AdventureWorksConnection");

        string inventoryUpdate =
```

```
@"UPDATE Production.ProductInventory
SET Quantity = Quantity - 1
WHERE rowguid IN
  (SELECT TOP(1) rowguid
   FROM Production.ProductInventory
   WHERE Quantity > 0
   AND ProductID IN
       (SELECT ProductID
        FROM Production.Product
        WHERE ProductNumber = '" + productNumber + "'))";

    // Execute the update statement and verify that it updated one row
    // If it did, then return true.
    // If it did not, then either the product does not exist,
    // or there are none in stock, so return false
    int numRowsChanged = (int)dbAdventureWorks.ExecuteNonQuery(
        CommandType.Text, inventoryUpdate);

    return (numRowsChanged == 1);
}

// On an exception, indicate failure
catch (Exception e)
{
    return false;
}
}
```

> **Note** The code for this method is available in the file DecrementStock.txt located in the Chapter 8 folder. As with previous examples using SQL statements, this method is greatly simplified for clarity (and because this is a book about WCF rather than how to write database access code) and does no checking for a SQL Injection attack or any other potential hazards.

The purpose of this method is to verify that the specified product is available and then update the stock level for this product. If you recall from Chapter 1, "Introducing Windows Communication Foundation," a product can be stored in more than one location and so have more than one row in the ProductInventory table. The rather complicated-looking SQL UPDATE statement in this method updates the first row for the product that it finds in the ProductInventory table and that has a quantity of greater than zero. If the update fails to modify a row, this method returns *false* to indicate either insufficient stock (all rows have a zero for the quantity) or that no such product exists (there are no rows). If the update changes exactly one row, then this method returns *true* to indicate success.

> **Note**   Strictly speaking, the service should save the value in the rowguid column of the row it updates in the ProductInventory table, so that the corresponding row can be incremented again if the user decides to remove the item from the shopping cart later. This functionality is left as an exercise for you to perform in your own time.
>
> It is also possible for this method to cause a database deadlock if multiple service instances execute it simultaneously. In this situation, SQL Server picks one of the transactions (referred to rather prosaically as the "victim" by SQL Server) and aborts it, releasing any locks held and hopefully enabling other concurrent transactions to complete. This will cause the UPDATE operation to fail and the *ExecuteNonQuery* command to throw an exception. If this happens, the method returns *false*. The important point to learn from this is that using transactions ensures that the database will remain consistent, even in the face of unforeseen eventualities.

8. In the AddItemToCart method, change the code that increments the volume of an item in the shopping cart also to update the stock level in the database, as shown in bold below:

```
...
// If so, increment the volume
if (item != null)
{
    if (decrementStock(productNumber))
    {        item.Volume++;
        return true;
    }
    else
    {
        return false;
    } }
...
```

9. Modify the *else* statement to check that sufficient stock is available in the database before retrieving the details of the product from the database, as shown in bold below:

```
...
// Otherwise retrieve the details of the product from the database
else if (decrementStock(productNumber))
{
    // Connect to the AdventureWorks database
    ...
} else
{
    return false;
}
catch (Exception e)
{
    ...
}
```

Leave the block of code that connects to the database and retrieves the product details untouched. Be sure to add the additional *else* statement to the end of the block, immediately before the *catch* block, as shown above.

10. Add an *OperationBehavior* attribute to the RemoveItemFromCart method, setting the *TransactionScopeRequired* property to *true* and the *TransactionAutoComplete* property to *false*. The method should look like this:

```
[OperationBehavior(TransactionScopeRequired=true,
                   TransactionAutoComplete=false)]
public bool RemoveItemFromCart(string productNumber)
{
    ...
}
```

> **Note**   If you have the time, you might care to add the appropriate code to this method to increment the stock level in the database after removing the item from the shopping cart.

11. Add another *OperationBehavior* attribute to the GetShoppingCart method, setting the *TransactionScopeRequired* property to *true* and the *TransactionAutoComplete* property to *false*:

```
[OperationBehavior(TransactionScopeRequired=true,
                   TransactionAutoComplete=false)]
public bool GetShoppingCart()
{
    ...
}
```

The GetShoppingCart method does not actually query or modify the database but could be (and probably would be) called by the client application during a transaction. It is important that this method does not commit the transaction, hence the need to set the *TransactionAutoComplete* property to *false*. You cannot set the *TransactionAutoComplete* property to *false* without setting the *TransactionScopeRequired* property to *true*.

12. Add a final *OperationBehavior* attribute to the Checkout method, setting the *TransactionScopeRequired* property to *true* and the *TransactionAutoComplete* property to *false*:

```
[OperationBehavior(TransactionScopeRequired=true,
                   TransactionAutoComplete=false)]
public bool Checkout()
{
    ...
}
```

Having modified the code in the service, you must also change the configuration of the service endpoint to enable the WCF runtime to "flow" transactions from the client application into the service. Information about transactions is included in the headers of the SOAP messages sent by client applications invoking the operations.

Configure the ShoppingCartService service to flow transactions from client applications

1. Edit the App.config file for the ShoppingCartHost project by using the WCF Service Configuration Editor.

2. In the WCF Service Configuration Editor, in the left pane, click the Bindings folder. In the right pane, click the New Binding Configuration link.

3. In the Create a New Binding dialog box, select the netTcpBinding binding type, and then click OK.

4. In the right pane, change the *Name* property of the binding to *ShoppingCartServiceNetTcpBindingConfig*. In the General section of the pane, set the *TransactionFlow* property to *True*. Verify that the *TransactionProtocol* property is set to *OleTransactions*.

   The *TransactionFlow* property indicates that the service should expect to receive information about transactions in the SOAP messages it receives.

   The *TransactionProtocol* property specifies the transaction protocol the service should use. By default, endpoints based on the TCP transport use the internal DTC protocol when performing distributed transactions. However, you can configure them to use transactions that follow the WS-AtomicTransaction protocol by changing this property to WSAtomicTransactionOctober2004 (you can probably guess the date of the WS-AtomicTransaction specification to which WCF conforms).

5. In the left pane, in the Services folder expand the ShoppingCartService.ShoppingCartServiceImpl node, expand the Endpoints folder, and then click the ShoppingCartServiceNetTcpEndpoint node. In the right pane, set the *BindingConfguration* property of the endpoint to *ShoppingCartServiceNetTcpBindingConfig*.

6. Save the configuration file, and then exit the WCF Service Configuration Editor.

7. In Visual Studio 2005, double-click the App.config file in the ShoppingCartHost project to display it in the code view window. Locate the connection string that the service uses for connecting to the *AdventureWorks* database. Modify this connection string to include support for multiple active result sets:

```
<connectionStrings>
  <add name="AdventureWorksConnection" connectionString=
    "Database=AdventureWorks;Server=(local)\SQLEXPRESS;Integrated Security=SSPI;
MultipleActiveResultSets=True;"
    providerName="System.Data.SqlClient" />
</connectionStrings>
```

   SQL Server 2005 requires you to enable multiple active result sets, also known as MARS, to operate with DTC in this environment.

You have configured the ShoppingCartService service to expect the client application to invoke operations within the scope of a transaction. You now need to modify the client application to actually create this transaction.

Create a transaction in the client application

1. In Visual Studio 2005, add a reference to the *System.Transactions* assembly to the ShoppingCartClient project.

2. Edit the Program.cs file in the ShoppingCartClient project, and add the following *using* statement to the list at the top of the file:

```
using System.Transactions;
```

3. In the Main method, surround the statements that invoke the operations in the ShoppingCartService service with the *using* block shown in bold below:

```
TransactionOptions tOpts = new TransactionOptions();
tOpts.IsolationLevel = IsolationLevel.RepeatableRead;
tOpts.Timeout = new TimeSpan(0, 1, 0);
using (TransactionScope tx =
    new TransactionScope(TransactionScopeOption.RequiresNew, tOpts))
{
    // Add two water bottles to the shopping cart
    proxy.AddItemToCart("WB-H098");
    proxy.AddItemToCart("WB-H098");

    // Add a mountain seat assembly to the shopping cart
    proxy.AddItemToCart("SA-M198");

    // Query the shopping cart and display the result
    string cartContents = proxy.GetShoppingCart();
    Console.WriteLine(cartContents);

    // Buy the goods in the shopping cart
    proxy.Checkout();
    Console.WriteLine("Goods purchased");
}
    // Disconnect from the ShoppingCartService service
proxy.Close();
```

You can create a new transaction in several ways: a service can initiate a new transaction automatically by setting the *TransactionScopeRequired* attribute of the *OperationBehavior* property to *true* as described earlier, an operation can explicitly start a new transaction by creating a *CommittableTransaction* object, or the client application can implicitly create a new transaction. In a WCF client application, the recommended approach is to use a *TransactionScope* object.

When you create a new *TransactionScope* object, any transactional operations that follow are automatically enlisted into a transaction. If the WCF runtime detects that there is no active transaction when you create a new *TransactionScope* object, it can initiate a new transaction and performs the operations in the context of this transaction. In this case, the transaction remains active until the *TransactionScope* object is destroyed. For this reason, it is common practice to use a *using* block to explicitly delimit the scope of a transaction.

The TransactionScopeOption parameter to the TransactionScope constructor deter-mines how the WCF runtime uses an existing transaction. If this parameter is set to *TransactionScopeOption.RequiresNew*, the WCF runtime will always create a new transac-tion. The other values you can specify are *TransactionScopeOption.Required*, which will only create a new transaction if there is not already another transaction in scope (referred to as the "ambient transaction"), and *TransactionScopeOption.Suppress*, which causes all operations in the context of the *TransactionScope* object to be performed with-out using a transaction (operations will not participate in the ambient transaction, if there is one).

The transaction isolation level of any new transactions should match the requirements of the service. You can specify the isolation level by creating a *TransactionOptions* object and referencing it in the TransactionScope constructor, as shown in the code. You can also specify a timeout value for transactions. This can improve the responsiveness of an application, as transactions will not wait for an indeterminate period for resources locked by other transactions to become available—the WCF runtime throws an excep-tion that the client application should be prepared to handle.

4. Add the *if* block and statement shown below around the code that invokes the Checkout operation:

```
// Buy the goods in the shopping cart if (proxy.Checkout())
{    tx.Complete();
    Console.WriteLine("Goods purchased"); }
```

By default, when the flow of control leaves the *using* block (either by the natural flow of the code or because of an exception), the transaction will be aborted and the work it per-formed undone. This is probably not what you want! Calling the Complete method on the *TransactionScope* object before destroying it indicates that work has been completed successfully and that the transaction should be committed. In the ShoppingCartService service, the Checkout method returns *true* if the checkout operation is successful, *false* otherwise. If the Checkout method fails and returns *false*, the Complete method will not be called and any changes made to the database by the transaction will be rolled back.

> **Note** Calling the Complete method does not actually guarantee that your work *will* be committed. It indicates only that the work performed inside the transaction scope was successful and *can* be committed in the absence of any other problems. You can nest transaction scopes; you can create a new *TransactionScope* object inside the *using* statement of another *TransactionScope* object. If the nested *TransactionScope* object cre-ates a new transaction (called a nested transaction), calling the Complete method on the nested *TransactionScope* object commits the nested transaction *with respect to* the transaction (called the parent transaction) used by the outer *TransactionScope* object. If the parent transaction aborts, then the nested transaction will also be aborted.

5. In an earlier exercise, you modified the contract for the ShoppingCartService by adding the *TransactionFlow* attribute to each operation. You must therefore update the proxy

that the client application uses to ensure that the proxy sends the details of transactions to the service. You can either perform this task by regenerating the code for the proxy class by using the svcutil utility (Chapter 7 contains the steps for doing this) or you can modify the code manually. In this example it is instructive to perform this task by hand and edit the code yourself, as follows:

❑ Open the ShoppingCartServiceProxy.cs file in the ShoppingCartClient project.

❑ Add the following *using* statement to the top of the file:

```
using System.ServiceModel;
```

❑ Locate the *ShoppingCartService* interface. This is the first interface in the *ShoppingCartClient.ShoppingCartService* interface.

❑ Add the *TransactionFlow* attribute to each method in this interface, as shown in bold below. Do not change any other code or attributes in this interface (the properties of the OperationContractAttribute for each method have been omitted, for clarity—leave these intact in your code):

```
public interface ShoppingCartService
{
    [System.ServiceModel.OperationContractAttribute(…)]
    [TransactionFlow(TransactionFlowOption.Mandatory)]
    bool AddItemToCart(string productNumber);

    [System.ServiceModel.OperationContractAttribute(…)]
    [TransactionFlow(TransactionFlowOption.Mandatory)]
    bool RemoveItemFromCart(string productNumber);

    [System.ServiceModel.OperationContractAttribute(…)]
    [TransactionFlow(TransactionFlowOption.Mandatory)]
    string GetShoppingCart();

    [System.ServiceModel.OperationContractAttribute(…)]
    [TransactionFlow(TransactionFlowOption.Mandatory)]
    bool Checkout();
}
```

The final step is to configure the endpoint for the client application to send information about its transactions across the network to the service.

Configure the client application to flow transactions to the ShoppingCartService service

1. Edit the App.config file for the ShoppingCartClient project by using the WCF Service Configuration Editor.

2. In the WCF Service Configuration Editor, in the left pane, click the Bindings folder. In the right pane, click the New Binding Configuration link.

3. In the Create a New Binding dialog box, select the netTcpBinding binding type and then click OK.

4. In the right pane, change the *Name* property of the binding to *ShoppingCartClientNetTcp-BindingConfig*. In the General section of the pane, set the *TransactionFlow* property to *True* and verify that the *TransactionProtocol* property is set to *OleTransactions*.

5. In the left pane, select the *NetTcpBinding_ShoppingCartService* node in the Endpoints folder under the Client folder. In the right pane, set the BindingConfguration property of the endpoint to *ShoppingCartClientNetTcpBindingConfig*.

6. Save the configuration file and then exit the WCF Service Configuration Editor.

You can now test the transactional version of the ShoppingCartService service and the client application.

Test the transactional implementation of the ShoppingCartService service

1. On the Windows Start menu, open the Control Panel, click Performance and Maintenance, click Administrative Tools, and then double-click Component Services.

    The Component Services console appears. You can use this console to monitor the transactions being processed by DTC.

> **Note**   If you are using Windows Vista, open Windows Explorer, move to the C:\Windows\System32 folder, and then double-click the file comexp.msc to start the Component Services console.

2. In the Component Services console, expand the Component Services node, expand the Computers folder, right-click the My Computer node and then click Stop MS DTC. Right-click the My Computer node and then click Start MS DTC.

    Stopping and restarting DTC clears its statistics, so you can more easily monitor the progress of your transactions.

> **Note**   The Component Services console under Windows Vista does not provide the facility for stopping and restarting MS DTC, so you will have to work without clearing the statistics.

3. Under the My Computer node, expand the Distributed Transaction Coordinator folder and then click Transaction Statistics.

> **Note**   Under Windows Vista, expand the Local DTC node in the Distributed Transaction Coordinator folder, and then click Transaction Statistics.

    The right pane displays the statistics, which should all currently be set to zero (unless you are using Windows Vista).

4. Return to Visual Studio 2005, and start the solution without debugging.

> **Note**   If a Windows Security Alert appears, click Unblock to allow the service to use TCP port 9080.

In the ShoppingCartClient console window displaying the message "Press ENTER when the service has started," press Enter.

The client application displays the shopping cart containing two water bottles and a mountain seat assembly, followed by the "Goods purchased" method. However, there also appears to be a problem as the application throws an exception reporting, "The transaction has aborted":

Press Enter to close the client application console window. In the host application console window, press Enter to stop the service.

5.   Switch to the Component Services console. It should confirm that the one transaction you have performed since you restarted DTC has aborted:

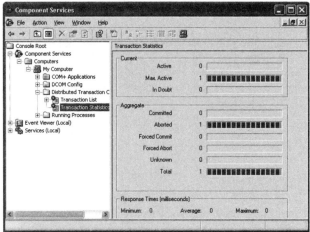

The problem is actually quite subtle. Remember that the Complete method of a *TransactionScope* object indicates only that the transaction can be committed. However, before committing a transaction, the transaction must have actually done some work and completed this work successfully. Although the AddItemToCart operation invoked in the ShoppingCartService service clearly updates the database, it never actually indicates that the work was successfully completed. The same is true of the other operations. Consequently, when the runtime examines the state of the transaction created for the *TransactionScope* object, in the absence of any information indicating success, it decides to abort the transaction and rollback the changes.

You need to make some modifications to the ShoppingCartService service to indicate when a transaction has completed successfully. Bear in mind that you can complete a transaction only once, so in the shopping cart scenario, the best place to do this is in the Checkout method.

6. In Visual Studio 2005, edit the ShoppingCartService.cs file in the ShoppingCartService project and find the Checkout method towards the end of the file. The *OperationBehavior* attribute for this method currently sets the *TransactionAutoComplete* property to *false*. You could set this property to *true*, and this would cause the transaction to complete successfully at the end of the method, as long as it did not throw an unhandled exception (if the method throws an exception that you handle in the same method, the transaction will not abort). But in the real world, you would probably want to be a bit more selective than this; for example, the transaction should only commit if this method ascertains that the user has a valid account with Adventure-Works, for billing purposes. However, for this exercise you will simply add a statement that indicates that the transaction can be committed.

Modify the code in the Checkout method as shown in bold below:

```
[OperationBehavior(TransactionScopeRequired = true,
                   TransactionAutoComplete = false)]
public bool Checkout()
{
    // Not currently implemented
    // - just indicate that the transaction completed successfully
    // and return true
    OperationContext.Current.SetTransactionComplete();
    return true;
}
```

The *OperationContext* object provides access to the execution context of the operation. The SetTransactionComplete method of the *Current* property indicates that the current transaction has completed successfully and can be committed when the client application calls the Complete method of the *TransactionScope* object containing this transaction. If you need to abort the transaction, just exit the method without calling the SetTransactionComplete method, as you did before.

> **Note**   Calling the SetTransactionComplete method indicates that you have finished all the transactional work. If a transaction spans multiple operations, you cannot invoke any further operations that have the *TransactionScopeRequired* property of the *OperationBehavior* attribute set to *true* and that execute in the same transaction scope. Addi-

tionally, you can call the SetTransactionComplete method only once in a transaction. A subsequent call to this method inside the scope of the same transaction will raise an exception. Finally, if you call the SetTransactionComplete method, but later fail to call the Complete method of the *TransactionScope* object, the transaction will be silently rolled back.

7. Start the solution without debugging. In the ShoppingCartClient console window, press Enter.

   This time, the client application executes without reporting the message, "The transaction has aborted."

8. Press Enter to close the client application console window. In the host application console window, press Enter to stop the service.

9. Return to the Component Services console. This time, you can see that the transaction committed:

10. To verify that the database is being updated, open a Visual Studio 2005 command prompt window, and move to the Microsoft Press\WCF Step By Step\Chapter 8 folder under your \My Documents folder. Type the following command:

    ```
    StockLevels
    ```

    This command executes a script that queries the *AdventureWorks* database, displaying the current stock level of water bottles and mountain seat assemblies:

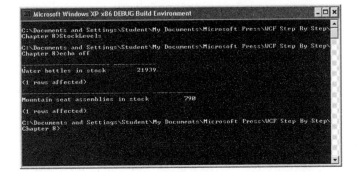

Make a note of these stock levels.

> **Note**   Your stock levels might be different from those shown in this image.

11. Leave the command prompt window open and return to Visual Studio 2005. Start the solution again without debugging. In the ShoppingCartClient console window, press Enter. When the client application has finished, press Enter to close the client application console window. In the host application console window, press Enter to stop the service.

12. Return to the command prompt window and execute the *StockLevels* command again. Verify that the stock level for water bottles has decreased by two, and the stock level for mountain seat assemblies has decreased by one.

13. Examine the transaction statistics in the Component Services console. You should see that the number of committed transactions is now 2.

14. Close the Component Services console.

Implementing WS-AtomicTransaction Transactions

The NetTcpBinding binding uses OLE transactions and Microsoft's own protocol for communicating through DTC to other Microsoft-specific services, such as SQL Server. In a heterogeneous environment, you cannot use OLE transactions. Instead, you should use a more standardized mechanism such as the WS-AtomicTransaction protocol. When using the NetTcpBinding or NetNamedPipeBinding bindings, you can explicitly specify which transaction protocol to use by setting the *TransactionProtocol* property that these bindings provide. With the HTTP family of bindings, the WCF runtime itself selects the transaction protocol based on the Windows configuration, the transport you are using, and the format of the SOAP header used to flow the transaction from the client application to the service. For example, a WCF client application connecting to a WCF service through an endpoint based on the "http" scheme will use OLE transactions. If the computers hosting the WCF client application and WCF service are configured to support the WS-AtomicTransaction protocol over a specific port, and the client application connects to the service through an endpoint based on the "https" scheme that uses this port, then transactions will follow the WS-AtomicTransaction protocol.

The choice of transaction protocol should be transparent to your services and client applications. The code that you write to initiate, control, and support transactions based on the WS-AtomicTransaction protocol is the same as that for manipulating OLE transactions; the same service can execute using OLE transactions or WS-AtomicTransaction transactions, depending on how you configure the service.

> **Important**   The BasicHttpBinding binding does not support transactions (OLE or WS-AtomicTransaction).

If you wish to use the implementation of the WS-AtomicTransaction protocol provided by the .NET Framework 3.0 with the HTTP bindings, you must configure support for the WS-AtomicTransaction protocol in DTC.

> **Note**   If you are using Windows XP, Service Pack 2, you must install the hotfix for adding WS-AtomicTransaction support to DTC. You can download this hotfix from the Microsoft Web site at *http://www.microsoft.com/downloads/details.aspx?familyid=86B93C6D-0174-4E25-9E5D-D949DC92D7E8&displaylang=en.*

The .NET Framework 3.0 contains a command line tool called wsatConfig.exe that you can use to configure WS-AtomicTransaction protocol support. The Microsoft Windows SDK provides a graphical user interface component that performs the same tasks, and that plugs into the Component Services console, as shown in Figure 8-1. You can access this interface by opening the Properties dialog box for My Computer and clicking the WS-AT tab.

The implementation of the WS-AtomicTransaction protocol over HTTP requires mutual authentication, integrity, and confidentiality for all messages. This means that you must use the HTTPS transport. If the WCF service listens on a port other than 443 (the default HTTPS port), you should specify the port in the WS-AT tab. You must also provide a certificate that the service can use to encrypt messages. Additionally, the WS-AT tab lets you specify which users are authorized to access your service, identifying these accounts by their Windows credentials or certificates.

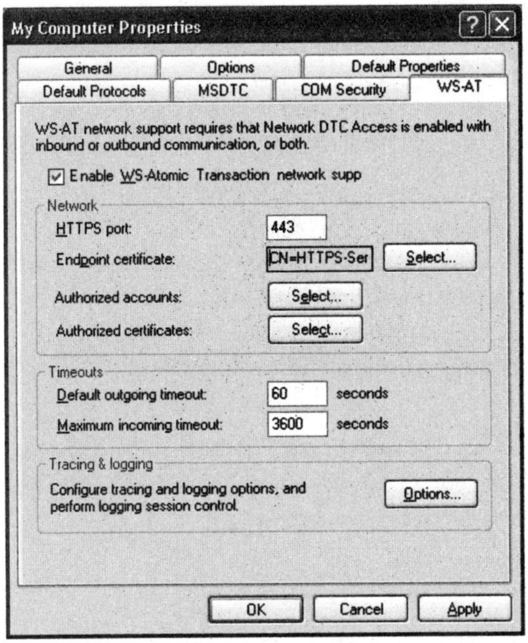

Figure 8-1   The WS-AtomicTransaction configuration tab in the Component Services console.

> **Note**   You must register the assembly that implements the user interface before you can use it in the Component Services console. From a command prompt window, move to the \Program Files\Microsoft SDKs\Windows\V6.0\Bin folder and type the following command:
>
> ```
> regasm /codebase WsatUI.dll
> ```

> **More Info**   See Chapter 5, "Protecting a WCF Service over the Internet," for more details about configuring SSL and using certificates to identify users.

Designing a WCF Service to Support Transactions

The previous sections have shown you how to implement transactions in a WCF service, but there are a number of issues you should be aware of when designing a WCF service that requires transactions.

Transactions and Service Instance Context Modes

If you set the *TransactionAutoComplete* property of the *OperationBehavior* attribute of one or more methods in a WCF service to *false*, you must use the PerSession service instance context mode. This is because the WCF runtime needs to maintain transactional state between calls to operations. If you set the *TransactionAutoComplete* property to *true* for every operation, the

WCF runtime does not need to maintain transactional state as it completes the current transaction at the end of each operation, and you can use the PerCall and Single service instance context modes.

If you use the PerSession instance context mode, WCF provides two additional properties you can specify as part of the *ServiceBehavior* attribute:

- *ReleaseServiceInstanceOnTransactionComplete*. If you set this property to *true*, the WCF runtime will automatically end the session and recycle the service instance at the end of each transaction. If a client application invokes another operation, it must create and connect to a new instance of the service, as described in Chapter 7. Setting this property to *false* allows a session to handle multiple transactions. The default value of this property is *true*.

- *TransactionAutoCompleteOnSessionClose*. If you set this property to *true*, the WCF runtime will automatically complete the current transaction when the client application closes the session. The default value for this property is *false*.

Transactions and Messaging

A transactional operation sends information back to the client application about the state of the transaction. All the operations that you have defined so far have followed the request/response model; the client application sends a request and waits for a response from the service. You will see in Chapter 11, "Invoking WCF Service Operations Asynchronously," that you can define one-way operations that do not send a response back to the client application. One-way operations cannot be transactional.

Transactions and Multi-Threading

You saw in Chapter 7 that a WCF service can enable multiple concurrent calls to operations if you set the *ConcurrencyMode* property of the *ServiceBehavior* attribute to *ConcurrencyMode.Multiple*. You should note the following points when attempting to use this mode:

- The *TransactionAutoComplete* property of the *OperationBehavior* attribute must be set to *true* for every operation in the service. Transactions cannot span multiple operations.

- The *ReleaseServiceInstanceOnTransactionComplete* property of the *ServiceBehavior* attribute for the service must be set to *false*. You must explicitly release the service instance by closing the connection from the client.

- The *TransactionAutoCompleteOnSessionClose* property of the *ServiceBehavior* property for the service must be set to *true*. All transactions on all threads must be terminated when the session closes.

Long-Running Transactions

Transactions lock resources. To minimize the impact on other users and to maintain through-put and concurrency, you should design transactions to be as short-lived as possible. Avoid performing tasks such as waiting for user input while executing a transaction.

In a business-to-business scenario, this is not always possible. It is common for inter-business transactions to take a considerable period of time (possibly days). Such long-running transactions require you to adopt an alternative strategy. The most common solution is for a service to perform any updates and release any locks on resources immediately, effectively treating each modification as a singleton transaction in its own right. The service should maintain a list of changes it has made. At some later point, if the service needs to rollback these changes, it can consult this list and perform updates that reverse their effect. This undo operation is sometimes referred to as a "compensating transaction."

Using compensating transactions has a number of issues. For example, it might not be possible to undo an operation if another user has made further changes in the interim. Additionally, other users can see the changes that have been made, so if you undo these changes, other users' transactions might cause some inconsistencies.

Detailed discussion of creating and rolling back long-running transactions is outside the scope of this book, but Microsoft provides support for defining compensating transactions by using Windows Workflow Foundation.

> **More Info**   For further details about Microsoft Windows Workflow Foundation, see the Windows Workflow Foundation Web site at *http://msdn.microsoft.com/winfx/technologies/workflow/default.aspx*.

Summary

In this chapter, you have seen how to define and control transactions in a WCF client application and service. An application can enlist in an existing transaction, or create a new transaction, by instantiating a *TransactionScope* object with the appropriate parameters. Transactions can flow from a client application, across the network, to the service. You can specify the trans-actional requirements of a WCF service by using the *ServiceBehavior* and *OperationBehavior* attributes. The operations in a WCF service can indicate that the transaction can be committed, by executing the OperationContext.Current.SetTransactionComplete method. An application can then finish a transaction by calling the Complete method of the *TransactionScope* object.

You have seen how to configure a WCF service and client application to include information about the transactions they are performing in the SOAP messages that they send and receive. You have also learned how using transactions can affect the design of a WCF service.

Chapter 9
Implementing Reliable Sessions

After completing this chapter, you will be able to:

- Explain how to implement reliable sessions in a WCF service and client application.
- Describe how the WS-ReliableMessaging protocol works with the WCF runtime.
- Create a custom binding that implements replay detection.

Most of the time, apart from when you are performing the exercises in this book, when you build WCF client applications and services, you will expect them to be deployed to different computers and communicate with each other across a connecting network. This is a principal reason for using WCF, after all. Aside from security issues, the other main problem with networks is that they can be unreliable. It is very easy for a cable or wireless connection to be interrupted and for messages to be intercepted, interfered with, or just lost. This is clearly unacceptable.

Additionally, if a WCF service is running using the PerSession service instance mode, a conversation between a client application and the WCF service can comprise several messages. In a wide area network such as the Internet, different messages can take different routes when traveling to their destination, and so it is possible for messages to arrive in a different sequence from that in which they were sent. It could be important for a service to process messages in the same order that the client sent them, rather than the order that they were received, so the client application and service must agree on a protocol to use for indicating the order of messages.

Messages traveling across an open network are vulnerable. They can be intercepted, corrupted, diverted, or have a variety of other nasty things happen to them. Several of the Web service (WS-*) specifications are intended to help protect messages, and you have seen how WCF implements some of these specifications in earlier chapters. Another specification that is relevant when you need to send messages reliably is WS-ReliableMessaging. Another common security issue is the "replay attack," in which a third party intercepts messages and repeatedly forwards them on to the intended destination.

In this chapter, you will look at the ways in which you can use WCF to provide reliable messaging and configure replay detection.

Using Reliable Sessions

To handle the problems of lost messages, or messages arriving in the wrong order, the OASIS organization has proposed the WS-ReliableMessaging specification. This specification defines an interoperable protocol for transmitting messages in a reliable manner between a single source and a single destination. Messages can pass through any number of intermediary sites en route to the destination. WCF provides an implementation of this protocol that attempts to ensure that all messages sent from the source will arrive at the destination and without duplication (in other words, exactly once). The protocol implemented by the WCF runtime also attempts to detect missing messages and resend them if possible. At worst, the WCF runtime will throw an exception if a message disappears irrevocably.

WCF optionally supports sequencing, ensuring that messages are processed by the destination in the order that they were sent—the messages might arrive in a different order, but the WCF infrastructure can buffer them to present them to a service in the correct sequence.

> **More Info** For detailed information about the WS-ReliableMessaging specification, see the Web Services Reliable Messaging Protocol document on the Microsoft Web site at *http://msdn.microsoft.com/library/en-us/dnglobspec/html/WS-ReliableMessaging.pdf.*

It is important to understand that reliable messaging as specified by the WS-ReliableMessaging specification does not imply any form of message persistence or message queuing. The protocol requires that both the source application sending the message and the destination application receiving the message are running at the same time. If it is not possible to receive messages, either because the destination application is not running or because of a network failure, the source application will receive an error. In other words, when using reliable messaging, the WCF runtime will guarantee to deliver a message if it can, or it will alert the sender if it cannot—WCF will not silently lose messages.

> **More Info** Message queuing implements its own form of reliable messaging through the use of transactions and message durability rather than the WS-ReliableMessaging protocol. You will learn about using message queues as a transport mechanism for WCF messages in Chapter 11, "Implementing OneWay and Asynchronous Operations."

Implementing Reliable Sessions with WCF

Configuring reliable messaging with a WCF service is a very straightforward task. The WS-ReliableMessaging protocol generates a number of additional messages used by the WCF runtime on the client and service to coordinate their activities, and it is instructive to enable tracing to help you understand how it all works.

Enable reliable sessions in the ShoppingCartService service and client application

1. Using Visual Studio 2005, open the solution file ShoppingCartService.sln located in the Microsoft Press\WCF Step By Step\Chapter 9\ShoppingCartService folder under your \My Documents folder.

This solution contains a copy of the completed ShoppingCartService, and Shopping-CartServiceHost and ShoppingCartClient projects from Chapter 8, "Supporting Transactions." Remember that the ShoppingCartService service exposes a TCP endpoint and requires the client application to create a transaction to maintain the integrity of the database.

> **Note**   This set of exercises uses the NetTcpBinding binding and transport level security. This enables you to easily examine the messages and headers generated by the reliable messaging protocol. Reliable messaging works with the WSHttpBinding over an HTTP endpoint with message level security in exactly the same way. However, in this configuration the messages are intermingled with other messages negotiating the various security tokens, and the messages also contain encrypted data and additional headers making it more difficult to pick out the elements associated with reliable messaging.

2. In Solution Explorer, edit the App.config file for the ShoppingCartHost project by using the WCF Service Configuration Editor.

3. In the WCF Service Configuration Editor, in the Bindings folder, select the Shopping-CartServiceNetTcpBindingConfig binding configuration. In the right pane, scroll down to display the ReliableSession Properties section and then set the *Enabled* property to *True*. Verify that the *Ordered* property is set to *True*, and note that the *InactivityTimeout* property is set to 10 minutes by default.

The WCF runtime uses the *Ordered* property to determine whether to pass messages to the service in the same order that the client sent them; this is an optional but useful feature of reliable messaging. The WCF runtime will wait for the time period specified by the *InactivityTimeout* property between messages before deciding that something has gone wrong and messages have gone missing. If this timeout expires, the WCF runtime sends a "sequence terminated" SOAP fault message to the client application (which it might not receive if the client application is no longer running or communications have failed) and then terminates the session, rolling back any changes that have occurred if the service uses transactions.

> **Note**   If you are using the NetTcpBinding or NetNamedPipeBinding bindings you must also verify that the *TransferMode* property in the General section of the binding configuration page is set to *Buffered*.
>
> The *TransferMode* property specifies that the WCF runtime buffers complete messages in memory before passing them to the service or sending out responses. The TCP and named pipe transports, also support streaming, which enables you to send large messages as a series of small chunks. In this mode, the receiver does not have to wait for the sender to finish transmitting the message before it can start processing it. Using streaming removes the need for holding large messages in memory and can improve scalability. However, the implementation of reliable sessions in WCF requires that an entire message has been received before it can be processed, so buffering is mandatory.

> If you are using the WSHttpBinding binding, messages are automatically buffered (the HTTP protocol does not support streaming).
>
> Incidentally, transactions and message-level security also require WCF to buffer messages before transmitting them.

4. You will examine the messages generated by the WS-ReliableMessaging protocol, so the next step is to configure tracing.

   In the left pane, click the Diagnostics folder. In the right pane, click the EnableMessageLogging link.

5. In the left pane, expand the Diagnostics folder and then click the Message Logging node. In the right pane, set the *LogEntireMessage* property to *True* and set the *LogMalformedMessages* property to *False*.

6. In the left pane, expand the Listeners folder and then click the ServiceModelMessageLogggingListener node. In the right pane, change the path in the *InitData* property to refer to the file app_messages.svclog in the Microsoft Press\WCF Step By Step\Chapter 9 folder under your My Documents folder.

7. Save the configuration file and then exit the WCF Service Configuration Editor.

8. The binding configuration for the client endpoint must match the properties used by the service endpoint.

   In Solution Explorer, edit the App.config file for the ShoppingCartClient project. Display the properties for the ShoppingCartClientNetTcpBindingConfig binding configuration, and set the *Enabled* property in the ReliableSession Properties section to *True*. Verify that the *Ordered* property is set to *True*, and the *InactivityTimeout* property is set to 10 minutes.

   Reliable messaging in the client application can cause a timeout and throw an exception if it doesn't receive any messages within the period specified by the *InactivityTimeout* property. However, a client application normally only receives messages in response to a request (in Chapter 14, "Using a Callback Contract to Publish and Subscribe to Events," you will see that it is also possible for a client application to receive messages at other times). It is possible for a client application to become quiescent on the network, but remain active even if it is not sending messages to a service (it might be busy displaying data, or gathering user input, for example). Similarly, it was mentioned earlier that a WCF service can timeout if it doesn't receive any messages within the period specified by its own *InactivityTimeout* property. To prevent this happening unnecessarily, the WCF runtime on the client computer will periodically send a "keep alive" message to the service if the client application has not sent any messages recently. The point at which this happens is approximately half the value of the InactivityTimeout period specified in the client application configuration file. This "keep alive" message actually serves a dual purpose: it lets the service know the client application is still running, and it probes to make sure that the service is still accessible. The WCF runtime on the client computer expects the WCF runtime on the server computer to reply with an acknowledgement message, and if this acknowledgement is not received within the period specified by the *Inactivi-tyTimeout* property, the WCF runtime on the client application assumes that the service has died and generates a "sequence terminated" SOAP fault message that the client application should handle.

9. Save the configuration file and then exit the WCF Service Configuration Editor.

Examine the trace messages generated by the client application

1. Start the solution without debugging. In the ShoppingCartClient console window displaying the message "Press ENTER when the service has started," press Enter.

   The client application executes as before, displaying the shopping cart containing two water bottles and a mountain seat assembly, followed by the "Goods purchased" method. Press Enter to close the client application console window. In the host application console window, press Enter to stop the service and close the application.

2. Start the Service Trace Viewer (in the Windows Start menu, point to All Programs, point to Microsoft Windows SDK, point to Tools, and then click Service Trace Viewer).

3. In the Service Trace Viewer, open the app_messages.svclog file in the WCF Microsoft Press\Step By Step\Chapter 9 folder under your My Documents folder.

4. In the left pane, click the Message tab. Click the first message. In the lower right pane, click the Message tab. Examine the contents of this message; it should look like this. (The format of the message has been adjusted to fit on the page. Your *MessageID* and *Identifier* properties will be different from those shown here):

```
<s:Envelope …>
  <s:Header>
    <a:Action s:mustUnderstand="1">
      http://schemas.xmlsoap.org/ws/2005/02/rm/CreateSequence
    </a:Action>
    <a:MessageID>
      urn:uuid:fe0e4bbe-4eeb-4e85-85f0-46a133195754
    </a:MessageID>
    <a:To s:mustUnderstand="1">
      net.tcp://localhost:9080/ShoppingCartService
    </a:To>
  </s:Header>
  <s:Body>
    <CreateSequence xmlns="http://schemas.xmlsoap.org/ws/2005/02/rm">
      <AcksTo>
        <a:Address>
          http://www.w3.org/2005/08/addressing/anonymous
        </a:Address>
      </AcksTo>
      <Offer>
        <Identifier>
          urn:uuid:e170f8ff-4715-4ace-bc81-76a2a6e63245
        </Identifier>
      </Offer>
    </CreateSequence>
```

```
      </s:Body>
    </s:Envelope>
```

The WS-ReliableMessaging protocol organizes messages in a conversation between a client application and a service by associating them with a unique identifier known as a sequence number. The first message in the protocol is this CreateSequence message, sent by the WCF runtime on the client computer. This message initiates the reliable session. All messages in the same reliable session must share the same set of identifiers, and the body of this message contains a unique identifier generated by the WCF runtime (highlighted in bold) that the service should use when responding to the client application.

5. In the left pane, click the second message, and then examine the contents of this message in the lower right pane. It should look like this:

```
<s:Envelope …>
  <s:Header>
    <a:Action s:mustUnderstand="1">
       http://schemas.xmlsoap.org/ws/2005/02/rm/CreateSequenceResponse
    </a:Action>
    <a:RelatesTo>
      urn:uuid:fe0e4bbe-4eeb-4e85-85f0-46a133195754
    </a:RelatesTo>
    <a:To s:mustUnderstand="1">
      http://www.w3.org/2005/08/addressing/anonymous
    </a:To>
  </s:Header>
  <s:Body>
    <CreateSequenceResponse xmlns="http://schemas.xmlsoap.org/ws/2005/02/rm">
      <Identifier>
        urn:uuid:efae0f85-cd33-438e-a8f1-bc6e0818de1e
      </Identifier>
      <Accept>
        <AcksTo>
          <a:Address>
            net.tcp://localhost:9080/ShoppingCartService
          </a:Address>
        </AcksTo>
      </Accept>
    </CreateSequenceResponse>
  </s:Body>
</s:Envelope>
```

This is the CreateSequenceResponse message, sent back to the client by the WCF runtime on the service computer. Note that the body of this message also contains an identifier (shown in bold). The WCF runtime on the client must provide this identifier when sending further messages to the service.

6. Examine the contents of third message. It should look like this (some elements have been removed for clarity):

```
<s:Envelope …>
  <s:Header>
    <r:AckRequested>
```

```
      <r:Identifier>
        urn:uuid:efae0f85-cd33-438e-a8f1-bc6e0818de1e
      </r:Identifier>
    </r:AckRequested>
      <r:Sequence s:mustUnderstand="1">
        <r:Identifier>
        urn:uuid:efae0f85-cd33-438e-a8f1-bc6e0818de1e
      </r:Identifier>
      <r:MessageNumber>
        1
      </r:MessageNumber>
    </r:Sequence>
    …
  </s:Header>
  <s:Body>
    <AddItemToCart xmlns="http://adventure-works.com/2007/03/01">
      <productNumber>
        WB-H098
      </productNumber>
    </AddItemToCart>
  </s:Body>
</s:Envelope>
```

This is the first AddItemToCart message sent by the client application. The key thing to notice in this message is the *<Sequence>* block, shown in bold. The identifier in this block is the same as the identifier returned in the CreateSequenceResponse message by the service. All messages transmitted from the client application to the service participating in the reliable session must include this information in the SOAP header. They should also include a message number—in this case message "1"—enabling the WCF runtime on the server computer to ensure that messages are passed to the service in the correct order. You should also notice that the SOAP header includes an *<AckRequested>* block. When the WCF runtime on the server computer receives this message it must send an acknowledgement message back to the client computer so that the client knows it has been received.

7. Examine the contents of the fourth message. It should look like this:

```
<s:Envelope …>
  <s:Header>
    <r:SequenceAcknowledgement>
      <r:Identifier>
        urn:uuid:efae0f85-cd33-438e-a8f1-bc6e0818de1e
      </r:Identifier>
      <r:AcknowledgementRange Lower="1" Upper="1">
      </r:AcknowledgementRange>
      <netrm:BufferRemaining xmlns:netrm="http://schemas.microsoft.com/ws/2006/05/rm">
        8
      </netrm:BufferRemaining>
    </r:SequenceAcknowledgement>
    <a:Action s:mustUnderstand="1">
      http://schemas.xmlsoap.org/ws/2005/02/rm/SequenceAcknowledgement
    </a:Action>
    …
  </s:Header>
```

```
  <s:Body></s:Body>
</s:Envelope>
```

This is the acknowledgement message from the WCF runtime on the server computer, back to the WCF runtime on the client computer. The service has verified that it has received the AddItemToCartMessage.

8. Look at the fifth message:

```
<s:Envelope …">
  <s:Header>
    <r:AckRequested>
      <r:Identifier>
        urn:uuid:e170f8ff-4715-4ace-bc81-76a2a6e63245
      </r:Identifier>
    </r:AckRequested>
    <r:Sequence s:mustUnderstand="1">
      <r:Identifier>
        urn:uuid:e170f8ff-4715-4ace-bc81-76a2a6e63245
      </r:Identifier>
      <r:MessageNumber>
        1
      </r:MessageNumber>
    </r:Sequence>
    <a:Action s:mustUnderstand="1">
      http://adventure-works.com/2007/03/01/ShoppingCartService/AddItemToCartResponse
    </a:Action>
      …
  </s:Header>
  <s:Body>
    <AddItemToCartResponse xmlns="http://adventure-works.com/2007/03/01">
      <AddItemToCartResult>
        true
      </AddItemToCartResult>
    </AddItemToCartResponse>
  </s:Body>
</s:Envelope>
```

This is the AddItemToCartResponse message, indicating that the service successfully added the specified item to the shopping cart. Again, notice how this message requires the client to acknowledge its receipt, that the identifier used in the *<Sequence>* block is the identifier specified by the client at the start of the session, and that this is also message "1" (in the opposite direction from the client message). If you examine the sixth message, you will see that it is the acknowledgement for this AddItemToCartReponse message from the client sent back to the service.

9. Examine messages seven through fourteen. You can see that things settle down at this point, and the conversation consists of request messages sent by the client application and the response messages sent back from the service. These messages all contain a *<Sequence>* block with the appropriate identifier. Each message also has a message number, which is incremented for each new message in each direction (the next message in

the sequence sent from the client application to the service is message "2," and the response message sent by the service back to the client is also message "2").

> **Note** If it helps, think of the request/response messages as a series of two synchronized one-way conversations. Each message traveling in one direction forms part of a sequence, and the messages in this sequence are numbered starting at 1. The messages traveling in the opposite direction form part of a different sequence and are also numbered starting at 1. The message numbers do not tie messages together; response message 1 might or might not be the response for request message 1.

As an optimization mechanism, after the initial request/response messages the message acknowledgements are incorporated into the next request or response messages sent by the client application or service—the header in a message being sent contains the acknowledgement for the previous message received.

> **Note** The *<SequenceAcknowledgement>* block in messages seven through fourteen also includes a *BufferRemaining* element. As already mentioned, to handle messages arriving out of order, the WCF runtime buffers them before handing them off to the application. If a message with a high message number is received when the runtime was expecting a lower message number, the higher numbered message will be held in a buffer until the lower numbered message has been received and passed to the application. The WCF runtime provides a finite number of buffers for a session. If a client application sends a large volume of messages to a service and many arrive out of order, the WCF runtime on the server computer may run out of buffers and start to drop messages (they are resent when more space is available). Therefore, when acknowledging a message, the WCF runtime also provides the number of free buffers it currently has in the *BufferRemaining* element. The WCF runtime on the client computer can examine this value and suspend sending messages if this number minus the number of messages the client has sent but have not yet been acknowledged (they are in transit) drops below a certain threshold (currently 2). As the WCF runtime on the server receives the missing messages it can pass them to the service and hopefully free up some of the buffers. Subsequent acknowledgement messages from the service should indicate that more buffer space is available, and the WCF runtime on the client computer can resume sending messages. This is a WCF-specific feature—if an application built using another technology does not understand this element, it will be ignored.

10. Examine message fifteen. It should look like this:

```
<s:Envelope …>
  <s:Header>
    <r:SequenceAcknowledgement>
      <r:Identifier>
        urn:uuid:e170f8ff-4715-4ace-bc81-76a2a6e63245
      </r:Identifier>
      <r:AcknowledgementRange Lower="1" Upper="5">
      </r:AcknowledgementRange>
      <netrm:BufferRemaining xmlns:netrm="http://schemas.microsoft.com/ws/2006/05/rm">
        8
      </netrm:BufferRemaining>
```

```
      </r:SequenceAcknowledgement>
      <r:Sequence s:mustUnderstand="1">
        <r:Identifier>
          urn:uuid:efae0f85-cd33-438e-a8f1-bc6e0818de1e
        </r:Identifier>
        <r:MessageNumber>
          6
        </r:MessageNumber>
        <r:LastMessage>
        </r:LastMessage>
      </r:Sequence>
      <a:Action s:mustUnderstand="1">
        http://schemas.xmlsoap.org/ws/2005/02/rm/LastMessage
      </a:Action>
      <a:To s:mustUnderstand="1">
        net.tcp://localhost:9080/ShoppingCartService
      </a:To>
    </s:Header>
    <s:Body>
    </s:Body>
  </s:Envelope>
```

This is the LastMessage message. It is sent by the WCF runtime on the client computer to indicate that this is the final message in the sequence. This message is sent when the client application starts to close the session. The WCF runtime on the server computer acknowledges this message (see message sixteen) and then sends its own LastMessage message to indicate that it has also finished (message seventeen). The WCF runtime on the client computer sends an acknowledgement (message eighteen).

11. Examine message nineteen:

```
<s:Envelope …>
  <s:Header>
    <a:Action s:mustUnderstand="1">
      http://schemas.xmlsoap.org/ws/2005/02/rm/TerminateSequence
    </a:Action>
      …
  </s:Header>
  <s:Body>
    <TerminateSequence xmlns="http://schemas.xmlsoap.org/ws/2005/02/rm">
      <Identifier>
        urn:uuid:e170f8ff-4715-4ace-bc81-76a2a6e63245
      </Identifier>
    </TerminateSequence>
  </s:Body>
</s:Envelope>
```

This is the TerminateSequence message. The WCF runtime on the server computer sends this message to indicate that it is not going to send any more messages using the sequence specified by the identifier and that the WCF runtime on the client computer can release any resources associated with this session. The WCF runtime on the client computer also sends a TerminateSequence message to the server (message twenty), identifying the sequence used by the client to send messages to the server. At the end of this exchange, the session terminates.

12. Close the Microsoft Service Trace Viewer and delete the trace file.

These exercises should make two things apparent to you:

- It is very easy to implement reliable messaging with WCF. You just set a few properties of the binding configuration. You don't need to write any additional code; it is all transparent to your client applications and services.

- Reliable sessions can generate a significant amount of additional network traffic, both in terms of the extra protocol messages and the increased size of each message. The more messages a client application sends in a session, the smaller this overhead becomes proportionally. However, if you use short sessions, comprising a single request and response for example, each request sent by a client application establishes a new reliable session that is thrown away after a response has been received. This is expensive, and in this situation you should consider very carefully whether you really need reliable messaging or whether you should rework the client application to make more efficient use of reliable sessions.

Reliable messaging works well with the PerCall service instance context mode. Although the WCF runtime creates a new service instance for each request, it creates the sequence for the reliable session when the client application makes the first call to the service in the session, and only terminates the sequence when the session ends. Ideally, you should set the *Session-Mode* property of the service contract to *SessionMode.Required* to ensure that the client application actually establishes a session.

You should also be aware that not all binding configurations support the WS-ReliableMessaging protocol. The ones that do are netTcpBinding, wsDualHttpBinding (this binding always uses reliable messaging, you cannot disable it), wsFederationHttpBinding, and wsHttpBinding. The MSMQ bindings, msmqIntegrationBinding and netMsmqBinding, implement their own version of reliable messaging based on message persistence and queuing technologies rather than WS-ReliableMessaging. The common bindings that do not support reliable messaging include basicHttpBinding, netNamedPipeBinding, and netPeerTcpBinding.

Note You can also create custom bindings that support reliable sessions. You will see how to define a custom binding later in this chapter, and also in Chapter 10, "Programmatically Controlling the Configuration and Communications."

Detecting and Handling Replay Attacks

In Chapter 4, "Protecting an Enterprise WCF Service," you learned a little about replay attacks. In a replay attack, a hacker intercepts and stores messages flowing over the network and then sends them at some time in the future. At best this can become a nuisance if, for example, a hacker repeatedly replays the same intercepted purchase order sent by a genuine customer to an online bookstore; the bookstore receives hundreds of orders and sends the books to the customer who has not ordered them. At worst, it can lead to large-scale fraud; consider an attacker intercepting a request to credit his bank account and then repeatedly replaying this message to the bank's servers.

Using reliable sessions can help to mitigate simple replay attacks, as each message must provide a valid sequence identifier and a unique message number. When the session has completed, the sequence identifier becomes invalid, so any subsequent attempt to replay the message should be rejected by the receiver. However, consider the following hypothetical scenario. If a session is long-running, it might be possible for an attacker to edit the *<Sequence>* block in an intercepted message, modify the message number, set it to some value higher than the message that was received, and then forward this message to the service if the session is still active. When the application hosting the service receives this message, if no message with this number has yet been received, the host will buffer it and then pass it to the service when all the intermediate messages have been received. When a genuine message from the client with this message number is subsequently received, the genuine message will be rejected. How can you handle this situation?

You can use transport-level security to encrypt messages as they traverse the network from machine to machine. Additionally, many implementations of transport-level security include automatic replay detection of packets at the transport layer. But remember that transport-level security operates on a point-to-point basis, and when a service receives the message, it has unrestricted access to its contents. If the service is expected to forward the request on to a service running elsewhere, it can modify the message before it does so. The usual way to protect data, if you cannot trust any intermediate services, is to use message level security. However, message level security is predominantly concerned with protecting the body of a message rather than the data in message headers, which is where the sequence identifiers and message numbers are held.

> **More Info**   Review Chapter 4 and Chapter 5, "Protecting a WCF Service over the Internet," for more information about implementing message level security with WCF.

So, to prevent a reply attack, the receiver requires a more secure mechanism than simple sequence identifiers and message numbers for uniquely identifying messages. Fortunately, WCF provides just such a mechanism.

Configuring Replay Detection with WCF

When you enable replay detection, the WCF runtime generates a random, unique, signed, time-stamped identifier for each message. These identifiers are referred to as *nonces*. On receiving a message, a service can use the signature to verify that the nonce has not been corrupted and extract and examine the timestamp to ascertain that the message was sent *reasonably* recently (the service can allow for a certain amount of clock-skew between computers and should also recognize that it takes a little time for data to physically traverse the network from the client application). The service can then save the nonce in a cache. When another message is received, the service can retrieve the nonce from the message header. If a matching nonce is found in its cache then this is a copy of an earlier message and should be discarded. If it is not, the message can be processed and its nonce added to the cache.

The WCF security channel implements replay detection by default, although the relevant properties for configuring it are not immediately visible when using the standard WCF bindings. However, it is quite simple to create a custom binding that makes them available. You will adopt this approach in the following exercises.

Create a custom binding for the ShoppingCartService service

1. In Visual Studio 2005, edit the App.config file for the ShoppingCartHost project by using the WCF Service Configuration Editor.

2. In the left pane, click the Bindings folder. In the right pane, click the New Binding Configuration link. In the Create a New Binding dialog box, select customBinding and then click OK.

   In the right pane, change the *Name* property to *ShoppingCartServiceCustomBindingConfig*.

   If you recall from Chapter 2, "Hosting a WCF Service," the WCF runtime creates a channel stack for sending and receiving messages. Incoming messages arrive at a particular address (such as a port or a URL) using an appropriate transport (such as TCP or HTTP). When you host a service, the WCF runtime "listens" for incoming request messages sent by client applications to the specified address by using a transport channel. Incoming messages pass through the transport channel to an encoding channel, which parses the message, and the WCF runtime can then invoke the relevant operation in the service using the information in this parsed data. Outgoing response messages are encoded by the encoding channel (a message can be encoded as text, or as binary data), before being passed to the transport channel for transmission back to the client application.

   A channel stack must always have at least these two channels: a transport channel and an encoding channel. When you create a new custom binding, the WCF Service Configuration Editor automatically adds elements for using the HTTP transport and text encoding. You have been using the TCP transport in previous exercises in this chapter, so you will change the transport channel.

3. In the lower right pane, select the *httpTransport stack* element and then click Remove. Click Add. In the Adding Binding Element Extension Sections dialog box, select tcp-Transport and then click Add.

   A point worth emphasizing from Chapter 2 is that the order of the channels in the channel stack is important. The transport channel must always be the final item, and it is conventional for the encoding channel to be placed immediately above the transport channel. Verify that the *tcpTransport* element is in position 2 in the list and the *textMessageEncoding* element is in position 1. If the positions are different, use the Up and Down buttons to swap them over.

4. Click Add in the lower right pane. In the Adding Binding Element Extension Sections dialog box, select security and then click Add. Use the Up and Down buttons to place the security element in position 1 at the top of the stack, above the *textMessageEncoding* element.

5. In the left pane, click the security node underneath the ShoppingCartServiceCustomBindingConfig node. In the right pane, set the *AuthenticationMode* property to *SecureConversation*. This mode uses the protocol defined by the WS-SecureConversation specification to establish a secure session between the service and client applications (see the sidebar after this exercise for details).

6. In the right pane, click the Service tab. Verify that the *DetectReplays* property is set to *True* by default.

7. Examine the *ReplayCacheSize* property.

   When implementing replay detection, the WCF runtime on the server computer will cache nonces in memory. The value of this property determines the maximum amount of memory it will use, specified as a number of cached nonces. When this limit is reached, the oldest nonce is removed from the cache before a new one is added. The default value should be sufficient, but you might want to consider reducing it if memory is at a premium. However, don't make it so small that nonces are discarded too quickly as you could render the service vulnerable to replay attacks again.

8. Examine the *ReplayWindow* and *MaxClockSkew* properties.

   The ReplayWindow specifies the time for which nonces are considered valid. If the timestamp in a received nonce is outside the time window specified here, it is discarded as being too old. However, WCF recognizes that the system clock on different computers might not be completely synchronized, and the *MaxClockSkew* property enables you to specify the maximum clock difference to allow. It is also possible that the timestamp for a nonce could appear to be for a short time in the future if the clock on the server computer is running slow, so the *MaxClockSkew* property allows the service to accept nonces with a future timestamp provided they are within the range specified.

> **Note** The *security custom binding* element enables you to configure replay detection for client applications as well, by using the properties in the Client tab.

9. In the left pane, click the ShoppingCartServiceCustomBindingConfig node.

   The ShoppingCartService service uses transactions and reliable sessions, so you must add channels that implement these features:

❑ In the lower right pane, click Add. In the Adding Binding Element Extension Sections dialog box, select reliableSession and then click Add.

❑ Repeat this process and add the *transactionFlow* element to the binding.

❑ Rearrange the channel stack so that the *transactionFlow* element is in position 1, the *reliableSession* element is in position 2, the security element is in position 3, the *textMessageEncoding* element is in position 4, and the *tcpTransport* element is in position 5, as shown in the following image. This is the recommended order for these channels:

10. In the left pane, expand the ShoppingCartService.ShoppingCartServiceImpl service in the Services folder, right-click the Endpoints folder, and then click New Service Endpoint. In the right pane, set the properties of this endpoint using the values in this table:

Property	Value
Name	ShoppingCartServiceCustomEndpoint
Address	net.tcp://localhost:9090/ShoppingCartService
Binding	customBinding
BindingConfiguration	ShoppingCartServiceCustomBindingConfig
Contract	ShoppingCartService.IShoppingCartService

11. Save the file, and then exit the WCF Configuration Editor.

The WS-SecureConversation Specification

The WS-SecureConversation specification is yet another specification being developed by members of OASIS. It enables two participants (a service and a client application) to establish and share a security context for exchanging multiple messages (a conversation) in a secure and optimal manner without needing to include comprehensive security credential information in every message. Participants exchange and validate credentials at the start of the session, and negotiate security tokens derived from the authorized credentials. Subsequent messages in the conversation contain these derived tokens rather than a complete set of credentials to enable the recipient to authenticate the source. The process of validating these derived tokens is faster than fully authenticating each message from the original set of credentials.

The WS-SecureConversation specification builds on other WS-* specifications, such as WS-Security, so you can create a security context based on a variety of authentication and encryption mechanisms, as described in Chapter 4.

For detailed information about the WS-SecureConversation specification, see the Web Services Secure Conversation Language (WS-SecureConversation) document on the Microsoft Web site at *http://msdn.microsoft.com/library/en-us/dnglobspec/html/WS-secureconversation.pdf*.

You can now add a corresponding binding to the client application and then configure the client to use this binding.

Create a custom binding for the WCF client application

1. In Visual Studio 2005, edit the App.config file for the ShoppingCartClient project by using the WCF Service Configuration Editor.

2. In the left pane, add a new customBinding binding configuration to the Bindings folder and set the *Name* property to *ShoppingCartClientCustomBindingConfig*.

3. Remove the *httpTransport* element and replace it with a *tcpTransport* element.

4. Add a security element. Set the *AuthenticationMode* property of this security element to *SecureConversation*.

5. Add a *reliableSession* and a *transactionFlow* element to the custom binding.

6. Rearrange the channel stack so that the *transactionFlow* element is in position 1, the *reliableSession* element is in position 2, the security element is in position 3, the *textMessageEncoding* element is in position 4, and the *tcpTransport* element is in position 5.

7. In the left pane, add a new endpoint to the Endpoints folder under the Client folder. Set the properties for this endpoint using the following values:

Property	Value
Name	CustomBinding_ShoppingCartService
Address	net.tcp://localhost:9090/ShoppingCartService
Binding	customBinding
BindingConfiguration	ShoppingCartClientCustomBindingConfig
Contract	ShoppingCartClient.ShoppingCartService.ShoppingCartService

8. Save the file, and then exit the WCF Configuration Editor.

9. In Visual Studio 2005, edit the Program.cs file in the ShopingCartClient project. In the Main method, change the statement that creates the *proxy* object to reference the CustomBinding_ShoppingCartService endpoint, as shown in bold below:

```
static void Main(string[] args)
{
    …
    try
    {
        // Connect to the ShoppingCartService service
        ShoppingCartServiceClient proxy = new
            ShoppingCartServiceClient("CustomBinding_ShoppingCartService");
        …
    }
    …
}
```

10. Start the solution without debugging. In the ShoppingCartClient console window displaying the message "Press ENTER when the service has started," press Enter.

    The client application executes exactly as before, except that this time it is using the custom binding, with replay detection enabled, to communicate with the ShoppingCartService service.

11. Press Enter to close the client application console window. In the host application console window, press Enter to stop the service.

Summary

In this chapter, you have configured a WCF service and client application to communicate by using a reliable session. You have seen how WCF implements the protocol defined by the WS-ReliableMessaging specification and how it uses sequences, message numbers, and acknowledgement messages to verify that messages have been received and assembled in the correct order. You have also seen how to create a custom binding that enables you to configure replay detection.

Chapter 10

Programmatically Controlling the Configuration and Communications

After completing this chapter, you will be able to:

- Describe the main elements of the WCF Service Model.
- Create bindings by using code.
- Implement a custom service behavior and add it to a service.
- Connect to a service from a client application by using the service contract.
- Send messages directly to a service without using a proxy object.

By now, you should have a good understanding of how to create WCF client applications and services and how to configure them so that they can communicate with each other. A compelling feature of WCF is the ability to perform many of these tasks by using configuration files. Behind the scenes, the WCF runtime takes this configuration information and uses it to build an infrastructure that can send and receive messages using specified protocols, encoding them in the appropriate manner, and directing them to the appropriate methods implementing operations in a service.

There will inevitably be occasions when you need to perform configuration tasks programmatically, possibly because an application or service needs to adapt itself dynamically according to its environment without intervention from an administrator or maybe for security reasons if you don't want a user to be able to modify the configuration for an application. For example, you might not want an administrator to be able to enable or disable metadata publishing for a service. It is also instructive to see the sorts of things the WCF runtime does when it executes your client applications and services. So, in this chapter you will look at how to create and use bindings in code and how to send and receive messages programmatically.

The WCF Service Model

WCF provides a comprehensive infrastructure for sending and receiving messages by creating a number of objects that manage and control the communications. This infrastructure is extensible, and you can augment it with your own functionality if you need to customize the way it works. For example, in Chapter 9, "Implementing Reliable Sessions," you saw how to compose the channels provided with WCF into a custom binding. If you have a very specific requirement or need to transmit messages using a protocol that has no corresponding channel in the *.NET Framework 3.0* class library, you can develop your own channel (or buy one from a third party) and then easily integrate it into your configuration without needing to modify the code for a service or client application. You can also customize other parts of the WCF infrastructure, such as the way that WCF maps incoming messages to operations. You will see some examples of this in Chapter 13, "Routing Messages."

More Info Detailed discussion about creating a custom channel is beyond the scope of this book. For information about creating custom channels, see the Building Custom Channels page on the Microsoft .NET Framework 3.0 Community Web site at *http://wcf.netfx3.com/content/BuildingCustomChannels.aspx*.

For more information about how to add your own functionality to the WCF infrastructure, consult the topics in the "Extending WCF" section of the Microsoft Windows SDK Documentation.

This section introduces you to some of the main components in the WCF infrastructure, which is sometimes referred to as the *WCF Service Model*.

Services and Channels

You can think of a binding as a description of the channels in a channel stack. When a host application starts a service running, the WCF runtime uses the bindings defined for each endpoint to instantiate a *ChannelListener* object and a channel stack. A *ChannelListener* object connects an endpoint to the channel. The WCF runtime creates a *ChannelListener* object for each URI on which the service can accept messages. When a request message arrives at a URI, the corresponding *ChannelListener* object receives the message and passes it to the transport channel at the bottom of the corresponding channel stack. To the transport channel, a message is nothing more than a stream of bytes; it makes no attempt to understand the contents of the message. The transport channel passes the message to the next channel in the stack, which by convention is an encoding channel.

The purpose of an encoding channel is to parse the incoming request message and convert it into a format that the channels above it in the channel stack can understand—usually SOAP. When sending an outgoing response message, the encoding channel converts a SOAP message passed in from the channels above it in the stack into a specified format for transmission by the transport channel. The *.NET Framework 3.0* class library provides encoding channels for converting between SOAP messages and plain text, binary data, and an optimized format called the Message Transmission Optimization Mechanism, or MTOM. You will learn more about MTOM in Chapter 12, "Implementing a WCF Service for Good Performance." The transport and encoding channels are mandatory parts of a binding. Above the encoding channel, you can add channels handling reliability, security, transactions, and other non-functional aspects of SOAP messaging.

> **Note** The binary encoding channel implements a WCF-specific encoding. You cannot use it to communicate with non-WCF client applications and services, so you should only use it in situations where interoperability is not an issue. MTOM is an OASIS approved specification and should be used if you need to transmit data in a binary format in an interoperable manner.
>
> Additionally, each transport channel will load a default encoding channel if you don't specify one in the channel stack. The HTTP and HTTPS transport channels load the text encoding channel, but the TCP channel defaults to using the binary encoding channel.

When an incoming request message reaches the top of the channel stack, a *ChannelDispatcher* object takes the message, examines it, and passes it to an *EndpointDispatcher* object that invokes the appropriate method in the service, passing the data items in the message as parameters to the method. *ChannelDispatcher* and *EndpointDispatcher* objects are created automatically when you use a *ServiceHost* object to run a service.

> **Note** It is possible to associate multiple endpoints with the same URI. When a WCF service receives a message, the *ChannelDispatcher* will query the *EndpointDispatcher* for each endpoint in turn to establish which one, if any, can process the message. You will learn more about this process in Chapter 13.

When a method implementing an operation in a service finishes, the data it returns passes back through the channel stack to the transport channel where it is transmitted back to the client application. The WCF runtime on the client builds a similar structure to that used by the service, except that it is slightly simpler, as it does not have to listen for requests or manage multiple instances of the application in the way that a service does. The WCF runtime for the client creates a *ChannelFactory* object and uses this object to construct a channel from the binding definition. The proxy object in the client application is responsible for converting method calls into outgoing request messages and passing them to the channel for transmission. Incoming response messages received on the transport channel work their way back up through the channel stack, where the proxy object converts them into the format expected by the client code and returns them as the results of the original method call.

Behaviors

You can customize the way in which components in the WCF infrastructure operate by applying behaviors. For example, the .NET Framework 3.0 provides a number of built-in endpoint behaviors you can use to modify the way in which the endpoint serializes data, how it batches operations together in a transaction, the specific credentials it uses when sending messages or receiving messages, and so on. You can also attach behaviors to other objects in the WCF runtime, such as the service instance created by the *ServiceHost* object. As another example, WCF supplies the serviceDebug service behavior that you can use to specify that the service should transmit complete error information to the client application in the event of an exception.

WCF provides different sets of behaviors for customizing different types of objects, and they each have a scope that depends on the type of object they apply to. For example, you use service behaviors for modifying the behavior of an entire service, operation behaviors for influencing the way in which individual methods in a service are invoked, and contract behaviors for affecting the way in which all operations in a contract are called. You can define your own custom behaviors, and you will see an example of a custom service behavior later in this chapter.

The .NET Framework 3.0 enables you to apply behaviors by using a configuration file, declaratively by specifying an attribute, or imperatively by adding code to a service that instantiates the behavior and sets its properties. Not all behaviors are available through all mechanisms. The general rule is that you can only change behaviors that are critical to the way in which a service functions (such as operation behaviors) by using an attribute or writing code. These behaviors are the concern of the developers building a service rather than an administrator configuring it. On the other hand, WCF exposes the behaviors that are a matter of administrative policy rather than implementation strategy through the configuration file.

Composing Channels into Bindings

The channels in a channel stack implement the various protocols and specifications used by SOAP messaging. The binding used by a client application should correspond to the binding implemented by the service that the client application communicates with; if a channel is omitted, or placed in a different position in the channel stack, there is the possibility that either the client application or the service will not be able to interpret messages correctly.

In Chapter 2, "Hosting a WCF Service," you were first introduced to the predefined bindings in the .NET Framework 3.0, such as basicHttpBinding, wsHttpBinding, and netTcpBinding. These predefined bindings combine channels in configurations that meet the requirements of many common scenarios. The .NET Framework 3.0 contains classes that correspond to these bindings in the *System.ServiceModel* namespace, and these classes expose properties that enable you to configure the channels used by these bindings. You can also create your own custom bindings by combining binding elements and setting the properties of each of these binding elements to determine exactly which channels the WCF runtime uses.

You build a custom binding by adding binding elements to a *CustomBinding* object. The predefined bindings restrict the channels in a binding to various meaningful combinations. When you create a custom binding, you must ensure that you combine binding elements in a sensible manner. To some extent, the WCF runtime protects you and will throw an exception if, for example, you try and add two encoding binding elements to a binding. However, the WCF runtime is not able to perform complete sanity checking of your bindings, especially if you are using custom bindings. If you get it wrong, the client application and service might not understand each other's messages, which will consequently cause faults, timeouts, and exceptions.

The order of the binding elements in a custom binding is also important. It has been mentioned before that the transport channel must be at the bottom of the stack, followed by the encoding channel. Microsoft recommends that you layer channels according to the function that they perform. Table 10-1 lists the layers and the channels appropriate to each layer. The class names for the binding element classes associated with the corresponding channels provided by the .NET Framework 3.0 in each layer are shown in italics:

Table 10-1   Recommended Channel Organization

Layer	Function	Channel Binding Element Class
1 (*top*)	Transaction Flow	TransactionFlowBindingElement
2	Reliable Sessions	ReliableSessionBindingElement
3	Security	AsymmetricSecurityBindingElement, SymmetricSecurityBindingElement, or TransportSecurityBindingElement, and others created by factory methods in the SecurityBindingElement class.
4	Stream Upgrades	SslStreamSecurityBindingElement or WindowsStreamSecurityBindingElement
5	Encoding	BinaryMessageEncodingBindingElement, MtomMessageEncodingBindingElement, or TextMessageEncodingBindingElement
6 (*bottom*)	Transport	HttpTransportBindingElement, HttpsTransportBindingElement, PeerTransportBindingElement, TcpTransportBindingElement, NamedPipeTransportBindingElement, MsmqTransportBindingElement, or MsmqIntegrationBindingElement

This table shows the common binding elements that you have met in earlier chapters in this book. There are others, and you will see some of them later. Most of these binding elements are self-explanatory, but some warrant a little more explanation.

- The *SecurityBindingElement* class acts as a factory for security binding elements and exposes methods that you can use to create channels that implement them. You will see an example of this in the exercise that follows this section.

- The *AsymmetricSecurityBindingElement* and *SymmetricSecurityBindingElement* classes represent channels that implement message level security. The *TransportSecurityBindingElement* class represents a channel that implements transport level security. (For more information about message level and transport level security, refer back to Chapter 4, "Protecting an Enterprise WCF Service.") However, you are more likely to use channels for specific scenarios, such as *CreateAnonymousForCertificateBindingElement*, which creates a symmetric binding element that supports anonymous client authentication and certificate-based server authentication. You can create these channels by using the factory methods of the *SecurityBindingElement* class.

■ Stream upgrades such as the *SslStreamSecurityBindingElement* and *WindowsStreamSecurityBindingElement* classes do not actually represent channels but rather objects that can modify the way in which data is transmitted over the network. You can use them in conjunction with a transport that supports a stream-oriented protocol, such as TCP and named pipes. A stream upgrade operates on a stream of data rather than individual WCF messages. For example, the *WindowsStreamSecurityBindingElement* class enables you to specify that data should be encrypted and/or signed before being transmitted. Another example (not currently implemented by the .NET Framework 3.0) would be to use a streaming upgrade channel that compresses the data using a specified algorithm before transmission.

When you use a configuration file to create a binding, you are not necessarily aware of which binding elements you are using. For example, when you specify a *<security>* element, the "mode" attribute determines whether the WCF runtime uses a message level *<security binding>* element or a transport level one. Setting other attributes in the *<security>* element enable the WCF runtime to determine exactly which of the many possible security binding elements it should use when constructing the channel. When you create a binding programmatically, you have to be explicit.

That's the theory. The exercises that follow show how to put some of what you have just read into action.

Programmatically create and use a binding in the ShoppingCartService service

1. Using Visual Studio 2005, open the solution file ShoppingCartService.sln located in the Microsoft Press\WCF Step By Step\Chapter 10\ShoppingCartService folder under your \My Documents folder.

   This solution contains a copy of the ShoppingCartService, and ShoppingCartClient projects from Chapter 9. The ShoppingCartHost project is a little different though. The binding and service endpoint information for the ShoppingCartService service has been removed, leaving only the connection string for the *AdventureWorks* database. Additionally, the Main method in the Program.cs file is currently empty.

2. In Solution Explorer, edit the Program.cs file in the ShoppingCartHost project. Add the following *using* statement to the list at the top of the file:

   ```
   using System.ServiceModel.Channels;
   ```

   The *System.ServiceModel.Channels* namespace contains the classes defining the various channels and bindings provided by the WCF.

3. In the Main method in the *Program* class, add the following statement:

   ```
   CustomBinding customBind = new CustomBinding();
   ```

   This statement creates a new, empty custom binding object. You will add binding elements to the custom binding object in the next step.

> **Note**   If you want to use one of the standard bindings, you can create it in much the same way. For example, to create a standard HTTP binding object for the wsHttpBinding binding configuration, you could use:
>
> ```
> WSHttpBinding httpBind = new WSHttpBinding();
> ```

4. The ShoppingCartService service uses transactions and requires reliable sessions. Create the binding elements that correspond to the channels that implement the transaction and reliable messaging protocols, set their properties, and then add them to the custom binding as follows:

```
TransactionFlowBindingElement txFlowBindElem = new TransactionFlowBindingElement();
txFlowBindElem.TransactionProtocol = TransactionProtocol.OleTransactions;
customBind.Elements.Add(txFlowBindElem);

ReliableSessionBindingElement rsBindElem = new ReliableSessionBindingElement();
rsBindElem.FlowControlEnabled = true;
rsBindElem.Ordered = true;
customBind.Elements.Add(rsBindElem);
```

The transaction flow binding element is configured to use OLE transactions; the alternative is to specify WSAtomicTransactionOctober2004, which implements the WS-AtomicTransactions specification. Refer back to Chapter 8, "Supporting Transactions," for further details.

The reliable sessions binding element enables flow control and ensures that the order of messages is preserved, as described in Chapter 9.

It is worth emphasizing again that the order in which you add the elements to the custom binding is important. Binding elements higher up the channel stack must be added to the custom binding before those that occur lower down in the stack.

5. The ShoppingCartService service also needs to implement secure conversations and replay detection. Use the *SecurityBindingElement* class to create a *SecureConversation BindingElement,* as follows:

```
SecurityBindingElement secBindElem =
    SecurityBindingElement.CreateSecureConversationBindingElement(
        SecurityBindingElement.CreateSspiNegotiationBindingElement());
secBindElem.LocalServiceSettings.DetectReplays = true;
customBind.Elements.Add(secBindElem);
```

The secure conversation protocol uses a handshaking mechanism between the client application and the service to establish a security context token that both parties can use to authenticate the messages that pass between them. This handshake also needs to be secured, and the security binding element passed as a parameter to the CreateSecureBindingElement method specifies how to protect the handshake messages that flow while negotiating the security context. The code in this exercise uses SOAP SSPI negotiation to authenticate messages while handshaking (this is the default).

After creating the security binding element, the code enables server-side replay detection before adding it to the custom binding.

6. Add binding elements that implement a text encoding channel and a TCP transport channel, like this:

```
customBind.Elements.Add(new TextMessageEncodingBindingElement());

TcpTransportBindingElement tcpBindElem = new TcpTransportBindingElement();
tcpBindElem.TransferMode = TransferMode.Buffered;
customBind.Elements.Add(tcpBindElem);
```

The reliable sessions channel requires that messages are buffered by the transport. The transport channel must be the last item in the custom binding.

7. Add code to create a *ServiceHost* object, as follows:

```
ServiceHost host = new ServiceHost(typeof(ShoppingCartService.ShoppingCartServiceImpl));
```

This should be a familiar statement to you, but you now appreciate what a *ServiceHost* object does: it constructs the channel, it manages the lifetimes of various instances of the service defined by the specified type, and it ensures that client requests are dispatched to the correct service instance. It performs these tasks in conjunction with *ChannelListener*, *ChannelDispatcher*, and *EndpointDispatcher* objects that it creates by using the code you will add in the following steps.

8. Previously, you specified the endpoint definition for the ShoppingCartService in the application configuration file, and the *ServiceHost* constructor used this information to construct an endpoint and a *ChannelListener*. You no longer have this information in the application configuration file, so add the endpoint by using code, as shown below:

```
host.AddServiceEndpoint(typeof(ShoppingCartService.IShoppingCartService),
    customBind, "net.tcp://localhost:9090/ShoppingCartService");
```

The parameters to the AddServiceEndpoint method are the service contract that the service implements, the binding, and the URI for the listener.

9. You can now start the service running. Add the following statements to the Main method:

```
host.Open();
Console.WriteLine("Service running");
Console.WriteLine("Press ENTER to stop the service");
Console.ReadLine();
```

The Open method starts a *ChannelListener* object listening for client requests. When a request arrives, the ChannelListener passes it to the channel. The *ChannelDispatcher* object retrieves the message from the top of the channel and passes it, through the EndpointDispatcher, to an instance of the ShoppingCartService service.

10. Start the solution without debugging. In the ShoppingCartClient console window displaying the message "Press ENTER when the service has started," press Enter.

The client application runs exactly as before, creates a shopping cart, adds two water bottles and a mountain seat assembly, and then purchases the goods.

11.   Press Enter to close the client application console window. In the host application console window, press Enter to stop the service.

Inspecting Messages

An interesting feature of the WCF service model is the ability to intercept messages as they are dispatched to a service method, and again as they leave the service method prior to traversing the channel and being transmitted back to the client application. You can perform this task by creating a message inspector; you create a class that implements the *IDispatchMessageInspector* interface and insert it into the WCF infrastructure by using a behavior. The behavior that you use determines the scope of the message interception. If you specify message interception as a service behavior, all messages sent to the service will be intercepted. You can also apply message interception by using operation, endpoint, or contract behaviors, in which case interception applies only to the specified operation, endpoint, or contract.

You can implement message inspection in a client application or a service. In the exercise that follows, you will see how to create a message inspector and integrate it into the dispatch mechanism of the WCF runtime for the service. To continue in the spirit of this chapter, you will perform these tasks programmatically.

Create a message inspector for the ShoppingCartService service

1.   In Visual Studio 2005, select the ShoppingCartService project in Solution Explorer. In the Project menu, click Add Class, and add a new class file called ShoppingCartInspector.cs to the project.

2.   In the ShoppingCartInspector.cs file, add the following *using* statements to the list at the top:

```
using System.ServiceModel.Dispatcher;
using System.ServiceModel.Description;
```

3.   Modify the definition of the *ShoppingCartInspector* class to implement the *IDispatchMessageInspector* interface, as follows:

```
public class ShoppingCartInspector : IDispatchMessageInspector
{
}
```

The *IDispatchMessageInspector* interface defines two methods that enable you to view and modify messages flowing into and out of the service.

4.   In the code view window, right-click IDispatchMessageInspector, point to Implement Interface, and then click Implement Interface.

Visual Studio 2005 generates stubs for the two methods in the *IDispatchMessageInspector* interface. These methods are called AfterReceiveRequest, which is invoked immediately before the service method is called, and BeforeReplySend, which runs when the service method has completed. Notice that the first parameter to both methods is a reference to a *Message* object. This is the message that has just been received or is about to be sent. The important point to realize is that you can modify the contents of this message, and any changes you make will be passed to the service method or returned to the client application depending on whether this is an inbound message (AfterReceiveRequest) or an outbound message (BeforeSendReply). For this reason, you should be especially careful that you don't add any code that inadvertently changes the contents of messages.

5. Remove the *throw* statement in the AfterReceiveRequest method, and replace it with the code shown in bold below:

```
public object AfterReceiveRequest(
    ref System.ServiceModel.Channels.Message request,
    System.ServiceModel.IClientChannel channel,
    System.ServiceModel.InstanceContext instanceContext)
{
    Console.WriteLine("Message received: {0}\n{1}\n\n",
        request.Headers.Action, request.ToString());
    return null;
}
```

The first statement displays the action that identifies the message, followed by the message itself.

It is sometimes useful to be able to correlate messages in the AfterReceiveRequest method with the corresponding response sent by the BeforeSendReply method. If you examine the BeforeSendReply method, you will see that it has a second parameter called *correlationState*. If you need to correlate request and reply messages, you can create a unique identifier in the AfterReceiveRequest method and return it. The WCF runtime will pass this same identifier in as the *correlationState* parameter to the BeforeSendReply-Method. In this example, you are not correlating request and reply messages, so the AfterReceiveRequest method simply returns *null*.

> **Caution**   The *Message* object contains a SOAP message, comprising XML text. You can use the generic GetBody<> method to parse the contents of the message and retrieve the data in the *<Body>* element, like this:
>
> ```
> System.Xml.XmlElement data =
>     request.GetBody<System.Xml.XmlElement>();
> ```
>
> However, the GetBody<> method is destructive. You can use it only once on a message, so doing this destroys the message, and the service method receives incorrect data. To examine a message safely, use the CreateBufferedCopy method of the request message to create a *MessageBuffer* object containing a copy of the message. You can then extract the copy of the message from this *MessageBuffer* object by using the CreateMessage method, like this:
>
> ```
> MessageBuffer requestBuffer = request.CreateBufferedCopy(10000);
> Message requestCopy = requestBuffer.CreateMessage();
> ```

6. Replace the *throw* statement in the BeforeSendReply method with the code shown in bold below:

```
public void BeforeSendReply(ref System.ServiceModel.Channels.Message reply,
    object correlationState)
{    Console.WriteLine("Reply sent: {0}\n{1}\n\n",
        reply.Headers.Action, reply.ToString());
}
```

This statement displays the action and the reply message on the console.

You will integrate the ShoppingCartInspector into the WCF runtime by using a service behavior. Sadly, there is no built-in "IntegrateShoppingCartInspector" service behavior in WCF. Fortunately, it is not difficult to write it yourself.

Create a service behavior for the ShoppingCartService service

1. Add the following class to the ShoppingCartInspector.cs file, underneath the *Shopping-CartInspector* class:

```
public class ShoppingCartBehavior: IServiceBehavior
{
}
```

The *IServiceBehavior* interface defines three methods that a class must implement to be able to act as a service behavior in the WCF infrastructure.

2. In the code view window, right-click IServiceBehavior, point to Implement Interface, and then click Implement Interface.

Visual Studio 2005 adds the following three methods to the *ShoppingCartBehavior* class:

- ❑ AddBindingParameters. Some behaviors can take additional data items as parameters to the binding elements, and an administrator or developer can supply this information in *the BindingParameterCollection* passed to this method. The WCF runtime invokes the AddBindingParameters method once for each URI that the service is listening on. The ShoppingCartBehavior service behavior does not require this facility.

- ❑ ApplyDispatcherBehavior. This method enables you to modify the behavior of *ServiceHost* object hosting the service. The *ServiceHost* object is passed in as the second parameter to this method. Use this method to perform tasks such as adding custom error handlers or message inspector objects into the runtime. The Shopping-CartBehavior service behavior will use this method to insert the message inspector into the processing path for each *EndpointDispatcher* object used by the service.

- ❑ Validate. The WCF runtime invokes this method to verify that the service meets your own custom requirements. For example, you can examine the service description passed in as the first parameter and if it does not conform to expectations (it doesn't specify how to handle faults, for example), you can reject the contract and throw an exception. The ShoppingCartBehavior service behavior does not use this feature either.

3. Comment out the *throw* statements in the AddBindingParameters and Validate methods. Replace the *throw* statement in the ApplyDispatchBehavior method with the code shown in bold below:

```
public void ApplyDispatchBehavior(ServiceDescription serviceDescription,
    System.ServiceModel.ServiceHostBase serviceHostBase)
{
    foreach (ChannelDispatcher chanDispatcher in
        serviceHostBase.ChannelDispatchers)
    {
        foreach (EndpointDispatcher epDispatcher in
            chanDispatcher.Endpoints)
        {
            epDispatcher.DispatchRuntime.MessageInspectors.Add(
                new ShoppingCartInspector());
        }
    }
}
```

This block of code iterates through each *EndpointDispatcher* object for each *ChannelDispatcher* object created by the *ServiceHost* object and adds a *ShoppingCartInspector* object into the *MessageInspectors* collection of each endpoint. Subsequently, whenever an *EndpointDispatcher* object dispatches a service method or whenever a service method returns to the *EndpointDispatcher* object, the message will pass through the *ShoppingCartInspector* object.

4. The final step is to apply the ShoppingCartBehavior to the ShoppingCartService when it runs. Open the Program.cs file in the ShoppingCartHost project and add the code shown below in bold between the statement that adds the service endpoint to the service and the statement that opens the service:

```
...
host.AddServiceEndpoint(typeof(ShoppingCartService.IShoppingCartService),
    customBind, "net.tcp://localhost:9090/ShoppingCartService");
host.Description.Behaviors.Add(new ShoppingCartService.ShoppingCartBehavior());
host.Open();
...
```

5. Start the solution without debugging. In the ShoppingCartClient console window, press Enter.

The client application runs as before (albeit a little more slowly). However, the console window running the service host now displays the SOAP messages being sent and received, like this:

6. Press Enter to close the client application console window. In the host application console window, press Enter to stop the service.

Controlling Client Communications

You have now seen how to configure the channel stack for a service and how to create a behavior that can modify the way in which the WCF runtime processes messages. In this section, you will examine how to programmatically connect a client application to a service, send messages, and process responses.

Connecting to a Service Programmatically

When a client application runs and connects to a service, the WCF runtime creates an infrastructure that is a simplified mirror of that created for the service. When you use a proxy object to connect to a service, behind the scenes the WCF runtime creates a binding object using the binding elements specified in the configuration file, and an endpoint based on the selected endpoint definition, and then uses these items to construct a *ChannelFactory* object. The WCF runtime uses the *ChannelFactory* object to instantiate the channel stack and connect it to the URI specified by the endpoint. When the client application invokes operations through the proxy object, the WCF runtime routes these requests through the channel stack and transmits them to the service. When a response message arrives from the service, it passes back up through the channel stack to the WCF runtime, and the proxy object then passes it back to the client application code.

You can create a client proxy class for a service by using the svcutil utility to query the metadata for the service and generate an assembly that you can add to the client project (you have performed this task at regular intervals during the exercises in this book). For security reasons, the administrator managing the host computer running a WCF service can elect to disable service metadata publishing. However, the WCF service developer can distribute an assembly containing the service contract, and you can use this to create a proxy object instead of using svcutil. In the next exercise, you will see how to connect to a service by using the service contract to create a proxy object at runtime.

> **Note** You can also use the svcutil to generate the proxy class from an assembly containing the service interface (you will use this technique in later chapters), but performing this task by using code provides you with additional flexibility and helps you to understand how the proxy class generated by using svcutil actually works.

Connect to the ProductsService service by using a service contract

1. In Visual Studio 2005, close the ShoppingCartService solution and then open the ProductsService solution in the Microsoft Press\WCF Step By Step\Chapter 10\ProductsServiceV2 folder under your \My Documents folder.

   This solution contains a copy of the ProductsService service and ProductsServiceHost application from Chapter 6, "Maintaining Service Contracts and Data Contracts," and a version of the ProductsClient application that has most of the code from the Program.cs file removed. The application configuration file and the file containing the proxy class definition have also been removed from the client application.

2. In Solution Explorer, open the ProductsServiceContract.cs file in the ProductsClient project and examine its contents. This file contains the definition of the service contract for the ProductsService service, IProductsServiceV2, and the associated data contracts (it was copied from the ProductsService.cs file in the ProductsService project). It does not contain any code that implements the service.

3. In Solution Explorer, open the Program.cs file in the ProductsClient project. This file contains the basic framework for the client application in the Main method, but the code that connects to the service and invokes operations is currently missing.

4. Add the following using statement to the list at the top of the file:

   ```
   using System.ServiceModel.Security;
   ```

5. In the Main method, in the *try* block, add the statements shown in bold below:

   ```
   ...
   try
   {
       NetTcpBinding tcpBinding = new NetTcpBinding(SecurityMode.Message);
       NetTcpSecurity tcpSec = tcpBinding.Security;
       tcpSec.Message.AlgorithmSuite = SecurityAlgorithmSuite.Basic128;
       tcpSec.Message.ClientCredentialType = MessageCredentialType.Windows;
   }
   ...
   ```

   The *NetTcpBinding* class implements the standard TCP binding. The ProductsService service exposes a TCP endpoint with the URI, "net.tcp://localhost:8080/TcpProductsService." If you examine the application configuration file for the ProductsServiceHost project, you will see that the binding configuration for the service endpoint uses message level security, with 128-bit encryption of messages and Windows authentication. The code you have just added sets the corresponding security properties for the *NetTcpBinding* object in the client application.

6. Add the following statement:

```
EndpointAddress address = new EndpointAddress(
    "net.tcp://localhost:8080/TcpProductsService");
```

The *EndpointAddress* object encapsulates the address that the client application uses to communicate with the service.

7. Add the code shown below:

```
Products.IProductsServiceV2 proxy =
    ChannelFactory<Products.IProductsServiceV2>.CreateChannel(
        tcpBinding, address);
```

The generic *ChannelFactory* class creates a channel by calling the static CreateChannel method. The new channel uses the binding specified in the first parameter and connects to the address provided in the second parameter. The value returned is a reference to the channel just created. A channel has a type based on the service contract. In this case, the channel is assigned to a variable of type Products.IProductsServiceV2. Remember that IProductsServiceV2 is the interface implemented by the service contract in the ProductsServiceContract.cs file. You can create channels based on any interface that is annotated with the *ServiceContract* attribute.

8. You can now invoke methods through the proxy variable. Add the following statements that invoke the ListSelectedProducts operation to retrieve a list of bicycle frames and display the results:

```
Console.WriteLine("Test 1: List all bicycle frames");
List<string> productNumbers = proxy.ListSelectedProducts("Frame");
foreach (string productNumber in productNumbers)
{
    Console.WriteLine("Number: " + productNumber);
}
Console.WriteLine();
```

There is one very subtle difference between this code and the corresponding code you used in Chapter 6: the value returned by the ListSelectedProducts method is now returned as a *List<string>* object rather than the array of strings passed back when using the generated proxy.

9. Close the connection to the service by setting the proxy variable to *null*, as follows:

```
proxy = null;
```

The complete code for the Main method should look like this (comments have been added to help clarify the code):

```
static void Main(string[] args)
{
    Console.WriteLine("Press ENTER when the service has started");
    Console.ReadLine();

    try
    {
        // Create the TCP binding and configure security
```

```
NetTcpBinding tcpBinding = new NetTcpBinding(SecurityMode.Message);
NetTcpSecurity tcpSec = tcpBinding.Security;
tcpSec.Message.AlgorithmSuite = SecurityAlgorithmSuite.Basic128;
tcpSec.Message.ClientCredentialType =
    MessageCredentialType.Windows;

// Create an endpoint
EndpointAddress address = new EndpointAddress(
    "net.tcp://localhost:8080/TcpProductsService");

// Build the channel for communicating with the service
Products.IProductsServiceV2 proxy =
    ChannelFactory<Products.IProductsServiceV2>.CreateChannel(
        tcpBinding, address);

// Obtain a list of all bicycle frames
Console.WriteLine("Test 1: List all bicycle frames");
List<string> productNumbers = proxy.ListSelectedProducts("Frame");
foreach (string productNumber in productNumbers)
{
    Console.WriteLine("Number: " + productNumber);
}
Console.WriteLine();

// Close the connection to the service
proxy = null;
}

catch (Exception e)
{
    Console.WriteLine("Exception: {0}", e.Message);
}

Console.WriteLine("Press ENTER to finish");
Console.ReadLine();
}
```

10.   Build the solution, and then exit Visual Studio 2005.

Before you run the client application, you must make one configuration change to the security of your computer: you must add your user account to the WarehouseStaff group. This is because the ProductsService service expects the user requesting the ListSelectedProducts operation to be a member of this group.

Configure security and test the client application

1.   On the Windows Start menu, right-click My Computer and then click Manage.

The Computer Management console appears.

2.   In the Computer Management console, expand the Local Users and Groups node in the System Tools folder, and then click the Groups folder. In the right pane, right-click the WarehouseStaff group and then click Add to Group.

The WarehouseStaff Properties window appears.

3. In the WarehouseStaff Properties window, click Add.

   The Select Users window appears.

4. In the Select Users window, enter the name of your own user account and then click OK.

5. In the WarehouseStaff Properties window, click OK.

6. Close the Computer Management console.

7. Log off from Windows and log back in again.

   This step is necessary for Windows to recognize your new membership of the WarehouseStaff group.

8. Start Visual Studio 2005, and open the ProductsService solution again.

9. Start the solution without debugging. In the ProductsServiceHost form, click Start. In the client console window, press Enter.

   The client application connects to the service, requests a list of bicycle frames, and displays the results, like this:

10. Press Enter in the client console window to close the client application. In the ProductsServiceHost form, click Stop and then close the form.

Using the *ClientBase Abstract* Class

In earlier chapters, you used the *ClientCredentials* property of the proxy object to specify the credentials to send to the service. The *Products.IProductsServiceV2* interface does not include this functionality. If you need to provide credentials other than your current Windows identity, you must define a class that extends the *System.ServiceModel.ClientBase* generic abstract class. This class incorporates the client-side *ChannelFactory* infrastructure through a series of constructors. You can expose whichever of the base class constructors are appropriate for your situation. The class should also provide an implementation of the interface that defines service contract. You can use the *Channel* property of the base class to route method calls through the channel to the service in each method implementing the service interface. The code below shows an example, creating a *ClientBase* class based on the Products.IProductsServiceV2 service contract and implementing the methods of the *Products.IProductsServiceV2* interface. This example also implements one of the ten available *ClientBase* constructors:

```
class ProductsServiceProxy : ClientBase<Products.IProductsServiceV2>,
                             Products.IProductsServiceV2
{
    public ProductsServiceProxy(Binding binding, EndpointAddress address) :
        base(binding, address)
    {
    }

    #region IProductsServiceV2 Members

    public List<string> ListSelectedProducts(string match)
    {
        return base.Channel.ListSelectedProducts(match);
    }

    public Products.Product GetProduct(string productNumber)
    {
        return base.Channel.GetProduct(productNumber);
    }

    public int CurrentStockLevel(string productNumber)
    {
        return base.Channel.CurrentStockLevel(productNumber);
    }

    public bool ChangeStockLevel(string productNumber, int newStockLevel,
                                 string shelf, int bin)
    {
        return base.Channel.ChangeStockLevel(productNumber, newStockLevel,
                                             shelf, bin);
    }

    public void UpdateProductDetails(Products.Product product)
    {
        base.Channel.UpdateProductDetails(product);
    }

    #endregion
}
```

You can instantiate this class and use it as your proxy object. The *ClientBase* class provides the *ClientCredentials* property that you can use to specify the credentials to transmit to the service by using the following familiar code:

```
ProductsServiceProxy proxy = new ProductsServiceProxy(tcpBinding, address);
proxy.ClientCredentials.Windows.ClientCredential.UserName = "Fred";
```

```
proxy.ClientCredentials.Windows.ClientCredential.Password = "Pa$$w0rd";
proxy.ClientCredentials.Windows.ClientCredential.Domain = "LON-DEV-01";
```

If you examine the code for any client proxy class generated by using the svcutil utility, you will see that it follows this approach.

Sending Messages Programmatically

A major objective of WCF is to provide a platform for interoperability. You can build WCF client applications that communicate with services created by using other, non-WCF technologies, such as Java. In this situation, if the administrator of the computer hosting the service disables service metadata publishing, the service developer is unlikely to provide you with a .NET Framework assembly containing the service contract. However, if you have documentation describing the SOAP messages that the service can accept and the responses the service emits, you can still access the service from a WCF client application; you can send messages directly through the channel. This is a very low-level, but extremely flexible approach that also gives a valuable insight into how the WCF runtime on the client converts proxy object method calls into SOAP messages. This is the subject of the final exercise in this chapter.

Send a message and process the response in the client application

1. In Visual Studio 2005, close the ProductsService solution and then open the SimpleProductsService solution in the Microsoft Press\WCF Step By Step\Chapter 10\SimpleService folder under your \My Documents folder.

    This solution contains a simplified version of the ProductsService service called SimpleProductsService. The settings in the app.config file cause the host application, SimpleProductsServiceHost, to publish the service with an HTTP endpoint using the BasicHttpBinding binding at the URI http://localhost:8040/SimpleProductsService/SimpleProductsService.svc.

2. Open the ProductsService.cs file in the SimpleProductsService project. Locate the *ISimpleProductsService* interface defining the service contract. It looks like this:

    ```
    // Simplified service contract
    [ServiceContract(Namespace="http://adventure-works.com/2006/09/30",
                     Name="SimpleProductsService")]
    public interface ISimpleProductsService
    {
        [OperationContract(Name = "ListProducts")]
        List<string> ListProducts();
    }
    ```

    The service contract defines a single operation: ListProducts (this is the same as the corresponding operation in the original ProductsService service). Note the namespace and name of the service contract. WCF uses the service contract namespace and name in conjunction with the name of the operations to define the SOAP messages, or actions, that the service publishes. In this case, the service will accept and process SOAP messages with an action of "http://adventure-works.com/2006/09/30/SimpleProductsSer-vice/ListProducts." Also, notice that the return type is List<string>, so the service will return a SOAP message containing a serialized list of strings.

> **Note** If you don't want to base the name of an action on the name and namespace properties of the service contract, you can provide your own name by specifying the *Action* and *ReplyAction* properties for the *OperationContract* attribute. You will learn more about the *Action* and *ReplyAction* properties in Chapter 13.

3. Edit the Program.cs file in the ProductsClient project. The Main method in this project currently creates a default *BasicHttpTcpBinding* and an *EndpointAddress* object. The URI in this endpoint is http://localhost:8040/SimpleProductsService/SimpleProductsService.svc; this is the address that the SimpleProductsService is configured to listen on.

   Add the following *using* statement to the list at the top of the file:

   ```
   using System.ServiceModel.Channels;
   ```

4. In the *try* block in the Main method, add the following statements shown in bold immediately after the code that creates the *EndpointAddress* object:

   ```
   ...
   EndpointAddress address = new EndpointAddress(
       "http://localhost:8040/SimpleProductsService/SimpleProductsService.svc");

   IChannelFactory<IRequestChannel> factory =
       httpBinding.BuildChannelFactory<IRequestChannel>();
   factory.Open(); ...
   ```

   The first statement creates a client-side *ChannelFactory* object that the client application can use for sending and receiving messages. The Open method instantiates the channel factory ready for building the channel stack.

   A channel implements interfaces that specify the messaging model that it supports. A channel can be an input channel, an output channel, an input and output channel (a duplex channel), a special form of output channel known as a *request channel*, or an equivalent input channel known as a *reply channel*. These interfaces are collectively referred to as channel shapes. The shapes available to a transport channel depend on several factors, including the type of the transport channel and the current value of its properties. For example, a TCP transport channel cannot act as a reply channel if it uses the buffered transfer mode; it can only operate as a bi-directional duplex channel in this case. However, the HTTP protocol operates using a send/receive pattern, and by default the HTTP transport channel conforms to the request channel shape in a client application, and the reply channel shape in a service.

5. The next step is to create the channel stack by using the channel factory. Add the following statements to perform this task:

   ```
   IRequestChannel channel = factory.CreateChannel(address);
   channel.Open();
   ```

6. You can now send messages and receive replies through the channel stack. You create a message by using the static CreateMessage method of the *Message* class. Add the following statement to your code:

```
Message request = Message.CreateMessage(MessageVersion.Soap11,
    "http://adventure-works.com/2006/09/30/SimpleProductsService/ListProducts");
```

When creating a message, you must specify the message version and a string specifying the requested action. The SOAP messaging specification has undergone several changes since it was first released, and the various bindings in WCF support different versions of the specification. The BasicHttpBinding binding is intended to be compatible with SOAP 1.1 messaging. The constant *MessageVersion.Soap11* indicates that the message should be formatted according to this specification. As discussed earlier, the action string combines the namespace and name of the service with the name of the operation.

The CreateMessage method is overloaded. This is the simplest version. Other overloads enable you to specify parameters to send to messages and to generate SOAP fault messages (useful if you are creating a service using this low-level mechanism).

7. To send a message by using the request/response pattern, you use the Request method of the channel. Add the statements shown below to your code:

```
Message reply = channel.Request(request);
Console.Out.WriteLine(reply);
```

The Request method blocks until a response is received from the service. The incoming response message is passed back as the return value from the Request method. After the application has received the response, the client simply displays it to the console.

8. At this point, you can send further requests to the service, but this simple client application will simply disconnect and finish. Add these statements to your code immediately before the end of the *try* block.

```
request.Close();
reply.Close();
channel.Close();
factory.Close();
```

Messages, channels, and channel factories all consume resources, so you should close them when you have finished using them.

9. Start the solution without debugging. In the ProductsServiceHost form, click Start. In the client application console window, press Enter.

The client application sends the ListProducts request to the service, which responds with a message containing a list of products. The client application displays the SOAP message containing this list, which has the following format:

```
<s:Envelope xmlns:s="http://schemas.xmlsoap.org/soap/envelope/">
  <s:Header />
  <s:Body>
    <ListProductsResponse xmlns="http://adventure-works.com/2006/09/30">
```

```
            <ListProductsResult
    xmlns:a="http://schemas.microsoft.com/2003/10/Serialization/Arrays"
    xmlns:i="http://www.w3.org/2001/XMLSchema-instance">
            <a:string>AR-5381</a:string>
            <a:string>BA-8327</a:string>

            …

            <a:string>VE-C304-S</a:string>
            <a:string>WB-H098</a:string>
          </ListProductsResult>
        </ListProductsResponse>
      </s:Body>
    </s:Envelope>
```

You can use the generic GetBody<> method of the reply message to parse the contents, as described earlier in this chapter.

10. Press Enter to close the client application console window. In the ProductsServiceHost form, click Stop and then close the form.

Summary

In this chapter, you have examined some of the internal mechanisms that the WCF runtime uses to send and receive messages. You have seen how to create bindings in code and how to use a *ServiceHost* object to create a channel for listening for requests. You have also seen how to use a *ChannelFactory* object in a client application for sending requests and receiving responses. You have learned how you can use a message inspector to examine the messages flowing from the channel stack into a service and how to create a service behavior for modifying the way in which the WCF runtime manages a service. You have also examined ways of sending messages from a client to a service if you don't have access to a proxy class generated by using the svcutil utility: you can create your own proxy or you can use the low-level messaging interface.

Chapter 11

Implementing OneWay and Asynchronous Operations

After completing this chapter, you will be able to:

- Explain the behavior of OneWay operations, and how they are impacted by service behavior and binding properties.

- Implement OneWay operations in a WCF service, and invoke them from a WCF client application.

- Implement asynchronous operations in a WCF service, and invoke operations asynchronously in a WCF client application.

- Explain the difference between invoking an operation asynchronously and implementing an operation that supports asynchronous execution.

- Use a message queue to send requests to a service asynchronously.

WCF client applications and services frequently follow the request/response messaging pattern for performing operations; the client application issues a request and then waits patiently while the message crosses the network, the service receives and processes the message, the service generates a reply, and the reply wends its way back across the network to the client application. If the client application does not require the service to send a response, then waiting for one is a waste of time and can impact the responsiveness of the client application. In this situation, you might find that a OneWay operation can improve performance of the client application.

If the client application does require a response but can safely perform other tasks while waiting for this response, then you should use asynchronous method invocation. This technique enables the client application to send a request and then continue execution. When a reply message arrives from the service, a separate thread in the client application handles the response.

OneWay operations and asynchronous operations both require that the client application and the service are running at the same time. If this is not the case, then you should consider using message queues as the transport medium between the client application and the service. A message queue can provide durable storage for messages. However, you must design client applications and services carefully if you are planning on using message queues, as the request/response messaging pattern is not appropriate in this case.

In this chapter, you will look in detail at these three options for invoking operations in a WCF service and maximizing the scope for parallelism in your applications.

> **Note**   It is also possible for a client to provide a callback method for a service. The service can send a message that invokes this method. WCF client applications and services can use this mechanism to implement events, enabling the service to notify a client application of some significant occurrence. You will examine this feature in more detail in Chapter 14, "Using a Callback Contract to Publish and Subscribe to Events."

Implementing OneWay Operations

When a client application invokes a OneWay operation, it can continue running without waiting for the service to complete the operation. You can indicate that an operation is OneWay by specifying the OneWay behavior in the operation contract. The simplest way to achieve this is to set the *IsOneWay* property to *true* in the *OperationContract* attribute when defining the operation. You will see an example of this in the exercises in this section.

The Effects of a OneWay Operation

Marking an operation as OneWay has several implications. The most important one is that such an operation cannot pass any data back to the client application; it must return a *void* and cannot have parameters marked as *out* or *ref*. When a OneWay operation starts running in the service, the client application has no further contact with it and will not even be aware of whether the operation was successful or not. If the operation raises an exception that would normally generate a SOAP fault message, this SOAP fault message is simply discarded and never sent to the client.

> **Note**   If you invoke a OneWay operation by using the Request method of an *IRequestChannel* object as described in Chapter 10, "Programmatically Controlling the Configuration and Communications," the value of the response message returned will be *null*.

Invoking a OneWay operation is not simply a matter of generating a message and throwing it at an endpoint where, hopefully, the service is listening. Although a client application does not know when a OneWay operation has completed (successfully or not), it is still important for the client application to know that the service has received the message. If the service is not listening on the specified endpoint, the client will be alerted with an exception. Additionally, if the service is very busy, it might not be able to accept the message immediately. Some transports implement a buffering mechanism for requests and will not accept further messages if the number of outstanding requests is too big. For example, the TcpTransport channel has a configurable property called *ListenBacklog* that specifies the maximum number of connection requests that can be pending. If this number is exceeded, then subsequent requests will be blocked until the number of pending requests drops; the client application will wait until the request is accepted. If you want to be absolutely certain that the service has received the message and that the transport has not just buffered it, you can invoke the OneWay operation in a reliable session. The service will send back an acknowledgement to the client when it starts processing the message, as described in Chapter 9, "Implementing Reliable Sessions." Reliable messaging has some other beneficial side effects on OneWay operations, as you will see in the exercise.

OneWay Operations and Timeouts

There are several possible failure points when sending messages over a network. If a client application does not receive a response to a request within a specified period of time, the WCF runtime on the client computer assumes that something has gone wrong and throws a System.TimeoutException to the client application. The duration of this timeout period is configurable as the *SendTimeout* property of the client binding and has a default value of 1 minute. If a client application invokes a OneWay operation, the service only needs to accept the message within this time period; it does not have to complete processing the message in this time.

Malicious users have often exploited OneWay operations to perform Denial of Service attacks; they bombard a service with a large number of requests, causing it to grind to a halt as it attempts to process all the messages. Bindings have a *ReceiveTimeout* property, which is used by the WCF runtime managing the service. If an operation takes longer than the amount of time specified by this value to complete, the WCF runtime aborts the operation and throws a Timeout exception. The default value for the *ReceiveTimeout* property is 10 minutes. This is a long time, and you should consider changing this value unless you genuinely have operations that could take this long to perform.

In the following exercises, you will implement a OneWay operation and investigate what happens when you invoke it from a client application. To provide another variation in the host environment, you will create a new WCF service that runs using the ASP.NET Development Web Server supplied with Visual Studio 2005. Developers frequently use this environment when building new Web services and then deploy them to IIS when they are complete. The Web service you will create will provide administrative functions for the AdventureWorks organization.

The first operation you will implement enables an administrator to request a report of the current day's sales. This report could take several minutes to run, and you don't want to hold up the administrator while this is happening, so you will implement this feature as a OneWay operation.

Create the AdventureWorks administrative operations service

1. Using Visual Studio 2005, create a new Web site using the WCF Service template. In the New Web Site dialog box, select File System from the Location drop-down list box and set the location to the Microsoft Press\WCF Step By Step\Chapter 11\AdventureWorksAdmin folder under your \My Documents folder. Make sure you set the Language to Visual C#.

2. In Solution Explorer, select the C:\...\AdventureWorksAdmin\ project. In the Properties window, set the *Use dynamic ports* property to *False* and set the Port number to 9090.

    By default, the ASP.NET Development Web Server picks an unused port when it starts running. For this exercise, it is useful to know in advance exactly which port the service will use, and disabling the *dynamic ports* property enables you to specify a fixed port.

3. In Solution Explorer, expand the App_Code folder and edit the Service.cs file.

4. In the code view window, remove everything underneath the *using* statements (leave the *using* statements intact).

5. Add a new service contract called *IAdventureWorksAdmin* to the file. In the *ServiceContract* attribute, set the *Namespace* property to *http://adventure-works.com/2007/01/01* (pretend it is January 1st, and that you use the recommended approach of incorporating the creation date into namespaces), and set the *Name* property to *AdministrativeService*, like this:

```
[ServiceContract(Namespace="http://adventure-works.com/2007/01/01",
                 Name="AdministrativeService")]
public interface IAdventureWorksAdmin
{
}
```

6. Add an operation called GenerateDailySalesReport, shown below in bold, to the service contract. Mark it as a OneWay operation by setting the *IsOneWay* property of the *OperationContract* attribute to *true*:

```
public interface IAdventureWorksAdmin
{
    [OperationContract(IsOneWay = true)]
    void GenerateDailySalesReport(string id);
}
```

    Notice that this method returns a *void*. All OneWay methods must be void methods. OneWay methods can take parameters, as long as they are not marked with the *ref* or *out* modifiers. The parameter passed to the GenerateDailySalesReport method will contain a string that you will use to identify an invocation of the operation.

7. In Solution Explorer, right-click the C:\...\AdventureWorksAdmin\ project, and then click Add Reference. In the Add Reference dialog box, add a reference to the *PresentationFramework* assembly and then click OK.

8. Add a class called *IAdventureWorksAdmin* to the file, underneath the service contract. This class should implement the *IAdventureWorksAdmin* interface and provide the GenerateDailySalesReport method, as follows:

```
public class AdventureWorksAdmin : IAdventureWorksAdmin
{
    public void GenerateDailySalesReport(string id)
    {
        // Simulate generating the report
```

```
    // by sleeping for 1 minute and 10 seconds
    System.Threading.Thread.Sleep(70000);
    string msg = String.Format("Report {0} generated", id);
    System.Windows.MessageBox.Show(msg);
    }
}
```

In this version of the WCF service, you will simulate the process of generating the report by sleeping for 70 seconds (you will understand why I have selected a duration of just over 1 minute in the next exercise). When the report has been generated, the method displays a message box.

> **Important** The message box displayed by this method is primarily so you can observe when the method completes. You should never incorporate interactive message boxes like this in a production service. If you need to output messages for testing or debugging purposes, you should generally use the System.Diagnostics.Debug.WriteLine method and send messages to a trace listener.

9. In Solution Explorer, edit the Service.svc file. Modify this file to refer to the *Adventure-WorksAdmin* class, as shown in bold below:

```
<% @ServiceHost Language=C# Debug="true" Service="AdventureWorksAdmin" CodeBehind="~/
App_Code/Service.cs" %>
```

10. In Solution Explorer, edit the Web.config file by using the WCF Service Configuration Editor.

11. In the WCF Service Configuration Editor, select the MyService service in the Services folder. In the right pane, change the *Name* property of the service to *AdventureWorksAdmin*.

    Notice that this service also has a behavior defined called returnFaults. You will examine this behavior later in this exercise.

12. In the left pane, expand the service (the name will still appear as MyService until you click it), expand the Endpoints folder, and click the endpoint labeled (Empty Name). In the right pane, verify that this endpoint uses the wsHttpBinding binding. Set the *Name* property of the endpoint to *AdventureWorksAdminHttpBinding* and set the *Contract* property to *IAdventureWorksAdmin*.

13. In the left pane, add a new binding configuration to the Bindings folder based on the wsHttpBinding binding type.

14. In the right pane displaying the properties of the new binding, set the *Name* property to *AdventureWorksAdminHttpBindingConfig*. It should never take more than 5 minutes to generate the daily report, so set the *ReceiveTimeout* property to 00:05:00.

15. In the left pane, return to the AdventureWorksAdminHttpBinding endpoint. In the right pane, set the *BindingConfiguration* property to *AdventureWorksAdminHttpBindingConfig*.

16. In the left pane, expand the Advanced folder, expand the ServiceBehaviors folder. Note that the service has a behavior called returnFaults.

    This is the service behavior mentioned earlier. If you examine this service behavior using the WCF Configuration Editor, you will see that it contains a *<serviceDebug>* element with the *IncludeExceptionDetailInFaults* property set to *True*. Leave this element intact for the time being, but bear in mind that you should disable this property of the behavior, or remove the behavior, before deploying the service to a live environment.

17. Select the returnFaults behavior and then click Add in the right pane. In the Adding Behavior Element Extension Sections dialog box, click serviceMetadata, and then click Add. In the left pane, click the *<serviceMetadata>* element that has just been added to the returnFaults service behavior. In the right pane, set the *HttpGetEnabled* property to *True* (leave the *HttpsGetEnabled* property set to *False*).

    This element enables metadata publishing for the service. You will query the metadata for the service when you build the client application for testing this service.

18. Save the configuration file and exit the WCF Service Configuration Editor.

19. In Visual Studio 2005, start the solution without debugging.

    If you have not made any mistakes so far, the ASP.NET Development Server will start (if it is not already running) and display an icon in the bottom right corner of the Windows taskbar. Internet Explorer will run, navigate to the site *http://localhost:9090/Adventure-WorksAdmin/Service.svc*, and display the page describing how to generate the WSDL description for the service and how to use the service in a client application, like this:

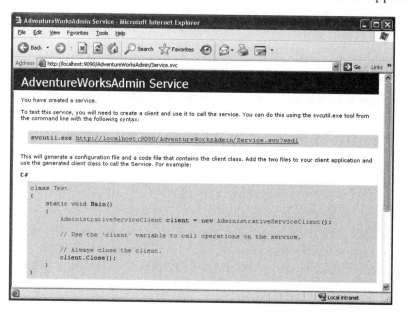

> **Tip**   If Internet Explorer displays a blank page, manually enter the address
> *http://localhost:9090/AdventureWorksAdmin/Service.svc* in the address bar and
> press Enter to display the page for the service.

20. Close Internet Explorer and return to Visual Studio 2005.

21. In Solution Explorer, right-click the C:\...\AdventureWorksAdmin\ project and then
    click Start Options. In the Start Options page, select the option "Don't open a page. Wait
    for a request from an external application," and then click OK.

    When you start this project in subsequent exercises, you just need the service to start
    running but don't want Internet Explorer to open.

Create a WCF client application for testing the AdventureWorks administrative operations service

1. In Visual Studio 2005, add a new project to the AdventureWorksAdmin solution. In the
   Add New Project dialog box, select the Visual C# project types, select the Console Application template, set the Name to AdventureWorksAdminTestClient, and save it in the
   Microsoft Press\WCF Step By Step\Chapter 11 folder under your \My Documents
   folder.

2. In Solution Explorer, right-click the AdventureWorksAdminTestClient project and then
   click Add Service Reference. In the Add Service Reference dialog box, type http://local-
   host:9090/AdventureWorksAdmin/Service.svc in the Service URI text box, type AdventureWorksAdmin in the Service reference name text box, and then click OK.

   This step generates the client proxy for the AdventureWorksAdmin WCF service and
   adds it to the AdventureWorksAdminTestClient project. It also creates an application
   configuration file.

3. Open the app.config file and examine its contents. Note that Visual Studio 2005 has
   added and configured a binding for communication with the AdventureWorksAdmin
   service called AdventureWorksAdminHttpBinding.

4. In Solution Explorer, in the AdventureWorksAdminTestClient project, open the file Pro-
   gram.cs. Add the following *using* statement to the list at the start of the file:

   ```
   using AdventureWorksAdminTestClient.AdventureWorksAdmin;
   ```

   The proxy class generated in the previous step is in this namespace.

5. Add the statements shown below in bold to the Main method:

   ```
   static void Main(string[] args)
   {    try
       {
           AdministrativeServiceClient proxy =
               new AdministrativeServiceClient
                   ("AdventureWorksAdminHttpBinding");
   ```

```
        Console.WriteLine("Requesting first report at {0}", DateTime.Now);
        proxy.GenerateDailySalesReport("First Report");
        Console.WriteLine("First report request completed at {0}",
            DateTime.Now);
        Console.WriteLine("Requesting second report at {0}", DateTime.Now);
        proxy.GenerateDailySalesReport("Second Report");
        Console.WriteLine("Second report request completed at {0}",
            DateTime.Now);

        proxy.Close();
    }
    catch (Exception e)
    {
        Console.WriteLine("Exception: {0}", e.Message);
    }
    Console.WriteLine("Press ENTER to finish");
    Console.ReadLine();
}
```

This code creates a proxy object and then invokes the GenerateDailySalesReport operation twice in quick succession, displaying the date and time before and after each request.

6. In Solution Explorer, right-click the AdventureWorksAdmin solution and then click Set Startup Projects. In the Property Pages dialog box, select the Multiple startup projects option. Set the action for both projects to Start, and then click OK.

7. Start the solution without debugging.

The request for the first report completes quickly (it might take a few seconds, depending on whether the WCF service is still running or Visual Studio 2005 needs to start it, but it will be less than the 70 seconds that the operation runs for), but the second request causes the client application to stop. If you wait for 1 minute, the client application eventually times out with an error (the default value of the *SendTimeout* property of the binding is 1 minute):

You should also notice that the AdventureWorksAdmin service successfully completes the first request and displays a message box:

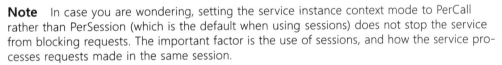

Report First Report generated

OK

Click OK to close the message box. If you wait for another 70 seconds, the message box for the second request appears as well. This shows that the request was actually received successfully by the AdventureWorksAdmin service, although something appears to have gone awry with the client application.

Click OK to close the second message box, and press Enter to close the client application console window.

So, what went wrong? The problem lies partly in the fact that the service uses sessions, and partly in the concurrency mode of the service. If you disable sessions (by using a binding that does not support them, or by setting the *SessionMode* property of the *ServiceContract* attribute of the *IAdventureWorksAdmin* interface to *SessionMode.NotAllowed*), then the concurrent calls to the service are not blocked. However, sessions are a useful feature, especially if you want to make effective use of transactions, or control the sequencing of operations. Consequently, many services make a lot of use of them. If you recall from Chapter 7, "Maintaining State and Sequencing Operations," services that use sessions are single-threaded by default. This behavior causes the service to block the second request from the client application until the first has completed processing.

> **Note** In case you are wondering, setting the service instance context mode to PerCall rather than PerSession (which is the default when using sessions) does not stop the service from blocking requests. The important factor is the use of sessions, and how the service processes requests made in the same session.
>
> The blocking problem is also exacerbated by the fact that the AdventureWorksAdmin service uses the HTTP transport, which does not support request queuing like the TCP transport does. If you had used a TCP endpoint, the client would be able to continue as soon as the second request would be queued by the transport channel, rather than waiting for it to be accepted by the service. The second request would still not be processed until the first had completed, however.

In the next exercise you will see how to address this situation.

Resolve the blocking problem with the OneWay request in the WCF client application

1. In Solution Explorer, edit the Service.cs file in the App_Code folder in the C:\...\AdventureWorksAdmin\ project. Add the *ServiceBehavior* attribute shown below in bold to the *AdventureWorksAdmin* class:

```
[ServiceBehavior(ConcurrencyMode=ConcurrencyMode.Multiple)]
public class AdventureWorksAdmin : IAdventureWorksAdmin
```

```
{
    ...
}
```

As described in Chapter 7, the *ConcurrencyMode* property of the *ServiceBehavior* attribute enables you to change the threading model used by the session. Selecting the value *ConcurrencyMode.Multiple* allows the service to process multiple concurrent requests in the same session, although you must ensure that the code you write in each method is thread-safe (as it is in this example).

2. Start the solution without debugging.

   This time, both requests are submitted successfully (the client application displays the message "Second report request completed at ..."), but the client application now stops and times out at the end of the Main method:

   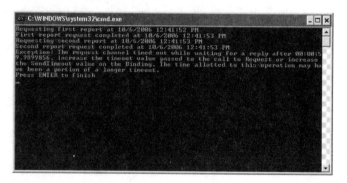

   Press Enter to close the client console window, and press OK when the two message boxes displayed by the service appear.

   This time, the blockage is caused by a combination of the security implemented by the service and the call to the Close method of the proxy. Remember that the wsHttpBinding binding uses sessions and message-level security by default. When terminating a session, the client application and service exchange messages to ensure that the session terminates in a secure and controlled manner. The client application will not finish until this message exchange completes, and the service does not send its final message until all operations have completed, and hence a timeout occurs. Two possible solutions are to disable security (absolutely not recommended) or to switch to transport-level security (which requires installing a certificate and configuring HTTPS). However, there is another workaround available if you want to use message-level security; you can use reliable sessions.

3. In the C:\...\AdventureWorksAdmin\ project, edit the web.config file by using the WCF Service Configuration Editor. In the WCF Service Configuration Editor, expand the Bindings folder and select the AdventureWorksAdminHttpBindingConfig binding configuration. In the right pane, set the *Enabled* property in the *ReliableSession* Properties section to *True*. Save the file, and close the WCF Service Configuration Editor.

4. Follow the same procedure to edit the app.config file of the client application and enable reliable sessions in the AdventureWorksAdminHttpBinding binding configuration.

5. Start the solution without debugging.

   The client should successfully send both requests and close the session without timing out.

In Chapter 9, you investigated the acknowledgement messages sent by the reliable sessions protocol implemented by WCF. The purpose of this protocol is to assure both parties (the client and the service) that the messages they have sent have been received. When the client application closes its session, it does not need to wait for the service to actually complete its processing as long as the service has acknowledged all messages sent by the client application; the Close method can complete before the service actually terminates the session.

> **Note** If you need to implement OneWay operations but cannot guarantee the thread-safety of the corresponding methods, you *should not* set the *ConcurrencyMode* attribute of the service to *ConcurrencyMode.Multiple*. Just enable reliable sessions.
>
> When you enable reliable sessions, the client will not wait for a single-threaded service to accept each message before continuing; instead, the client will be able to carry on as soon as the service has acknowledged the message. Message acknowledgements are generated by the WCF runtime hosting the service before the message is dispatched to the service instance; so they are not blocked by a single-threaded service instance.
>
> If you are curious, try disabling multiple-threading for the AdventureWorksAdmin service, but keep reliable sessions enabled and then run the solution. The client application will run without blocking. However, you should observe the difference in the behavior of the service. Previously, both calls to the GenerateDailySalesReport method executed concurrently, and the second message box appeared a couple of seconds after the first. If you use reliable messaging rather than multiple threads, the method calls run sequentially, and the second message box will appear at least 70 seconds after the first.

Recommendations for Using OneWay Methods

You have seen that OneWay methods are a very useful mechanism for improving the performance of a client application by enabling it to continue executing without waiting for the service to complete processing operation requests. However, to maximize the concurrency between a client application and a service, you should bear in mind the following points, summarizing what you have seen in the exercises:

■ Services that don't use sessions provide the greatest degree of parallelism by default. If a service requires or allows sessions, then depending on how the transport used by the binding buffers messages, the service can block OneWay requests if it is already busy processing a message in the same session. This is true even if the service uses the PerCall service instance context mode; it is the fact that the service uses sessions that causes the service to block requests.

■ Services that use sessions can set the concurrency mode to enable multi-threading, but you must ensure that the operations in the service are thread-safe. Enabling multi-threading allows the service to execute requests in the same session simultaneously.

■ Enable reliable sessions to allow a client application to close a connection to a service before the service has completed processing of all outstanding requests.

Invoking and Implementing Operations Asynchronously

A OneWay operation is useful for "fire and forget" scenarios, where the client application does not expect the service to pass back any information. However, many operations do not fit into this scheme of working and return data to the client application. To cater for these situations, WCF supports asynchronous operations and the IAsyncResult design pattern. WCF enables you to implement the IAsyncResult design pattern in two ways: in the client application invoking the operation and in the WCF service implementing the operation.

> **More Info** The IAsyncResult design pattern is commonly used throughout the .NET Framework and is not peculiar to WCF. For details, see the topic "Asynchronous Programming Design Patterns" in the .NET Framework Developer's guide, available in the Microsoft Visual Studio 2005 Documentation, and also online at http://msdn2.microsoft.com/en-us/library/ms228969.aspx.

Invoking an Operation Asynchronously in a Client Application

WCF enables you to generate a version of the proxy class that a client application can use to invoke operations asynchronously; you can use the */async* flag with the svcutil utility when creating the proxy class. When you specify this flag, svcutil generates *begin* and *end* pairs of methods for each operation. The client application can invoke the *begin* method to initiate the operation. The *begin* method returns after sending the request, but a new thread created by the .NET Framework runtime in the client waits for the response. When you invoke the *begin* method, you also provide the name of a callback method. When the service finishes the operation and returns the results to the client proxy, the new thread executes this callback method. You use the callback method to retrieve the results from the service. You should also call the *end* method for the operation to indicate that you have processed the response.

It is important to understand that you do not need to modify the service in any way to support this form of asynchronous programming. Indeed, the service itself does not necessarily have to be a WCF service; it could be a service implemented by using other technologies. The code making the operation appear asynchronous to the client application is encapsulated inside the proxy generated on the client side and the .NET Framework runtime. All the threading issues are handled by code running in the WCF runtime on the client. As far as the service is concerned, the operation is being invoked in the exact same, synchronous manner that you have seen in all the preceding chapters in this book.

Implementing an Operation Asynchronously in a WCF Service

As mentioned earlier, WCF also enables you to implement an operation that can execute asynchronously. In this case, the service provides its own pair of *begin* and *end* methods that constitute the operation. The code in the client application invokes the operation through the proxy object using the ordinary operation name (not the *begin* method). The WCF runtime transparently routes the operation to the *begin* method, so the client application is not necessarily aware that the service implements the operation as an asynchronous method.

As a variation, the developer of the service can add logic to the *begin* method to choose whether the operation should run synchronously or asynchronously. For example, if the current workload of the service is light, it might make sense to perform the operation synchronously to allow it to complete as soon as possible. As the workload increases, the service might choose to implement the operation asynchronously. Implementing operations in this manner in a service can increase the scalability and performance of a service without the need to modify client applications. It is recommended that you implement any operation that returns data to a client application after performing a lengthy piece of processing in this way.

> **Important**   You should understand the important distinction between asynchronous operation invocation in the client application and asynchronous operation implementation in the service. Asynchronous invocation in the client application enables the client to initiate the operation and then continue its own processing while waiting for a response. Asynchronous implementation in the service enables the service to offload the processing to another thread, or sleep while waiting for some background process to complete. A client application invoking an operation implemented asynchronously in the service still waits for the operation to complete before continuing.

You can specify that an operation supports asynchronous processing by setting the *AsyncPattern* property to *true* in the *OperationContract* attribute when defining the operation and providing a pair of methods that follow a prescribed naming convention and signature and that implement the IAsyncResult design pattern.

In the next set of exercises, you will add another operation called CalculateTotalValueOfStock to the AdventureWorksAdmin service. The purpose of this operation is to determine the total value of every item currently held in the AdventureWorks warehouse. This operation could take a significant time to run, so you will implement it as an asynchronous method.

Add an asynchronous operation to the AdventureWorks administrative service

1. In Visual Studio 2005, edit the Service.cs file in the App_Code folder in the C:\...\AdventureWorksAdmin\ project. Add the following operation, shown in bold, to the IAdventureWorksAdmin service contract:

```
[ServiceContract(Namespace="http://adventure-works.com/2007/01/01",
                Name="AdministrativeService")]
public interface IAdventureWorksAdmin
{
```

```
[OperationContract(IsOneWay = true)]
void GenerateDailySalesReport(string id);

[OperationContract(AsyncPattern = true)]
IAsyncResult BeginCalculateTotalValueOfStock(string id,
                                             AsyncCallback cb,
                                             object s);
int EndCalculateTotalValueOfStock(IAsyncResult r);
}
```

This operation consists of two methods: BeginCalculateTotalValueOfStock and EndCalculateTotalValueOfStock. Together, they constitute a single asynchronous operation called CalculateTotalValueOfStock. It is important that you name both methods in the operation following this convention for them to be recognized correctly when you build the client proxy. You can specify whatever parameters the operation requires in the *begin* method (in this case, the client application will pass in a string parameter to identify each invocation of the operation), but the final two parameters must be an AsyncCallback referencing a callback method in the client application and an *object* holding state information provided by the client application. The return type must be IAsyncResult. The *end* method must take a single parameter of type IAsyncResult, but the return type should be the type appropriate for the operation. In this case, the CalculateTotalValueOfStock operation returns an *int* containing the calculated value.

The other key part of this operation is the *AsyncPattern* property of the *OperationContract* attribute. You only apply the *OperationContract* attribute to the *begin* method. When you generate the metadata for this service (when building the client proxy, for example), this property causes the *begin* and *end* methods to be recognized as the implementation of a single asynchronous operation.

2. In Solution Explorer, right-click the App_Code folder in the C:\...\AdventureWorksAdmin\ project and then click Add Existing Item. Add the file AsyncResult.cs, located in the Microsoft Press\WCF Step By Step\Chapter 11\Async folder under your \My Documents folder.

3. Open the AsyncResult.cs file and examine its contents. It contains a single generic class called *AsyncResult* that implements the *IAsyncResult* interface. Detailed discussion of this class and the *IAsyncResult* interface is outside the scope of this book, but the purpose of the *AsyncResult* class is to provide synchronization methods and state information required by other classes that implement asynchronous methods. For this exercise, the important members of the *AsyncResult* class are:

    ❑ *Data*. This property provides access to the data returned by the asynchronous operation. In this example, the CalculateTotalValueOfStock operation will populate this property and return the *AsyncResult* object to the client application when it executes the *end* method.

    ❑ AsyncResult. This is the constructor. It take two parameters which it stores in private fields. The service will use the *synchronous* parameter to indicate whether it really is invoking the operation synchronously, and the *stateData* parameter will be a reference to the object passed in as the final parameter to the *begin* method (it is important to save this object, as it has to be returned to the client application to enable it to complete processing).

4. Return to the Service.cs file in the App_Code folder. Add the following delegate to the *AdventureWorksAdmin* class:

```
private delegate void AsyncSleepCaller(int millisecondsTimeout);
```

You will use this delegate in the methods that you will add in the next steps.

5. Add the following method to the *AdventureWorksAdmin* class:

```
// CalculateTotalValueOfStock operation
// Service can elect to perform the operation
// synchronously or asynchronously
public IAsyncResult BeginCalculateTotalValueOfStock(string id,
    AsyncCallback callback, object state)
{
    AsyncResult<int> calcTotalValueResult;

    // Generate a random number.
    // The value generated determines the "complexity" of the operation
        Random generator = new Random();

    // If the random number is even, then the operation is simple
    // so perform it synchronously
    if ((generator.Next() % 2) == 0)
    {
        calcTotalValueResult = new AsyncResult<int>(true, state);
        System.Threading.Thread.Sleep(20000);
        System.Windows.MessageBox.Show(
            "Synchronous sleep completed");
        calcTotalValueResult.Data = 5555555;
        calcTotalValueResult.Complete();
    }
    // Otherwise, the operation is complex so perform it asynchronously
    else
    {
        // Perform the operation asynchronously
        calcTotalValueResult = new AsyncResult<int>(false, state);
        AsyncSleepCaller asyncSleep = new
            AsyncSleepCaller(System.Threading.Thread.Sleep);
        IAsyncResult result = asyncSleep.BeginInvoke(30000,
            new AsyncCallback(EndAsyncSleep), calcTotalValueResult);
    }

    callback(calcTotalValueResult);
    System.Windows.MessageBox.Show(
        "BeginCalculateTotalValueOfStock completed for " + id);
    return calcTotalValueResult;
}
```

Note   You can find this code in the file BeginCalculateTotalValueOfStock.txt in the Async folder under the Chapter 11 folder.

Again, the exact details of how this method works are outside the scope of this book (strictly speaking, it has nothing to do with WCF). But to summarize, the method generates a random number, and if this number is even it performs the operation synchronously, otherwise it performs it asynchronously. In the synchronous case, the code creates a new *AsyncResult* object, sleeps for 20 seconds to simulate the time taken to perform the calculation, and then populates the *AsyncResult* object with the result—5555555. In the asynchronous case, the code also creates an *AsyncResult* object, but spawns a thread that sleeps for 30 seconds in the background. It does not populate the *AsyncResult* object, as this happens when the background, when the sleeping thread, wakes up later. In both cases, the code invokes the callback method in the client application, passing the *AsyncResult* object as its parameter. The client application will retrieve the results of the calculation from this object. The same *AsyncResult* object is also returned as the result of this method (this is a requirement of the IAsyncResult design pattern).

The method also displays message boxes helping you to trace the execution of the method and establish whether the operation is running synchronously or asynchronously.

6. Add the *end* method shown below to the *AdventureWorksAdmin* class:

```
public int EndCalculateTotalValueOfStock(IAsyncResult r)
{
    // Wait until the AsyncResult object indicates the
    // operation is complete
    AsyncResult<int> result = r as AsyncResult<int>;
    if (!result.CompletedSynchronously)
    {
        System.Threading.WaitHandle waitHandle = result.AsyncWaitHandle;
        waitHandle.WaitOne();
    }

    // Return the calculated value in the Data field
    return result.Data;
}
```

Note   You can find this code in the file EndCalculateTotalValueOfStock.txt in the Async folder under the Chapter 11 folder.

This method is invoked when the *begin* method completes. The purpose of this method is to retrieve the result of the calculation from the *Data* property in the *AsyncResult* object passed in as the parameter. If the operation is being performed asynchronously, it might not have completed yet. (Applications invoking the *begin* method for an asynchronous operation can call the *end* method at any time after the *begin* finishes, so the *end* method should ensure that the operation has completed before returning.) In this case, the method waits until the *AsyncResult* object indicates that the operation has finished before extracting the data and returning.

7. Add the following method to the *AdventureWorksAdmin* class:

```
private void EndAsyncSleep(IAsyncResult ar)
{
    // This delegate indicates that the "complex" calculation
    // has finished
    AsyncResult<int> calcTotalValueResult =
        (AsyncResult<int>)ar.AsyncState;
    calcTotalValueResult.Data = 9999999;
    calcTotalValueResult.Complete();

    System.Windows.MessageBox.Show("Asynchronous sleep completed");
}
```

> **Note**   You can find this code in the file EndAsyncSleep.txt in the Async folder under the Chapter 11 folder.

If the *begin* method decides to perform its task asynchronously, it simulates performing the calculation by creating a new thread and sleeping for 30 seconds. The EndAsync-Sleep method is registered as a callback when the background sleep starts, and when the 30 seconds have expired, the operating system reawakens the thread and invokes this method. This method populates the *Data* field of the *AsyncResult* object, and then indicates that the operation is now complete. This releases the main thread in the service, waiting in the *end* method, and allows it to return the data to the client application.

Notice that the values returned are different if the service performs the operation synchronously (5555555) and asynchronously (9999999).

8. Rebuild the solution.

Invoke the CalculateTotalValueOfStock operation in the WCF client application

1. In the AdventureWorksAdminTestClient project, expand the Service References folder, right-click the AdventureWorksAdmin.map file, and then click Update Service Reference.

   This action generates a new version of the client proxy, including the CalculateTotalValueOfStock operation.

2. Expand the AdventureWorksAdmin.map file, and open the AdventureWorksAdmin.cs file. In the code view window, examine the updated proxy. Notice that the new operation is called CalculateTotalValueOfStock and that there is no sign of the *begin* and *end* methods that implement this operation; the fact that this operation is implemented asynchronously is totally transparent to the client application.

3. Edit the Program.cs file. Remove the statements in the *try* block that invoke the GenerateDailySalesReport operation and the Console.WriteLine statements, and replace them with the following code shown in bold:

```
try
{
    AdministrativeServiceClient proxy =
        new AdministrativeServiceClient("AdventureWorksAdminHttpBinding");

    int totalValue = proxy.CalculateTotalValueOfStock("First Calculation");
    Console.WriteLine("Total value of stock is {0}", totalValue);

    totalValue = proxy.CalculateTotalValueOfStock("Second Calculation");
    Console.WriteLine("Total value of stock is {0}", totalValue);

    totalValue = proxy.CalculateTotalValueOfStock("Third Calculation");
    Console.WriteLine("Total value of stock is {0}", totalValue);

    proxy.Close();
}
```

These statements simply invoke the CalculateTotalValueOfStock method three times and display the results. Hopefully, the service will execute at least one of these calls in a different manner from the other two (either synchronously or asynchronously).

4. Start the solution without debugging.

If you are unlucky, you will have to wait for 20 seconds before you see the first message box appear.

This is because the random number generator in the BeginCalculateTotalValueOfStock method produced an even number and is executing the method synchronously. This should be followed by the following message box:

You will see the result (5555555) displayed in the client application console window as soon as you click OK in the message box.

If you only see the second message box, the BeginCalculateTotalValueOfStock has decided to execute the method asynchronously. You will then have to wait for up to 30 seconds after closing the message box, until you see the following one:

The value 9999999 should also appear in the client application console window.

5. Press Enter to close the client application console window.

This is all very well, but so far, we have gone to a lot of trouble to allow the service to determine the best strategy for running a potentially lengthy or expensive operation, although as far as the client application is concerned, everything is still synchronous; each call to the CalculateTotalValueOfStock operation was blocked until it completed. Well, you can also enable asynchronous operations on the client, by regenerating the proxy with the /async flag as mentioned earlier. This is what you will do in the next exercise.

Invoke the CalculateTotalValueOfStock operation asynchronously

1. Open a Windows SDK CMD Shell window and move to the Microsoft Press\WCF Step By Step\Chapter 11\AdventureWorksAdminTestClient\Service References folder under your \My Documents folder.

2. In the CMD Shell window, type the following command:

```
svcutil http://localhost:9090/AdventureWorksAdmin/Service.svc
/namespace:*,AdventureWorksAdminTestClient.AdventureWorksAdmin /async
```

This command creates a version of the client proxy that includes asynchronous versions of each of the operations in the service contract.

> **Tip** If the *svcutil* command fails with the message "No connection could be made because the target machine actively refused it," then the ASP.NET Development Web Service has probably shut down. You can restart it by running the solution.

3. Return to Visual Studio 2005 and examine the AdventureWorksAdmin.cs file under AdventureWorksAdmin.map in the Service References folder.

> **Tip** If you still have this file open in the code view window from earlier, close the file and reopen it to refresh the display.

You should see that the client proxy now contains *begin* and *end* methods for all of the operations in the service contract (and not just the CalculateTotalValueOfStock operation). Remember that these changes are only implemented in the client proxy and that the service is not actually aware of them.

4. Edit the Program.cs file in the AdventureWorksAdminTestClient project. Remove the statements that invoke the CalculateTotalValueOfStock operation and the Console.WriteLine statements and replace them with the following code:

```
proxy.BeginCalculateTotalValueOfStock("First Calculation",
    CalculateTotalValueCallback, proxy);
proxy.BeginCalculateTotalValueOfStock("Second Calculation",
    CalculateTotalValueCallback, proxy);
proxy.BeginCalculateTotalValueOfStock("Third Calculation",
    CalculateTotalValueCallback, proxy);
```

This code invokes the client-side asynchronous version of the CalculateTotalValueOfStock method three times. The results will be handled by a method called CalculateTotalValueCallback, which you will add next. A reference to the proxy is passed in as the state parameter.

5. Delete the *proxy.Close* statement from the *try* block in the Main method.

If you close the proxy at this point, the WCF runtime will destroy the channel stack on the client side before the asynchronous calls have completed, and the client application will be unable to obtain the responses from the service.

6. Add the following method immediately after the end of the Main method in the *Program* class:

```
static void CalculateTotalValueCallback(IAsyncResult asyncResult)
{
    int total = ((AdministrativeServiceClient)asyncResult.AsyncState).
        EndCalculateTotalValueOfStock(asyncResult);
    Console.WriteLine("Total value of stock is {0}", total);
}
```

This is the callback method. When the CalculateTotalValueOfStock operation completes, the proxy will run this method. It retrieves the object passed back from the service (this is the state object, which is a reference to the proxy passed in by the client application as the third parameter in the BeginCalculateTotalValueOfStock method), and uses this object to invoke the EndCalculateTotalValueOfStock method. The value returned by the *end* method is the calculated total value of the stock from the service.

7. Start the solution without debugging.

The client application starts, and then immediately displays the message "Press ENTER to finish." This is because the calls to the BeginCalculateTotalValueOfStock method are no longer blocking the client application.

Do not press Enter just yet, but allow the application to continue running. After 20 or 30 seconds, you should see the message boxes that appeared in the previous exercise, indicating whether the service is executing each request synchronously or asynchronously.

The results of the calculations should appear in the client console window as the operations complete.

8. After all three results have been displayed, press Enter to close the client application console window.

From these exercises, you should now fully understand the difference between invoking an operation asynchronously in a client application and implementing an operation that supports asynchronous processing in the service. A developer can decide whether to implement an operation as a pair of methods implementing the IAsyncResult design pattern independently from any client applications. These methods appear as a single operation to the client application, and the implementation is totally transparent. Equally, if a developer creating a WCF client application wishes to invoke operations asynchronously, all she needs to do is generate a proxy using the */async* flag with the svcutil utility. Whether the client application invokes an operation synchronously is transparent to the service. You should also realize that although a client application can invoke an operation asynchronously, the service may choose to implement the operation synchronously, and vice versa. The result is complete flexibility on the part of both client applications and services.

There is one final point worth making. You can define synchronous and asynchronous versions of the same operation in a service contract, like this:

```
[ServiceContract(…)]
public interface IAdventureWorksAdmin
{
    …

    // Synchronous operation
    [OperationContract]
    int CalculateTotalValueOfStock(string id);

    // Asynchronous version
    [OperationContract(AsyncPattern = true)]
    IAsyncResult BeginCalculateTotalValueOfStock(string id,
                                                 AsyncCallback cb,
                                                 object s);
    int EndCalculateTotalValueOfStock(IAsyncResult r);
}
```

However, if you do this, both operations appear as the same action (CalculateTotalValueOfStock) if you examine the WSDL description of the service. WCF will not throw an exception but will always use the synchronous version of the operation in favor of the asynchronous version (WCF assumes that the synchronous version achieves faster throughput). So, don't define synchronous and asynchronous versions of the same operation in the same service contract.

Using Message Queues

Message queues are the ultimate in asynchronous technology. Message queues can provide a durable, reliable, transacted transport for messages. Furthermore, a client application sending messages, and a service receiving them, do not have to be running at the same time. There is a price you pay for this flexibility though: message queues are an inherently one-way transport, so implementing applications and services that send requests and expect to receive responses requires a lot of careful design. Message queues are also slower than other transports, primarily because of their reliability and durability; the Windows operating system stores messages in files on disk. This means that messages held in a message queue can survive machine shutdown and power failure, at the cost of the additional I/O involved in creating and transmitting them.

> **Note**   You can specify that messages are not durable if performance is more important than reliability. So-called *volatile* messages are cached in memory rather than disk and consequently do not survive machine restarts or crashes.

If you have already built message queuing applications using Microsoft Message Queue (MSMQ), you will appreciate that although the programming model is straightforward, it is fundamentally different compared to the programming practices you adopt when building a more traditional client/server application. However, one of the goals of WCF is to provide a consistent model for sending and receiving irrespective of the underlying transport, so using message queues with WCF is very similar to using most other transports, but is somewhat different from the message queuing techniques you might have used in the past.

In the final set of exercises in this chapter, you will see just how easy it is to use message queues as a transport for asynchronous one-way operations.

Implement a WCF service that uses message queuing

1. Using Visual Studio 2005, open the solution file AdventureWorksAdmin.sln located in the Microsoft Press\WCF Step By Step\Chapter 11\MSMQ folder under your \My Documents folder.

   This solution contains two projects: AdventureWorksAdminHost, which is a self-hosted version of the AdventureWorksAdmin WCF service, and AdventureWorksAdminTestClient, which is a client application for testing the service.

2. In Solution Explorer, open the file Service.cs in the AdventureWorksAdminHost project.

   This is the code that defines and implements the service contract. It should look familiar, as it is very similar to the service you created in the first set of exercises in this chapter. The service contains a single operation, GenerateDailySalesReport. Notice that the operation contract still specifies that this is a OneWay operation. This is important as all operations in a service accessed through a message queue must be OneWay operations.

Also note that the implementation of the GenerateDailySalesReport method now only waits for 10 seconds (pretend that you are running on a faster machine than before, so the processing takes less time).

3. Open the HostController.xaml file. This is a version of the Windows Presentation Foundation form that you previously used to host the ProductsService service.

4. Open the code behind this form in the file HostController.xaml.cs. The logic in this form is the same as before. The only difference is that this form now hosts the AdventureWorksAdmin service.

5. Add a new application configuration file to the AdventureWorksAdminHost project, and then edit this file by using the WCF Service Configuration Editor.

6. In the WCF Service Configuration Editor, create a new service and set the *Name* property to *AdventureWorksAdmin* (this is the name of the class implementing the service).

7. Add an endpoint to this service. Set the *Name* property to *AdventureWorksAdminMsmqEndpoint*, set the *Address* property to *net.msmq://localhost/private/AdventureWorksAdmin*, set the *Binding* property to *netMsmqBinding*, and set the *Contract* property to *IAdventureWorksAdmin*.

The format for a message queuing URI consists of the scheme "net.msmq" followed by the name of the queue. MSMQ identifies queues using a syntax very similar to HTTP URLs, although the semantics are a little different. The "private" part of the URI indicates that this is a private message queue, meaning that it can only be accessed from applications running on the local computer. If you are using a computer that is a member of a Windows domain, you can also create public message queues that can be accessed by code running on other computers. The actual name of the message queue is "AdventureWorksAdmin."

> **More Info**   For a detailed description of message queues, see the topic "Using Messaging Components" in the Microsoft Windows SDK documentation, and also on the Microsoft Web site at *http://msdn2.microsoft.com/en-us/library/fzc40kc8.aspx*.

8. Add a new binding configuration using the netMsmqBinding binding type. Set the *Name* property of this binding configuration to *AdventureWorksAdminMsmqBindingConfig*.

You can set binding properties that control many aspects of the way the message queue works. For example, the *Durable* property determines whether messages should be capable of surviving process failure or machine shutdown and restart; setting this property to *False* makes messages volatile. The *ExactlyOnce* property is the MSMQ analog of reliable messaging for other transports. Setting this property to *True* guarantees that messages will be received once and once only; messages will not be lost, or inadvertently retrieved twice by concurrent instances of the service from the message queue. Setting this property to *True* requires that the message queue is transactional.

9. Modify the security settings of the binding configuration, and set the *Mode* property to *None*.

Message queues support message level security and transport level security, although the implementation of transport level security is peculiar to MSMQ and does not require you to configure SSL. If you implement message level security, you can specify the client credential type. You should note that the authentication mechanism implemented by MSMQ message level security requires that the message queue server must be configured to provide a certificate for the message queue used by the binding.

> **Important**   For simplicity, this example uses a local, unprotected private message queue that is accessible only on the host computer. In a production environment, you will probably use public queues, which should be protected by using transport or message level security.

10. Return to the AdventureWorksAdminMsmqEndpoint endpoint definition you added in step 7. Set the *BindingConfiguration* property to *AdventureWorksAdminMsmqBinding Config*.

11. Save the configuration file, and exit the WCF Configuration Editor.

12. In Visual Studio 2005, build the AdventureWorksAdminHost project. Do not try and build the entire solution, as the client application is not yet complete; this is your next task.

Send messages to a message queue in a WCF client application

1. Open a Microsoft Windows SDK CMD Shell window, and move to the Microsoft Press\WCF Step By Step\Chapter 11\MSMQ\AdventureWorksAdminHost\bin\Debug folder under your \My Documents folder. Type the following commands to generate the client proxy from the service contract compiled into the *AdventureWorksAdminHost.exe* assembly:

```
svcutil AdventureWorksAdminHost.exe
svcutil /namespace:*,AdventureWorksAdminTestClient.AdventureWorksAdmin adventure-
works.com.2007.01.01.wsdl *.xsd /out:AdventureWorksAdminProxy.cs
```

2. Return to Visual Studio 2005, and add the AdventureWorksAdminProxy.cs file that you have just created to the AdventureWorksAdminTestClient project.

3. Open the Program.cs file in the AdventureWorksAdminTestClient project. Again, this code should look very familiar, as it is almost identical to the client application you developed in the first set of exercises in this chapter for testing OneWay operations. There is an additional prompt "Press ENTER to send messages" in the *try* block, and you must specify a binding to use when instantiating the proxy. Before you do this, you must create an application configuration file and define the binding you are going to use.

4. Add a new application configuration file to the AdventureWorksAdminTestClient project and edit it by using the WCF Service Configuration Editor.

5. In the WCF Service Configuration Editor, add a new client endpoint with the properties shown in the following table:

Property	Value
Name	AdventureWorksAdminMsmqEndpoint
Address	net.msmq://localhost/private/AdventureWorksAdmin
Binding	netMsmqBinding
Contract	AdventureWorksAdminTestClient.AdventureWorksAdmin.AdministrativeService

6. Add a binding configuration based on the netMsmqBinding type. Set the *Name* property of this binding configuration to *AdventureWorksAdminMsmqBindingConfig*. Change the security settings of the binding configuration, and set the *Mode* property to *None*.

7. Return to the AdventureWorksAdminMsmqEndpoint endpoint definition and set the *BindingConfiguration* property to *AdventureWorksAdminMsmqBindingConfig*.

8. Save the configuration file and exit the WCF Service Configuration Editor.

9. In the Program.cs file, modify the statement that creates the proxy object and replace the text "INSERT ENDPOINT HERE" with the name of the MSMQ endpoint, as shown in bold below:

```
AdministrativeServiceClient proxy =
    new AdministrativeServiceClient("AdventureWorksAdminMsmqEndpoint");
```

That completes the code. You can now create the message queue and test the client application and service.

Create the AdventureWorksAdmin queue and test the service

1. On the Windows Start menu, right-click My Computer and then click Manage.

   The Computer Management console starts.

2. In the Computer Management console, expand the Services and Applications node in the left pane, expand the Message Queuing node, right-click the Private Queues folder, point to New, and then click Private Queue.

3. In the New Private Queue dialog box, type AdventureWorksAdmin in the Queue name text box, check the Transactional box, and then click OK.

> **Note**   If you don't want the overhead of transactional message queues, you must set the *ExactlyOnce* property of the binding configuration for the netMsmqBinding binding to *False*.

4. Leave the Computer Management console open, and return to Visual Studio 2005.

5. Start the solution without debugging. In the client console window, press Enter to send the two GenerateDailySalesReport messages but don't start the service running yet. Notice that the client successfully sends the messages even though the service is not running. Press Enter to close the client console window.

6. Return to the Computer Management console. Expand the AdventureWorksAdmin queue in the Private Queues folder under Message Queuing, and then click the Queue messages folder. Two messages should be displayed in the right pane:

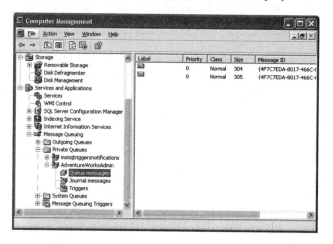

   Tip   If no messages appear, click Refresh on the Action menu to update the display.

If you double-click a message, you can display its properties, including the text in the body of the message.

7. In the AdventureWorksAdminHost form for the service host application, click Start.

The service starts running, retrieves each message from the queue in turn, and processes them (remember that each message takes at least 10 seconds to process). The operation displays a message box after each message is processed.

Stop the service and close the AdventureWorksAdminHost form after the second message box has been displayed.

8. Return to the Computer Management console displaying the messages in the message queue. On the Action menu, click Refresh to update the display. Both messages should disappear as they have now been removed from the message queue by the WCF service.

Close the Computer Management console.

MSMQ provides an easy-to-use mechanism for implementing asynchronous operations. However, the netMsmqBinding binding restricts you to implementing OneWay operations. If a service needs to send a response, it can do so asynchronously by sending a message to a queue to which the client application can connect. This involves implementing a different message for each client (for privacy) and correlating messages, so the client application knows which response corresponds to which request.

> **More Info**   For more information and an example of using message queues to implement asynchronous request/response messaging, see the topic "Two-Way Communication" in the Windows SDK documentation, which is also available on the Microsoft Web site at *http://windowssdk.msdn.microsoft.com/en-us/library/ms752264.aspx.*

Summary

In this chapter, you have seen three ways to send and process messages to improve the response time of a service and exploit multiple threads. You should use OneWay messaging for long-running operations that do not return any data. For operations that do pass information back to the client application, you can generate a client proxy using the svcutil utility with the /async option and invoke these operations asynchronously from the client. A service can also choose to implement a long-running operation asynchronously, independent from the way in which the client application actually invokes the operation, by setting the *AsyncPattern* property of the operation contract to *True*, and then implementing the IAsyncResult design pattern. If client applications and services execute at different times, you can use message queuing and the MSMQ transport.

Chapter 12
Implementing a WCF Service for Good Performance

After completing this chapter, you will be able to:

- Manage service scalability by using throttling to control use of resources.

- Use the Message Transmission Optimization Mechanism (MTOM) to transmit messages containing binary data in a standardized, efficient manner.

- Explain how to enable streaming for a binding and design operations that support streaming.

Good performance is a key factor in most applications and services. You can help to ensure that a WCF service maintains throughput, remains responsive, and is scalable by thoughtful design, by selecting the appropriate features that meet this design. Examples that you have met so far include careful use of transactions, session state, reliable messaging, and asynchronous operations.

There are other aspects that can impact performance, such as security. You have seen, in earlier chapters, that implementing message level security and secure conversations results in a complex exchange of messages negotiating the protocol to use and the exchange of identity information. Messages themselves are bigger as a result of the additional security information included in the message headers, which means they take longer to traverse the network and require more memory to process. Encryption and decryption are also very resource intensive tasks. However, these are all necessary parts of a secure system, and most people are willing to sacrifice some performance in return for ensuring that their data and identity information remain private. (If decryption were quick and easy to perform, it would also be fairly useless; the more resources it takes to decrypt a message, results in a better protected message.)

An important aspect of maintaining performance is to ensure that a service does not exhaust the resources available on the host computer, as this will cause the system to slow down and possibly stop altogether. WCF provides service throttling to help control resource utilization. Using this feature can greatly aid the scalability of your service. You can also use WCF in conjunction with load-balanced servers. Chapter 13, "Routing Messages," describes a simple implementation of this technique using WCF. You can also build a load-balancing infrastructure based on Microsoft Windows Network Load Balancing, although the details of this technology are outside the scope of this book.

> **More Info**   For further information about Microsoft Windows Network Load Balancing, see the Load Balancing page on the Microsoft Windows Server TechCenter Web site at *http://technet2.microsoft.com/windowsserver/en/technologies/nlb.mspx*.

Using the appropriate encoding mechanism when transmitting data can also have a significant effect on performance. You have seen how WCF supports text and binary encoding of messages. Binary encoding is often more compact and incurs less network overhead, but the format is proprietary and cannot easily be used with applications and services running on non-Microsoft platforms. However, WCF also supports MTOM, which provides a standardized, interoperable format for transmitting large blocks of binary data.

MTOM is useful if you know how much data the service is going to transmit. Some services emit long data blocks of indeterminate size. This type of data is best transmitted as a stream, and WCF provides support for outputting streams from a service.

In this chapter, you will examine how to use service throttling to assist in maintaining scalability, how to encode data by using MTOM to reduce the overhead of transmitting large binary data objects, and how to enable streaming to make best use of network bandwidth.

Using Service Throttling to Control Resource Use

You can use service throttling to prevent over-consumption of resources in a WCF service. If you recall from Chapter 10, "Programmatically Controlling the Configuration and Communications," when a message received by a service host reaches the top of the channel stack, it passes to a *ChannelDispatcher* object, which in turn passes it to the appropriate *EndpointDispatcher* object, which invokes the corresponding method in the appropriate service instance. However, before forwarding the request to the *EndpointDispatcher* object, the *ChannelDispatcher* object can examine the current load on the service and elect to hold the request back if the request would cause the service to exceed the permissible load. The request is blocked and held in an internal queue until the load on the service eases. The *ChannelDispatcher* object has a property called *ServiceThrottle* that you can use to help control how the *ChannelDispatcher* decides whether to block and queue requests or let them execute. The *ServiceThrottle* property is an instance of the *ServiceThrottle* class, and this class itself exposes three further integer properties:

- *MaxConcurrentInstances*. This property specifies the maximum number of concurrent service instances that the service host will permit.

- *MaxConcurrentCalls*. This property specifies the maximum number of concurrent messages that the service host will process. If a client application makes a large number of concurrent calls, either as the result of invoking OneWay operations or by using client-side multi-threading, it can quickly monopolize a service. In this scenario, you might want to limit each client to a single thread in the service by setting the *ConcurrencyMode* property of the service to *ConcurrencyMode.Single*. The client application can continue running asynchronously and should remain responsive to the user, but requests submitted by the client application will be processed in a serial manner by the service.

- *MaxConcurrentSessions*. This property specifies the maximum number of concurrent sessions that the service host will permit. Client applications are responsible for establishing and terminating sessions and can make several calls to the service during a session. Clients creating long-running sessions can result in other clients being blocked, so keep sessions as brief as possible and avoid performing tasks such as waiting for user input.

Configuring Service Throttling

By default, the *ServiceThrottle* property of the *ChannelDispatcher* object is *null* and the WCF runtime uses its own default values for the maximum number of concurrent instances, calls, and sessions. To control scalability, you should arrange for the WCF runtime to create a *ServiceThrottle* object and explicitly set these properties to values suitable for your environment, taking into account the expected number of concurrent client applications and the work that they are likely to perform. You can perform this task in code by creating a *ServiceThrottlingBehavior* object, setting its properties (the *ServiceThrottlingBehavior* class provides the same properties as the *ServiceThrottle* class), and adding it to the collection of behaviors attached to the *ServiceHost* object, as described in Chapter 10. You must do this before opening the *ServiceHost* object. The following code shows an example:

```
// Required for the ServiceThrottlingBehavior class
using System.ServiceModel.Description;
...
ServiceHost host = new ServiceHost(…);
ServiceThrottlingBehavior throttleBehavior = new ServiceThrottlingBehavior();
throttleBehavior.MaxConcurrentCalls = 40;
throttleBehavior.MaxConcurrentInstances = 20;
throttleBehavior.MaxConcurrentSessions = 20;
host.Description.Behaviors.Add(throttleBehavior);
host.Open();
...
```

However, be warned that the values of the properties in a *ServiceThrottle* object can have a drastic affect on the response time and throughput of a WCF service. You should actively monitor the performance of the WCF service and be prepared to change these settings if the computer hosting the service is struggling. Additionally, clients blocked by limits that are set too low can result in an excessive number of time-outs or other errors occurring in the client application or the channel stack, so be prepared to catch and handle them.

Note   At the time of writing, the default value for the maximum number of concurrent instances is 21474836467 (Int32.MaxValue), the default value for the maximum number of concurrent calls is 16, and the default value for the maximum number of concurrent sessions is 10. However, these values may change in subsequent releases of WCF.

A more flexible way to create a *ServiceThrottle* object and set its properties is to add a service behavior that contains the *<serviceThrottling>* element to the service configuration file. This is the approach that you will adopt in the following exercise.

Apply Throttling to the ShoppingCartService Service

1. Using Visual Studio 2005, open the solution file ShoppingCartService.sln located in the Microsoft Press\WCF Step By Step\Chapter 12\Throttling folder under your \My Documents folder.

   This solution contains a simplified non-transactional version of the ShoppingCartService service that does not actually update the database, and an extended version of the client application that opens multiple concurrent sessions to the service.

   > **Note**   The rationale behind not updating the database or using transactions is to allow you to concentrate on the throttling semantics of a service and not worry about any potential locking and concurrency issues in the database. In the real world, you have to take all of these factors into account.

2. Open the ShoppingCartService.cs file in the ShoppingCartService project. Notice that the service specifies that sessions are required in the *ServiceContract* attribute of the *IShoppingCartService* interface and that the *ServiceBehavior* attribute of the *ShoppingCartServiceImpl* class specifies the PerSession instance context mode.

3. Examine the AddItemToCart method in this class. This method starts with a WriteLine statement that displays the method name. A corresponding WriteLine statement has been added at each point that the method can terminate. You will use these statements to trace the progress of each instance of the service as it runs. Also notice that the method contains the statement *System.Threading.Thread.Sleep(5000)* immediately after the first WriteLine statement. Although this method still queries the database, it no longer performs updates for reasons described earlier. This statement slows the method down by waiting for 5 seconds, simulating the time taken to perform the database update (assume the database update operation is very time consuming), and making it a little easier to observe the effects of the service throttling parameters. The other public methods, RemoveItemFromCart, GetShoppingCart, and Checkout, have been amended in the same way.

4. Open the Program.cs file in the ShoppingCartClient project, and locate the doClientWork method. This method contains code that creates a new instance of the proxy object and then invokes the various operations in the ShoppingCartService service, in much the same way as you have seen in earlier chapters. The method contains WriteLine statements displaying its progress to the console. The output includes a number that identifies the client. The client connects to the service using a standard TCP binding.

5. Examine the Main method. This method asynchronously calls the doClientWork method ten times, passing in the client number as the parameter. Each call creates a new thread. This simulates ten different but identifiable clients connecting to the service at the same time.

6. Open the Program.cs file in the ShoppingCartHost project. This is the application that hosts the service. Add the following *using* statement to the top of the file:

```
using System.ServiceModel.Dispatcher;
```

This namespace contains the *ServiceThrottle* and *ChannelDispatcher* classes.

7. Add the code shown below in bold to the Main method, immediately after the statement that opens the *ServiceHost* object:

```
host.Open();

ChannelDispatcher dispatcher =
    (ChannelDispatcher)host.ChannelDispatchers[0];
ServiceThrottle throttle = dispatcher.ServiceThrottle;
if (throttle == null)
    Console.WriteLine("Service is using default throttling behavior");
else
    Console.WriteLine("Instances: {0}\nCalls: {1}\nSessions: {2}",
        throttle.MaxConcurrentInstances, throttle.MaxConcurrentCalls,
        throttle.MaxConcurrentSessions);

Console.WriteLine("Service running");
```

This code retrieves a reference to the *ChannelDispatcher* object used by the service (the service has only a single binding, so the WCF runtime creates only a single *ChannelDispatcher* when the service opens). The code then examines the *ServiceThrottle* property of this *ChannelDispatcher* object. If it is *null*, then the administrator or developer has not specified any customized throttling settings so the service uses the default values. If the *ServiceThrottle* property is not *null*, then the service is using a customized throttling behavior and the values provided by the administrator or developer are displayed.

8. Start the solution without debugging. In the service console window, notice that the service is using the default throttling behavior.

Press Enter in the client console window.

The client console window displays ten messages of the form "Client *n*: 1st AddItemToCart," where *n* is the number identifying the instance of the client. In the service console window, notice that the message "AddItemToCart operation started" appears ten times in succession, as shown in the following image:

This indicates that the service is handling all ten clients simultaneously. As each method completes, the service displays "AddItemToCart operation completed" messages and the clients invoke further operations. At this point, the output becomes a little more chaotic, but the important point is that in this "unthrottled" state the service has not prevented any of the ten clients from invoking operations at the same time (the default value for the maximum number of concurrent calls is greater than 10).

When the clients have finished (the message "Client *n*: Goods Purchased" has appeared ten times), press Enter to close the client console window. Press Enter to close the service console window.

9. In Visual Studio 2005, edit the App.config file in the ShoppingCartHost project by using the WCF Service Configuration Editor.

10. In the WCF Service Configuration Editor, expand the Advanced Folder and then click the Service Behaviors folder. In the right pane, click the New Service Behavior Configuration link.

   A new behavior appears in the right pane. Change the *Name* property of this behavior to *ThrottleBehavior*.

11. In the right pane, click Add and add a *serviceThrottling* element to the behavior.

12. Double-click the *serviceThrottling* behavior element you have just added.

   The properties for this element appear: *MaxConcurrentCalls*, *MaxConcurrentInstances*, and *MaxConcurrentSessions*. Each property displays its default value:

13. Change the value of the *MaxConcurrentCalls* property to 3.

14. In the left pane, click the ShoppingCartService.ShoppingCartServiceImpl node in the Services folder. In the right pane, set the *BehaviorConfiguration* property to *ThrottleBehavior*.

15. Save the configuration file, but leave the WCF Service Configuration Editor open.

16. In Visual Studio 2005, start the solution without debugging. In the service console window, you should see that the service is now using the throttling behavior you have just defined rather than the default settings.

    Press Enter in the client console window.

    In the client console window, all ten clients output the message "Client n:1st AddItemToCart," but the service console shows something different from before; initially only three "AddItemToCart operation started" messages appear. This is because the service now supports only three concurrent operation calls. Each request that occurs after this is queued by the *ChannelDispatcher*. As each call finishes, displaying "AddItemToCart operation completed," the *ChannelDispatcher* releases the next request from its queue, and you see the message "AddItemToCart operation started" appear for the next client. Thereafter, each time an operation completes, the *ChannelDispatcher* releases the next request. You should see alternating "completed" and "started" messages until the clients have finished their work, as the time taken for the service to process each request is at least 5 seconds, and this is longer than the time taken for each client to send the next request when the previous one completes.

> **Note**   The *ChannelDispatcher* releases requests from its queue on a first-come first-served basis. Currently, WCF does not allow you to specify that the requests for one client should have a higher priority than another.

    Press Enter to close the client console window, and then press Enter to close the service console window.

17. Return to the WCF Service Configuration Editor and click the *serviceThrottling* service behavior element in the left pane. In the right pane, increase the *MaxConcurrentCalls* property to 16 (the default value) and set the *MaxConcurrentSessions* property to 3. Save the configuration file, but leave the WCF Service Configuration Editor open.

18. In Visual Studio 2005, start the solution without debugging. In the service console window, you should see that the service is using the updated throttling behavior.

    Press Enter in the client console window.

    Again, in the client console window, all ten clients output the message "Client n: 1st AddItemToCart," and the service console window shows three calls to the AddItemToCart operation starting and completing. However, when these calls complete, if you observe the messages in the client console window, you will see that only clients 0, 1, and 2 invoke the AddItemToCart operation the second time; the other clients are held pending by the *ChannelDispatcher* because it has reached the maximum number of concurrent sessions it will allow. Clients 0, 1, and 2 complete their cycle of work calling AddItemToCart a third time, followed by the GetShoppingCart operation and the Checkout operation. Only when Checkout completes and a client closes its session before terminating does the next client actually get to continue. You should see messages occurring in batches of three in the client console window (three "2nd AddItemToCart" messages, three "3rd AddItemToCart" messages, and so on), as each set of three sessions executes.

Some of the later sessions might report the exception "The operation did not complete within the allotted time-out of 00:01:00. ...," as the time between them submitting the initial AddItemToCart request and the service allowing that request to be handled exceeds the time-out limit specified for the client binding.

> **Note**   Although the *ChannelDispatcher* queues the requests to create each session in the order it receives them, once a session starts running, there is no guarantee that it will be serviced before or after any other running session in this example. For example, when sessions for clients 3, 4, and 5 are running, you might see messages indicating that operations for client 4 execute before those of client 3; this is due to the scheduling algorithm in the operating system deciding when to execute each thread in the client and in the service.

Press Enter to close the client console window, and then press Enter to close the service console window.

19.   Return to the WCF Service Configuration Editor. In the right pane, set the *MaxConcurrentSessions* property to 10 (the default value). Save the configuration file, and close the WCF Service Configuration Editor.

This exercise has shown you the effects of using service throttling to control the maximum number of concurrent calls and sessions that a service will permit. To what values should you set the service throttling properties? I am afraid that there is no simple answer. You need to test your service against a realistic workload and observe whether client applications are blocked for extended periods. Remember that the purpose of service throttling is to prevent your service from being inundated with a flood of requests that it does not have the resources to cope with. You should set the service throttling properties to ensure that, when a client request is accepted and execution actually starts, the computer hosting the service has sufficient resources available to be able to complete the operation before the client times out, as this would hinder overall performance further. In a transactional environment, aborted client requests generate even more work for the service, as it then has to rollback all the transactional work it has performed.

WCF and Service Instance Pooling

The WCF runtime creates service instances to handle client requests. If the service is using the PerSession instance context mode, the instance can last for several operations. If the service is using the PerCall instance context mode, each operation call results in a new service instance, which is discarded and destroyed when the operation ends. Creating and destroying instances are expensive, potentially time-consuming tasks. Service instance pooling would be very useful in this scenario.

When using instance pooling, the WCF runtime would create a pool of service instance objects when the service starts. When using the PerCall instance context mode, as client applications invoke operations, the WCF runtime would retrieve a pre-created service instance from the pool and return it to the pool when the operation completes. When using the PerSession instance context mode, the same semantics apply, but the WCF runtime would obtain a service instance from the pool at the start of the session and return it at the end of the session. For security purposes, any data held by the service instance (fields in the class defining the service implementation) would be cleared as the instance was returned to the pool.

As you might have gathered from the tone of the previous paragraph, WCF does not provide service instance pooling directly, but it is possible to extend WCF by defining your own custom behavior that implements pooling. WCF supplies the *IInstanceProvider* interface in the *System.ServiceModel.Dispatcher* namespace that you can use to define your own service instance dispatch mechanism. This is a useful technique, but the details are outside the scope of this book, although Chapter 10 provides an example of how to implement a service behavior. For more information, see the topic "Pooling" in the Microsoft Windows SDK Documentation. This topic is also available on the Microsoft Web site at *http://msdn2.microsoft.com/en-gb/library/ms751482(en-us).aspx.*

Transmitting Data by Using MTOM

A SOAP message usually contains a message body, which is held in an XML format. This body contains the data for a request being transmitted to a service or the information being returned in response to a request back to a client application. The actual structure of the information in the message body is specified by the WSDL description of the operation, which is in turn derived from the operation contract you specify in your services. For example, the ProductsService service that you created in Chapter 1, "Introducing Windows Communication Foundation," defined the ChangeStockLevel operation in the IProductsService service contract like this:

```
[ServiceContract]
public interface IProductsService
{
    ...
    [OperationContract]
    bool ChangeStockLevel(string productNumber, int newStockLevel, string
                          shelf, int bin);
}
```

When a client application invokes the ChangeStockLevel operation, the WCF runtime constructs a message that looks like this:

```
<s:Envelope xmlns:a="http://www.w3.org/2005/08/addressing"  xmlns:s="http://www.w3.org/2003/
05/soap-envelope">
    <s:Header>
        ...
    </s:Header>
    <s:Body>
        <ChangeStockLevel xmlns="http://tempuri.org/">
            <productNumber>WB-H098</productNumber>
            <newStockLevel>25000</newStockLevel>
            <shelf>N/A</shelf>
            <bin>40101</bin>
        </ChangeStockLevel>
    </s:Body>
</s:Envelope>
```

You can see that the message body contains the parameters for the operation, encoded as an XML infoset. This scheme works well for parameters that have easily definable representations. However, remember that the XML message is transmitted as a series of text characters when it traverses the network, and non-text data, such as the *<newStockLevel>* and the *<bin>* elements in the example above, is being converted to and from a text representation as it is sent and received. This conversion incurs an overhead at two levels:

1. It takes time, memory, and computational power to convert from the binary representation of an integer (in the case of the *<newStockLevel>* and the *<bin>* elements) to text and back again.

2. The text representation of the data as it crosses the network might be less compact than the original binary representation; the bigger the number, the longer the text representation.

In this example, this overhead is minimal. However, how would you handle lengthy binary data, such as an image? One possible solution is to convert the binary data into a text representation containing the corresponding series of "0" and "1" characters. But consider the overhead of this approach. Converting a megabyte of binary data into a string a million characters long requires a significant amount of memory and time. What actually happens in this case is that WCF converts the binary data into a Base64 encoded string rather than a string of "0" and "1" characters. The result is a more compact text representation of the data. However, on average, the Base64 encoding mechanism results in a string that is approximately 140% of the length of the original data. Additionally, this data has to be converted back into its original binary format by the recipient of the data. Clearly, it makes sense to find an alternative representation when transmitting messages that include large amounts of binary data.

MTOM is a specification that provides just such a facility. When you use MTOM to transmit a message that includes binary data, the binary data is not encoded as text but is transmitted unchanged as an attachment to the message following the format of the Multipurpose Internet Mail Extension (MIME) specification. Any text information in the original message is encoded as an XML infoset as before, but binary information is represented as a reference to the MIME attachment, as depicted in Figure 12-1:

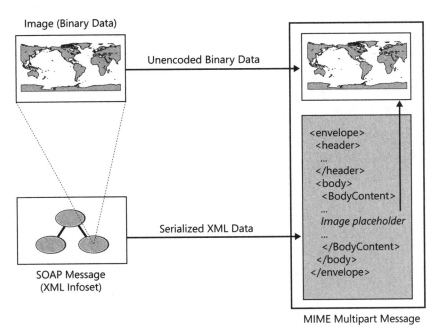

Figure 12-1   Encoding a message containing binary data.

> **Note**   MTOM supersedes previous proposed standards that you might have heard of, such as the Direct Internet Message Encapsulation protocol (DIME) and the WS-Attachments specification. Don't confuse DIME with MIME.

As always, security is an important consideration. When signing MTOM messages, WCF computes a signature that includes the data in any MIME attachments. If any part of the message, including the MIME attachments, is changed between sending and receiving the message, the signature will be invalid. For more details about signing messages, refer back to Chapter 4, "Protecting an Enterprise WCF Service."

In WCF, MTOM is handled by a specific encoding channel. If you are using any of the standard HTTP bindings (basicHttpBinding, wsDualHttpBinding, wsFederationHttpBinding, or wsHttpBinding), you can change the *MessageEncoding* property of the binding configuration to MTOM to use the MTOM encoding channel. Other transports, such as TCP, MSMQ, and Named Pipes, use their own proprietary binary encodings by default. The corresponding standard bindings do not have a *MessageEncoding* property, so if, for example, you want to use MTOM over TCP, you must create your own custom binding.

Sending Large Binary Data Objects to a Client Application

Consider this scenario: Adventure-Works wants, to extend the functionality available in the ShoppingCartService WCF service to enable a user to be able to view photographs of the products supplied by Adventure-Works. The database contains images of the products held as binary data. The developers have built a prototype service called ShoppingCartPhotoService that provides an operation called GetPhoto. This operation retrieves the image data from the database and returns it to the client application. In the following exercise, you will see how to encode binary data using MTOM over HTTP when transmitting the photographic data from the service back to the client application.

Use MTOM to transmit photographic images from the ShoppingCartService service

1. Using Visual Studio 2005, open the solution file MTOMService.sln located in the Microsoft Press\WCF Step By Step\Chapter 12\MTOM folder under your \My Documents folder.

   This solution contains a prototype WCF service called ShoppingCartPhotoService that implements the proposed GetPhoto operation. The ShoppingCartPhotoService service is hosted by using the ASP.NET Development Web Server provided with Visual Studio 2005. The solution also contains a basic WPF client application that displays data in a WPF form.

2. Open the ShoppingCartPhotoService.cs file in the App_Code folder in the C:\...\MTOM-Service\ project.

   Examine the *IShoppingCartPhotoService* interface defining the service contract. This interface contains the GetPhoto operation. This operation enables a client application to request the photograph of a product given its name. The photograph itself is passed back to the client application in the photo parameter, which is marked as *out*. The type of this parameter is *byte[]*, because the photographic images are held as raw binary data in the database. The return value is a Boolean indicating whether the operation was successful or not.

   If you have time, look at the implementation of the GetPhoto method in the *ShoppingCartPhotoServiceImpl* class. There is nothing specific to WCF in this method; all it does is query the Production.ProductPhoto table in the database to find the photograph for the specified product (for clarity, this method does not perform any checks to deter SQL Injection attacks). The photograph is held as a *varbinary* column of unspecified length in the database, so the code reads the contents of this column in manageable chunks and then pieces these chunks together to construct the *byte* array that is passed back to the client application.

> **Note** The size of the chunks used by this method is specified by the *chunkSize* integer constant. The developer can increase or decrease the value of this constant to determine the optimal chunk size.

3. Open the Window1.xaml file in the ShoppingCartGUIClient application. This XAML file defines a WPF form that contains an image control occupying the main part of the form, together with a label, a text box, and a button. The user types a product number into the text box and clicks the "Get Photo" button.

4. Open the Window1.xaml.cs code file behind this form (expand the Window1.xaml node in Solution Explorer to display the file). The onGetPhotoClick method in this file runs when the user clicks the "Get Photo" button. The code in this method creates an instance of the client proxy, reads the product number typed in by the user, creates a new *byte* array, and then invokes the GetPhoto operation passing in the *byte* array and the product number as parameters. If the operation returns *true*, the method uses the *byte* array containing the data for the photograph and uses it to populate a *BitmapImage* object, which it then displays in the image control on the WPF form.

5. Start the solution without debugging. The ShoppingCartPhotoService starts the ASP.NET Development Web Server and starts listening on port 9080.

    When the ShoppingCartGUIClient form appears, type **WB-H098** in the product number text box and then click Get Photo. An image showing a pair of water bottles appears in the image control on the form, like this:

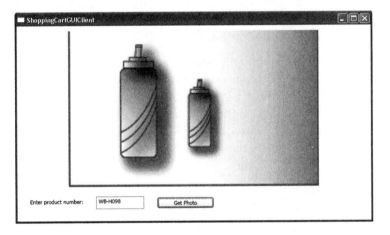

    Type **PU-M044** in the product number text box and then click Get Photo. This time the image displays a picture of a mountain pump.

6. Close the client form and return to Visual Studio 2005.

7. In Solution Explorer, edit the Web.config file in the C:\...\MTOMService\ project by using the WCF Service Configuration Editor.

8. In the left pane, right-click the Diagnostics folder. In the right pane, click the Enable MessageLogging link.

9. In the left pane, expand the Diagnostics folder and click the Message Logging node. In the right pane, set the *LogEntireMessage* property to *True*.

10. In the left pane, expand the Sources folder under Diagnostics and then click the System.ServiceModelMessageLogging node. In the right pane, set the Trace level to Verbose.

11. Click the Diagnostics node again in the left pane. In the right pane, click the Enable Tracing link. In the left pane, click System.ServiceModel in the Sources folder, and in the right pane, set the Trace level to Verbose.

12. Save the configuration file, but leave the WCF Service Configuration Editor open.

13. In Visual Studio 2005, start the solution again without debugging. Using the ShoppingCartGUIClient form, retrieve and display the photographs for products WB-H098 and PU-M044 and then close the ShoppingCartGUIClient form. Stop the ASP.NET Web Development Server by right-clicking the ASP.NET Development Server icon in the Windows taskbar and then clicking Stop.

14. Start the Service Trace Viewer in the Tools program group in the Microsoft Windows SDK program group. In the Service Trace Viewer, open the file web_messages.svclog in the Microsoft Press\WCF Step By Step\Chapter 12\MTOM\MTOMService folder under your \My Documents folder.

15. In the left pane, click the Message tab. Four messages are listed; one for each request and response. Click the first message. In the lower right pane, click the Message tab and scroll down to display the body of the message. You should see that this is the message requesting the photograph for product WB-H098.

16. In the left pane, click the second message. In the lower right pane, examine the message body. This is the response containing the photographic data in the *<photo>* element. You can see that this data consists of a long string of characters containing the Base64 encoding of the binary data. Examine the remaining messages; the third message is the request for the photograph of product PU-M044, and the fourth is the response containing the Base64 encoded image data.

17. Open the web_tracelog.svclog file, and then click the Activity tab in the left pane. This file contains a log of the work performed by the WCF runtime, and the Activity pane displays a list of all the tasks the WCF runtime on the service performed.

18. Locate and click the first item named "Process action 'http://adventure-works.com/2007/03/01/ShoppingCartService/GetPhoto.'" The upper right pane displays the tasks performed by this activity, including receiving the message over the channel, opening an instance of the service, executing the operation, creating a response message, sending the response message, and finally, closing the service instance.

19. In the upper right pane, scroll down and click the task "A message was written." The lower right pane displays information about the message. In the *Message* Properties and Headers section, note that the *Encoder* property is "application/soap+xml; charset=utf-8." This indicates that the message was encoded as text:

20. On the File menu click Close All, but leave the Service Trace Viewer running.

21. Return to the WCF Service Configuration Editor editing the Web.config file for the ShoppingCartPhotoService service. In the left pane, click the ShoppingCartPhotoServiceBindingConfig binding configuration in the Bindings folder. This is the binding configuration used by the HTTP endpoint. In the right pane, change the *MessageEncoding* property from *Text* to *MTOM*. Save the configuration file and then close the WCF Service Configuration Editor.

22. In Visual Studio 2005, edit the app.config file in the ShoppingCartGUIClient project using the WCF Service Configuration Editor. In the left pane, click the WSHttpBinding_ShoppingCartPhotoService binding configuration in the Bindings folder. In the right pane, change the *MessageEncoding* property to *MTOM*. Save the configuration file and then close the WCF Service Configuration Editor.

23. Using Windows Explorer, delete the files web_messages.svclog and web_tracelog.svc in the Microsoft Press\WCF Step By Step\Chapter 12\MTOM\MTOMService folder under your \My Documents folder.

24. In Visual Studio 2005, start the solution without debugging. Fetch and display the photographs for products WB-H098 and PU-M044. Close the ShoppingCartGUIClient form, and then stop the ASP.NET Web Development Server.

25. In the WCF Service Trace Viewer, open the web_tracelog.svclog file. In the Activity pane, locate and click the first item named "Process action 'http://adventure-works.com/2007/03/01/ShoppingCartService/GetPhoto.'" In the upper right pane, locate and click the task "A message was written." In the lower right pane, examine the *Encoder* property in the *Message* Properties and Headers section. This time the *Encoder* property is set to

"multipart/related; type='application/xop+xml.'" This indicates that the service sent a MIME multipart message:

26. Close the WCF Service Trace Viewer.

> **Note** If you examine the SOAP messages in the web_messages.svclog file, you might be surprised, and possibly disappointed, to see that the *<photo>* parameter returned in the GetPhotoResponse message always appears to be encoded as a Base64 string embedded in the message. Do not be fooled. MTOM is actually transparent to WCF SOAP message logging in much the same way that it is transparent to your own applications, and so it is not aware that the *<photo>* parameter is being transmitted as an attachment. If you really want to see the SOAP message in its raw format with the attachment, you must use a network analyzer, such as Windows Netmon.

You have seen that configuring a binding to use the MTOM encoding is a very straightforward task. Using MTOM does not affect the functionality of your applications, and you don't have to make any special coding changes to use it.

Streaming Data from a WCF Service

MTOM is useful for encoding large binary data objects in messages, but if these objects become too large they can consume significant amounts of memory in the computer hosting the WCF service and the client applications that receive them. Additionally, very large messages can take a long time to construct and transmit, and it is possible that the client application could time-out while waiting for a response containing a large binary object.

In many cases, it does not make sense to even attempt to try and package up data into a single message. Consider a WCF service that provides an operation that emits audio or video data. In this scenario, it is far more efficient to send the data as a stream than to try and send it as one big chunk. Streaming enables the client application to start receiving and processing bytes of data before the service has transmitted the end of the message, resolving the need to create large buffers for holding an entire message in the service and the client application, and resolving the time-out issue.

Enabling Streaming in a WCF Service and Client Application

WCF provides streaming support for operations by enabling you to modify the *TransferMode* property of binding configurations based on the basicHttpBinding, netTcpBinding, or net-NamedPipeBinding bindings. If you need to use a binding other than these, you must create a custom binding with a transport channel element that exposes the *TransferMode* property (basically, this means using *<HttpTransportBindingElement>*, *<HttpsTransportBindingElement>*, *<TcpTransportBindingElement>*, or *<NamedPipeTransportBindingElement>*). For further information on creating and using a custom binding, refer back to Chapter 10.

You can set the *TransferMode* property to one of the following values:

- *Buffered.* This is the default transfer mode. Messages are completely constructed in memory and transmitted only when they are complete.

- *StreamedRequest.* Request messages are streamed, but response messages are buffered.

- *StreamedResponse.* Response messages are streamed, but request messages are buffered.

- *Streamed.* Request and response messages are all streamed.

Designing Operations to Support Streaming

There is more to streaming than just changing the *TransferMode* property of a binding, and not all operations are conducive to streaming. To support request streaming, an operation can take only a single input parameter, and this parameter must either be a stream object (a descendent of the *System.IO.Stream* class) or be serializable using the encoding mechanism specified by the binding. To support response streaming, an operation must either have a *non-void* return type or a single *out* parameter, and, like the input parameter, the type of this return type or parameter must either be a stream object or be serializable. As an example, here is the service contract for a version of the GetPhoto operation from the ShoppingCartPhotoService service that supports streaming:

```
public interface IShoppingCartPhotoService
{
    [OperationContract(Name = "GetPhoto")]
    byte[] GetPhoto(string productNumber);
}
```

If you enable message logging, you will see that the body of the response message appears like this:

```
<s:Envelope xmlns:s="http://www.w3.org/2003/05/soap-envelope"
xmlns:a="http://www.w3.org/2005/08/addressing">
  <s:Header>
    ...
  </s:Header>
  <s:Body>... stream ...</s:Body>
</s:Envelope>
```

> **Note** A version of the ShoppingCartPhotoService that uses streaming is available in the Microsoft Press\WCF Step By Step\Chapter 12\Streaming folder under your \My Documents folder. The solution contains a project called StreamingHost that implements the GetPhoto operation, a console application called StreamingServiceHost that hosts the service and configures a TCP binding with the *TransferMode* property set to enable streaming, and a GUI client application called StreamingGUIClient that exercises the GetPhoto operation.

Security Implications of Streaming

Message level security features such as signing and encryption require the WCF runtime to have access to the entire message. When you enable streaming for a binding, this is no longer possible, so you must use transport level security instead.

Additionally, you cannot use reliable messaging. This feature depends on buffering so that the protocol can acknowledge delivery of complete messages and optionally order them (if ordered delivery has been specified for the binding). This is only really an issue for bindings based on the HTTP transport, as the TCP protocol and named pipes typically provide their own inherently reliable delivery mechanisms that are independent of the WCF implementation of the WS-ReliableMessaging protocol.

One final point concerning security: by default, bindings created by WCF allow a maximum received message size of 64Kb. If a message being received exceeds this limit, the WCF runtime throws an exception and aborts the operation. This limit is primarily intended to reduce the scope for Denial of Service attacks. This value is sufficient for most message-oriented operations but is too low for many streaming scenarios. In these cases, you will need to increase the value of the *MaxReceivedMessageSize* property of the binding. However, be aware that this is a global setting for the binding and so affects all operations exposed by the service through this binding.

Summary

In this chapter, you have seen how to use service throttling to control the requests submitted to a service and ensure that a service does not overcommit itself and attempt to handle too many concurrent operations. You have also seen how to use MTOM to optimize the way in which WCF encodes large binary objects for transmission. Finally, you have seen how to design operations and services that support streaming.

Chapter 13
Routing Messages

After completing this chapter, you will be able to:

- Describe how the WCF runtime for a service dispatches messages to operations.
- Build a WCF service that transparently routes client requests to other WCF services.
- Describe how WCF conforms to the WS-Addressing specification.

When a client application sends a message to a WCF service, it sends the request through an endpoint. If you recall, an endpoint specifies three pieces of information: an address, a binding, and a contract. The address indicates where the message should go; the binding identifies the transport, format, and protocols to use to communicate with the service; and the contract determines the messages that the client can send and the responses it should expect to receive. A service can expose multiple endpoints, each associated with the same or a different contract. When a WCF service receives a message, it has to examine the message to determine which service endpoint should actually process it. You can customize the way in which WCF selects the endpoint to use, and this provides a mechanism for you to change the way in which WCF routes messages within a service.

Sometimes it is useful to forward messages to entirely different services for handling. Suppose that client applications send requests to various WCF services hosted by an organization, but all of these requests actually go through the same front-end service, which acts as a firewall to the real WCF services. The front-end service can run on a computer forming part of the organization's perimeter network, and the computers hosting the real WCF service servers can reside in a protected network inside the organization. The front-end service can act as a router, forwarding requests on the real services by examining the action or address in each message. This mechanism is known as address-based routing. The front-end service can also filter messages, detecting rogue requests and blocking them, depending on the degree of intelligence you want to incorporate into the front-end service logic.

An alternative scheme is to route messages based on their contents rather than the action being requested. This mechanism is known as content-based routing. For example, if you are hosting a commercial service, you might offer different levels of service to different users depending on the fees that they pay you. A "premium" user (paying higher fees) could have requests forwarded to a high-performance server for a fast response, whereas a "standard" user (not paying as much) might have to make do with a lower level of performance. The client application run by both categories of user actually sends messages to the same front-end service, but the front-end service examines some aspect of the message, such as the identity of the user making the request, and then forwards the message to the appropriate destination.

A front-end service can also provide other features such as load-balancing. Requests from client applications arrive at a single front-end server, which uses a load-balancing algorithm to distribute requests evenly across all servers running the WCF service.

In this chapter, you will look at techniques you can use to handle scenarios such as these.

How the WCF Service Runtime Dispatches Operations

Before looking in detail at how you can build a WCF service that routes messages to other services, it is useful to explain a little more about what happens when a WCF service actually receives a request message from a client application.

ChannelDispatcher and EndpointDispatcher Objects Revisited

In Chapter 10, "Programmatically Controlling the Configuration and Communications," you saw that the WCF runtime for a service creates a channel stack for each distinct address and binding combination used to communicate with the service. Each channel stack has a *ChannelDispatcher* object and one or more *EndpointDispatcher* objects. The purpose of the *ChannelDispatcher* object is to determine which *EndpointDispatcher* object should handle the message. The role of the *EndpointDispatcher* object is to convert the message into a method call and invoke the appropriate method in the service.

> **Note**   This is a very simplified view of the WCF Service Model. The *EndpointDispatcher* object does not directly invoke the method in the service itself. It uses a number of other helper objects instantiated by the WCF runtime. These objects have their own specific responsibilities for converting the message into a method call, selecting the appropriate service instance, handling the value returned by the method, and all the other low-level tasks associated with executing an operation. The WCF runtime is highly customizable, and you can replace many of the standard objects provided by WCF that perform these tasks with your own implementations.

Each address and binding combination exposed by a service can be shared by multiple endpoints. For example, the configuration file for the ProductsServiceV2 solution from Chapter 6, "Maintaining Service Contracts and Data Contracts," defined the following service and endpoints:

```
<services>
  <service … name="Products.ProductsServiceImpl">
    <endpoint
      address="https://localhost:8000/ProductsService/ProductsService.svc"
      binding="basicHttpBinding" name="ProductsServiceHttpEndpoint"
      contract="Products.IProductsService" />
    <endpoint address="net.tcp://localhost:8080/TcpProductsService"
      binding="netTcpBinding" name="ProductsServiceTcpBinding"
      contract="Products.IProductsService" />
    <endpoint
```

```
      address="http://localhost:8010/ProductsService/ProductsService.svc"
      binding="wsHttpBinding" name="ProductsServiceWSHttpEndpoint"
      contract="Products.IProductsService" />
    <endpoint
      address="https://localhost:8000/ProductsService/ProductsService.svc"
      binding="basicHttpBinding" name="ProductsServiceHttpEndpointV2"
      contract="Products.IProductsServiceV2" />
    <endpoint address="net.tcp://localhost:8080/TcpProductsService"
      binding="netTcpBinding" name="ProductsServiceTcpBindingV2"
      contract="Products.IProductsServiceV2" />
    <endpoint
      address="http://localhost:8010/ProductsService/ProductsService.svc"
      binding="wsHttpBinding" name="ProductsServiceWSHttpEndpointV2"
      contract="Products.IProductsServiceV2" />
  </service>
</services>
```

Notice that this configuration defines six endpoints, but that there are only three distinct address/binding combinations. Consequently, this configuration causes the WCF runtime to create three channel stacks, each with its own *ChannelDispatcher* object. Each channel stack is associated with two possible endpoints; one for each of the contracts available through that channel stack. The WCF runtime creates two *EndpointDispatcher* objects for each channel stack and adds them to the collection of *EndpointDispatcher* objects associated with the *ChannelDispatcher* object. Figure 13-1 shows the relationship between the endpoints, channel stacks, and dispatcher objects for this service.

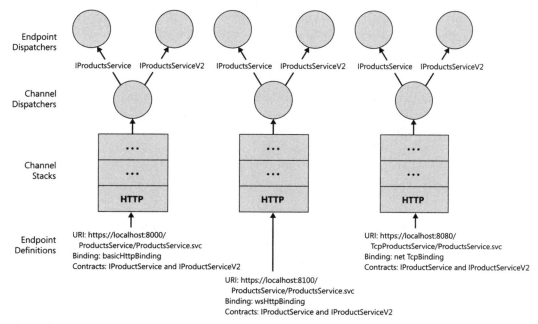

Figure 13-1   Channels and Dispatchers for the ProductsServiceImpl service.

When the service receives a message on a channel, the *ChannelDispatcher* object at the top of the channel stack queries each of its associated *EndpointDispatcher* objects to determine which endpoint can process the message. If none of the *EndpointDispatcher* objects can accept the message, the WCF runtime raises the *UnknownMessageReceived* event on the *ServiceHost* object hosting the service. Chapter 3, "Making Applications and Services Robust," describes how to handle this event.

EndpointDispatcher Objects and Filters

How does an *EndpointDispatcher* object indicate that it can process a message? Well, an *EndpointDispatcher* object exposes two properties that the *ChannelDispatcher* can query. These properties are *AddressFilter* and *ContractFilter*.

The *AddressFilter* property is an instance of the *EndpointAddressMessageFilter* class. The *EndpointAddressFilterMessage* class provides a method called Match that takes a message as its input parameter and returns a Boolean value indicating whether the *EndpointDispatcher* object recognizes the address contained in the header of this message or not.

The *ContractFilter* property is an instance of the *ActionMessageFilter* class. This class also provides a Match method that takes a message as its input parameter, and it returns a Boolean value indicating whether the *EndpointDispatcher* object can handle the action specified in the message header. Remember that the action identifies the method that the *EndpointDispatcher* will invoke in the service instance if it accepts the request. Internally, the *ActionMessageFilter* object contains a table of actions, held as strings, and all the Match method does is iterate through this table until it finds a match or reaches the end of the table.

The Match method in *both* filters must return *true* for the *ChannelDispatcher* object to consider sending the message to the *EndpointDispatcher* object for processing. It is also possible for more than one *EndpointDispatcher* object to indicate that it can handle the message. In this case, the *EndpointDispatcher* class provides the *FilterPriority* property. This property returns an integer value, and an *EndpointDispatcher* object can indicate its relative precedence compared to other *EndpointDispatcher* objects by returning a higher or lower number. If two matching endpoints have the same priority, the WCF runtime throws a MultipleFilter-MatchesException exception.

The WCF runtime creates the *EndpointAddressFilterMessage* and *ActionMessageFilter* objects for each *ChannelDispatcher* object based on the endpoint definitions in the service configuration file (or in code, if you are creating endpoints dynamically by using the AddServiceEndpoint method of the *ServiceHost* object, as described in Chapter 10). You can override these filters by creating your own customized instances of these objects with your own address and table of actions and inserting these filters when the WCF runtime builds the service prior to opening it. One way to do this is to create a custom behavior, as you did when adding the message inspector in Chapter 10.

By default, the *EndpointDispatcher* invokes the method corresponding to the action in the service contract. However, you can modify the way in which the *EndpointDispatcher* processes an operation request by creating a class that implements the *IDispatchOperationSelector* interface and assigning it to the *OperationSelector* property of the *DispatchRuntime* object referenced by the *DispatchRuntime* property of the *EndpointDispatcher*. This interface contains a single method called SelectOperation:

public string SelectOperation(ref Message message).

You can use this method to examine the message and return the name of a method that the *EndpointDispatcher* should invoke to handle it. This is useful if you want to manually control the way in which the dispatching mechanism works.

> **More Info**   The Custom Demux sample included with the WCF samples in the Microsoft Windows SDK provides more information on creating an endpoint behavior class that overrides the contract filter and operation selector for an endpoint dispatcher. This sample is based on the MsmqIntegrationBinding binding, but the general principles are the same for other bindings. You can find this sample online at *http://windowssdk.msdn.microsoft.com/en-us/library/ms752265.aspx*.

To summarize, the dispatching mechanism provides a highly customizable mechanism for determining which endpoint should process a message. You can make use of this knowledge to build services that can transparently route messages to other services.

Routing Messages to Other Services

The WCF runtime makes it a relatively simple matter to build a WCF service that accepts *specific messages* and sends them to another service for processing (I shall refer to this type of service as a *front-end service* from here on in this chapter). All you need to do is define a front-end service with a service contract that mirrors that of the target service. The methods defining the operations in the front-end service can perform any pre-processing required, such as examining the identity of the user making the request or the data being passed in as parameters, and then forward the request on to the appropriate target service.

However, creating a generalized WCF service that can accept *any messages* and route them to another service running on a different computer requires a little more thought. There are at least three issues that you need to handle:

1. The service contract. A WCF service describes the operations it can perform by defining a service contract. For a service to accept messages, they must be recognized by the ContractFilter of one or more *EndpointDispatcher* objects. At first glance, therefore, it would appear that any front-end service that accepts messages and forwards them on to another service must implement a service contract that is the same as that of the target service. Though it is acceptable when routing messages to a single service, if a WCF ser-

vice is acting as a front-end for many other services this situation can quickly become unmanageable, as the front-end service has to implement service contracts that match all of these other services.

2. The contents of messages. In some ways this issue is related to the first problem. If a front-end service has to implement the service contracts for a vast array of other services, it also has to implement any data contracts that these other services use, describing how data structures are serialized into the bodies of the messages. Again, this can quickly become an unwieldy task.

3. The contents of message headers. Apart from the data in the body, a message also contains one or more message headers. These message headers contain information such as encryption tokens, transaction identifiers, and many other miscellaneous items used to control the flow of data and manage the integrity of messages. A front-end service must carefully manage this information in order to appear transparent to the client application sending requests and the services that receive and process those requests.

Fortunately, there are reasonably simple solutions to at least some of these problems. In the following exercises, you will see how to build a very simple load-balancing router for the ShoppingCartService service. You will run two instances of the ShoppingCartService service, and the load-balancing router will direct requests from client applications transparently to them. The load-balancing routing will implement a very simple algorithm, sending alternate requests to each instance of the ShoppingCartService service. Although all three services in this exercise will be running on the same computer, it would be very easy to arrange for them to execute on different machines, enabling you to spread the workload across different processors.

You will start by re-familiarizing yourself with the ShoppingCartService service and modifying it to execute in a more traditional Internet environment.

Revisit the ShoppingCartService service

1. Using Visual Studio 2005, open the ShoppingCartService solution in the Microsoft Press\WCF Step By Step\Chapter 13\Load-Balancing Router folder under your \My Projects folder.

    This solution contains a copy of the ShoppingCartService and ShoppingCartService-Host projects from Chapter 7, "Maintaining State and Sequencing Operations," and the ShoppingCartClient project containing a client application for testing the service in a multi-user environment.

2. In the ShoppingCartService project, open the ShoppingCartService.cs file. Examine the *ServiceBehavior* attribute for the *ShoppingCartServiceImpl* class. Note that this version of the service uses the PerCall instance context mode; this is the stateless version of the service. The operations in the service make use of the saveShoppingCart and restoreShoppingCart methods to serialize users' shopping carts as XML files.

3. Open the Program.cs file in the ShoppingCartServiceHost project. This is the service host application. All it does is start the service running by using a *ServiceHost* object and then waiting for the user to press Enter to close the host.

4. Open the App.config file in the ShoppingCartServiceHost project. Notice that the service host creates an HTTP endpoint with the URI http://localhost:7080/ShoppingCartService/ShoppingCartService.svc. The endpoint uses the wsHttpBinding binding. The binding configuration specifies message level security; the client application is expected to provide a Windows username and a password for accessing the service. Close the App.config file when you have finished examining it.

5. Open the Program.cs file in the ShoppingCartClient project. This is a multi-threaded client application. Each thread runs the doClientWork method. This version of the client application creates two threads.

   Examine the doClientWork method. You can see that this method creates a proxy for connecting to the ShoppingCartService service and provides credentials for Fred and Bert, depending on which thread the method is running in. The method then exercises the methods in the ShoppingCartService service.

6. Open the App.config file in the ShoppingCartClient project, and verify that the client application uses an endpoint with the same URI and binding as the service (http://localhost:7080/ShoppingCartService/ShoppingCartService.svc). Close the App.config file when you have finished.

7. Start the solution without debugging. In the client console window, press Enter when the message "Service running" appears in the service console window.

   As the two client threads perform their tasks, they output messages in the client console window displaying their progress. Both threads add two water bottles and a mountain seat assembly to the shopping basket, display it, and then invoke the Checkout operation. The result should look like this (your output might appear in a slightly different sequence):

After both "Goods purchased" messages have appeared, press Enter to close the client console window. In the service console window, press Enter to stop the service.

In an Internet environment, for reasons of speed and interoperability, you are more likely to protect the ShoppingCartService by using transport level security than message level security. In the next exercise, you will reconfigure the service and client application to use transport level security. You will reuse the HTTPS-Server certificate that you created in Chapter 4, "Protecting an Enterprise WCF Service," to provide the necessary protection.

> **Note**   In general, you should avoid reusing the same certificate for protecting multiple services in a production environment. However, I don't want you to have to uninstall too many test certificates on your computer when you have finished reading this book.

Reconfigure the ShoppingCartService service to use transport level security

1. Using Microsoft Management Console and the Certificates snap-in, find the thumbprint of the HTTPS-Server certificate. (If you cannot remember how to do this, refer back to the exercise "Configure the WCF HTTP endpoint with an SSL certificate" in Chapter 4.)

2. Open a Windows SDK CMD Shell window, and run the following command to associate the certificate with port 7080, replacing the string following the *–h* flag with the thumbprint of the HTTPS-Server certificate on your computer:

```
httpcfg set ssl –i 0.0.0.0:7080 –h c390e7a4491cf97b96729167bf50186a4b68e052
```

> **Note**   On Windows Vista, use the following command, replacing the value for the *certhash* parameter with the thumbprint of the HTTPS-Server certificate:
>
> ```
> netsh http add sslcert ipport=0.0.0.0:7080
> certhash= c390e7a4491cf97b96729167bf50186a4b68e052
> appid={00112233-4455-6677-8899-AABBCCDDEEFF}
> ```

3. Leave the CMD Shell window open and return to Visual Studio 2005.

4. Edit the App.config file in the ShoppingCartServiceHost project by using the WCF Service Configuration editor.

   ❑ Change the *Address* property of the ShoppingCartServiceHttpEndpoint endpoint in the Endpoints folder to use the https scheme.

   ❑ Edit the ShoppingCartServiceHttpBindingConfig binding configuration in the Bindings folder, click the Security tab, and change the *Mode* property to *Transport*. Set the *TransportClientCredentialType* property to *Basic*.

   ❑ Save the file and exit the WCF Configuration Editor.

5. Open the App.config file in the ShoppingCartClient project by using the WCF Service Configuration Editor.

   ❑ In the Bindings folder, create a new binding configuration for the wsHttpBinding type. Set the *Name* property of the binding configuration to *ShoppingCartClientHt-*

tpBindingConfig. Click the Security tab and set the *security Mode* property to *Transport*, and set the *TransportClientCredentialType* property to *Basic*.

❑ Change the *Address* property of the WSHttpBinding_ShoppingCartService endpoint to use the https scheme, and set the *BindingConfiguration* property of the endpoint to *ShoppingCartClientHttpBindingConfig*.

❑ Save the file and exit the WCF Configuration Editor.

6. In Visual Studio 2005, edit the Program.cs file in the ShoppingCartClient project. Because the certificate used to protect the communications with the service was not issued by a recognized certification authority, you need to add the code you used before (in Chapter 4), to bypass the certificate validation. Add the following *using* statements to the top of the file:

```
using System.Security.Crytography.X509Certificates;
using System.Net;
```

7. Add the *PermissiveCertificatePolicy* class to the file, immediately after the *Program* class. The code for this class is available in the PermissiveCertificatePolicy.txt file in the Chapter 13 folder.

8. In the doClientWork method in the *Program* class, add the following statement shown in bold immediately before the code that creates the proxy object:

```
...
PermissiveCertificatePolicy.Enact("CN=HTTPS-Server");
ShoppingCartServuceClient proxy =
    new ShoppingCartServiceClient("WSHttpBinding_ShoppingCartService");
...
```

9. Change the statements that populate the *ClientCredentials* property of the proxy to provide the username and password for Fred and Bert as tokens available to Basic authentication rather than Windows authentication:

```
...
if (clientNum == 0)
{
    proxy.ClientCredentials.UserName.UserName = "Bert";
    proxy.ClientCredentials.UserName.Password = "Pa$$w0rd";
}
else
{
    proxy.ClientCredentials.UserName.UserName = "Fred";
    proxy.ClientCredentials.UserName.Password = "Pa$$w0rd";
}
...
```

10. Start the solution without debugging. In the client console window, press Enter when the message "Service running" appears in the service console window.

Verify that the client application runs exactly as before. When the client application has finished, press Enter to close the client console window. Press Enter to close the service console window.

You now have a version of the ShoppingCartService service that a client application can connect to by using transport level security. The next step is to run multiple instances of this service and create another service that routes messages from the client application transparently to one of these instances.

Create the ShoppingCartRouter service

1. Add a new project to the ShoppingCartService solution using the WCF Service Library template (make sure you select the Visual C# project types). Name the project Shopping-CartServiceRouter, and save it in the Microsoft Press\WCF Step By Step\Chapter 13\Load-Balancing Router folder under your \My Projects folder.

2. In the ShoppingCartServiceRouter project, rename the Class1.cs file as ShoppingCart-ServiceRouter.cs.

3. Open the ShoppingCartServiceRouter.cs file. Add the following *using* statements to the list at the top of the file:

```
using System.ServiceModel.Channels;
using System.ServiceModel.Dispatcher;
using System.ServiceModel.Description;
using System.Security.Cryptography.X509Certificates;
using System.Net;
```

4. Remove the extensive comments describing how to host the WCF service and the sample code for the IService1 service contract, the *service1* class, and the DataContract1 data contract. Leave the empty *ShoppingCartServiceRouter* namespace in place.

5. Add the service contract shown below to the *ShoppingCartServiceRouter* namespace:

```
[ServiceContract(Namespace = "http://adventure-works.com/2007/03/01",
                 Name = "ShoppingCartServiceRouter")]
public interface IShoppingCartServiceRouter
{
    [OperationContract(Action="*", ReplyAction="*")]
    Message ProcessMessage(Message message);
}
```

Understanding this rather simple-looking service contract is the key to appreciating how the router works.

In the earlier discussion, you saw that the problems that you have to overcome when designing a generalized front-end service that can forward any message on to another service concern the service contract and the contents of messages passing through the service. A service contract defines the operations that the service can process. Under normal circumstances, the WSDL description for an operation combines the *Namespace* and *Name* properties from the *ServiceContract* attribute with the name of the operation to the generate identifier, or action, defining the request message that a client application should send to invoke the operation, and the identifier, or reply action, for the response message that the service will send back. For example, the AddItemToCart operation in the ShoppingCartService service is identified like this:

```
http://adventure-works.com/2007/03/01/ShoppingCartService/AddItemToCart
```

When the WCF runtime constructs each *EndpointDispatcher* for a service, it adds the actions that the corresponding endpoint can accept to the table referenced by the *ContractFilter* property.

If you explicitly provide a value for the *Action* property of the *OperationContract* attribute when defining an operation, the WCF runtime uses this value instead of the operation name. If you specify a value of "*" for the *Action* property, the WCF runtime automatically routes all messages to this operation, regardless of the value of the action specified in the header of the message sent by the client application. Internally, the WCF runtime for the service replaces the *ActionMessageFilter* object referenced by the *ContractFilter* property of the *EndpointDispatcher* object with a *MatchAllMessageFilter* object. The Match method of this object returns true for all non-null messages passed to it, so the *EndpointDispatcher* will automatically indicate that it can accept all requests sent to it (the *AddressFilter* property is still queried by the *ChannelDispatcher,* however). In this exercise, when the ShoppingCartClient application sends AddItemToCart, RemoveItemFromCart, GetShoppingCart, and Checkout messages to the ShoppingCartRouter service, it will accept them all and the *EndpointDispatcher* will invoke the ProcessMessage method.

You should also pay attention to the signature of the ProcessMessage method. The WCF runtime on the client packages the parameters passed into an operation as the body of a SOAP message. Under normal circumstances, the WCF runtime on the service converts the body of the SOAP message back into a set of parameters that are then passed into the method implementing the operation. If the method returns a value, the WCF runtime on the service packages it up into a message and transmits it back to the WCF runtime on the client, where it is converted back into the type expected by the client application.

The ProcessMessage method is a little different as it takes a *Message* object as input. In Chapter 10, you saw that the *Message* class provides a means for transmitting and receiving raw SOAP messages. When the WCF runtime on the service receives a message from the client application, it does not unpack the parameters but instead passes the complete SOAP message to the ProcessMessage method. It is up to the ProcessMessage method to parse and interpret the contents of this *Message* object itself.

Similarly, the value returned by the ProcessMessage method is also a *Message* object. The ProcessMessage method must construct a complete SOAP message containing the data in the format expected by the client application and return this object. This response message must also include a ReplyAction in the message header corresponding to the ReplyAction expected by the WCF runtime on the client. Usually, the WCF runtime on the service adds a ReplyAction based on the name of the service and the operation. For example, the message that the ShoppingCartService service sends back to a client application in response to an AddItemToCart message is identified like this:

```
http://adventure-works.com/2007/03/01/ShoppingCartService/AddItemToCartResponse
```

If you set the *ReplyAction* property of the *OperationContract* attribute to "*", the WCF runtime on the service expects you to provide the appropriate ReplyAction yourself and add it to the message header when you create the response message. In this case, you will pass the ReplyAction returned from the ShoppingCartService back to the client application unchanged.

6. Add the *ShoppingCartServiceRouterImpl* class to the *ShoppingCartServiceRouter* namespace:

```
[ServiceBehavior(InstanceContextMode = InstanceContextMode.PerCall,
                ValidateMustUnderstand = false)]
public class ShoppingCartServiceRouterImpl : IShoppingCartServiceRouter
{
}
```

This class will contain the implementation of the ProcessMessage method. If you are familiar with the SOAP protocol, you will be aware that you can include information in message headers that the receiving service must recognize and be able to process. In this example, the ShoppingCartServiceRouter service is not actually going to process the messages itself, it is simply going to forward them to an instance of the ShoppingCart-Service service. It therefore does not need to examine or understand the message headers and should pass them on unchanged. Setting the *ValidateMustUnderstand* property of the *ServiceBehavior* attribute to *false* turns off any enforced recognition and validation of message headers by the service.

7. Add the following private fields to the *ShoppingCartServiceRouterImpl* class:

```
private static IChannelFactory<IRequestChannel> factory = null;
private EndpointAddress address1 = new EndpointAddress(
    "https://localhost:7080/ShoppingCartService/ShoppingCartService.svc");
private EndpointAddress address2 = new EndpointAddress(
    "https://localhost:7090/ShoppingCartService/ShoppingCartService.svc");
private static int routeBalancer = 1;
```

The ShoppingCartServiceRouter service actually acts as a client application to two instances of the ShoppingCartService service, sending them messages and waiting for responses. The generalized nature of the ProcessMessage method requires you to connect to the ShoppingCartService service using the low-level techniques described in Chapter 10 rather than by using a proxy object. You will use the *IChannelFactory* object to create channel factory for opening channels to each instance of the ShoppingCartSer-vice. Notice that channels for sending messages over the HTTP transport use the IRe-questChannel shape (refer back to Chapter 10 for a description of channel shapes).

The *EndpointAddress* objects specify the URI for each instance of the ShoppingCartSer-vice service. You will configure the ShoppingCartServiceHost application to run two instances of the ShoppingCartService service at these addresses in a later step.

The ProcessMessage method will use the routeBalancer variable to determine which instance of the ShoppingCartService service to send messages to.

8. Add the static constructor shown below to the *ShoppingCartServiceRouterImpl* class:

```
static ShoppingCartServiceRouterImpl()
{
    try
    {
        PermissiveCertificatePolicy.Enact("CN=HTTPS-Server");
        WSHttpBinding service = new WSHttpBinding(SecurityMode.Transport);
        factory = service.BuildChannelFactory<IRequestChannel>();
        factory.Open();
    }
    catch (Exception e)
    {
        Console.WriteLine("Exception: {0}", e.Message);
    }
}
```

The ShoppingCartServiceRouter service uses the PerCall instance context mode, so each request from the ShoppingCartClient application creates a new instance of the service (for scalability). The ProcessMessage method will use a *ChannelFactory* object to open a channel with the appropriate instance of the ShoppingCartService service. *ChannelFactory* objects are expensive to create and destroy, but all instances can reuse the same *ChannelFactory* objects. Building these objects in a static constructor ensures that they are created only once.

Also, notice that the *ChannelFactory* object is constructed by using a *WSHttpBinding* object with the security mode set to Transport. This matches the security requirements of the ShoppingCartService service.

> **Note**   The code also includes a statement that invokes the PermissiveCertificatePolicy.Enact method to bypass the security checks for the certificate used to protect communications with the ShoppingCartService service (you will add the *PermissiveCertificatePolicy* class to this service in a later step). You should not include this statement in a production environment.

9. Add the ProcessMessage method to the *ShoppingCartServiceRouterImpl* class, as follows:

```
public Message ProcessMessage(Message message)
{
    IRequestChannel channel = null;

    Console.WriteLine("Action {0}", message.Headers.Action);
    try
    {
        if (routeBalancer % 2 == 0)
        {
            channel = factory.CreateChannel(address1);
            Console.WriteLine("Using {0}\n", address1.Uri);
        }
        else
        {
            channel = factory.CreateChannel(address2);
```

```
                    Console.WriteLine("Using {0}\n", address2.Uri);
                }
                routeBalancer++;

                channel.Open();
                Message reply = channel.Request(message);
                channel.Close();
                return reply;
            }
            catch (Exception e)
            {
                Console.WriteLine(e.Message);
                return null;
            }
        }
    }
```

This method contains several *Console.WriteLine* statements that enable you to follow the execution in the service console window when the service runs.

The *if* statement in the *try* block implements the load-balancing algorithm; if the value in the routeBalancer variable is even, the method creates a channel for forward requests to address1 (https://localhost:7080/ShoppingCartService/ShoppingCartService.svc), otherwise it creates a channel for address2 (https://localhost:7090/ShoppingCartService/ShoppingCartService.svc). The method then increments the value in the routeBalancer variable. In this way, the ProcessMessage method sends all requests alternately to one instance or the other of the ShoppingCartService service.

The Request method of the *IRequestChannel* class sends a *Message* object through the channel to the destination service. The value returned is a *Message* object containing the response from the service. The ProcessMessage method returns this message unchanged to the client application.

> **Important**   Note that the code explicitly closes the *IRequestChannel* object before the method finishes. This object is local to the ProcessMessage method and so is subject to garbage collection when the method finishes, and if it was open at that time, it would be closed automatically. However, you can never be sure when the Common Language Runtime is going to perform its garbage collection, so leaving the *IRequestChannel* object open holds a connection to the service open for an indeterminate period, possibly resulting in the service refusing to accept further connections if you exceed the value of *MaxConcurrentInstances* for the service (Refer back to Chapter 12, "Implementing a WCF Service for Good Performance," for more details.)

Remember that the *Message* object sent by the client application can contain security and other header information. The ProcessMessage method makes no attempt to examine or change this information, and so the destination service is not even aware that the message has been passed through the ShoppingCartServiceRouter service. Similarly, the ProcessMessage method does not modify the response in any way, and the router is transparent to the client application. However, there is nothing to stop you from adding code that modifies the contents of a message or a response before forwarding it. This opens up some interesting security considerations, and you should ensure that you deploy the ShoppingCartServiceRouter service in a secure environment.

10. Add the *PermissiveCertificatePolicy* class to the file, immediately after the *ShoppingCart-ServiceRouterImpl* class. The code for the *PermissiveCertificatePolicy* class is available in the PermissiveCertificatePolicy.txt file in the Chapter 13 folder.

11. Build the ShoppingCartServiceRouter project.

Configure the ShoppingCartServiceHost application

1. Edit the App.config file for the ShoppingCartServiceHost project by using the WCF Service Configuration Editor.

2. Click the Services folder in the left pane. In the right pane click the Create a New Service link. Use the values in the table below as the response to the various questions in the New Service Element Wizard:

Page	Prompt	Response
What is the service type of your service?	Service type	ShoppingCartServiceRouter.ShoppingCartServiceRouterImpl
What service contract are you using?	Contract	ShoppingCartServiceRouter.IShoppingCartServiceRouter
What binding config-uration do you want to use?	Existing binding configuration	ShoppingCartServiceHttpBindingConfig_wsHttpBinding
What is the address of your endpoint?	Address	https://localhost:7070/ShoppingCartService/ShoppingCartService.svc

> **Note**   Make sure you include the "s" in the "https" scheme when specifying the address of the endpoint.

3. In the Services folder, note that there are now two services. Expand the Endpoint folder for the ShoppingCartService.ShoppingCartServiceImpl service. Select the Shopping-CartServiceHttpEndpoint service endpoint. In the right pane, change the name of this endpoint to ShoppingCartServiceHttpEndpoint1.

4. Add another endpoint to the ShoppingCartService.ShoppingCartServiceImpl service. Use the values in the following table to set the properties for this endpoint.

Property	Value
Name	ShoppingCartServiceHttpEndpoint2
Address	https://localhost:7090/ShoppingCartService /ShoppingCartService.svc
Binding	wsHttpBinding
BindingConfiguration	ShoppingCartServiceHttpBindingConfig
Contract	ShoppingCartService.IShoppingCartService

5. Save the configuration file and exit the WCF Service Configuration Editor.

6. Using Solution Explorer, add a reference to the ShoppingCartServiceRouter project to the ShoppingCartServiceHost project.

7. Edit the Program.cs file in the ShoppingCartServiceHost project. In the Main method, add the following statements, shown in bold, which create and open a new *ServiceHost* object for the ShoppingCartServiceRouter service:

```
...
ServiceHost host = new ServiceHost(…)
host.Open();
ServiceHost routerHost = new ServiceHost(
    typeof(ShoppingCartServiceRouter.ShoppingCartServiceRouterImpl));
routerHost.Open();
Console.WriteLine("Service running");
...
```

8. The ShoppingCartServiceRouter service listens to port 7070, and the second instance of the ShoppingCartService service listens to port 7090. Both of these services require transport level security. Return to the CMD Shell window you opened earlier, and run the following commands to associate the HTTPS-Server certificate with ports 7070 and 7090, replacing the string following the –h flag with the thumbprint of the HTTPS-Server certificate on your computer:

```
httpcfg set ssl –i 0.0.0.0:7070 –h c390e7a4491cf97b96729167bf50186a4b68e052
httpcfg set ssl –i 0.0.0.0:7090 –h c390e7a4491cf97b96729167bf50186a4b68e052
```

> **Note** On Windows Vista, use the following commands, replacing the value of the *certhash* parameter with the thumbprint of the HTTPS-Server certificate:
>
> ```
> netsh http add sslcert ipport=0.0.0.0:7070
> certhash= c390e7a4491cf97b96729167bf50186a4b68e052
> appid={00112233-4455-6677-8899-AABBCCDDEEFF}
> ```
>
> ```
> netsh http add sslcert ipport=0.0.0.0:7090
> certhash= c390e7a4491cf97b96729167bf50186a4b68e052
> appid={00112233-4455-6677-8899-AABBCCDDEEFF}
> ```

9. Close the CMD Shell window and return to Visual Studio 2005.

Reconfigure the client application to use the ShoppingCartRouter service

1. Edit the App.config file for the ShoppingCartClient project. Change the address of the WSHttpBinding_ShoppingCartService endpoint to refer to port 7070, like this:

    ```
    https://localhost:7070/ShoppingCartService/ShoppingCartService.svc
    ```

    This is the address of the router.

2. Save the configuration file.

3. Start the solution without debugging. In the client console window, press Enter when the message "Service running" appears in the service console window.

    The client application should function exactly as before. However, if you examine the service console window, you can see that the router has forwarded the messages to the two instances of the ShoppingCartService service in turn; the addresses alternate between port 7090 and port 7080:

4. When the client application has finished, press Enter to close the client console window. Press Enter to close the service console window.

WCF and the WS-Addressing Specification

When using the WSHttpBinding binding, the mechanism that WCF uses to identify message actions, route a message to a service, and send a response message back follows to the WS-Addressing specification. This specification defines a standard format for the message header, containing information such as the action, the address of the destination service, and the return address for any response, which conforming services should use in a SOAP message. As long as a message contains addressing information in this standard format, neither the service nor the client application cares about the technology used to create the message. This is a key factor enabling WCF client applications and services to interoperate with applications and services running on other platforms; you can use WCF to build a router for Web services developed using other languages and running on platforms other than Windows, as long as these Web services also follow the WS-Addressing specification.

Here is an example showing the addressing header of a typical message sent by the Shopping-CartClient application to the ShoppingCartServiceRouter service:

```
<s:Envelope xmlns:s="http://www.w3.org/2003/05/soap-envelope" xmlns:a="http://
schemas.xmlsoap.org/ws/2004/08/addressing">
  <s:Header>
    <a:Action s:mustUnderstand="1">
      http://adventure-works.com/2007/03/01/ShoppingCartService/AddItemToCart
    </a:Action>
    <a:MessageID>
     urn:uuid:5705a3a1-21ca-4e83-b279-dc223a0274a9
    </a:MessageID>
    <a:ReplyTo>
      <a:Address>
        http://www.w3.org/2005/08/addressing/anonymous
      </a:Address>
    </a:ReplyTo>
    <a:To s:mustUnderstand="1">
      https://localhost:9070/ShoppingCartService
    </a:To>
  </s:Header>
  <s:Body>
    ...
  </s:Body>
</s:Envelope>
```

Much of the information in this header should be reasonably clear, although there are one or two points that require further explanation. In particular, you might expect the Address in the *<ReplyTo>* element to contain the address of the client endpoint. The question is: what is the address of the client endpoint? In many cases, you cannot easily specify the information for a reply address in a manner that is meaningful in a SOAP header (several applications might share the same address, or the address might even vary between the time the application sends the message and the time the service responds). For this reason, the WS-Addressing specification allows a client application to insert this "anonymous" placeholder instead. However, the client application must provide some alternative mechanism of providing an address to enable the service to send it a response. The way in which the client application and service negotiate the reply address is independent of the WS-Addressing specification and frequently depends on the underlying transport mechanism. For example, the client might expect the service to reply using the same connection that the client used to send the initial request. The exact details of how this happens are beyond the scope of this book.

The other noteworthy part of the WS-Addressing header is the *<MessageID>* element. Each message that the client application sends has a unique identifier. When a service responds, it should include this same identifier in a *<RelatesTo>* element in the response header. A typical response to an AddItemToCart message from the ShoppingCartService service looks like this:

```
<s:Envelope xmlns:s="http://www.w3.org/2003/05/soap-envelope" xmlns:a="http://
schemas.xmlsoap.org/ws/2004/08/addressing">
  <s:Header>
    <a:Action s:mustUnderstand="1">
```

```
    http://adventure-works.com/2007/03/01/ShoppingCartService/AddItemToCartResponse
  </a:Action>
  <a:RelatesTo>
   urn:uuid:5705a3a1-21ca-4e83-b279-dc223a0274a9
  </a:RelatesTo>
 </s:Header>
 <s:Body>
   ...
 </s:Body>
</s:Envelope>
```

When the client application receives this response message, it can use the information in the *<RelatesTo>* element to correlate the response with the original request.

> **More Info**   You can find a detailed description of the WS-Addressing specification on the Microsoft Web Services and Other Distributed Technologies Developer Center at *http://msdn.microsoft.com/webservices/webservices/understanding/specs/default.aspx?pull= /library/en-us/dnglobspec/html/ws-addressing.asp*.

The WS-Referral Specification and Dynamic Routing

The approach to building a router described in this chapter works well, but the routes it defines are static; the addresses of the services are hard-coded into the router. The next evolutionary step is to build a dynamic router that routes messages to services that register themselves with the router. This is actually a common scenario, and the WS-Referral specification defines a protocol that enables a SOAP router to dynamically configure and modify its paths for routing messages. The WS-Referral specification describes a standard set of messages that services can use to register themselves with a SOAP router, and the messages to which they are interested. The SOAP router can store this information in a *referral cache*. When a client application sends a request message to the SOAP router, the router can query the referral cache, obtain the address of a service that can handle the message, and forward the request to this service.

WCF does not provide explicit support for the WS-Referral specification, but if you are interested in this approach to message routing, you should look at the Intermediary Router sample included with the WCF samples in the Microsoft Windows SDK. This sample is also available online at *http://windowssdk.msdn.microsoft.com/en-us/library/ms751497.aspx*.

> **More Info**   For a detailed description of the WS-Referral specification, see the Web Services Referral Protocol page at *http://msdn2.microsoft.com/en-us/library/ms951244.aspx*.

Summary

In this chapter, you have seen how the WCF runtime for a service determines how to handle an incoming message. The *ChannelDispatcher* object receiving the message queries each of its *EndpointDispatcher* objects in turn. An *EndpointDispatcher* exposes the *AddressFilter* and *ContractFilter* properties that the *ChannelDispatcher* can use to ascertain whether the *EndpointDispatcher* can accept the message. The *EndpointDispatcher* selected to process the message invokes the appropriate method in the service. You can customize the way in which the *EndpointDispatcher* accepts and processes messages by providing your own *AddressFilter* and *ContractFilter* objects and implementing the *IDispatchOperationSelector* interface.

You have also seen how to define a very generalized WCF service that can act as a router for other services, implementing a method that can accept almost any message and forwarding it for processing elsewhere.

Finally, you have seen how the infrastructure provided by WCF conforms to the WS-Addressing specification, when using the WSHttpBinding binding. This enables you to accept and route messages to and from applications and services created by using other technologies.

Chapter 14

Using a Callback Contract to Publish and Subscribe to Events

After completing this chapter, you will be able to:

- Define a callback contract enabling a WCF service to call back into a client application.

- Create a client application that implements a callback contract.

- Use a callback contract to build a simple mechanism for alerting client applications about significant events.

The examples and exercises that you have seen so far in this book have concentrated on the client/server model of processing. In this model, a server provides a service that waits passively for a request from a client application, handles that request, and then optionally sends a response back to the client application. The client application is the active participant, making requests and effectively determining when the service should perform its work. While this is the most common model, WCF supports other processing schemes, such as peer-to-peer networking and client callbacks.

In the peer-to-peer scenario, there are no passive services. All applications are autonomous clients that can communicate with each other as equals (or peers). There is no client/server relationship, and applications should be prepared to handle messages sent to them at any time.

> **More Info** Peer-to-peer technologies are an integral part of Windows Vista but require you to manually install Peer Networking services if you are using Windows XP. You must also configure the peer-to-peer infrastructure. WCF provides the PeerChannel for communicating between peers and defines the NetPeerTcpBinding binding to enable you to configure the communication parameters. Detailed discussion of using WCF to build peer-to-peer applications is outside the scope of this book, but the Windows SDK documentation provides information and examples in the Peer to Peer Networking section, under Windows Communication Foundation. You can find further information about configuring and building peer-to-peer applications and services online in the Windows Peer-to-Peer Networking site at *http://www.microsoft.com/technet/itsolutions/network/p2p/default.mspx*. Additionally, you can find a good overview and introduction to building peer-to-peer applications on the MSDN Web site at *http://msdn.microsoft.com/msdnmag/issues/06/10/PeerToPeer*.

Using client callbacks, a service can invoke a method in a client application, in essence inverting the client/server relationship between the client application and the service. In this chapter, you will look at how to define a client callback and how to use it to implement a simple eventing mechanism for alerting interested client applications about a change of state in the service.

Implementing and Invoking a Client Callback

A client callback is an operation implemented by a client application that a service can invoke. This is a reverse of the more traditional mechanism for exchanging messages and requires that the client application is listening for requests from the service. However, while a service listens to an endpoint, using the WCF service infrastructure established when the host application opens a *ServiceHost* object, a client application does not use a *ServiceHost* object, and it normally only expects to receive messages in response to explicit requests that it sends. The question is how can a client application listen for requests and at the same time continue its own processing? WCF provides two features that you can use to implement this functionality: callback contracts and duplex channels.

Defining a Callback Contract

A callback contract specifies the operations that a service can invoke in a client application. A callback contract is very similar to a service contract inasmuch as it contains operations marked with the *OperationContract* attribute. The main syntactic difference is that you do not decorate it with the *ServiceContract* attribute. Here is an example:

```
public interface IProductsServiceCallback
{
    // Inform the client application that the price of the specified
    // product has changed
    [OperationContract]
    void OnPriceChanged(Product product);
}
```

Client applications are expected to provide an implementation of each method in the callback contract. You reference a callback contract from a service contract defining the operations implemented by the service by using the *CallbackContract* property of the *ServiceContract* attribute, like this:

```
[ServiceContract(…, CallbackContract=typeof(IProductsServiceCallback)]
public interface IProductsServiceV3
{
    // Any method in this contract can invoke the OnPriceChanged method
    // in the client application
    [OperationContract]
    List<string> ListSelectedProducts(string match);
    …

    [OperationContract]
    bool ChangePrice(string productNumber, decimal price);
    …
}
```

The service can invoke any of the operations in the callback contract from methods implementing the service contract. You can only associate a single callback contract with a service contract.

Implementing an Operation in a Callback Contract

The callback contract defines the operations that the service can invoke in a client application, but you must also provide a means for the service to actually invoke these operations. If you create a client proxy class for the service by using the svcutil utility, the class is based on the generic *System.ServiceModel.DuplexClientBase* class (an ordinary client proxy extends the *ClientBase* generic class, as described in Chapter 10, "Programmatically Controlling the Configuration and Communications"). An abbreviated version of the proxy code for the *IProductsServiceV3* interface looks like this:

```
[System.ServiceModel.ServiceContractAttribute(...,
    CallbackContract=typeof(ProductsServiceCallback))]
public interface ProductsService
{
    [System.ServiceModel.OperationContractAttribute(Action=...,
                                                    ReplyAction=...)]
    string[] ListSelectedProducts(string match);
    ...
    [System.ServiceModel.OperationContractAttribute(Action=...,
                                                    ReplyAction=...)]
    bool ChangePrice(string productNumber, decimal price);
    ...
}
 public interface ProductsServiceCallback
{
    [OperationContractAttribute(Action=...)]
    void OnPriceChanged(Product product);
}
public partial class ProductsServiceClient :
    DuplexClientBase<ProductsService>, ProductsService
{
    ProductsServiceClient(InstanceContext callbackInstance) :
            base(callbackInstance)
    {
    }

    public ProductsServiceClient(InstanceContext callbackInstance,
        string endpointConfigurationName) :
            base(callbackInstance, endpointConfigurationName)
    {
    }
    // Other constructors not shown
    ...
    public string[] ListSelectedProducts(string match)
    {
        return base.Channel.ListSelectedProducts(match);
    }
    ...
    bool ChangePrice(string productNumber, decimal price);
    {
        return base.Channel.ChangePrice(productNumber,price);
    }
    ...
}
```

The bold statements highlight the important differences between this code and the code for a proxy that does not define a callback contract. The client application must provide a class that implements the *ProductsServiceCallback* interface, including the OnPriceChanged method.

The *ProductsServiceClient* proxy class extends the *DuplexClientBase<ProductsService>* class and defines a number of constructors that the client application can use to instantiate a proxy object. The code fragment shows only two of these constructors, but the main feature is that they all expect you to provide an *InstanceContext* object as the first parameter. This is the key property that enables the service to invoke the operation in the client application.

You should already be familiar with the concept of instance context for a service; each instance of a service runs in its own context holding the state information (instance variables and pieces of system information) for that instance. Different instances of a service have their own context. The WCF runtime creates and initializes this context automatically when it instantiates the service instance. A client application implementing a callback contract must also provide an instance context that the service can use to invoke the operations in this instance of the client. You create and provide this context, wrapped up as an *InstanceContext* object, to the constructor of the proxy. When the client application sends a request message to the service, the WCF runtime automatically sends the client context with the request. If the service needs to invoke an operation in the callback contract, it uses this context object to direct the call to the appropriate instance of the client application (you will see how to do this shortly).

Here is the code for part of a client application that implements the *ProductsServiceCallback* interface defined in the client proxy:

```
class Client : ProductsServiceCallback, IDisposable
{
    private ProductsServiceClient proxy = null;

    public void DoWork()
    {
        // Create a proxy object and connect to the service
        InstanceContext context = new InstanceContext(this);
        proxy = new ProductsServiceClient(context, …);
        …

        // Invoke operations
        bool result = proxy.ChangePrice(…);
        …
    }
    public void Dispose()
    {
        // Disconnect from the service
        proxy.Close();
    }
    // Method specified in the ProductsServiceCallback interface
    public void OnPriceChanged(Product product)
    {
```

```
Console.WriteLine("Price of {0} changed to {1}",
    product.Name, product.ListPrice);
    }
}
```

The parameter specified for the InstanceContext constructor (*this*) is a reference to the object implementing the ProductsServiceCallback contract. The statement that creates the proxy object in the DoWork method references this *InstanceContext* object. If the service invokes the OnPriceChanged operation through this context object, the WCF runtime will call the method on this instance of the client application.

Notice that the *client* class also implements the *IDisposable* interface. The Dispose method closes the proxy. A service could potentially call back into the client application at any time after the *Client* object has sent an initial message. If the client application closes the proxy immediately after sending requests to the service in the DoWork method, the service will fail if it attempts to call back into the *Client* object. The *Client* object continues to exist after the DoWork method finishes, and closing the proxy in the Dispose method enables a service to invoke operations in the *Client* object at any time until the client application terminates or it explicitly disposes the *Client* object.

Invoking an Operation in a Callback Contract

To invoke an operation in a callback contract, a service must obtain a reference to the client application object implementing the callback contract. This information is available in the operation context for the service. You can access the operation context through the static *OperationContext.Current* property, which returns an *OperationContext* object. The *Operation-Context* class provides the generic GetCallbackChannel method, which in turn returns a reference to a channel that the service can use to communicate with the instance of the client application that invoked the service. The value returned by the GetCallbackChannel method is a typed reference to the callback contract, and you can invoke operations through this reference, like this:

```
// WCF service class that implements the service contract
public class ProductsServiceImpl : IProductsServiceV3
{
    …
    public bool ChangePrice(string productNumber, decimal price)
    {
        // Update the price of the product in the database
        …
        // Invoke the callback operation in the client application
        IProductsServiceCallback callback = OperationContext.Current.
            GetCallbackChannel<IProductsServiceCallback>();
        callback.OnPriceChanged(GetProduct(productNumber));
        …
    }
}
```

It is possible that the client application could terminate between invoking the operation in the service and the service calling back into the service, especially if the operation in the service is a one-way operation. You should therefore check to ensure that the callback channel has not been closed before invoking a callback operation:

```
IProductsServiceCallback callback = OperationContext.Current.
    GetCallbackChannel<IProductsServiceCallback>();
if (((ICommunicationObject)callback).State == CommunicationState.Opened)
{
    callback.OnPriceChanged(GetProduct(productNumber));
}
```

All WCF channels implement the *ICommunicationObject* interface. This interface provides the *State* property, which you can use to determine whether the channel is still open or not. If the value of this property is anything other than *CommunicationState.Opened,* then the service should not attempt to use the callback.

 Note   Channels exhibit the same set of states and state transitions that a *ServiceHost* object does (the *ServiceHost* class indirectly implements the *ICommunicationObject* interface). Refer to Chapter 3, "Making Applications and Services Robust," for a description of these states.

Reentrancy and Threading in a Callback Operation

If a service invokes an operation in a callback contract, it is possible for the client code implementing that contract to make another operation call into the service. By default, the WCF runtime in the client handling the callback contract executes using a single thread, and calling back into the service could possibly result in the service blocking the thread processing the initial request. In this case, the WCF runtime detects the situation and throws an InvalidOperationException exception, with the message "This operation would deadlock because the reply cannot be received until the current Message completes processing." To prevent this situation from arising, you can set the concurrency mode of the class implementing the callback contract in the client application either to enable multiple threading (if the client application code is thread-safe) or enable reentrancy (if the client application code is not thread-safe, but the data it uses remains consistent across calls). You achieve this by applying the *CallbackBehavior* attribute to the class in the client application implementing the callback contract and setting the *ConcurrencyMode* property to *ConcurrencyMode.Multiple* or *ConcurrencyMode.Reentrant*:

```
[CallbackBehavior(ConcurrencyMode = ConcurrencyMode.Reentrant)]
class Client : ProductsServiceCallback, IDisposable
{
    ...
}
```

Implementing a Duplex Channel

Not all bindings support client callbacks. Specifically, you must use a binding that supports bidirectional communications; either end of the connection must be able to initiate communications, and the other end must be able to accept them. Transports such as TCP and named pipes are inherently bidirectional, and you can use the NetTcpBinding and NetNamedPipeBinding bindings with a client callback. However, the model implemented by the HTTP protocol does not support this mode of operation, so you cannot use the BasicHttpBinding or WSHttpBinding bindings. This sounds like a major shortcoming if you want to build an Intranet system based on the HTTP transport. However, WCF provides the WSDualHttpBinding binding for this purpose. The WSDualHttpBinding binding establishes two HTTP channels (one for sending requests from the client application to the service, and the other for the service to send requests to the client application) but hides much of the complexity from you, so you can treat it as a single bidirectional channel.

There are some important differences between the WSHttpBinding binding and the WSDualHttpBinding binding. Specifically, the WSDualHttpBinding binding does not support transport level security, but it always implements reliable sessions (you cannot disable them).

Using a Callback Contract to Implement Events

One of the principal uses of a callback contract is to provide a service with a means to inform a client application of a significant occurrence. You can use callbacks to implement an eventing mechanism; the service can advertise events and provide operations to enable client applications to subscribe to these events or unsubscribe from them. The service can use the callback contract to send a message to each subscribing client when an event occurs. You will see how to do this later, but first you need to define, implement, and test a callback contract that can act as the basis for an eventing mechanism.

Add a callback contract to the ProductsService service and invoke a callback operation

1. Using Visual Studio 2005, open the solution file ProductsService.sln located in the Microsoft Press\WCF Step By Step\Chapter 14\ProductsServiceV3 folder under your \My Documents folder.

   This solution contains version 3 of the ProductsService service. This service contains the operations ListSelectedProducts, GetProduct, CurrentStockLevel, ChangeStockLevel, and a new operation called ChangePrice, which a client application can invoke to change the price of a product. The solution also contains a WPF application for hosting the service, and a client application that you will use to test the ProductsService service and provide an implementation of a callback contract.

2. In Solution Explorer, open the ProductsService.cs file in the ProductsService project. Add the following callback contract to the file, immediately before the *IProductsServiceV3* interface defining the service contract:

```
// Callback interface for propagating "price changed" event
public interface IProductsServiceCallback
{
    [OperationContract(IsOneWay = true)]
    void OnPriceChanged(Product product);
}
```

This callback contract contains a single operation called OnPriceChanged. You will modify the ChangePrice operation in the ProductsService service to invoke this operation in a later step. The purpose of this operation is to inform the client of a change in the price of the product passed in as the parameter. Notice that this operation is defined as a one-way operation; all it does is alert the client application and does not return any sort of response.

3. Modify the *ServiceContract* attribute for the *IProductsServiceV3* interface to reference this callback contract, as shown in bold below:

```
// Version 3 of the service contract
[ServiceContract(Namespace = "http://adventure-works.com/2006/08/31",
                 Name = "ProductsService",
                 CallbackContract = typeof(IProductsServiceCallback))]
public interface IProductsServiceV3
{
    ...
}
```

The value to the *CallbackContract* property must be a type, so this code uses the *typeof* operator to return the type of the *IProductsServiceCallback* interface.

4. Locate the ChangePrice method at the end of the *ProductsServiceImpl* class (the *ProductsServiceImpl* class implements the IProductsServiceV3 service contract). This method updates the *AdventureWorks* database with the new product price, returning *true* if the update was successful, *false* otherwise (the method performs very limited error checking). Modify the code near the end of the method to invoke the OnPriceChanged operation in the callback contract if the update succeeds, as shown in bold below:

```
...
if (numRowsChanged != 0)
{
    IProductsServiceCallback callback = OperationContext.Current.
        GetCallbackChannel<IProductsServiceCallback>();
    callback.OnPriceChanged(GetProduct(productNumber));
    return true;
}
else
{
    return false;
}
...
```

5. Build the ProductsService project.

The next step is to implement the callback contract in the client application, but first you need to generate the proxy code for the client.

Generate the client proxy and implement the callback contract

1. Generate a proxy class for the client application by using the following procedure:

    ❑   Open a Visual Studio 2005 Command Prompt window and move to the ProductsServiceV3\ProductsService\bin folder in the Microsoft Press\WCF Step By Step\Chapter 14 folder under your \My Projects folder.

    ❑   In the Visual Studio 2005 Command Prompt window, run the command:

    ```
    svcutil ProductsService.dll
    ```

    ❑   Run the command:

    ```
    svcutil /namespace:*,ProductsClient.ProductsService adventure-
    works.com.2007.03.01.wsdl *.xsd /out:ProductsServiceProxy.cs
    ```

2. Leave the Visual Studio 2005 Command Prompt window open and return to Visual Studio 2005. Add the ProductsServiceproxy.cs file in the ProductsServiceV3\ProductsService\bin folder to the ProductsClient project.

3. Edit the Program.cs file in the ProductsClient project. Add the following *using* statement to the list at the top of the file:

    ```
    using ProductsClient.ProductsService;
    ```

4. Add the following class to the *ProductsClient* namespace, below the *Program* class:

    ```
    class Client : ProductsServiceCallback, IDisposable
    {
    }
    ```

    ProductsServiceCallback is the interface in the proxy that defines the callback contract.

5. Add the private proxy variable, the public TestProductsService method, and the public Dispose method shown below to the *Client* class. Replace the text "LON-DEV-01" in the statement that specifies the security domain for client credentials with the name of your own computer:

    ```
    private ProductsServiceClient proxy = null;

    public void TestProductsService()
    {
        // Create a proxy object and connect to the service
        proxy = new ProductsServiceClient(new InstanceContext(this),
            "WSDualHttpBinding_IProductsServiceV3");
        proxy.ClientCredentials.Windows.ClientCredential.Domain = "LON-DEV-01";
        proxy.ClientCredentials.Windows.ClientCredential.UserName = "Fred";
        proxy.ClientCredentials.Windows.ClientCredential.Password = "Pa$$w0rd";

        // Test the operations in the service
    ```

```
        try
        {
            // Obtain a list of frames
            Console.WriteLine("Test 1: List all frames");
            string[] productNumbers = proxy.ListSelectedProducts("Frame");
            foreach (string productNumber in productNumbers)
            {
                Console.WriteLine("Number: {0}", productNumber);
            }
            Console.WriteLine();

            // Fetch the details for a specific frame
            Console.WriteLine("Test 2: Display the details of a frame");
            Product product = proxy.GetProduct("FR-M21S-40");
            Console.WriteLine("Number: {0}", product.ProductNumber);
            Console.WriteLine("Name: {0}", product.Name);
            Console.WriteLine("Color: {0}", product.Color);
            Console.WriteLine("Price: {0}", product.ListPrice);
            Console.WriteLine();

            // Modify the price of this frame
            Console.WriteLine("Test 3: Modify the price of a frame");
            if (proxy.ChangePrice("FR-M21S-40", product.ListPrice + 10))
            {
                product = proxy.GetProduct("FR-M21S-40");
                Console.WriteLine("Price changed. New price: {0}",
                                    product.ListPrice);
            }
            else
            {
                Console.WriteLine("Price change failed");
            }
            Console.WriteLine();
        }

        catch (Exception e)
        {
            Console.WriteLine("Exception: {0}", e.Message);
        }
    }

    public void Dispose()
    {
        // Disconnect from the service
        proxy.Close();
    }
```

 Note   This code is available in the file Client.txt located in the Chapter 14 folder.

The TestProductsService method connects to the ProductsService using an instance of the proxy, fetches and displays a list of bicycle frames, displays the details for a specific frame, and updates the price of that frame. The Dispose method, which is part of the *IDisposable* interface, closes the proxy when the *Client* object is disposed.

Notice that the statement that creates the proxy object creates a new instance of the *InstanceContext* class as the first parameter to the constructor. The WCF runtime uses this information to construct the information in the operation context on the service, to enable the service to locate the client object when it calls the GetCallbackChannel method. The client application connects to the ProductsService by using the WSDualHttpBinding (you will configure this binding later), using message level security and Windows identities.

6. Add the following OnPriceChanged method to the *Client* class, after the Dispose method:

```
public void OnPriceChanged(Product product)
{
    Console.WriteLine("Callback from service: Price of {0} changed to {1}",
        product.Name, product.ListPrice);
}
```

This method implements the operation in the *ProductsServiceCallback* interface defining the callback contract.

7. In the Main method in the *Program* class, add the statements shown below in bold to create a new instance of the *Client* class and call the TestProductsService method:

```
static void Main(string[] args)
{
    Console.WriteLine("Press ENTER when the service has started");
    Console.ReadLine();

    Client client = new Client();
    client.TestProductsService();

    Console.WriteLine("Press ENTER to finish");
    Console.ReadLine();
}
```

Configure the WCF service and client application to use the WSDualHttpBinding binding

1. Edit the App.config file in the ProductsServiceHost project by using the WCF Configuration Editor.

2. In the left pane, add a new endpoint to the Products.ProductsServiceImpl service. Set the properties of this endpoint using the values in this table:

Property	Value
Name	ProductsServiceDualHttpEndpoint
Address	http://localhost:8050/ProductsService/ProductsService.svc
Binding	wsDualHttpBinding
Contract	Products.IProductsServiceV3

> **Note**   By default, the wsDualHttpBinding binding implements message level security and uses Windows identities.

3. Save the configuration and then exit the WCF Service Configuration Editor.

4. Add a new application configuration file called App.config to the ProductsClient project.

5. Edit the App.config file in the ProductsClient project by using the WCF Service Configuration Editor.

6. In the left pane, add a new endpoint to the Endpoints folder in the Client folder. Set the properties of this endpoint using the values in this table:

Property	Value
Name	WSDualHttpBinding_IProductsServiceV3
Address	http://localhost:8050/ProductsService/ProductsService.svc
Binding	wsDualHttpBinding
Contract	ProductsClient.ProductsService.ProductsService

7. Save the configuration and then exit the WCF Service Configuration Editor.

8. Edit the Program.cs file in the ProductsClient project. Add the statements shown below in bold to the TestProductsService method of the *Client* class, between the code that creates the proxy object and the statements that set the client credentials:

```
proxy = new ProductsServiceClient(new InstanceContext(this),
                                "WSDualHttpBinding_IProductsServiceV3");
WSDualHttpBinding binding = (WSDualHttpBinding)proxy.Endpoint.Binding;
binding.ClientBaseAddress =
    new Uri("http://localhost:8040/ProductsService/" +
            Guid.NewGuid().ToString());
proxy.ClientCredentials.Windows.ClientCredential.Domain = "LON-DEV-01";
```

When a WCF client application uses the WSDualHttpBinding binding, the WCF runtime creates two one-way channels using the HTTP transport. By default, the WCF runtime attempts to create a temporary endpoint for the client application to listen for incoming requests by using port 80. If you are running Internet Information Services, then port 80 will already be in use, and when the client attempts to connect to the service it will receive the exception "HTTP could not register URL http://+:80/Temporary_Listen_Address/.../ because TCP port 80 is being used by another application." You can force the WCF runtime to use a different URL and port by setting the *ClientBaseAddress* property of the binding. In the example in this exercise, the WCF runtime creates the temporary address based on the URL *http://localhost:8040/ProductsService/*. The address is supplemented with a GUID to ensure it is unique (if two instances of the client application execute simultaneously on the same computer, as you will be doing later, they cannot both share the same callback URL).

> **Note** This code is only necessary if you are using the WSDualHttpBinding binding. The other bindings that support callbacks (NetTcpBinding and NetNamedPipeBinding) automatically provide two-way communications.

9. Start the solution without debugging. In the ProductsServiceHost form, click Start. In the client application console window, press Enter.

   The client application displays a list of frames, followed by the details for the frame with product number FR-M21S-40. The code then adds 10 to the price of the frame and invokes the ChangePrice operation with this new price. Notice that after Test 3 starts, the message "Callback from service: Price of LL Mountain Frame – Silver, 40 changed to 364.0500" appears, output by the OnPriceChanged operation invoked by the service, as shown in the following image:

(Console window: C:\WINDOWS\system32\cmd.exe)

```
Number: FR-M21S-42
Number: FR-M21S-44
Number: FR-M21S-48
Number: FR-M21S-52
Number: FR-M21B-42
Number: FR-M21B-44
Number: FR-M21B-48
Number: FR-M21B-52
Number: FR-M63S-38
Number: FR-M21B-40
Number: FR-M21S-40

Test 2: Display the details of a frame
Number: FR-M21S-40
Name: LL Mountain Frame – Silver, 40
Color: Silver
Price: 354.0500

Test 3: Modify the price of a frame
Callback from service: Price of LL Mountain Frame – Silver, 40 changed to 364.05
00
Price changed. New price: 364.0500

Press ENTER to finish
```

> **Note** The price displayed might be different if you have previously modified the data in the AdventureWorks database. The important points are that this message appears, and that the price has increased by 10 from the value displayed in Test 2.

The client application outputs the message "Price changed. New price: 364.0500" after the ChangePrice operation completes (and after the message displayed by the OnPriceChanged method).

10. Press Enter to close the client application console window. In the ProductsServiceHost form, click Stop, and then close the form.

The callback contract enables the service to confirm to the client application that the product price has changed, but the client application probably already knew this because it initiated the change! It is arguably more important for other concurrent instances of the client application to be informed of this update. Now that you have seen how to implement and invoke a client callback and test that it works as expected, you can extend this idea to invoke the callback operation in other instances of the client application. To do this, the service must have a reference to each client application instance. In the following exercises, you will modify the ProductsService service to enable client application instances to register their interest in product price changes by adding a subscribe operation. The purpose of this operation is simply to cache a reference to the client application instance that the service can use later to invoke the OnPriceChanged operation. You will also add an unsubscribe operation to enable a client application instance to remove itself from the list that the service notifies.

Add subscribe and unsubscribe operations to the WCF service

1. In Visual Studio 2005, edit the ProductsService.cs file in the ProductsService project.

2. Add the SubscribeToPriceChangedEvent and UnsubscribeFromPriceChangedEvent methods shown below in bold to the end of the IProductsServiceV3 service contract:

```
[ServiceContract(Namespace = "http://adventure-works.com/2006/08/31",
                 Name = "ProductsService",
                 CallbackContract = typeof(IProductsServiceCallback))]
public interface IProductsServiceV3
{
    ...
    // Subscribe to the "price changed" event
    [OperationContract]
    bool SubscribeToPriceChangedEvent();
    // Unsubscribe from the "price changed" event
    [OperationContract]
    bool UnsubscribeFromPriceChangedEvent();
}
```

Client applications will use the SubscribeToPriceChangedEvent operation to declare an interest in product price changes and the UnsubscribeFromPriceChangedEvent operation to indicate that they are no longer interested in product price changes.

3. Add the following private variable to the *ProductsServiceImpl* class:

```
public class ProductsServiceImpl : IProductsServiceV3
{
    static List<IProductsServiceCallback> subscribers =
        new List<IProductsServiceCallback>();
    ...
}
```

The *ProductsServiceImpl* class will add references to client callbacks to this list for each client application instance that indicates its interest in product price changes.

4. Add the SubscribeToPriceChanged method shown below to the *ProductsServiceImpl* class:

```
public bool SubscribeToPriceChangedEvent()
{
    try
    {
        IProductsServiceCallback callback = OperationContext.Current.
            GetCallbackChannel<IProductsServiceCallback>();
        if (!subscribers.Contains(callback))
        {
            subscribers.Add(callback);
        }
```

```
        return true;
    }
    catch (Exception)
    {
        return false;
    }
}
```

This method obtains a reference to the callback contract for the client application instance invoking the operation and stores it in the subscribers list. If the callback contract reference is already in the list, this method does not add it again.

5. Add the UnsubscribeFromPriceChangedEvent method to the *ProductsServiceImpl* class, as follows:

```
public bool UnsubscribeFromPriceChangedEvent()
{
    try
    {
        IProductsServiceCallback callback = OperationContext.Current.
            GetCallbackChannel<IProductsServiceCallback>();
        subscribers.Remove(callback);
        return true;
    }
    catch (Exception)
    {
        return false;
    }
}
```

This method removes the callback reference for the client application instance invoking the operation from the subscribers list.

6. Add the private method shown below to the *ProductsServiceImpl* class:

```
private void raisePriceChangedEvent(Product product)
{
    subscribers.ForEach(delegate(IProductsServiceCallback callback)
    {
        if (((ICommunicationObject)callback).State ==
                CommunicationState.Opened)
        {
            callback.OnPriceChanged(product);
        }
        else
        {
            subscribers.Remove(callback);
        }
    });
}
```

This method iterates through all the callback references in the subscribers list. If the reference is still valid (the client application instance is still running), it invokes the OnPriceChanged operation, passing in the specified product as the parameter. If the reference is not valid, the method removes it from the list of subscribers.

7. In the ChangePrice method, comment out the statements that obtain the callback reference to the client application, invoke the OnPriceChanged method, and add a statement that calls the raisePriceChangedEvent method instead. Pass the product whose price has changed as the parameter to the raisePriceChangedEvent method, like this:

```
if (numRowsChanged != 0)
{
    //IProductsServiceCallback callback = OperationContext.Current.
    //    GetCallbackChannel<IProductsServiceCallback>();
    //callback.OnPriceChanged(GetProduct(productNumber));
    raisePriceChangedEvent(GetProduct(productNumber));
    return true;
}
```

When a client application instance changes the price of a product, all client application instances that have subscribed to the *"price changed"* event will be notified by running the OnPriceChanged method.

8. Rebuild the ProductsService project.

Update the WCF client application to subscribe to the "Price Changed" event

1. Regenerate the proxy class for the client application:

   ❑ In the Visual Studio 2005 Command Prompt window, run the command:

   ```
   svcutil ProductsService.dll
   ```

   ❑ Run the command:

   ```
   svcutil /namespace:*,ProductsClient.ProductsService adventure-
   works.com.2007.03.01.wsdl *.xsd /out:ProductsServiceProxy.cs
   ```

2. Close the Visual Studio 2005 Command Prompt window, and return to Visual Studio 2005. Delete the ProductsServiceproxy.cs file from the ProductsClient project and add the new version of this file from the ProductsServiceV3\ProductsService\bin folder.

3. Edit the Program.cs file in the ProductsClient project. Invoke the SubscribeToPriceChangedEvent operation as the first action inside the *try* block in the TestProductsService method in the Client class:

```
try
{
    proxy.SubscribeToPriceChangedEvent();

    // Obtain a list of frames
    Console.WriteLine("Test 1: List all frames");
    string[] productNumbers = proxy.ListSelectedProducts("Frame");
    ...
}
```

Whenever any instance of the client application updates the price of a product, the service will call the OnPriceChanged method in this instance of the client application.

4. Rebuild the ProductsClient project.

Test the "Price Changed" event in the WCF service

1. In Solution Explorer, right-click the ProductsServiceHost project, point to Debug, and click Start new instance. In the ProductsServiceHost form, click Start.

2. Using Windows Explorer, move to the Microsoft Press\WCF Step By Step\Chapter 14\ProductsClient\bin\Debug folder under your \My Documents folder.

   Apart from the executable and configuration files, you should notice a command file called RunClients.cmd. This command file simply runs the ProductsClient application concurrently, three times, each time opening a new window, like this:

   ```
   start ProductsClient
   start ProductsClient
   start ProductsClient
   ```

3. Double-click the RunClients.cmd file. Three console windows appear, one for each instance of the client application. In one console window, press Enter. Wait for the list of bicycle frames to appear, the details of frame FR-M21S-40 to be displayed, and the price of the frame to be changed. Verify that the message "Callback from service: Price of LL Mountain Frame – Silver, 40 changed to 374.0500" appears. Leave this command window open (*do not press Enter*).

4. In one of the other two console windows, press Enter. Again, wait while the list of frames and the details of frame FR-M21S-40 are displayed and the price of the frame is updated. Verify that the callback message appears in this client console window. Notice that a second callback message appears in the first client console window, also displaying the new price.

5. In the final console window, press Enter. Verify that when this instance of the client application updates the price of the bicycle frame and displays the callback message, the other two client console windows also output the callback message. The first client console window should display three callback messages, like this:

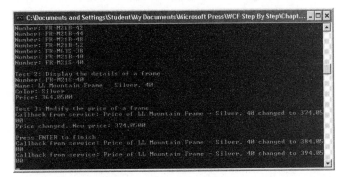

6. Press Enter in each of the client application console windows to close them. In the ProductsServiceHost form, click Stop, and then close the form.

Delivery Models for Publishing and Subscribing

Using a callback contract makes it very easy to implement a basic publication and subscription service based on WCF. You should be aware that you have been using a somewhat artificial and idealized configuration for these exercises. If you are implementing such a system in a large enterprise, or across the Internet, you have to consider issues of security and scalability and how they can impact the operation of a WCF service calling back into a client application. There are at least three well-known models that publication and subscription systems frequently implement, and you can use WCF to build systems based on any of them. Each model has its own advantages and disadvantages, as described in the following sections.

The Push Model

This is the model you have used in the exercises in this chapter. In this model, the publisher (the WCF service) sends messages directly to each subscriber (WCF client applications) through an operation in a callback contract. The service must have sufficient resources to be able to invoke operations in a potentially large number of subscribers simultaneously; the service could spawn a new thread for each subscriber if the callback operations return data or could make use of one-way operations if not. The primary disadvantage of this approach is security; the callback operations invoked by the service could be blocked by a firewall protecting client applications from unexpected incoming messages.

The Pull Model

In this model, the publisher updates a single, trusted third service with information about events as they occur. Each subscriber periodically queries this third service for updated information (they invoke an operation on the third service that returns the latest version of the data). This model is less prone to firewall blocking issues but requires more complexity on the part of the subscribers. There could also be scalability issues with the third service if a large number of subscribers query it too frequently. On the other hand, if a subscriber does not query the third site frequently enough, it might miss an event.

The Broker Model

This model is a hybrid combination of the first two schemes. The publisher updates a single, trusted third service with information about events as they occur. This third site is placed in a location, such as a perimeter network, trusted by the publishing service and the subscribing clients. Subscribers actually register with the third site rather than the site originating events. The third site calls back into subscribers when an event occurs. As well as reducing the likelihood of messages being blocked by a firewall, this model also resolves some of the scalability issues associated with subscribers polling for updated information too quickly.

> **Note**   You can also make use of Windows Network Load Balancing and clustering technologies to overcome some of the scalability concerns when using the Pull or Broker models.

Summary

In this chapter, you have seen how to use a callback contract to define operations that a client application can expose to a service. Implementing a callback contract requires the client application and service to connect with each other over a bidirectional channel that supports duplex communications; this means using the NetTcpBinding binding, the NetNamedPipe-Binding binding, the WSDualHttpBinding binding, or a custom binding based on the TCP or named pipe transports, or the HTTP transport with the *<CompositeDuplex>* binding element.

You can use a callback contract to help implement a publish and subscribe system, enabling a service to register instances of client applications that wish to be notified if a particular event occurs and then using an operation in the callback contract to inform the client application instances when the event actually happens.

Chapter 15
Managing Identity with Windows CardSpace

After completing this chapter, you will be able to:

- Describe the purpose of Windows CardSpace.
- Use Windows CardSpace with a WCF service to provide claims-based security.
- Summarize how you can employ claims-based security to implement a federated security scheme.

Security is an important, if not vital, feature of most commercial Web services and applications. Throughout this book you have seen some of the mechanisms that WCF provides to help you protect Web services and client applications. At the heart of these mechanisms is a scheme enabling a Web service to identify the user running the client application calling into the Web service. The means of identification is frequently a username and password, a certificate, or possibly a Kerberos token. After a Web service has established the identity of the user running the client application, it can then authorize or deny access to the operation requested by the user based on this identity. This use of identity to determine authorization has some interesting privacy implications—for example, if all a Web service needs to know is your age, do you really want to divulge your full identity? Consider the following real-world situations:

- Being a football fan, I used to regularly visit the supporters club of my local football team. On matchdays, you had to be a member of the club to be allowed in (at other times, anyone could enter). All members were issued with membership cards, and on entering the club, I was obliged to show my card to the person on the door. As long as I had this card and could show it, I could get in. The door attendant was never actually interested in the details on the card (my name and membership number), just the fact that I actually had one.

- If I pay for goods in a shop by using a credit card, the vendor does not need to know my full name, address, age, or even my inside leg measurement. She just needs to be confident that the credit card I am using is valid and that I have the necessary rights to use it (she will probably also do an initial visual check, just to make sure I am not using a credit card belonging to "Miss Jones" if I have a beard and a moustache, but on the Internet it is not yet possible to perform this type of validation). This scenario is actually a little more complicated than the previous one, as the vendor does not have access to the information needed to prove the validity of the card (strictly speaking, the door attendant at the football club cannot be totally sure that my membership card is not a forgery, but the quick examination performed by the door attendant usually provides an adequate level of security given the circumstances). Instead, the vendor asks the credit card company to verify my claim that this is my credit card, usually by asking me to type my pin number on a terminal connected to the credit card company's computers. The vendor then waits for the credit card company to respond that (1) the card is genuine and valid, and (2) I know the pin for the credit card and therefore I am probably the real card holder rather than some imposter who found it lying in the street (we all know this is not foolproof, but it is the best mechanism that the credit card companies have at this point).

These are two examples of claims-based security. A claim is simply a facet of my identity that is relevant to the operation being performed. In the first case, the door attendant was able to verify my claim that I was a member of the club by seeing that I had a membership card; possession of the card was taken as sufficient proof of my identity. In the second case, the vendor required my claim as the valid holder of the credit card be verified by a trusted third party.

You can apply claims-based security to Web services as well as real-world situations. In contrast to a traditional identity-based system, in a claims-based system, the Web service does not necessarily need to know who I am, just that I should be allowed to use it. WCF enables you to integrate claims-based security into your services and client applications by using Windows CardSpace. This is the subject of this chapter.

Using Windows CardSpace to Access a WCF Service

Windows CardSpace is a new technology incorporated into Windows Vista and is also available for Windows XP as part of the .NET Framework 3.0. Windows CardSpace is based on a number of WS-* standards, in particular WS-Trust, WS-MetadataExchange, and WS-SecurityPolicy. Consequently, the security mechanism that it implements is interoperable with Web services and client applications built using other technologies but that conform to these specifications.

Implementing Claims-Based Security

The world of claims-based security refers to three roles describing the participants involved in accessing a protected service:

- The *subject* is the user or entity trying to access the service. The subject provides evidence of suitable rights (a claim) to gain access. This must be a claim that the service can accept. In the credit card scenario described earlier, it would be no good trying to use my football supporters' club membership card when trying to pay for goods—the membership card might well be valid, but the vendor will not accept it.

- The *identity provider* is the organization or entity that issues the rights to assert a particular claim (or set of claims) to the subject and verifies the authenticity of any claims to exercise these rights made by the subject. In the credit card example, the identity provider is the credit card company issuing the card.

- The *relying party* is the organization or entity representing the protected service. The relying party asks the identity provider to verify that the claim made by the subject to the specified rights is valid. Again, in the credit card example, the relying party is the vendor selling me the goods that I am attempting to purchase.

> **Note**   From here on, I will refer to the information provided by a subject when attempting to prove its identity simply as a "claim." Identity providers are said to issue claims, services can demand verified claims, and subjects can submit claims when attempting to access a service.

Windows CardSpace comprises a Windows service, a set of components, and a framework for enabling identity providers to issue claims to a user, allowing the user to store and retrieve information about these claims in an accessible manner and providing assurance to a service that any claims asserted by a user are genuine. Windows CardSpace stores information about the set of claims (called a "claimset") issued by a provider as metadata in an Information Card. Windows CardSpace provides a graphical user interface enabling a user to manage and control her information cards.

A service that uses claims-based security specifies the claims it demands as part of its security policy. Windows CardSpace includes an identity selector component that can query this policy and then determine which of the user's cards have claims that match the policy. In the real world, you could use several different forms of identity to prove a claim, such as your age—your driver's license or your passport, for example. Similarly, when a service demands proof of one particular aspect of the user, there might be several information cards containing a corresponding claim from which the user can select. When a WCF client application attempts to access a service, the WCF runtime can invoke the identity selector component to determine and display the matching cards and the user can select which information card to use. The claims on the card then have to be verified by the identity provider before the client application can use them to access the service.

The complete sequence of operations that occur when a client application calls a Web service that uses Windows CardSpace to validate a user is as follows:

1. The client application attempts to invoke an operation or access a resource in a Web service.

2. The WCF runtime on the client invokes the identity selector component of Windows CardSpace. The identity selector queries the security policy of the Web service. The Web service returns information indicating the types of claims it can use to authenticate the user (for example, an email address or a pin number).

3. The identity selector examines the user's information cards and displays a list of cards that contain claims of the types specified by the Web service.

4. The user selects the information card to use.

5. The identity selector contacts the identity provider that issued the information card, passing it the metadata describing the claim on the user's information card and the claims demanded by the service.

6. The identity provider examines the metadata describing the claim and generates a token verifying that user's claim is valid. The identity provider sends this token back to the identity selector running on the client computer.

7. The identity selector asks the user to approve release of the token to the Web service.

8. If the user approves release, the identity selector sends the token to the Web service. The Web service examines the token to verify that the user's claim is valid. If the token is valid, the Web service can use the identity information in this token to determine whether the user is authorized to invoke the operation or access the resource.

All of this sounds quite complicated. Fortunately, WCF and Windows CardSpace shield you from much of this complexity, and it is actually quite straightforward to incorporate claims-based security into a WCF service. In the following set of exercises, you will configure the ShoppingCartService service to identify users by their email address.

Before we delve into the world of Windows CardSpace, I need to explain one more thing. In a real-world environment, you will most likely use information cards issued by commercial, trusted, third-party identity providers (such as credit card companies, banks, governments, or other organizations). Windows CardSpace also enables you to create self-issued cards. A self-issued card is a card that you create yourself by using the Windows CardSpace console, often for testing purposes (they have other uses as well). A self-issued card can contain a small but useful subset of claims, such as your name, home address, telephone number, and email address. In this case, you can think of the identity provider as the Windows CardSpace service running on your own computer. The exercises that follow make use of self-issued information cards, as I don't want you to have to obtain a commercial information card just for learning purposes. However, the technique is very similar when you use an information card issued by a trusted third party, as I will explain afterwards.

Important   A production Web service should not rely on claims asserted by self-issued information cards for authorizing access to sensitive data. It is very easy for a user to create a self-issued card with whatever values they want for the claims it contains.

Configure the ShoppingCartService service to use claims-based security

1. Using Visual Studio 2005, open the solution file ShoppingCartService.sln located in the Microsoft Press\WCF Step By Step\Chapter 15\ShoppingCartService folder under your \My Documents folder.

    This solution contains a completed version of the ShoppingCartService service, console host application, and test client application, from Chapter 9, "Implementing Reliable Sessions."

2. Edit the App.config file in the ShoppingCartHost project by using the WCF Configuration Editor.

3. In the left pane, add a new binding configuration to the Bindings folder. Select the wsFederationHttpBinding binding type. Change the name of the binding configuration to ShoppingCartServiceCardSpaceBindingConfig. The ShoppingCartService service uses reliable sessions and transactions, so set the *TransactionFlow* property to *True* and set the *Enabled* property in the *ReliableSession Properties* section to *True*.

> **Note**   You can also use claims-based security with the wsHttpBinding binding, but that binding supports only a limited set of claims. The wsFederationHttpBinding binding enables you to configure the service to specify a more extensive range.

4. In the left pane, click the ClaimTypes folder under the Security node for the ShoppingCartServiceCardSpaceBindingConfig binding configuration. Click the New button at the bottom of the right pane.

    In the Claim Type Element Editor, set the *ClaimType* property to *http://schemas.xmlsoap.org/ws/2005/05/identity/claims/emailaddress*. Verify that the *IsOptional* property is set to *False*, and then click OK.

    The claims specified in the *ClaimTypes* property of the binding configuration constitute the claims security policy for the service. Each type of claim is identified by a well-known URI—the URI you have specified here indicates an email address. You can add multiple claim types if you want to identify users based on more than one piece of information.

> **Note**   Apart from an email address, Windows CardSpace provides support for a number of other built-in claim types, such as a user's name, address, telephone number, and date of birth. For a full list of the built-in claim types and the corresponding URIs that Windows CardSpace recognizes, see the properties of the *ClaimTypes* class in the Windows SDK documentation.
>
> However, you are not restricted to this set of claims. A key objective of the WCF claims-based security model is that it is extensible and interoperable with systems developed by using other technologies. You can make use of claim types supported by identity providers other than Windows CardSpace, you just need to know the URI that identifies the claim types you want to use.

5. In the left pane, click the Security folder under the ShoppingCartServiceCardSpaceBindingConfig node. In the right pane, set the *IssuedTokenType* property to the value *urn:oasis:names:tc:SAML:1.0:assertion*.

    A WCF service uses the *IssuedTokenType* property to specify the type of token it expects to receive from the identity provider containing the claim information (identity providers can send tokens conforming to a number of different standard formats). In this case, the ShoppingCartService service expects a Secure Application Markup Language (SAML) 1.0 token.

6. A fundamental requirement of solutions based on Windows CardSpace is that client applications must be able to verify the identity of the Web service requesting the claim and the Web service must be able to trust the identity provider verifying the claim. This means that you should configure the requesting Web service with a certificate and provide the client application with a reference to this certificate. If you are using a third-party identity provider, it must also supply a certificate that the client application and Web service can use to confirm its identity (the identity provider signs tokens with its private key, so the Web service must have access to its public key in order to verify their signatures). Additionally, all messages must be encrypted, either at the message level or at the transport level.

> **More Info**   For more information about how you can use certificates to encrypt and sign messages and verify the authenticity of a service, refer back to Chapter 5, "Protecting a WCF Service over the Internet."

To create a certificate for the ShoppingCartService, open a Microsoft Windows SDK CMD Shell prompt, and use the makecert utility to create a new certificate for the service, like this:

```
makecert -sr LocalMachine -ss My -n CN=ShoppingCartService -sky exchange
```

7. Leave the CMD shell open, and return to the WCF Service Configuration Editor. In the left pane, add a new service behavior to the Service Behaviors folder in the Advanced folder. Name this behavior ShoppingCartServiceBehavior.

8. In the right pane, click Add, and add a <serviceCredentials> element to the behavior. In the left pane, expand the new serviceCredentials node, and click the serviceCertificate node. In the right pane, set the *FindValue* property to *ShoppingCartService* (this is the name of the certificate you have just created) and the *X509FindType* property to *FindBySubjectName*.

9. In this exercise, you are using an unverifiable self-issued information card rather than a card issued by a third-party identity provider. At run time, the SAML token containing the claim token is provided by the Windows CardSpace service running on the client application computer. Therefore, you need to configure the Web service to accept SAML tokens from an untrusted source (the user running the client application and who has issued the card to herself).

    In the left pane, click the issuedTokenAuthentication node under the serviceCredentials node. In the right pane, set the *AllowUntrustedRsaIssuers* property to *True*.

10. In the left pane, select the ShoppingCartService.ShoppingCartServiceImpl service in the Services folder. In the right pane, set the *BehaviorConfiguration* property to *ShoppingCartServiceBehavior*.

11. In the left pane, add a new endpoint to the Endpoints folder under the ShoppingCart-Service.ShoppingCartServiceImpl service. Set the properties of this endpoint using the values in the following table:

Property	Value
Name	ShoppingCartServiceHttpFederationEndpoint
Address	http://localhost:9050/ShoppingCartService /ShoppingCartService.svc
Binding	wsFederationHttpBinding
BindingConfiguration	ShoppingCartServiceCardSpaceBindingConfig
Contract	ShoppingCartService.IShoppingCartService

12. Save the configuration file, and close the WCF Service Configuration Editor.

The ShoppingCartService now expects the client application to provide the user's email address whenever it invokes an operation. You can use the email address to authorize the user and grant or deny them access to specific operations. You can perform this task in a variety of ways. The most direct technique is to explicitly examine the value of the claim in the token passed to the service, which is what you will do in the next exercise.

Amend the ShoppingCartService service to authorize users based on their email address

1. In Solution Explorer, edit the ShoppingCartService.cs file in the ShoppingCartService project.

2. Add the following *using* statements to the list at the top of the file:

```
using System.Security;
using System.IdentityModel.Claims;
using System.IdentityModel.Policy;
```

3. Add the following private array to the *ShoppingCartServiceImpl* class:

```
// The list of authorized users
private string[] authorizedUsers = { "Fred@Adventure-Works.com",
                                     "Bert@Adventure-Works.com" };
```

This array contains the email addresses of the users that the service will allow to access the service.

> **Note**   This code is for testing purposes only. In a production environment, you should consider storing the details of authorized users in a database rather than using a hard-coded array of strings.

4. Add the following private method to the *ShoppingCartServiceImpl* class to determine whether the claimset in the token passed to the service contains an email claim with an email address that corresponds to one of the authorized users:

```
// Authorize the user if their email address is in the authorizedUsers list
private bool authorizeUser()
{
    bool authorized = false;

    AuthorizationContext authContext =
      OperationContext.Current.ServiceSecurityContext.AuthorizationContext;
    foreach (ClaimSet claimSet in authContext.ClaimSets)
    {
        foreach (Claim emailClaim in
            claimSet.FindClaims(ClaimTypes.Email, Rights.PossessProperty))
        {
            foreach (string validUser in authorizedUsers)
            {
                if (String.Compare(emailClaim.Resource.ToString(),
                                   validUser, true) == 0)
                {
                    authorized = true;
                    break;
                }
            }
        }
    }
    return authorized;
}
```

When the WCF runtime for the service receives the tokenized claims from the client application, it matches the values for these claims against the security policy that it implements. The *AuthorizationContext* property of the service security context contains the results of this match. In this case, *AuthorizationContext* property should contain an email address claim with the email address provided by the information card sent by the client application.

> **Note** The *AuthorizationContext* property will also contain other claims resulting from the various WS-* protocols that Windows CardSpace uses, but the details are beyond the scope of this book.

The *AuthorizationContext* property comprises a collection of claimsets, and each claimset contains a collection of claims. This method iterates through each claimset looking for an email claim. If it finds one, it examines the value of the claim and compares it to each email address in the list of authorized users. Notice that the value of a claim is available through the *Resource* property. The type of this property is *Object,* and its contents are dependent on the type of the claim. An email claim is a string containing the authenticated email address of the user, so this method simply performs a case-insensitive string comparison. If the email address in the claim matches one of the authorized users, the authorizeUser method returns *true,* otherwise it returns *false.*

5. Locate the AddItemToCart method in the *ShoppingCartServiceImpl* class. At the start of the method, add a block of code that calls the authorizeUser method and throws a security exception if the user is not an authorized user, like this:

```
public bool AddItemToCart(string productNumber)
{
    // Check that the user is authorized
    // Throw a SecurityException if they are not
    if (!authorizeUser())
    {
        throw new SecurityException("Access denied");
    }    ...
}
```

6. Add the same statements to the start of the RemoveItemFromCart, GetShoppingCart, and Checkout methods.

7. Build the ShoppingCartService project.

You can now configure the client application to enable the user to select an information card and send the SAML token containing the user's email address to the ShoppingCartService service.

Implementing Custom Authorization

If you need to perform more extensive authorization checks than those shown in the exercise, the .NET Framework 3.0 provides the *ServiceAuthorizationManager* class in the *System.ServiceModel* namespace. The WCF runtime on the service calls the methods of this class to perform authorization checks whenever it processes a client request. However, this class is just a placeholder, which by default allows users to invoke all operations without restriction. To implement a more secure policy, extend this class by using inheritance and override its methods to perform your own custom authorization. You then register your implementation of the class with the WCF runtime by setting the *Authorization.ServiceAuthorizationManager* property of the service host object to an instance of your class, or by creating a service behavior in the service configuration file and specifying the name of your class in the *<serviceAuthorization>* element.

For a complete example, see the topic "How To: Create a Custom AuthorizationManager for a Service" in the Microsoft Windows SDK documentation.

Configure the ShoppingCartClient application to use Windows CardSpace to send a token identifying the user

1. Edit the App.config file in the ShoppingCartClient project by using the WCF Configuration Editor.

2. In the left pane, add a new binding configuration to the Bindings folder. Select the wsFederationHttpBinding binding type. Change the name of the binding configuration

to ShoppingCartClientCardSpaceBindingConfig. Set the *TransactionFlow* property to *True*, and set the *Enabled* property in the *ReliableSession* Properties section to *True*.

3. Add the claim type http://schemas.xmlsoap.org/ws/2005/05/identity/claims/emailaddress to the *ClaimTypes* collection under the Security node in the left pane. Verify that the *IsOptional* property is set to *False*.

> **Note** Hardcoding the claim type in this way removes the need for WCF runtime on the client computer to query the security policy of the service. This is acceptable if you know that the types of claims demanded by the service are not going to change very often. However, if the security policy of the service does change and it requires different claims, you must make corresponding updates to this configuration.

4. Set the *IssuedTokenType* property of the Security node to *urn:oasis:names:tc:SAML:1.0:assertion*.

5. Return to the CMD Shell window and type the following command:

```
certmgr -put -c -n ShoppingCartService -r LocalMachine -s My ShoppingCartService.cer
```

This command retrieves a copy of the ShoppingCartService certificate used by the WCF service to authenticate itself and creates a file called ShoppingCartService.cer. This file contains a copy of the certificate including its public key but *not* the private key.

Type the following command to import this certificate into the trusted people certificate store for the current user:

```
certmgr -add ShoppingCartService.cer -c -r CurrentUser -s TrustedPeople
```

6. Close the CMD Shell window and return to the WCF Service Configuration Editor. In the left pane, add a new endpoint behavior to the Endpoint Behaviors folder under the Advanced folder. Name this behavior ShoppingCartClientEndpointBehavior.

7. In the right pane, click Add, and add a *<clientCredentials>* element to the behavior. In the left pane, expand the clientCredentials node, expand the serviceCertificate node, and then click the authentication node. In the right pane, set the *CertificateValidationMode* property to *PeerTrust* and the *RevocationMode* property to *NoCheck*.

> **Note** You are using a test certificate issued by the certmgr tool rather than a recognized certification authority. You placed the certificate in the TrustedPeople store, and setting the validation mode to PeerTrust bypasses validation for certificates placed in this store.

8. In the left pane, add a new client endpoint to the Endpoints folder under the Client folder. Set the properties of this endpoint using the values in the following table:

Property	Value
Name	HttpFederationBinding_ShoppingCartService
Address	http://localhost:9050/ShoppingCartService/ShoppingCartService.svc
BehaviorConfiguration	ShoppingCartClientEnpointBehavior
Binding	wsFederationHttpBinding
BindingConfiguration	ShoppingCartClientCardSpaceBindingConfig
Contract	ShoppingCartClient.ShoppingCartService.ShoppingCartService

9. In the right pane, click the Identity tab. In the *CertificateReference* Properties section, set the *FindValue* property to *ShoppingCartService* and the *X509FindType* property to *FindBySubjectName*.

10. Save the configuration file, and close the WCF Service Configuration Editor.

11. In Solution Explorer, edit the Program.cs file in the ShoppingCartClient project. In the Main method in the *Program* class, change the statement that creates the proxy to use the HttpFederationBinding_ShoppingCartService endpoint, as follows:

```
// Connect to the ShoppingCartService service
ShoppingCartServiceClient proxy = new
    ShoppingCartServiceClient("HttpFederationBinding_ShoppingCartService");
```

The next stage is to create some information cards that you can use to test the ShoppingCart-Service service. You can do this using the Windows CardSpace application in the Control Panel.

Create information cards for testing the ShoppingCartService service

1. In Windows Control Panel, select the User Accounts category, and then start the Windows CardSpace application.

   The Windows CardSpace console starts and displays the Windows CardSpace–Welcome dialog box. Click Don't show me this page again, and then click OK.

2. If you have not yet created or installed any cards, the list of information cards will be empty apart from the Add a card icon. Click the Add a card icon, and then click the Add button that appears at the bottom of the console window.

3. In the Add a card window, click Create a Personal card.

4. In the Edit a new card window, specify *Valid ShoppingCartService Test Card* for the *Card Name* property, *Fred@Adventure-Works.com* for the *Email Address* property, and then click Save. The following image shows the details for the information card:

The new information card should appear in the list of cards in the Windows CardSpace console. The email address for this card represents a user that is authorized to access the operations in the ShoppingCartService service.

5. Add another personal card. In the Edit a new card window, specify *Invalid ShoppingCart-Service Test Card* for the *Card Name* property, *Sid@Adventure-Works.com* for the *Email Address* property, and then click Save. The email address for this card represents a user that is not authorized to invoke the operations in the ShoppingCartService service.

6. Close the Windows CardSpace console.

Test the ShoppingCartService service

1. In Visual Studio 2005, start the solution without debugging. Wait for the service to start and display the message "Service running." In the client application console window displaying the message "Press ENTER when the service has started," press Enter.

When the client application invokes the first operation in the ShoppingCartService service, the Windows CardSpace service intervenes and displays the Windows CardSpace console.

> **Note** The Windows CardSpace identity selector runs in a separate desktop session from the user to prevent other applications being able to interfere with it. For this reason, whenever the Windows CardSpace console appears, the user's desktop is dimmed and inaccessible.

Notice that Windows CardSpace recognizes that the certificate used by the Shopping-CartService service is not verified and displays the following warning:

> **Windows CardSpace**
>
> ⊙ Do you want to send a card to this site?
>
> Review the following site information and privacy statement to decide if you want to send a card to this site.
>
> ⚠ • This site does not meet Windows CardSpace requirements for a bank or major Internet business. To learn more, click Why is this important?
>
> Site information:
>
> **ShoppingCartService**
> *Organization name not verified*
> *Location not verified*
> View privacy statement
> Cards that are sent to this site may be sent to the site's designated agents.
>
> Site information verified by:
> Root Agency
>
> ⊙ Yes, choose a card to send
> ⊙ No, return to the site
>
> Tasks
> View certificate details
> View privacy statement
>
> Why is this important?
> Help

Click Yes, choose a card to send.

> **Important**   If Windows CardSpace displays this message when you access a commercial Web service, you should be very careful, as it indicates that the Web service's certificate might not have originated from a recognized certification authority. In this situation, you should probably click No and not send your credentials to the site.

2. Windows CardSpace displays a list of cards that contain email addresses and so match the claims required by the service. Select the Valid ShoppingCartService Test Card, and then click Send.

3. Windows CardSpace displays the details of the card that it will send to the Shopping-CartService service:

Click Send to confirm that this is the correct card.

The client application resumes and runs as it has done in previous chapters. The selected card contains an email address identifying a user that the ShoppingCartService service allows to invoke the various operations it implements. Notice that although the client application makes several calls to the service, Windows CardSpace intervenes only on the first call in the session.

> **Note** If you take more than one minute to select and send the card, the client application stops with the exception "The operation is not valid for the state of the transaction." This is because the AddItemToCart operation is part of a transaction initiated by the client application, and the transaction timeout specified by the client application is one minute. If this happens, stop the client application and service, restart the solution, and select the Valid ShoppingCartService Test Card when prompted by Windows CardSpace.
>
> Generally, it is not good practice to gather user input during a transaction. For situations such as this, you can programmatically request a token for a specific card in advance of the transaction starting and then supply this token when the first operation occurs. Note that the API that Windows CardSpace currently provides for performing these tasks is unmanaged and requires that you are familiar with C++.

4. Press Enter to close the client application console window, but leave the service running.

5. In Visual Studio 2005, in Solution Explorer, right-click the ShoppingCartClient project, point to Debug, and then click Start new instance. This action starts a new instance of the client application.

6. In the client application console window, press Enter. The Windows CardSpace appears again. This time, however, you don't get the warning that the Web service is using a sus-

pect certificate—this warning only appears the first time you access the service. Windows CardSpace also organizes the list of matching cards and informs you which cards you have previously sent to the Web service:

7. Select the Invalid ShoppingCartService Test Card, and then click Send. Click Send again to confirm that this is the card you want to use.

   This time the client application stops and reports the exception "Access is denied." The email address in this card identifies a user to which the ShoppingCartService service has not granted access.

8. Press Enter to close the client application console. Press Enter to close the service application console.

Using a Third-Party Identity Provider

In the previous exercises, Windows CardSpace acted as its own identity provider, verifying the claim made by the user before sending a SAML token containing the claim information to the service. I mentioned earlier that you might not want to rely on the veracity of self-issued cards in a commercial environment. Instead, you should use information cards issued by trusted third-party identity providers, such as banks, credit card companies, government agencies, and so forth. It is important to realize that the claims on an information card are simply a representation of a set of rights. The rights themselves are retained by the identity provider, and the identity provider can withdraw these rights at any time, rendering the user's information card invalid.

A user can request an information card from a third party as an out-of-band operation. If the third party approves the request, it can create an information card file and send it to the user.

This file is a signed XML file, containing data in a format that Windows CardSpace recognizes. The user can then install this file into Windows CardSpace using the "Install a Managed card" feature of the Windows CardSpace console (this is on the same page in the Windows CardSpace console that you use to create self-issued cards). If the user tries to create a card with a forged set of claims, the third party will not be able to verify those claims and will consequently not issue a token when the user attempts to use the card.

> **More Info**   Remember that Windows CardSpace is built on accepted WS-* protocols. Microsoft provides documentation on how Windows CardSpace uses these protocols and how to build non-WCF services that can interact with Windows CardSpace for issuing cards and verifying claims. For more information, see the document "A Guide to Integrating with Windows CardSpace v1.0," available at *http://download.microsoft.com/download/6/c/3 /6c3c2ba2-e5f0-4fe3-be7f-c5dcb86af6de/infocard-guide-beta2-published.pdf*.
>
> The Microsoft Windows SDK also includes the sample "Creating Managed Cards," which shows how to build an application that can create a signed XML file containing claims that a user can import into Windows CardSpace. This sample is available online at *http://msdn2.microsoft.com/en-us/library/aa967567.aspx*.

Configuring a WCF Client Application and Service to use a Third-Party Identity Provider

You have seen that an identity provider actually has to perform two related tasks: it issues claims, and it verifies that the claims submitted by a client application are genuine and issues a security token. The component of the identity provider that performs claims verification and issues tokens is usually referred to as a Security Token Service, or STS. In the exercises you performed earlier, Windows CardSpace provided the STS itself. You can also build your own STS. The details are outside the scope of this book, but the Microsoft Windows SDK includes a description of the process in the topic "How To: Create a Security Token Service." You can find this document online at *http://msdn2.microsoft.com/en-us/library/ms733095.aspx*.

When you use an STS other than that provided with Windows CardSpace, you must configure the client application with the address of this STS. The identity selector on the client computer uses this information to contact the STS and obtain a security token. You can provide this information programmatically or in the application configuration file. If you use the WCF Configuration Editor to edit the application configuration file, the key properties are in the Issuer page of the wsFederationHttpBinding configuration, shown in Figure 15-1.

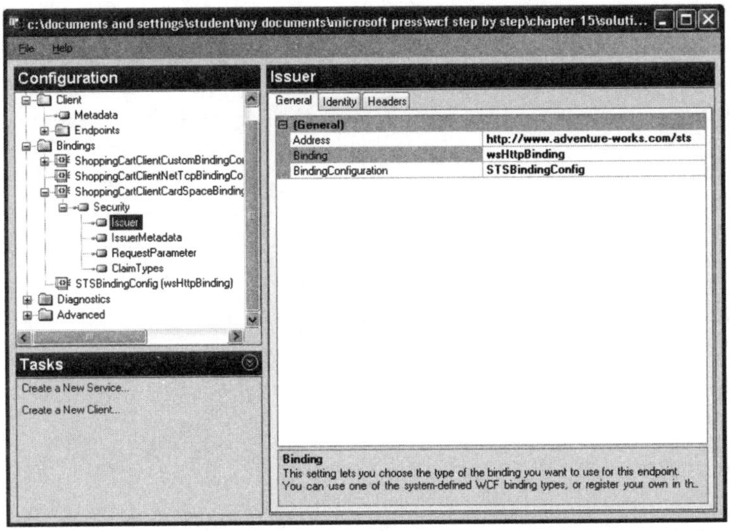

Figure 15-1   Configuring the Issuer properties for a WCF client application.

Specify the URI of the STS in the *Address* property. You can optionally provide a binding configuration if the STS has particular communications requirements, such as reliable sessions. The Identity tab enables you to indicate a certificate in the local certificate store to use for validating the identity of the STS.

The token issued by an STS can be in one of several formats. By default, the client application requests a token that conforms to the SAML 1.1 specification. However, if the WCF service expects a token in a different format, you can specify the token type in the *IssuedTokenType* property on the Security page. The STS should respond with a token of this type.

> **More Info**   For more information about these properties and how to set them programmatically rather than using an application configuration file, see the topic "How To: Create a WSFederationHttpBinding" in the Microsoft Windows SDK documentation. This information is also available online at *http://msdn2.microsoft.com/en-us/library/aa347982.aspx*.

Claims-Based Authentication in a Federated Environment

Claims-based authentication is an extremely powerful and flexible mechanism that you can use in a variety of scenarios. For example, suppose the Fabrikam organization wants to make one of its Web services available to users belonging to other partner companies, such as Adventure-Works, but not to the general public. One way to authenticate users from Adventure-Works attempting to access the Fabrikam service would be for Fabrikam to implement an STS and issue information cards for each employee of Adventure-Works. However, if Adventure-Works has a large number of employees, then maintaining a list of valid users in the Fabrikam system can quickly become an unmanageable task. Furthermore, should Fabrikam really be concerned with the details of who works for Adventure-Works? All the Fabrikam service requires is that the user is a verified employee of Adventure-Works but not any other details. If Fabrikam has several other partner organizations besides Adventure-Works, whose employees should also be able to access the Fabrikam service, then the scope of the problem multiplies.

To solve this problem, it can help to think of an STS as a service that converts claims of one type into claims of another. The WS-Trust specification on which the concept of an STS is based defines a "language" for requesting and issuing claims. An organization can implement an STS that verifies its employees' claims, and outputs tokens that can be used as claims for another STS belonging to another organization (the exact details of the WS-Trust specification are beyond the scope of this book). What does this mean, and how does it help? Look at the following possible solution to the problem of Fabrikam authenticating Adventure-Works employees.

The Fabrikam organization has an STS that issues a single claim to Adventure-Works, effectively stating that it recognizes any employee that Adventure-Works authenticates as an employee as being a valid user of the Fabrikam Web service. Adventure-Works implements its own STS. Users inside Adventure-Works have information cards issued by the Adventure-Works STS containing a claim asserting that they are valid employees of Adventure-Works (the "employee claim"). An application run by a user within Adventure-Works that requires access to the Fabrikam Web service actually sends the "employee claim" of the user to the Adventure-Works STS. This STS verifies that the user really is an employee and returns a token containing a verified "the user is an employee of Adventure-Works" claim. The application then sends this new claim to the STS inside the Fabrikam organization. The Fabrikam STS verifies the authenticity of this claim to establish that it is genuine and was issued by a recognized partner organization, and then issues another token containing an authenticated claim that the client application uses to access the Fabrikam Web service. Figure 15-2 depicts the flow of claims and security tokens.

The Fabrikam organization can issue similar claims to other partner companies, enabling their employees to access the Fabrikam service. If Fabrikam wishes to withdraw the rights of a partner company, it only needs to rescind a single claim. Of course, Fabrikam can issue individual claims to its own employees as well.

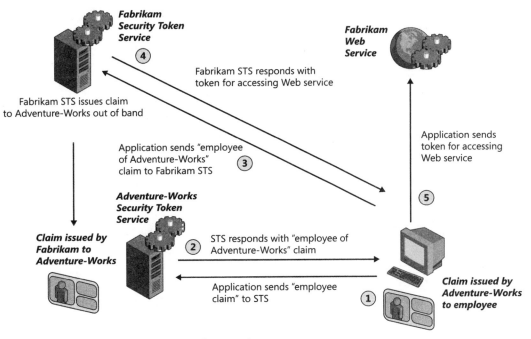

Figure 15-2   Cooperating Security Token Services.

> **Note**   This is a somewhat simplified view of the process, and there other security aspects that a scheme like this requires you to implement, such as authenticating and protecting the physical communications between organizations.

This mechanism is generally referred to as *federated security*. Each user is authenticated, but the authentication is the responsibility of the individual organizations to which they belong. Internally, each organization operates in an autonomous manner, implementing its own security policies and authenticating users in its own way.

A key aspect of federated security is the confidence that different organizations have with each other's authentication mechanisms. As long as an organization implements a strong security policy, partner organizations can trust that if it says "user x is valid" then that user is genuinely valid. Security is always a matter of confidence and trust. In the past, different organizations have tried to protect their systems from unauthorized access by using a wide variety of techniques, often based on proprietary protocols. This frequently becomes a problem as soon as organizations need to share information with each other, with ad hoc solutions that often open holes in the security infrastructure of these organizations. The increasing use of STSs and the adoption of the various WS-* protocols can help to standardize the way in which organizations protect their communications and their users, making their security mechanisms more interoperable. Windows CardSpace and WCF provide an important set of tools for helping to implement these mechanisms in a simple-to-use but robust manner.

Summary

In this chapter, you have seen how to use Windows CardSpace to implement claims-based security. You have learned how to configure a WCF client application and service to interact with Windows CardSpace and how to use a self-issued card to send a claim to a service. You have seen how a service can query the values of claims it has been sent in order to authorize access to operations. You have also looked at how to configure a client application and service to use a third-party STS for authenticating claims. Finally, you have seen how organizations can use claims-based authentication and STSs to implement federated security.

Chapter 16

Integrating with ASP.NET Clients and Enterprise Services Components

After completing this chapter, you will be able to:

- Create a WCF service that can interoperate with an ASP.NET client application.
- Integrate a COM+ application into a WCF solution.

A key feature of WCF is the ability to use it to build heterogeneous solutions, protecting your existing investment in existing components and software. WCF is based on commonly accepted WS-* standards and protocols. This enables you to create services that can communicate with client applications running on platforms other than Microsoft Windows and developed using other technologies, such as Java, as long as they conform to the same WS-* standards and use the same protocols. If you publish the metadata for your WCF service, many Java tools vendors provide utilities that can query this metadata and generate Java proxy classes, in much the same way that svcutil does. The converse situation is also true. You can use WCF to build client applications that connect to Java Web services, again as long as those Java Web services conform to the same WS-* standards and protocols as WCF. If these services publish their metadata, you can use the svcutil utility to generate proxy classes for these services. You may also have a number of components, services, and applications created using Microsoft technologies that predate WCF, such as COM+ and ASP.NET. Again, WCF protects your investment in these technologies by enabling you to integrate components built using them into a WCF solution. This chapter describes two common scenarios. First, you will see how to configure a WCF service to enable interoperability with an ASP.NET Web client application. Then you will learn how to integrate a COM+ application into a WCF solution by exposing it as a WCF service.

Creating a WCF Service that Supports an ASP.NET Client

Microsoft developed ASP.NET as a framework for building Web applications. It includes a large number of components that developers can incorporate into interactive Web pages and a structure for processing requests and generating Web pages in response to those requests. Part of the ASP.NET framework is concerned with building Web services. However, the Web services model implemented by ASP.NET now seems quite primitive, as it does not provide support for many of the WS-* protocols that have emerged in recent years. Consequently, ASP.NET Web services and client applications cannot easily make use of WS-* specifications covering features such as reliable sessions, transactions, or even message level security (ASP.NET provides its own implementation of some of these features, and you can use transport level security over the HTTPS transport to protect messages).

Microsoft subsequently released the Web Services Enhancements (WSE) as an add-on to ASP.NET. WSE includes support for some selected WS-* standards. WSE was really just a temporary solution, and you should consider using WCF for all new development. However, it is probably not feasible for your organization to stop using your existing ASP.NET services and applications while you build new versions using WCF. Furthermore, if your ASP.NET Web services and client applications are functioning perfectly, why should you replace them? You are far more likely to migrate Web services to WCF piecemeal, either as you need to add new features to a specific Web service or as you retire a service and replace it with a Web service implementing new functionality. Additionally, it might not be feasible or desirable to migrate ASP.NET Web client applications to WCF. Consequently, you might have a large number of ASP.NET Web client applications in everyday use in your organization that need to be able to connect to ASP.NET and WCF Web services. It is therefore important to understand how to support existing ASP.NET Web client applications in a WCF service.

> **Important**   The current release of WCF does not provide support for client applications that use partial trust; client applications (including ASP.NET Web services communicating with a WCF service) must run with full trust. This situation might change in the next release of WCF.

In the following exercise, you will see how to build a WCF service that can be accessed by an ASP.NET Web client application (it can also be accessed by a WCF client application, of course).

Examine an existing ASP.NET Web service and client application

1. Using Visual Studio 2005, open the solution file ASPNETProductsService.sln located in the Microsoft Press\WCF Step By Step\Chapter 16\ASPNETService folder under your \My Documents folder.

    This solution contains an ASP.NET Web site called ASPNETProductsService and a client application that uses this service.

> **Note**   In this exercise, pretend that the ASPNETProductsService Web service is a copy of a production Web service deployed elsewhere in your organization using IIS and transport level security. For ease of testing and configuration, this copy of the Web service executes using the ASP.NET Development Server supplied with Visual Studio 2005 and consequently does not support SSL and the HTTPS protocol. However, the Web client application can be configured to connect to the Web service over an HTTPS connection, and you *will* provide transport level security when you implement the WCF version of the Web service.

2. Using Solution Explorer, open the ASPNETProductsService.cs file in the App_Code folder in the C:\...\ASPNETProductsService project and examine its contents.

   This Web service should have a familiar look to it; it is an ASP.NET version of the ProductsService service, providing the ListSelectedProducts, GetProduct, CurrentStockLevel, and ChangeStockLevel Web methods.

   The file contains an implementation of the *Product* class, tagged with the *Serializable* attribute to enable the ASP.NET runtime to transfer instances back to the ASP.NET client application.

   Notice the namespace and name of the Web service (the *ASPNETProductsService* class); the WCF version of the Web service will use this same namespace to remain compatible with existing ASP.NET client applications:

```
[WebService(Namespace = "http://adventure-works.com/2005/01/01",
            Name = "ProductsService")]
public class ASPNETProductsService : System.Web.Services.WebService,
                                IProductsService
{
    ...
}
```

   The Web methods use ADO.NET rather than the Microsoft Enterprise Library for accessing the *AdventureWorks* database (the Web service was created before the Enterprise Library was available). The web.config file contains the connection string that the application uses to connect to the database. If you are not running a local instance of SQL Server Express, you will need to modify the *value* property of the configuration setting in this file to connect to the correct server.

3. In the C:\...\ASPNETProductsService project, right-click the file ASPNETProductsService.asmx, and then click View in Browser.

   Internet Explorer starts and displays the list of Web methods implemented by the service. Display the WSDL description of the Web service by appending the text "?wsdl" to the end of the address in the Address box, like this:

```
http://localhost:7080/ASPNETProductsService/ASPNETProductsService.asmx?wsdl
```

   In the WSDL document displayed by Internet Explorer, note the following points:

   ❑ The return type of the ListSelectedProducts Web method (List<string>) is serialized as a sequence of strings in a type named *ArrayOfString* in the *http://adventure-works/2005/01/01* schema.

   ❑ The Product type is also in the *http://adventure-works/2005/01/01* schema. It has four elements named, in order: *Name*, *ProductNumber*, *Color*, and *ListPrice*.

   ❑ The SOAP action for the ListSelectedProducts Web method is *http://adventure-works/2005/01/01/ListSelectedProducts*.

❑   The SOAP action for the GetProduct Web method is *http://adventure-works/2005/01/01/GetProduct.*

❑   The SOAP action for the CurrentStockLevel Web method is *http://adventure-works/2005/01/01/CurrentStockLevel.*

❑   The SOAP action for the ChangeStockLevel Web method is *http://adventure-works/2005/01/01/ChangeStockLevel.*

Close Internet Explorer when you have finished browsing the WSDL document and return to Visual Studio 2005.

4. In Solution Explorer, open the Program.cs file in the ASPNETProductsClient project. Again, you should recognize much of the code in this application. It connects to the ASP.NET Web service, and tests each of the Web methods in turn.

The client application makes use of a Web service proxy generated by Visual Studio 2005 using the *Add Web Reference* command. You will use this same proxy to connect to the WCF service later.

> **Note**   In the production environment, the Web service uses the ASPNETProductsService certificate to protect communications with the client application (this version of the Web service currently does not use this level of protection because it runs using the ASP.NET Development Server in this exercise). In a subsequent exercise, you will use a test certificate generated by using the makecert utility, so the client application contains code that invokes the Enact method of the *PermissiveCertificatePolicy* class to bypass certificate verification. Once again, it is worth emphasizing that this code is provided for testing purposes only, and you should never include the *PermissiveCertificatePolicy* class in a production environment.

5. Open the app.config file in the ASPNETProductsClient project. This configuration file contains the ASPNETProductsClient_ProductsService_ProductsService setting. This setting was generated by the *Add Web Reference* command. It specifies the address of the ASP.NET Web service.

6. Start the solution without debugging. The ASP.NET Development Server starts, and the client application runs. The client application console generates a list of bicycle frames, displays the details of a water bottle, displays the stock level of water bottles, and then updates this stock level.

Press Enter to close the client application console when the application finished.

You have now seen the existing ASP.NET Web service and client application. Your next task is to implement a WCF service that provides the same functionality. The ASP.NET client application must be able to connect to the WCF service and run unchanged (apart from modifying the configuration file to refer to the new service).

Implement a WCF service to replace the ASP.NET Web service

1. Add a new project to the solution, using the WCF Service Library template in the Visual C# .NET Framework 3.0 project types. Name the project WCFProductsService and save it in the Microsoft Press\WCF Step By Step\Chapter 16\WCFService folder under your \My Documents folder.

2. In Solution Explorer, rename the file Class1.cs as ProductsService.cs.

3. Edit the ProductsService.cs file, and remove all comments and code apart from the *using* statements at the top of the file.

4. Add a reference to the *System.Configuration* assembly to the WCFProductsService project.

5. Add the following using statements to the ProductsService.cs file:

```
using System.Data;
using System.Data.SqlClient;
using System.Configuration;
```

6. Copy the code for the *Product* class, the *IProductsService* interface, and the *ASPNETProductsService* class from the ASPNETProductsService.cs file in the App_Code file in the C:\...\ASPNETProductsService project to the ProductsService.cs file.

7. In the ProductsService.cs file, modify the definition of the *Product* class as follows:

   ❑ Replace the *Serializable* attribute for the *Product* class with the *DataContract* attribute.

   ❑ Set the *Namespace* property of this attribute to the namespace expected by the ASP.NET client application.

   ❑ Tag each member of the *Product* class with a *DataMember* attribute ensuring that the members are serialized in the order in which they appear in the class and that they have the correct names in the serialization stream.

   The *Product* class should look like this (the new additions are shown in bold):

```
// Data contract describing the details of a product
[DataContract (Namespace="http://adventure-works.com/2005/01/01")]
public class Product
{
    [DataMember(Order=0, Name="Name")]
    public string Name;

    [DataMember(Order = 1, Name = "ProductNumber")]
    public string ProductNumber;

    [DataMember(Order = 2, Name = "Color")]
    public string Color;

    [DataMember(Order=3, Name="ListPrice")]
    public decimal ListPrice;
}
```

8. By default, the WCF service will serialize the *List<string>* value returned by the ListSelectedProducts operation using a different type and schema from that expected by the ASP.NET client application, which expects an *ArrayOfString* type in the *http://adventure-works.com/2005/01/01* namespace. Add the following class to the ProductsService.cs file underneath the *Product* class:

```
// Data contract for seralizing a list of strings
// using the same schema as the ASP.NET Web service
[CollectionDataContract(Namespace = "http://adventure-works.com/2005/01/01")]
public class ArrayOfString : List<string>
{
}
```

9. Make the following modification to the *IProductsService* interface:

   ❑ Add the *ServiceContract* attribute shown below in bold. In this attribute, specify the appropriate namespace and name.

   ❑ Mark each operation with an *OperationContract* interface explicitly specifying the names of the Action and ReplyAction messages.

   ❑ Change the return type of the ListSelectedProducts operation to *ArrayOfString*.

   The *IProductsService* interface should look like this (the new additions are shown in bold):

```
// ASP.NET compatible version of the service contract
[ServiceContract(Namespace = "http://adventure-works.com/2005/01/01",
                 Name = "ProductsService",
                 SessionMode = SessionMode.Allowed)] public interface IProductsService
{
    // Get the product number of selected products
    [OperationContract(
        Action = "http://adventure-works.com/2005/01/01/ListSelectedProducts",
        ReplyAction =
"http://adventure-works.com/2005/01/01/ListSelectedProducts
        Response")]
    [TransactionFlow(TransactionFlowOption.Allowed)]
    ArrayOfString ListSelectedProducts(string match);

    // Get the details of a single product
    [OperationContract(
        Action = "http://adventure-works.com/2005/01/01/GetProduct",
        ReplyAction = "http://adventure-works.com/2005/01/01/GetProductResponse")]
    [TransactionFlow(TransactionFlowOption.Allowed)]
    Product GetProduct(string productNumber);

    // Get the current stock level for a product
    [OperationContract(
        Action = "http://adventure-works.com/2005/01/01/CurrentStockLevel",
        ReplyAction =
"http://adventure-works.com/2005/01/01/CurrentStockLevel
        Response")]
    [TransactionFlow(TransactionFlowOption.Allowed)]
```

```
    int CurrentStockLevel(string productNumber);

    // Change the stock level for a product
    [OperationContract(
        Action = "http://adventure-works.com/2005/01/01/ChangeStockLevel",
        ReplyAction =
"http://adventure-works.com/2005/01/01/ChangeStockLevel
        Response")]
    [TransactionFlow(TransactionFlowOption.Allowed)]
    bool ChangeStockLevel(string productNumber, int newStockLevel,
                          string shelf, int bin);
}
```

> **Note**   WCF can automatically generate names for the Action and ReplyAction mes-
> sages based on the *namespace* and *name* properties of the service contract, but it is
> better to be explicit in this case. Additionally, WCF includes the name of the service
> contract when it generates message names, whereas the ASP.NET client application
> only expects the messages to be named after the namespace. For example, the default
> message name generated by WCF for the action for the ListSelectedProducts opera-
> tion would be *http://adventure-works.com/2005/01/01/ProductsService/ListSelected-
> Products*. However, the ASP.NET client application is expecting the action message to
> be named *http://adventure-works.com/2005/01/01/ListSelectedProducts.*

10. Make the following changes to the definition of the *ASPNETProductsService* class:

    ❑ Replace the *WebService* attribute with the *ServiceBehavior* attribute, retaining exist-
       ing values for the *Namespace* and *Name* properties.

    ❑ *Do not* inherit from the *System.Web.Services.WebService* class. This is the base class
       used by ASP.NET Web services only.

    The definitions of the *ASPNETProductsService* class should look like this:

```
// WCF service class that implements the service contract
[ServiceBehavior(Namespace = "http://adventure-works.com/2005/01/01",
                 Name = "ProductsService")]
public class ASPNETProductsService : IProductsService
{
    ...
}
```

11. Make the following changes to the ListSelectedProducts method in the *ASPNETProd-
    uctsService* class:

    ❑ Remove the *WebMethod* attribute.

    ❑ Change the return type of this method to *ArrayOfString*.

    ❑ In the body of this method, amend the statement that returns an empty
       List<string> object to return an *ArrayOfString* object instead.

    ❑ Modify the statement that declares the productsList local variable. This variable
       must be an *ArrayOfString* rather than a *List<string>*.

```
public ArrayOfString ListSelectedProducts(string match)
{
    // Check for potential SQL Injection attack
    if (IsPotentialSqlInjectionAttack(match))
    {
        return new ArrayOfString();
    }

    // Read the configuration information for connecting to the
    ...

    // Create and populate a list of products
    ArrayOfString productsList = new ArrayOfString();
    ...
}
```

12. Remove the *WebMethod* attribute from the remaining operations—GetProduct, Current-StockLevel, and ChangeStockLevel.

13. In Solution Explorer, remove the C:\...\ASPNETProductsService project from the solution, and then build the WCFProductsService project.

You will use the familiar WPF application to host the WCF service. This will enable you to implement transport level security for testing purposes.

Configure the WCF host application and service

1. Add the ProductsServiceHost project located in the Microsoft Press\WCF Step By Step\Chapter 16\ProjectsServiceHost folder under your \My Documents folder to the solution.

2. Add a reference to the WCFProductsService project to the ProductsServiceHost project.

3. Open the App.config file in the ProductsServiceHost project.

   The configuration file defines a single service endpoint with an address of *https://local-host:8040/ProductsService/ProductsService.svc*. The binding this endpoint uses is basicH-ttpBinding. The BasicHttpBinding binding is designed for maximum interoperability with Web services and client applications that do not make use of any WS-* standards, such as ASP.NET client applications.

   At the end of the configuration file you will find the <appSettings> section. This section contains a single key setting called AdventureWorksConnection, with the value for the connection string for accessing the *AdventureWorks* database. If you are not using a local instance of SQL Server Express to host the database, you will need to modify this string.

4. Build the solution.

5. Open a Windows SDK CMD Shell prompt. Type the following command to create and install the certificate for the ASPNETProductsService service (refer back to Chapter 4, "Protecting an Enterprise WCF Service," for a detailed explanation of using certificates to provide transport level security):

```
makecert -sr LocalMachine -ss My -n CN=ASPNETProductsService -sky exchange
```

> **Tip**   To open a Windows SDK CMD Shell prompt, on the Windows Start menu point
> to All Programs, point to Microsoft Windows SDK, and then CMD Shell.

6. Using the Certificates snap-in in the Microsoft Management Console, retrieve the
    thumbprint for the ASPNETProductsService service from the Personal certificates store
    for the local computer (refer back to the section "Configure the WCF HTTP endpoint
    with an SSL certificate" in Chapter 4 for a detailed description of how to do this).

7. In the CMD Shell prompt, type the following command to associate the certificate with
    port 8040 (the port used by the WCF service), replacing the string of digits after the $-h$
    flag with the thumbprint of your certificate:

```
httpcfg set ssl -i 0.0.0.0:8040 -h cf60efed47ae63d73005c6cfa5807b3673176e98
```

> **Note**   Under Windows Vista, use the following *netsh* command, replacing the digits
> for the certhash parameter with the thumbprint of your certificate:
>
> ```
> netsh http add sslcert ipport=0.0.0.0:8000
> certhash= cf60efed47ae63d73005c6cfa5807b3673176e98
> appid={00112233-4455-6677-8899-AABBCCDDEEFF}
> ```

8. Close the CMD Shell prompt.

Test the ASP.NET client application

1. In Solution Explorer, right-click the ProductsServiceHost project, point to Debug, and
    then click Start new instance. In the ProductsServiceHost form, click Start.

2. Using Windows Explorer, move to the Microsoft Press\WCF Step By Step\Chapter
    16\ASPNETService\ASPNETProductsClient\bin\Debug folder under your \My Docu-
    ments folder. This folder contains the compiled assembly and configuration file for the
    ASP.NET client application.

3. Edit the configuration file ASPNETProductsClient.exe.config by using Notepad. In the
    <applicationSettings> section of this file, set the ASPNETProductsClient_Products
    Service_ProductsService setting to *https://localhost:8040/ProductsService/Products
    Service.svc*. This is the URL of the WCF service. Save the file, and then close Notepad.

4. In Windows Explorer, double-click the file ASPNETProductsClient.exe to start the
    ASP.NET client application.

    The client application runs exactly as before, except this time it is connecting to the WCF
    service rather than the ASP.NET Web service. You can verify this if you stop the WCF ser-
    vice and run the ASP.NET client application again; it should fail with the message
    "Exception: Unable to connect to the remote server."

The key to building a WCF service that can be accessed by applications created using other technologies is interoperability. You have seen throughout this book how WCF implements many of the standard WS-* standards and protocols, making it compatible with applications and services that adhere to these standards and protocols. To provide connectivity to older applications, like those created by using ASP.NET, you must ensure that you provide a binding that is compatible with the limited functionality available to these applications. For maximum interoperability, you should supply a binding that is compatible with applications that conform to the WS-I Basic Profile. When you are building a WCF service, this essentially means using the BasicHttpBinding binding and not mandating the use of message level security, transactions, or reliable messaging. However, there is nothing to stop you adding further bindings for other capable client applications to use that do enable these features.

The WS-I Basic Profile and WCF Services

The WS-I Basic Profile constitutes a set of recommendations for building interoperable Web services. It was defined by the Web Services Interoperability Organization and describes how a Web service should apply many of the core Web services specifications that are not covered by the WS-* specifications, such as the SOAP messaging format, generating a WSDL description of a Web service, and defining the metadata to enable Web service discovery using Universal Description, Discovery, and Integration (UDDI). The WS-I Basic Profile essentially describes the lowest common denominator for features that a Web service must provide and remain useful. Web services that conform to the WS-I Basic Profile will be interoperable with client applications and other Web services that also conform to the WS-I Basic Profile. (Web services that implement the WS-* specifications are only interoperable with other Web services that implement the same WS-*specifications.)

You can use the WCF BasicHttpBinding binding to configure and expose endpoints that the service can use to communicate with client applications and services that conform to the WS-I Basic Profile 1.1, including ASP.NET Web client applications.

You can download the specification for the WS-I Basic Profile 1.1 from the WS-I Web site at *http://www.ws-i.org/Profiles/BasicProfile-1.1-2004-08-24.html*.

Exposing a COM+ Application as a WCF Service

Any reasonably sized organization that has been using the Microsoft Windows platform for any length of time as the basis for their applications will doubtless have systems that make use of COM+ applications. The good news is that WCF enables you to leverage this technology and reuse your existing COM+ components by building a WCF service wrapper around them. The .NET Framework 3.0 includes a useful tool called ComSvcConfig, which enables you to integrate COM+ applications into the WCF service model (you can find this tool in the

C:\WINDOWS\Microsoft.NET\Framework\v3.0\Windows Communication Foundation folder). Additionally, the WCF Service Configuration Editor provides a graphical user interface to many of the features available in the ComSvcConfig utility.

In the final set of exercises, you will use the WCF Service Configuration Editor and the ComSvcConfig utility to configure a COM+ application and enable client applications to access it in the same way as a WCF service. The COM+ application provides an interface that is very similar to the ProductsService service you used in the previous exercise.

Deploy the Products COM+ application to the COM+ catalog

1. Using Visual Studio 2005, open the solution file Products.sln located in the Microsoft Press\WCF Step By Step\Chapter 16\Products folder under your \My Documents folder.

   This solution contains a COM+ version of the ProductsService service.

> **Note**   If you are interested in how this COM+ application has been structured, follow steps 2–4 below. However, this understanding is not crucial to the exercise, and if you have never implemented a COM+ application you can safely skip to step 5.

2. Using Solution Explorer, open the Products.cs file. In the *Products* namespace, examine the *Product* class. Notice that this class is very similar to the Product data contract you implemented in the WCF service. As with the ASP.NET Web service implementation, this class has been tagged with the *Serializable* attribute:

```
[Serializable]
public class Product
{
    public string Name;
    public string ProductNumber;
    public string Color;
    public decimal ListPrice;
}
```

3. Inspect the *IProductsService* interface. This interface defines the methods that the application exposes through COM+, in a manner very similar to a WCF service contract:

```
[ComVisible(true)]
[Guid("A04ED9CA-D61C-984B-AE4D-A164BDC90FD5")]
public interface IProductsService
{
    // Get the product number of selected products
    ICollection ListSelectedProducts(string match);

    // Get the details of a single product
    Product GetProduct(string productNumber);

    // Get the current stock level for a product
    int CurrentStockLevel(string productNumber);
```

```
// Change the stock level for a product
bool ChangeStockLevel(string productNumber, int newStockLevel,
                        string shelf, int bin);
}
```

Apart from the attributes required by COM+ to identify the component, the most important difference between this and the WCF version of the interface is the return type of the ListSelectedProducts method. In the WCF service contract, the corresponding operation returns a *List<string>* type. COM+ does not support generics, so this version of the method returns an untyped *ICollection* object.

4. Examine the *ProductsService* class. This class implements the *IProductsService* interface and is the equivalent of the service class in the WCF service. Additionally, this class descends from the *ServicedComponent* class—this is the base class for COM+ serviced components. Notice that this COM+ application does not expose a class interface (the only functionality available is that specified in the *IProductsService* interface), but it supports transactions (this is common practice for COM+ applications):

```
[ClassInterface(ClassInterfaceType.None)]
[Transaction(TransactionOption.Supported)]
public class ProductsService : ServicedComponent, IProductsService
{
    ...
}
```

5. In Solution Explorer, edit the app.config file. Like the ASP.NET Web service in the previous set of exercises, the Products COM+ application uses ADO.NET rather than the Microsoft Enterprise Library for accessing the *AdventureWorks* database. The app.config file contains the connection string that the application uses to connect to the database. If you are not running a local instance of SQL Server Express, you will need to modify the *value* property in this file to connect to the correct server.

6. Build the solution.

   The application compiles into an assembly called *Products.dll.* This assembly is signed because you will deploy it to the .NET Framework Global Assembly Cache. (The file holding the strong name key used for signing the assembly is called ProductsService.snk, visible in Solution Explorer.)

7. Open a Visual Studio 2005 Command Prompt window and move to the Microsoft Press\WCF Step By Step\Chapter 16\Products\Products\bin\Debug folder under your \My Documents folder.

Tip   To open a Visual Studio 2005 Command Prompt window, on the Windows Start menu point to All Programs, point to Microsoft Visual Studio 2005, point to Visual Studio Tools, and then click Visual Studio 2005 Command Prompt.

8. Type the following command to deploy the *Products.dll* assembly to the Global Assembly Cache:

    ```
    gacutil /i Products.dll
    ```

9. Start the Component Services console.

> **Tip**   To start the Component Services console under Windows XP, in the Start menu, click Control Panel, click Performance and Maintenance, click Administrative Tools, and then double-click Component Services.
>
> Under Windows Vista, type the command **mmc** in the Command Prompt window. In the Microsoft Management Console, on the File menu, click Open, and open the file comexp.msc in the C:\Windows\System32 folder.

10. In the Component Services Console, in the left pane expand the Component Service node, expand the Computers folder, expand My Computer, right-click the COM+ Applications folder, point to New, and then click Application.

     The COM+ Application Install Wizard starts.

11. In the "Welcome to the COM+ Application Install Wizard" page, click Next.

12. In the "Install or Create a New Application" page, click Create an empty application.

13. In the "Create Empty Application" page, type ProductsService for the name of the application, ensure that the Activation type is set to Server application, and then click Next.

14. In the "Set Application Identity" page, accept the default settings, and then click Next.

15. In the "Thank you for using the COM+ Application Install Wizard" page, click Finish.

     The ProductsService application should appear in the list of COM+ applications, as shown highlighted in the following image:

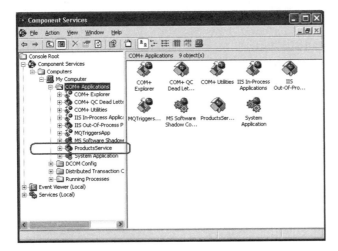

16. Expand the ProductsService application, right-click the Components folder, point to New, and then click Component.

    The Component Install Wizard starts.

17. In the "Welcome to the COM+ Component Install Wizard" page, click Next.

18. In the "Import or install a component" page, click Install new component(s).

19. In the "Select files to install" dialog box, move to the Microsoft Press\WCF Step By Step\Chapter 16\Products\Products\bin\Debug folder under your \My Documents folder. Click the *Products.dll* assembly, and then click Open.

20. In the "Install new components" page, verify that the Products.ProductsService component is correctly identified, as shown in the following image, and then click Next:

21. In the "Thank you for using the COM+ Component Install Wizard" page, click Finish.

22. Expand the Components folder under the ProductsService application in the Component Services console After a short delay, the Products.ProductsService component should appear:

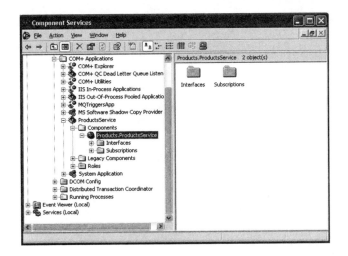

23. Leave the Component Services console open.

You can now configure the COM+ application to make it available like a WCF service. The simplest way to do this is to create a new WCF application configuration file and use the *Integrate* command in the WCF Service Configuration Editor. This command provides similar functionality to using the ComSvcConfig utility from the command line.

Configure the Products COM+ application as a WCF service

1. Start the WCF Service Configuration Editor.

> **Tip** To start the WCF Service Configuration Editor outside of Visual Studio 2005, on the Windows Start menu, point to All Programs, point to Microsoft Windows SDK, point to Tools, and then click Service Configuration Editor.

2. In the WCF Service Configuration Editor, on the File menu, point to Integrate, and then click COM+ Application.

The COM+ Integration Wizard starts.

3. In the "Which component interface would you like to integrate?" page, expand the ProductsService node, expand the Components folder, expand the Products.ProductsService component, expand the Interfaces folder, select the *IProductsService* interface, and then click Next:

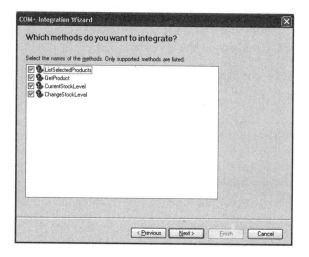

4. In the "Which methods do you want to integrate?" page, make sure that all four methods are selected, and then click Next.

5. In the "Which hosting mode would you like to use?" page, select COM+ hosted, and then click Next.

   Note that by default, the wizard also creates an endpoint for metadata exchange. Leave this option enabled.

6. In the "What communication mode do you want to use?" page, select HTTP, and then click Next.

7. In the "What is the base address of your service?" page, in the *Address* field, type http://localhost:9090/COMProductsService, and then click Next.

Note that this is the base address of the service and not its URI. The wizard will generate an endpoint URI based on the name of the interface, and append it to this base address. In this example, the URI of the service will actually be http://localhost:9090/COMProductsService/IProductsService.

> **Note**   If you are using Windows Vista, use the default port (port 80) rather than port 9090, and specify a base address of http://localhost/COMProductsService.

8. In the "The wizard is ready to create a service configuration page", click Next.

9. Verify that the wizard completes without reporting any errors, and then click Finish:

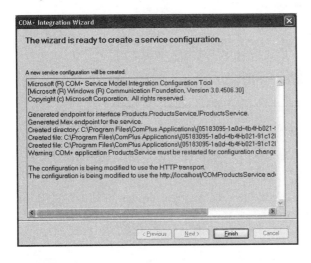

Note that when the wizard finishes, the configuration is *not* displayed in the WCF Service Configuration Editor.

10. In the WCF Service Configuration Editor, on the File menu, point to Open, and click COM+ Service.

A list of all COM+ applications configured as WCF services appears (just the ProductsService application in this case).

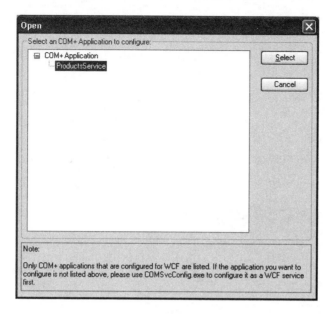

Click the ProductsService application, and then click Select.

The configuration for this service is loaded and displayed in the WCF Service Configuration Editor.

The service is named using the same globally unique identifiers GUIDs that COM+ uses to identify the COM+ application and class. Make a note of the first GUID in the service name.

11. Expand the service and verify that it has two endpoints. One is based on the wsHttp-Binding binding and is the endpoint that client applications connect to. The other is the metadata exchange endpoint.

   The COM+ component supports transactions, so the configuration file also includes transactional and nontransactional binding configurations for the wsHttpBinding and netNamedPipeBinding bindings. The binding configuration referenced by the HTTP endpoint refers to the binding that enables transactions by default.

12. In the left pane, expand the COM Contracts folder. This folder only appears for COM+ applications configured as WCF services. Expand the child folder named after a GUID, and then click the exposedMethods node.

   The right pane displays the four methods available through this configuration. You can hide methods from client applications by deselecting them in this page. Do not change anything.

13. Close the WCF Service Configuration Editor. Do not save any changes if you are prompted (the configuration was saved earlier by the COM+ Integration Wizard).

14. Using Windows Explorer, move to the C:\Program Files\ComPlus Applications folder. This folder contains folders for each configured COM+ application. Move to the folder with the same GUID as the application ID of the COM+ application (this is the GUID that you noted in step 10).

    This folder contains two files: a manifest file, and an application configuration file. The application configuration file is the file you have just created using the COM+ Integration Wizard in the WCF Service Configuration Editor.

    Open the application.config file using Notepad.

15. Leave Notepad open, and return to Visual Studio 2005. In Solution Explorer, open the app.config file in the Products project.

    Copy the appSettings section of this file to the Windows clipboard.

    Return to Notepad, and paste the contents of the Windows clipboard immediately after the opening <configuration> tag and before the <system.ServiceModel tag>, as shown in bold below:

```
<?xml version="1.0" encoding="utf-8"?>
<configuration>
    <appSettings>
        <add key="AdventureWorksConnection"
value="Database=AdventureWorks;Server=(local)\SQLEXPRESS;Integrated
Security=SSPI;"/>
    </appSettings>
    <system.serviceModel>

        …
    </system.serviceModel>
</configuration>
```

    The COM+ component needs this key/value pair to retrieve the connection string for connecting to the database.

> **Note** If you edited the connection string earlier, your value will differ from that shown here.

16. Save the file, and close Notepad.

You should now be able to use this COM+ application just like any WCF service.

Test the Products COM+ application

1. Start Internet Explorer and move to the URL *http://localhost:9090/COMProductsService*.

> **Note** If you are using Windows Vista, move to the URL *http://localhost/COMProductsService*.

Internet Explorer displays the page describing how to create a client application for the WCF service:

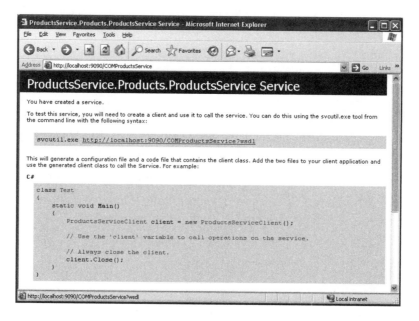

 Tip   If Internet Explorer displays the error message "The page cannot be displayed," then the COM+ application has probably shutdown due to inactivity. To restart the application, return to the Component Services console, right-click the ProductsService application in the COM+ Applications folder, and then click Start.

2. Click the link *http://localhost:9090/COMProductsService?wsdl*. The WSDL description of the service appears.

3. Close Internet Explorer.

4. In Visual Studio 2005, open the solution file ProductsClient.sln located in the Microsoft Press\WCF Step By Step\Chapter 16\ProductsClient folder under your \My Documents folder.

   This solution contains a copy of the client application for testing the ProductsService service. This code is not quite complete; you will add a statement to create the proxy object in a later step.

5. Open the Program.cs file. There is one small change to this code compared with the program you saw in previous chapters: the statement in the Main method that invokes the ListSelectedProducts operation returns the result into an *ICollection* object rather than a *List<string>*, for the reasons described earlier:

```
ICollection productNumbers = proxy.ListSelectedProducts("Frame");
```

6. In the Project menu, click Add Service Reference. In the Add Service Reference dialog box, enter http://localhost:9090/COMProductsService?wsdl for the service URI and ProductsService for the service reference name, and then click OK.

> **Note**   If you are using Windows Vista, specify http://localhost/ COMProductsService?wsdl for the service URI.

Visual Studio 2005 generates a proxy class for the service and adds it to the Services References folder in Solution Explorer. It also creates an application configuration file. If you examine this file, you will see that it contains a client endpoint for accessing the COMProductsService service called WSHttpBinding_IProductsService.

7. Add the following *using* statement to the list at the top of the Program.cs file:

```
using ProductsClient.ProductsService;
```

The proxy class you just generated is in this namespace.

8. In the Main method, add the statement shown in bold below, before the *try* block, to create the proxy object:

```
// Create a proxy object and connect to the service
ProductsServiceClient proxy = new
    ProductsServiceClient("WSHttpBinding_IProductsService");
```

9. Start the solution without debugging.

The client application functions as it has done in previous chapters, generating a list of bicycle frames, displaying the details of a water bottle, and displaying the stock level of water bottles and then modifying this stock level.

> **Tip**   If client application console displays an error containing the text "No connection could be made because the target machine actively refused it.", then the COM+ application has again probably shutdown due to inactivity. To restart the application, return to the Component Services console, right-click the ProductsService application in the COM+ Applications folder, and then click Start.

10. Press Enter to close the client application console window.

As far as the client application is concerned, there is little discernable difference between this implementation of the service and previous versions constructed using WCF. The fact that it is a COM+ application is transparent to the client application.

Summary

In this chapter, you have seen how to build WCF services that can interoperate with ASP.NET Web client applications and how to integrate COM+ applications into a WCF solution. WCF also supports a number of other integration and interoperability scenarios. For example, you can register and configure a WCF service with a COM moniker, enabling you to access it from a COM environment such as Microsoft Office VBA, Visual Basic 6.0, or Visual C++ 6.0. You can integrate WCF services with .NET Framework Remoting, and you can build WCF services that can interoperate with applications and services constructed using WSE. For more information, see the topic "Interoperability and Integration" in the Microsoft Windows SDK documentation. You can also find this topic online on the Microsoft Web site at *http://msdn2.microsoft.com/en-us/library/ms730017.aspx*.

Index

John Sharp

John Sharp is a Principal Technologist at Content Master (*http://www.contentmaster.com*), part of CM Group Ltd, a technical authoring company in the United Kingdom. He researches and develops technical content for training courses, seminars, and white papers. John is deeply involved with .NET Framework application development and interoperability. He has written papers and courses, built tutorials, and delivered conference presentations covering distributed systems and Web services, application migration and interoperability between Windows/.NET Framework and UNIX/Linux/Java, as well as development using the C# and J# languages. John has also authored *Microsoft Visual C# Step by Step*, and *Microsoft Visual J# Core Reference*, both published by Microsoft Press.

What do you think of this book?

We want to hear from you!

Do you have a few minutes to participate in a brief online survey?

Microsoft is interested in hearing your feedback so we can continually improve our books and learning resources for you.

To participate in our survey, please visit:

www.microsoft.com/learning/booksurvey/

...and enter this book's ISBN-10 number (appears above barcode on back cover*). As a thank-you to survey participants in the United States and Canada, each month we'll randomly select five respondents to win one of five $100 gift certificates from a leading online merchant. At the conclusion of the survey, you can enter the drawing by providing your e-mail address, which will be used for prize notification only.

Thanks in advance for your input. Your opinion counts!

* Where to find the ISBN-10 on back cover

ISBN-13: 000-0-0000-0000-0
ISBN-10: 0-0000-00000

00000

0 000000 000000

Example only. Each book has unique ISBN.

Microsoft
Press

www.microsoft.com/learning/booksurvey/